634

634

FISHES OF PENNSYLVANIA

FISHES OF PENNSYLVANIA

and the
Northeastern United States

EDWIN L. COOPER

THE PENNSYLVANIA STATE UNIVERSITY PRESS
UNIVERSITY PARK AND LONDON

Library of Congress Cataloging in Publication Data

Cooper, Edwin Lavern, 1919–
Fishes of Pennsylvania and the Northeastern United States.

Includes bibliography and index.
1. Fishes—Pennsylvania.   2. Fishes—Northeastern
States.   I. Title.
QL628.P4C66   1983   597.092'9748   82-18052
ISBN 0-271-00337-5

Designed by Dolly Carr

Printed in the United States of America

Contents

Preface

The study of the fishes of Pennsylvania has had a long history, beginning with some of the earliest ichthyologists to work in North America. Several species were originally described from material collected from local streams. The Academy of Natural Sciences of Philadelphia supported much of this early work and published many accounts of fishes by Cope, Baird, LeSueur, and Fowler, among others.

A detailed survey of the distribution of fishes within the several watersheds of Pennsylvania had not been made prior to 1956. For several years subsequent to this time, surveys of trout streams were conducted jointly by the Pennsylvania Fish Commission and the U.S. Fish and Wildlife Service as a basis for developing a fishery management plan for these waters. Many collections of fishes were preserved and donated to the Pennsylvania State University for identification and cataloguing. These collections have been added to by the author and many cooperators and form the basis for the present work. By the early 1970s it was perceived that most watersheds had been sampled sufficiently to project reasonable patterns of distribution for most fishes now believed to be present. It is hoped that this present summary of information will stimulate further work to help define the distribution of some of the rarer species which we have not had time to fully document.

A venture of this kind is possible only through the cooperation of many individuals, but a few should be singled out for special recognition. The planning of the original trout stream surveys should be credited to Joseph A. Boccardy, who also made many additional collecting trips with the author. To a former student and now colleague, Charles "Curt" Wagner, I owe a special note of appreciation for the many years of field and laboratory assistance in developing this book, when it did not interfere with his other avocations. And, to John E. Cooper goes the credit for transforming my crude drawings into recognizable graphics. The photographs of the fishes, for better or for worse, must remain the responsibility of the author.

To the many other persons who have had a hand in any stage of this work, from saving a rare species to the chores of typing and editing, I am very grateful.

And, I would be remiss in not recording the unstinting support of the Rockwell Foundation and the personal encouragement of Willard F. Rockwell, Jr., for our fishery research and education program at the Pennsylvania State University.

Ecological Description of Pennsylvania

Topography

The boundaries of this commonwealth include several physiographic divisions, of which the Appalachian Plateau Province and the Valley and Ridge Province predominate, except for a small area in southeastern Pennsylvania.[957] These divisions roughly divide the surface geology into rocks of various stratigraphic ages, although the surface exposures caused by lateral pressure, uplift, and folding sometimes create very complicated geological formations especially in the Valley and Ridge Province (Fig. 1).

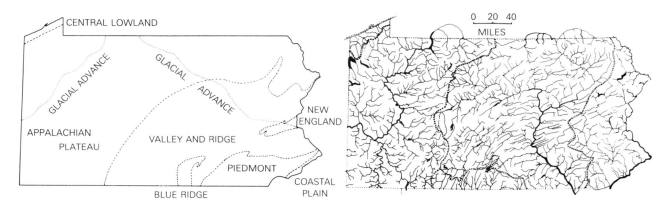

Figure 1. Physiographic divisions of Pennsylvania and extent of glacial advance.

Figure 2. Stream systems in Pennsylvania. Double-dotted lines indicate major divides separating the watersheds of the Great Lakes, Ohio, Susquehanna, Potomac, and Delaware.

Streams arising or flowing through Pennsylvania bear little relationship to the physiographic provinces as now recognized (Fig. 2). Their general courses were largely sculptured in late Tertiary time about 10–20 million years ago through sedimentary rocks which were being uplifted and tilted from the center of the state to the southeast. The northwest portion of the state was uplifted rather uniformly and remains as the Appalachian Plateau.

On the steeper slope toward the Atlantic Ocean, the streams eroded water gaps through what are now rather prominent ridges formed by lateral pressure and folding of the sedimentary rocks. These are especially prominent in a wide northeast to southwest belt (the Valley and Ridge Province) extending across the state.

Glacial History

Stream drainages probably remained relatively unchanged through millions of years of the Tertiary and early Quaternary until the advent of the ice ages in North America. Four separate advances and retreats of ice fronts, spanning the last 100,000 years or more of geological time, have been identified by geologists. Only the last three of these apparently reached Pennsylvania.

The earliest stage properly identified in Pennsylvania was the Kansan glaciation, followed by the Illinoian, and finally the Wisconsin, which retreated to the north some 15,000 years ago. The published record of these glacial events is voluminous, but it is fairly summarized in several investigations.[247,248,551,958,959,960]

The areas in Pennsylvania affected by glacial action are restricted to a small northwestern section extending from Warren County southwest to Beaver County, and a much larger northeastern section extending from McKean County southeast to Bucks County (Fig. 1).

Some of the major stream drainages such as the Delaware and the Potomac have remained relatively intact through the series of glacial advances and retreats across North America. In other cases, glaciers have altered stream flows by blocking preglacial outlets and reversing the flow of major river systems. For example, the Upper Allegheny, Tionesta, and Beaver-Monongahela drainages, which prior to glaciation flowed north into the Erian River (Fig. 3), have been captured by the Upper Ohio River and have reversed their flow to the south (Fig. 4).

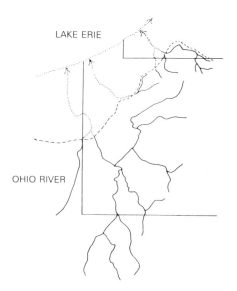

Figure 3. Preglacial drainage pattern (dotted lines) of western Pennsylvania. Dashed line shows farthest advance of glaciation.

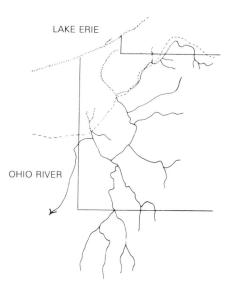

Figure 4. Postglacial drainage pattern of western Pennsylvania, showing effect of glaciation in reversing flow of the upper Ohio River.

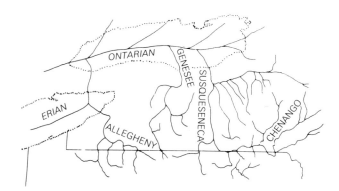

Figure 5. Preglacial drainage pattern of portions of New York and Pennsylvania; dotted lines outline Lakes Ontario and Erie.

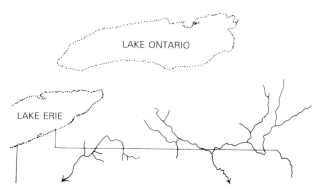

Figure 6. Postglacial drainage pattern of Allegheny and Susquehanna rivers as modified by glacial action.

As another example, the preglacial Susqueseneca River, draining the Finger Lakes region of New York and a small portion of northern Pennsylvania in a northerly direction into the Ontarian River (Fig. 5), was drastically altered by glaciation. Many valleys were dammed at their northern ends, creating the Finger Lakes, and a new outlet to the south was eroded near Horseheads, New York, to join the upper Susquehanna River near Towanda, Pennsylvania. This stream capture resulted in the reversal of considerable drainage in southern New York and northern Pennsylvania to the present Susquehanna River (Fig. 6). The connections of lakes and rivers associated with various glacial advances and retreats are regarded as major routes of dispersal of fishes from the Ohio River drainage through the Great Lakes drainage into the headwaters of the Susquehanna River.

Climate

The climate of Pennsylvania is moist and temperate with a mean annual precipitation of about 42 inches and a mean annual temperature of about 50°F. Weather systems usually move from west to east, with occasional hurricanes or other storms coming off the Atlantic Ocean from the southeast. The severe flood of the Susquehanna River in 1972 was the result of such a hurricane.

The topography of Pennsylvania influences the local climate to some extent. South and east of the mountains, winters are milder than to the northwest, and the growing season averages about 185 days. The Valley and Ridge Province is not high enough for true mountain climate, but the effects of radiation, such as valley warming and nocturnal cooling, increase the frequency of frosts in spring and fall. To the north and west, the Appalachian Plateau Province has a more typical continental climate, with frequent changes in weather brought in by the prevailing westerly flow. Here, winters are colder and more prolonged, and summers are generally cooler than on the Piedmont and Coastal Plain.

The rugged topography and sporadic, heavy rainfall over much of Pennsylvania create unstable flow patterns in the streams of many watersheds, causing rapid scouring and erosion. Johnstown, located at the confluence of several headwater tributaries of the Conemaugh River, is in one of these flood-prone areas caused by steep gradient and heavy rainfall of 46–50 inches per year.

Origin and Dispersal of the Fishes

Introduction of Exotics

Compared with the large number of native fishes in Pennsylvania, there are very few exotic species now maintaining populations by natural reproduction. Two of these, the common carp and the goldfish, have been so successful and have such a wide distribution in contiguous states that they must be considered as permanent, albeit unpopular, additions to our fauna. Two other species, the brown trout and the rainbow trout, are long-time residents, spawn successfully in natural environments, and are cultured and stocked by governmental agencies as important game species.

Several other species have been introduced with varying degrees of success in establishing natural populations. The kokanee (landlocked red salmon) presently is being maintained by stocking and natural reproduction in at least one lake in Pennsylvania. Two other salmonids (coho and chinook salmon) are being maintained by stocking in Lake Erie with spawning runs into tributary streams.

Three other game fishes (the Amur pike, striped bass, and redear sunfish) have been stocked recently in Pennsylvania waters, but it is too early to predict whether or not they will become permanent additions to our fauna.

In addition to these planned introductions, a few instances of exotics have been reported from our waters with unknown success in establishing natural populations. Although this list is probably incomplete, it includes the threadfin shad, the mosquitofish, and the ide, a European cyprinid.

Losses from Native Fauna

In 1948, Fowler [279] published the most recent list of the fauna known to have been collected in Pennsylvania. This list is based on his personal collections, and also on many earlier publications.[161,239,275] A more complete review of the literature and checklist of the fishes of the Susquehanna River drainage is given by Denoncourt and Cooper.[204]

Many species listed by these earlier workers are now thought to be extirpated from the Pennsylvanian portions of their range. No fewer than 16 of these extirpated species formerly were found in the Pennsylvanian waters of the Upper Ohio River and its tributaries, five species are missing from the Lake Erie drainage, five species are no longer found in the Delaware River drainage (mostly from below the fall line), and two species are missing from the Susquehanna River drainage (Table 1).

Many reasons may be cited for the loss of suitable habitat necessary to support these species, but extensive acid-mine drainage coupled with industrial pollution of major waterways probably accounted for the loss of many species in the Ohio River drainage. In the Delaware River drainage below the fall line, only a small amount of suitable habitat was originally present in Pennsylvania for species such as the pirate perch, mud sunfish, blackbanded sunfish, and the swamp darter. This area is now part of a large industrial complex in and near Philadelphia and the few remaining streams and swamps are badly polluted.

Table 1. Fishes listed by Fowler[274,277,279] for Pennsylvania watersheds, but not collected during the period 1958–1981.

Ohio River

Shovelnose sturgeon, *Scaphirhynchus platorynchus*
Paddlefish, *Polyodon spathula*

Shortnose gar, *Lepisosteus platostomus*
Skipjack herring, *Alosa chrysochloris*

Table 1 *continued*

Goldeye, *Hiodon alosoides*
River shiner, *Notropis blennius*
Blackchin shiner, *Notropis heterodon*
Bullhead minnow, *Pimephales vigilax*
River carpsucker, *Carpiodes carpio*
Highfin carpsucker, *Carpiodes velifer*
Blue sucker, *Cycleptus elongatus*
Blue catfish, *Ictalurus furcatus*
Black bullhead, *Ictalurus melas*
Longear sunfish, *Lepomis megalotis*
Sharpnose darter, *Percina oxyrhyncha*

Great Lakes

Mooneye, *Hiodon tergisus*
Cisco, *Coregonus artedii*

Lake whitefish, *Coregonus clupeaformis*
Lake chubsucker, *Erimyzon sucetta*
Greater redhorse, *Moxostoma valenciennesi*

Susquehanna River

Northern redbelly dace, *Phoxinus eos*
Blind silurid, *Gronias nigrilabris*

Delaware River

Ironcolor shiner, *Notropis chalybaeus*
Pirate perch, *Aphredoderus sayanus*
Mud sunfish, *Acantharchus pomotis*
Blackbanded sunfish, *Enneacanthus chaetodon*
Swamp darter, *Etheostoma fusiforme*

New Records of Occurrence

A few species now known to be present were not included in Fowler's 1948 list. It is highly likely that all of these were present in the area prior to 1948 but either had not been collected, had not been recognized as valid species, or were simply overlooked in the compilation. Most of these species are localized in distribution and are rare, such as the northern brook lamprey or the Iowa darter, but included are some rather widespread and common forms such as the Ohio lamprey and the channel darter (Table 2).

Table 2. Fishes collected in Pennsylvania watersheds during 1958–1981 in addition to those listed by Fowler.[279]

Ohio River

Ohio lamprey, *Ichthyomyzon bdellium*
Gravel chub, *Hybopsis x-punctata*
Ghost shiner, *Notropis buchanani*
Northern madtom, *Noturus stigmosus*
Spotted bass, *Micropterus punctulatus*
Iowa darter, *Etheostoma exile*
Channel darter, *Percina copelandi*

Great Lakes

Northern brook lamprey, *Ichthyomyzon fossor*
Spotted gar, *Lepisosteus oculatus*

Potomac River

Potomac sculpin, *Cottus girardi*

Diversity and Origin of Fossil Fishes

The oldest fossils of fishes occur as jawless, heavily armored ostracoderms in Ordovician rocks at least 425 million years old. Specimens of these fossils have been found in exposed beds in Colorado, Montana and South Dakota. A few investigators were inclined to dispute the extreme age of these fish fossils until it was clearly shown that the rocks also contained invertebrates characteristic of Ordovician strata in other parts of the world.[226]

In Pennsylvania, the type specimen of another jawless fish, *Americaspis americana* Claypole, was described from red rocks of upper Silurian age near the borough of New Bloomfield in Perry County.[130] This formation now goes by the name of the Landisburg Tongue.[208] Similar exposures of these Silurian rocks in northeastern Pennsylvania and elsewhere, known locally as the upper part of the Bloomsburg formation, have yielded many fine specimens of a closely related form, *Archegonaspis van ingeni* (Bryant). These fossil fishes seldom occur with other fossils in the sandstone beds, and are presumed to have inhabited a brackish or freshwater fluvial floodplain.[57]

By the Devonian period there had already been a proliferation of several primitive jawed forms such as the placoderms, scaled ganoids, and sharks that largely supplanted the jawless forms during this period known as the "Age of Fishes." In the 70 million years succeeding the Devonian period, which includes the Mississippian and the Pennsylvanian periods, the sharks became the dominant fishes in the oceans, with the few remaining placoderms, ganoids, lungfishes, and lobefins largely restricted to brackish estuaries and freshwater swamps. Because many rocks of these periods are exposed in Pennsylvania, numerous remains of these very primitive fish groups have been found and described here, ranging from isolated spines and scales to small slabs of shale containing up to five entire individuals.[668]

Only a few fossil fishes have been recorded in Pennsylvania from Permian rocks[805] or from Triassic rocks.[38,105] This is due, at least in part, to the lack of exposure of these rocks in Pennsylvania. But, many of the major fossil groups such as ostracoderms and placoderms became extinct by the close of the Permian, and others continued as small remnants of previously dominant groups such as the sharks.

In tracing the evolution of fishes from the Permian period to the present, we must look outside Pennsylvania for the record because of the complete absence of Jurassic, Cretaceous and Tertiary strata in the Appalachian highlands. It was during the Cretaceous period that great diversification of the rayfin fishes must have occurred, but the fossil record linking early rayfins with modern forms is scanty at best. However, the record is reasonably complete in Tertiary rocks of the Great Plains. Extensive collections of primitive gars, killifishes, suckers, minnows, catfishes, pirateperches, and perches have been found in Eocene beds from the Green River, Wyoming, site and elsewhere.

If we consider only the fossils of the Quaternary period (the last one million years of the geological record), fishes are very poorly known in North America, with only 95 species in 49 genera.[626] A few of these, such as sturgeons, gars, and the bowfin, have survived almost unchanged from their appearance during the Cretaceous period some 100 million years ago. Nearly half of the fossils recognized are minnows and suckers, which are also the dominant groups of living fishes of North America.

The fossil record of fishes found in Pennsylvania for the Quaternary period is almost non-existent. This is hardly surprising since Willard[957] shows only a small exposure of sands and gravels of this age present along the Delaware River in southeastern Pennsylvania. In 1849, a large number of bones were found in a cave on the Susquehanna River near Carlisle in Cumberland County. S. F. Baird identified these as a mixture of extinct (about 5%) and recent mammals together with some remains of fishes. Also, a small collection of bones found in Durham Cave on the Delaware River near Riegelsville, Pennsylvania, contained remains of sturgeon (*Acipenser sturio*) and catfish (*Amiurus atrarius*) together with the remains of many other recent vertebrates.[537] An extensive excavation of a limestone cave near the Delaware Water Gap (Hartman's Cave) yielded a mixture of fossil mammals, recent mammals, birds, turtles, snakes, snail shells, but no fishes. Since the author of this report comments that in mixed collections of extinct and recent remains found in these caves, "it is difficult, if not impossible, to ascertain how far the different species may have been cotemporaneous,"[537] we are left with the possibility that no fossils dating from the Quaternary period have yet been found in Pennsylvania.

Diversity and Origin of Recent Fishes

The present fish fauna of Pennsylvania includes no fewer than 159 species, representing 24 families. These may be grouped into two broad categories: 1) Primary fishes (119 species in 10 families) which are strictly freshwater, and 2) Secondary fishes (40 species in 14 families) which may be diadromous (American shad), salt tolerant (mummichog), or essentially freshwater representatives of marine groups (sculpins).[626] Thus our present fauna appears to be primarily of freshwater derivation, but with minor contributions from many marine families.

The freshwater group of species is closely associated with that of Eurasia, and presumably the two groups share common ancestral stocks. Such a derivation would be consistent with modern theory of continental drift.[167] Five families (pikes, mudminnows, minnows, suckers, and perches) contribute 81 species to our fauna. By comparison, there are no species of these families in South America; its fauna is dominated by characins, cichlids, and numerous families of freshwater catfishes. There is only one endemic species of characin (the banded tetra) in North America.[511] Very recently many exotics have been inadvertently introduced and are spreading through southern Florida.[165] Because of easy access to connecting waterways, these introductions are destined to become permanent contributions to the list of North American fishes.

Five other families of freshwater fishes in Pennsylvania (38 species) are endemic to North America. These range in the Pennsylvania fauna from single species in one family such as the bowfin and the trout-perch to two families with many representatives such as the bullhead catfishes, and the sunfishes.

The secondary fishes have representatives from many families ranging from very primitive forms such as lampreys to highly specialized forms such as sculpins. Many of these families have only one or two representatives in our fauna, but a large number have lost their close ecological relationship with the marine environment and are strictly freshwater. Examples of this group are the non-parasitic lampreys, gars, burbot, brook silverside, brook stickleback, freshwater drum, and the sculpins.

The present fish fauna of Pennsylvania thus owes its relative richness to several factors: 1) historical contributions from several watersheds, 2) diverse chemical and physical environments related to soils and topography derived from rocks of different ages, 3) temperate climatic conditions which offer both cold-water and warm-water habitats, and 4) introduction of exotic species by man.

Geographic Dispersal

The fish fauna of northeastern United States has been derived mostly from centers in the Mississippi lowlands, the southern Appalachian highlands, and the Atlantic coastal areas. The Appalachian mountains were apparently an effective barrier to east-west dispersal of fishes, resulting in considerable differences between the Atlantic coastal fauna and that of the Mississippi drainage. With these major centers of origin in mind, the present geographic distribution of fishes among the major watersheds of Pennsylvania and northeastern states is the result of many natural factors, such as glacial action, stream capture by erosional processes, changes in water level of the Atlantic Ocean, and changes in climate.

As the several glacial ice sheets advanced, many species found cold water refugia much further south than the present climate would indicate.[511] A few of these cold water forms, such as the longnose sucker and the burbot, closely followed the retreat of the glacier but were stranded as relict populations by moraines deposited by the retreating glacier. They are now found much further south than their normal range only in the cool headwater portions of the Youghiogheny River (longnose sucker) and the Allegheny River (burbot), two streams which were diverted from preglacial Great Lakes drainage to the present Ohio River drainage.

The Great Lakes drainage has had so many connections with the Mississippi River during the retreat of the Wisconsin glaciation that similarities between these two faunas are to be expected.[722] However, only a relatively few availed themselves of the Horseheads Outlet erosion channel from glacial Lake Newberry to the upper Susquehanna River. Among these are redside dace, pearl dace, stoneroller, spotfin shiner, rosyface shiner and the brook stickleback.[325] Several of these also moved through outlets from the Great Lakes to the Mohawk-Hudson drainage but did not make it into the Delaware drainage.[324] In Pennsylvania, the Delaware drainage is thus considerably more depauperate of fishes than the Susquehanna, its fauna being derived almost exclusively from northward dispersal from the Atlantic coastal plain as the glacier retreated to the north.

The widespread distribution of several species, such as the blacknose dace and banded killifish, and their recognition as separate subspecies, infers a northward dispersal from both the Mississippi lowlands and the Atlantic coastal plain. There is a convincing argument for the subspecies evolution and northern dispersal of two subspecies of *Esox americanus* from its original center in southern Appalachia; the redfin pickerel is now restricted to the Atlantic coast and the grass pickerel is found only in the Mississippi drainage.[177]

However, there are also widespread distribution patterns of some species that suggest a single derivation from Mississippi lowlands stocks, through Horseheads Outlet into the upper Susquehanna River and then rapid and widespread downstream colonization.[31] In this category are the river chub, the rosyface shiner, and the bluntnose minnow. Or, it is not unlikely that species have crossed watershed boundaries at more than one point through stream capture and have dispersed widely in this manner, as suggested for the river chub.[513]

In contrast to the slow natural dispersal of fish species, the original distribution of many fishes has been drastically altered by man. Within the past century, fish cultural activities and modern fish management have been so widespread and so pervasive that it is a wonder that natural distributions of any fishes are still discernible. Most game fishes and many forage fishes have been introduced outside their original range, and interesting extralimital populations now exist in Pennsylvania as well as other states.

The most noted example of this recent range extension is the banded darter, *Etheostoma zonale*, which somehow gained entrance to the Susquehanna River by way of Pine Creek in Potter County sometime during the late 1960s and rapidly colonized most of the mainstem riffles and many tributaries downstream into Maryland. The mimic shiner, *Notropis volucellus*, previously known only from the Ohio drainage, has recently turned up in the Susquehanna drainage at several localities near Harrisburg. The river chub, *Nocomis micropogon*, now is present in some of the streams tributary to Lake Wallenpaupack, Pike County, but nowhere else in the Delaware drainage. The stoneroller, *Campostoma anomalum*, was not found in the Delaware watershed of New York during a 1935 survey[325] but is now fairly abundant at several localities in this watershed.

The four-spined stickleback, *Apeltes quadracus*, has natural breeding populations in Harvey's Lake, Luzerne County, and in Big Spring Creek, Cumberland County; and the mummichog, *Fundulus heteroclitus*, has been found reproducing successfully at two headwater sites in the Susquehanna River above several dams. Introduction of these latter two species probably was the result of stocking by governmental agencies. The very recent successful introductions of the spottail shiner, *Notropis hudsonius*, and the white bass, *Morone chrysops*, into the Allegheny Reservoir, Warren County, possibly were derived from attempted introductions of the emerald shiner, *Notropis atherinoides*, into this reservoir from Lake Erie stocks. Despite the official disapproval of most of these transplantations, dispersal of other fishes will certainly be aided by man's activities in the future.

List of the Fishes

This list includes species which have been reported from the area and those whose reported range makes their presence possible in the near future. The list includes both native and some exotic species that have been acclimated at least temporarily. Detailed information on distribution will be found in the species accounts.

The major geographic divisions of the distribution maps represent the several watersheds in Pennsylvania. The details of the stream drainages have been omitted to focus attention on patterns of distribution that closely adhere to watershed boundaries. In all cases, specific collection sites are on record for each point plotted, and are available from the author.

Localities for which specimens either are catalogued, or have been personally identified by the author, are indicated by solid circles. Earlier reports of other localities have been plotted as solid triangles if these are consistent with the literature or if voucher specimens still exist. For the earlier reports, the publications indicated below have been very useful. These either identify the species and locality, or in many cases verify previous published records. Important publications are Cope,[161,164] Evermann and Bollman,[239] Fowler (many publications), Gilbert,[298] Jordan,[455] LeSueur,[546,547,548] McConnell,[599] Rafinesque,[732] Raney,[733] Scott and Smith,[840] Van Meter and Trautman.[916] In addition, several catalogued lots in the Academy of Natural Science of Philadelphia were plotted when literature records of these collections were not available.

In most cases, nomenclature and phylogenetic arrangement of families follows the fourth edition of "A List of Common and Scientific Names of Fishes from the United States and Canada."[798] The genera and species included in the accounts are arranged alphabetically for the convenience of most readers.

Petromyzontidae
    Ohio lamprey, *Ichthyomyzon bdellium* (Jordan)
    Northern brook lamprey, *Ichthyomyzon fossor* Reighard and Cummins
    Mountain brook lamprey, *Ichthyomyzon greeleyi* Hubbs and Trautman
    Silver lamprey, *Ichthyomyzon unicuspis* Hubbs and Trautman
    Least brook lamprey, *Lampetra aepyptera* (Abbott)
    American brook lamprey, *Lampetra appendix* DeKay
    Sea lamprey, *Petromyzon marinus* Linnaeus

Acipenseridae
    Shortnose sturgeon, *Acipenser brevirostrum* Lesueur
    Lake sturgeon, *Acipenser fulvescens* Rafinesque
    Atlantic sturgeon, *Acipenser oxyrhynchus* Mitchill
    Shovelnose sturgeon, *Scaphirhynchus platorynchus* (Rafinesque)

Polyodontidae
    Paddlefish, *Polyodon spathula* (Walbaum)

Lepisosteidae
    Spotted gar, *Lepisosteus oculatus* (Winchell)
    Longnose gar, *Lepisosteus osseus* (Linnaeus)
    Shortnose gar, *Lepisosteus platostomus* Rafinesque

Amiidae
    Bowfin, *Amia calva* Linnaeus

Anguillidae
    American eel, *Anguilla rostrata* (Lesueur)

Clupeidae
    Blueback herring, *Alosa aestivalis* (Mitchill)
    Skipjack herring, *Alosa chrysochloris* (Rafinesque)
    Hickory shad, *Alosa mediocris* (Mitchill)
    Alewife, *Alosa pseudoharengus* (Wilson)
    American shad, *Alosa sapidissima* (Wilson)
    Gizzard shad, *Dorosoma cepedianum* (Lesueur)

Hiodontidae
    Goldeye, *Hiodon alosoides* (Rafinesque)
    Mooneye, *Hiodon tergisus* Lesueur

Salmonidae
    Longjaw cisco, *Coregonus alpenae* (Koelz)
    Lake herring, *Coregonus artedii* Lesueur
    Lake whitefish, *Coregonus clupeaformis* Mitchill
    Pink salmon, *Oncorhynchus gorbuscha* (Walbaum)
    Coho salmon, *Oncorhynchus kisutch* (Walbaum)
    Sockeye salmon, *Oncorhynchus nerka* (Walbaum)
    Chinook salmon, *Oncorhynchus tshawytscha* (Walbaum)
    Round whitefish, *Prosopium cylindraceum* (Pallas)
    Rainbow trout, *Salmo gairdneri* Richardson

Atlantic salmon, *Salmo salar* Linnaeus
Brown trout, *Salmo trutta* Linnaeus
Arctic char, *Salvelinus alpinus* (Linnaeus)
Brook trout, *Salvelinus fontinalis* (Mitchill)
Lake trout, *Salvelinus namaycush* (Walbaum)

Osmeridae
Rainbow smelt, *Osmerus mordax* (Mitchill)

Umbridae
Central mudminnow, *Umbra limi* (Kirtland)
Eastern mudminnow, *Umbra pygmaea* (DeKay)

Esocidae
Redfin pickerel, *Esox americanus americanus* Gmelin
Grass pickerel, *Esox americanus vermiculatus* Lesueur
Northern pike, *Esox lucius* Linnaeus
Muskellunge, *Esox masquinongy* Mitchill
Chain pickerel, *Esox niger* Lesueur
Amur pike, *Esox reicherti* Dybowski

Cyprinidae
Central stoneroller, *Campostoma anomalum* (Rafinesque)
Goldfish, *Carassius auratus* (Linnaeus)
Redside dace, *Clinostomus elongatus* (Kirtland)
Rosyside dace, *Clinostomus funduloides* Girard
Lake chub, *Couesius plumbeus* (Agassiz)
Common carp, *Cyprinus carpio* Linnaeus
Silverjaw minnow, *Ericymba buccata* Cope
Tonguetied minnow, *Exoglossum laurae* (Hubbs)
Cutlips minnow, *Exoglossum maxillingua* (Lesueur)
Brassy minnow, *Hybognathus hankinsoni* Hubbs and Greene
Eastern silvery minnow, *Hybognathus regius* Agassiz
Bigeye chub, *Hybopsis amblops* (Rafinesque)
Streamline chub, *Hybopsis dissimilis* (Kirtland)
Silver chub, *Hybopsis storeriana* (Kirtland)
Gravel chub, *Hybopsis x-punctata* Hubbs and Crowe
Hornyhead chub, *Nocomis biguttatus* (Kirtland)
River chub, *Nocomis micropogon* (Cope)
Golden shiner, *Notemigonus crysoleucas* (Mitchill)
Comely shiner, *Notropis amoenus* (Abbott)
Satinfin shiner, *Notropis analostanus* (Girard)
Pugnose shiner, *Notropis anogenus* Forbes
Popeye shiner, *Notropis ariommus* (Cope)
Emerald shiner, *Notropis atherinoides* Rafinesque
Bridle shiner, *Notropis bifrenatus* (Cope)
River shiner, *Notropis blennius* (Girard)
Ghost shiner, *Notropis buchanani* Meek
Ironcolor shiner, *Notropis chalybaeus* (Cope)
Striped shiner, *Notropis chrysocephalus* (Rafinesque)
Common shiner, *Notropis cornutus* (Mitchill)
Bigmouth shiner, *Notropis dorsalis* (Agassiz)
Blackchin shiner, *Notropis heterodon* (Cope)

Blacknose shiner, *Notropis heterolepis* Eigenmann and Eigenmann
Spottail shiner, *Notropis hudsonius* (Clinton)
Silver shiner, *Notropis photogenis* (Cope)
Swallowtail shiner, *Notropis procne* (Cope)
Rosyface shiner, *Notropis rubellus* (Agassiz)
Spotfin shiner, *Notropis spilopterus* (Cope)
Sand shiner, *Notropis stramineus* (Cope)
Redfin shiner, *Notropis umbratilis* (Girard)
Mimic shiner, *Notropis volucellus* (Cope)
Northern redbelly dace, *Phoxinus eos* (Cope)
Southern redbelly dace, *Phoxinus erythrogaster* (Rafinesque)
Finescale dace, *Phoxinus neogaeus* (Cope)
Bluntnose minnow, *Pimephales notatus* (Rafinesque)
Fathead minnow, *Pimephales promelas* Rafinesque
Bullhead minnow, *Pimephales vigilax* (Baird and Girard)
Blacknose dace, *Rhinichthys atratulus* (Hermann)
Longnose dace, *Rhinichthys cataractae* (Valenciennes)
Creek chub, *Semotilus atromaculatus* (Mitchill)
Fallfish, *Semotilus corporalis* (Mitchill)
Pearl dace, *Semotilus margarita* (Cope)

Catostomidae
River carpsucker, *Carpiodes carpio* (Rafinesque)
Quillback, *Carpiodes cyprinus* (Lesueur)
Highfin carpsucker, *Carpiodes velifer* (Rafinesque)
Longnose sucker, *Catostomus catostomus* (Forster)
White sucker, *Catostomus commersoni* (Lacepede)
Blue sucker, *Cycleptus elongatus* (Lesueur)
Creek chubsucker, *Erimyzon oblongus* (Mitchill)
Lake chubsucker, *Erimyzon sucetta* (Lacepede)
Northern hogsucker, *Hypentelium nigricans* (Lesueur)
Smallmouth buffalo, *Ictiobus bubalus* (Rafinesque)
Bigmouth buffalo, *Ictiobus cyprinellus* (Valenciennes)
Spotted sucker, *Minytrema melanops* (Rafinesque)
Silver redhorse, *Moxostoma anisurum* (Rafinesque)
River redhorse, *Moxostoma carinatum* (Cope)
Black redhorse, *Moxostoma duquesnei* (Lesueur)
Golden redhorse, *Moxostoma erythrurum* (Rafinesque)
Shorthead redhorse, *Moxostoma macrolepidotum* (Lesueur)
Greater redhorse, *Moxostoma valenciennesi* Jordan

Ictaluridae
White catfish, *Ictalurus catus* (Linnaeus)
Blue catfish, *Ictalurus furcatus* (Lesueur)
Black bullhead, *Ictalurus melas* (Rafinesque)

Yellow bullhead, *Ictalurus natalis* (Lesueur)
Brown bullhead, *Ictalurus nebulosus* (Lesueur)
Channel catfish, *Ictalurus punctatus* (Rafinesque)
Mountain madtom, *Noturus eleutherus* Jordan
Stonecat, *Noturus flavus* Rafinesque
Tadpole madtom, *Noturus gyrinus* (Mitchill)
Margined madtom, *Noturus insignis* (Richardson)
Brindled madtom, *Noturus miurus* Jordan
Northern madtom, *Noturus stigmosus* Taylor
Flathead catfish, *Pylodictis olivaris* (Rafinesque)

Aphredoderidae
Pirate perch, *Aphredoderus sayanus* (Gilliams)

Percopsidae
Trout-perch, *Percopsis omiscomaycus* (Walbaum)

Gadidae
Burbot, *Lota lota* (Linnaeus)

Cyprinodontidae
Sheepshead minnow, *Cyprinodon variegatus* (Lacepede)
Banded killifish, *Fundulus diaphanus* (Lesueur)
Mummichog, *Fundulus heteroclitus* (Linnaeus)

Poeciliidae
Mosquitofish, *Gambusia affinis* (Baird and Girard)

Atherinidae
Brook silverside, *Labidesthes sicculus* (Cope)
Inland silverside, *Menidia beryllina* (Cope)

Gasterosteidae
Fourspine stickleback, *Apeltes quadracus* (Mitchill)
Brook stickleback, *Culaea inconstans* (Kirtland)
Threespine stickleback, *Gasterosteus aculeatus* (Linnaeus)
Blackspotted stickleback, *Gasterosteus wheatlandi* Putnam
Ninespine stickleback, *Pungitius pungitius* (Linnaeus)

Percichthyidae
White perch, *Morone americana* (Gmelin)
White bass, *Morone chrysops* (Rafinesque)
Striped bass, *Morone saxatilis* (Walbaum)

Centrarchidae
Mud sunfish, *Acantharchus pomotis* (Baird)
Rock bass, *Ambloplites rupestris* (Rafinesque)
Blackbanded sunfish, *Enneacanthus chaetodon* (Baird)
Bluespotted sunfish, *Enneacanthus gloriosus* (Holbrook)
Banded sunfish, *Enneacanthus obesus* (Girard)
Redbreast sunfish, *Lepomis auritus* (Linnaeus)
Green sunfish, *Lepomis cyanellus* Rafinesque
Pumpkinseed, *Lepomis gibbosus* (Linnaeus)
Warmouth, *Lepomis gulosus* (Cuvier)

Orangespotted sunfish, *Lepomis humilis* (Girard)
Bluegill, *Lepomis macrochirus* Rafinesque
Longear sunfish, *Lepomis megalotis* (Rafinesque)
Redear sunfish, *Lepomis microlophus* (Gunther)
Smallmouth bass, *Micropterus dolomieui* Lacepede
Spotted bass, *Micropterus punctulatus* (Rafinesque)
Largemouth bass, *Micropterus salmoides* (Lacepede)
White crappie, *Pomoxis annularis* Rafinesque
Black crappie, *Pomoxis nigromaculatus* (Lesueur)

Percidae
Eastern sand darter, *Ammocrypta pellucida* (Putnam)
Greenside darter, *Etheostoma blennioides* Rafinesque
Rainbow darter, *Etheostoma caeruleum* Storer
Bluebreast darter, *Etheostoma camurum* (Cope)
Iowa darter, *Etheostoma exile* (Girard)
Fantail darter, *Etheostoma flabellare* Rafinesque
Swamp darter, *Etheostoma fusiforme* (Girard)
Spotted darter, *Etheostoma maculatum* Kirtland
Least darter, *Etheostoma microperca* Jordan
Johnny darter, *Etheostoma nigrum* Rafinesque
Tessellated darter, *Etheostoma olmstedi* Storer
Tippecanoe darter, *Etheostoma tippecanoe* Jordan and Evermann
Variegate darter, *Etheostoma variatum* Kirtland
Banded darter, *Etheostoma zonale* (Cope)
Yellow perch, *Perca flavescens* (Mitchill)
Logperch, *Percina caprodes* (Rafinesque)
Channel darter, *Percina copelandi* (Jordan)
Gilt darter, *Percina evides* (Jordan and Copeland)
Longhead darter, *Percina macrocephala* (Cope)
Blackside darter, *Percina maculata* (Girard)
Sharpnose darter, *Percina oxyrhyncha* (Hubbs and Raney)
Shield darter, *Percina peltata* (Stauffer)
Slenderhead darter, *Percina phoxocephala* (Nelson)
River darter, *Percina shumardi* (Girard)
Sauger, *Stizostedion canadense* Cuvier
Walleye, *Stizostedion vitreum* (Mitchill)

Sciaenidae
Freshwater drum, *Aplodinotus grunniens* Rafinesque

Cottidae
Mottled sculpin, *Cottus bairdi* Girard
Slimy sculpin, *Cottus cognatus* Richardson
Potomac sculpin, *Cottus girardi* Robins
Spoonhead sculpin, *Cottus ricei* (Nelson)
Deepwater sculpin, *Myoxocephalus thompsoni* (Girard)

Glossary

Abbreviated-heterocercal tail. Axis of caudal fin upturned but not greatly extended; see text, bowfins.

Abdomen. The portion of the body which contains the viscera.

Abdominal pelvic fins. Placement of pelvic fins close to the anus.

Accessory rays. Short rays at origin of vertical fins.

Adipose eyelid. Tissue covering part of the eye; see text, herrings.

Adnate. Adipose fins joined along entire length to the back; see text, madtoms.

Alevin. Larval fish from time of hatching until free-swimming stage.

Allopatric. Organisims not occurring in the same geographical area.

Ammocoete. Immature growth stage of lampreys lacking adult dentition and functional eyes.

Anadromous. Migrating from the ocean to spawn in freshwater; see text, American shad.

Anal papilla. A protuberance in front of the genital pore; see text, darters.

Antrorse. Turned forward.

Articulated. Jointed, as in soft rays.

Axillary process. Elongated, membranous process at base of pelvic or pectoral fin.

Barb. Hook-like process on spines; see text, madtoms.

Barbel. Elongated, tapered projection of tissue, usually found about mouth or head.

Benthic. Living on the bottom.

Bicuspid. A tooth with two cusps on a single base.

Bifurcate. Divided into two branches.

Branched ray. A ray which divides distally into two or more parts.

Branchial. Of the gills.

Branchiostegal rays. A series of bones supporting the gill membranes under the head.

Buccal. Of the mouth.

Buccal disc. Head region of a lamprey including mouth and oral dentition.

Caducous. Scales which easily fall off; see text, gizzard shad.

Caecum. A blind sac opening off the intestine.

Cardioid scales. Heart-shaped, or odd-shaped scales; see pikes.

Carinate. Keeled, as the belly scales of shad.

Catadromous. Migrating from streams to spawn in the ocean; see text, American eel.

Caudal peduncle. Posterior part of body from anal fin base to end of hypural plate.

Cephalic lateral line system. Extension of sensory canal over head region.

Cheek. Lateral portion of head between eye and operculum.

Circumoral teeth. Teeth in the buccal funnel of a lamprey immediately surrounding the oral opening.

Circumorbitals. A series of small bones around the eye.

Compressed. Flattened laterally.

Crenate. With a notched margin, as the scales of sunfishes.

Ctenoid scale. Scales with teeth on posterior margins; see text, yellow perch.

Cuneate. Wedge shaped.

Cycloid scale. Scales without teeth on posterior margins; see text, trout.

Deciduous. Scales that fall off easily; see text, herrings.

Demersal. Referring to the habitat at the bottom of stream or lake.

Dentary. Principal bone of the lower jaw of fishes.

Denticulate. Having fine teeth.

Depressed. Flattened dorso-ventrally.

Depth. Vertical measurement of a part of a fish.

Distal. Portion of a structure most distant from the body.

Dorsad. Toward the back.

Elver. Juvenile eel after transformation from leptocephalus larva.

Emarginate. Having a slight indentation.

Endemic. The original or native geographic distribution.

Entire. Having no notches or indentations.

Esophagus. Part of the alimentary canal between the pharynx and the stomach.

Exotic. Transplanted and established outside its native range.

Extirpated. No longer occurring through natural reproduction; locally extinct.

Extraoral teeth. Teeth in the buccal funnel of a lamprey outside the circumoral row.

Falcate fin. Outer margin concave, as the anal fin of the golden shiner.

Fimbriate. Having a frilled edge.

Focus. Center of growth of a fish scale.

Fontanel. An unossified area in a skull bone; see text, suckers.

Frenum. A fleshy connection at midline of snout limiting extension of premaxillaries from snout.

Fulcral plate. Structure bordering the anterior rays of fins of sturgeons.

Fusiform. Spindle shaped.

Ganoid scales. Thick bony scales with outer layer of enamel-like ganoine; see text, gar.

Genital papilla. Protuberance near the anus which includes the genital opening.

Gill arches. Bony supports for the gills.

Gill cover. Opercular apparatus.

Gill rakers. Bony projections on anterior margin of gill arch.

Gill slits. Openings from pharynx to outside the body, covered in bony fishes by opercular apparatus.

Gonopodium. Intromittent sex organ of male livebearers; modified ray of anal fin.

Gravid. Bearing eggs at spawning time.

Guanine. Crystalline, reflective substance associated with skins and scales, responsible for white color.

Gular plate. One or more median bones on outside of head just behind the chin; see text, bowfin.

Haemal spine. Lower spine of a caudal vertebra.

Head length. Tip of snout or lower jaw to posterior edge of operculum.

Hemibranch. Rudimentary gill on inner side of the operculum.

Heterocercal tail. Axis of caudal fin turned up and extended, lobes of fin asymmetrical; see sturgeon.

Homocercal tail. Symmetrical externally, but with asymmetrical hypural plate; see text, largemouth bass.

Humeral process. Backward extension of the cleithrum; see text, catfishes.

Humeral scale. Large scale-like structure immediately behind the head above the pectoral origin; see text, darters.

Hypural plate. Series of modified haemal spines at base of tail which support fin rays.

Imbricated. Overlapping, like scales on a carp.

Inferior mouth. Mouth opening posterior to and below snout.

Infraorbital canal. Part of the sensory canal below the eye.

Insertion of fin. Posterior edge of base of vertical fins.

Intermuscular bone. Small bone lying in the connective tissue between adjacent myomeres, not connected to axial skeleton.

Interorbital canal. Part of the sensory canal system between the orbits in top of the head.

Interorbital width. Distance between inner margins of orbits.

Isocercal tail. Symmetrical dorso-ventrally, with tapering vertebra; see text, American eel.

Isthmus. Lower part of the head between the gill openings.

Keeled. Having a sharp, median ridge.

Kelt. Recently spawned salmon.

Labial. Pertaining to the lips.

Lacustrine. Lake habitat.

Lanceolate. Spear-shaped, tapering to a point.

Larva. Young stage of a fish when differing noticeably from the adult form.

Lateral line. Pored scales along sides connected to sensory canal.

Lateral line incomplete. Pored scales missing from a portion of the lateral sensory canal.

Lateral line complete. Lateral sensory canal with complete series of pored scales.

Leptocephalus. Flat, leaf-like larval stage of eel.

Lingual. Pertaining to the tongue.

Littoral. Bottom of a lake near the shore.

Mandible. Lower jaw.

Mandibular pores. Openings to sensory canal along ventral side of lower jaw.

Marginal teeth. Teeth in outer row of the buccal funnel of a lamprey near marginal fimbriae.

Maxillary. Posterior, lateral bones of upper jaw of most bony fishes.

Melanophore. Black pigment cell.

Mental. Pertaining to the tip of the chin, as the barbel of the burbot.

Meristic. Structures associated with body segments, see fin ray counts.

Molar-like. Teeth with flattened cusps, similar to human molar teeth.

Morphometric. Measurements of body parts.

Myomere. Lateral muscle segment bounded by myosepta; see text, lampreys.

Nape. The back of the fish just posterior to the head.

Nares. Openings into nasal sac.

Native. Original geographic range before modified by man.

Neural spine. Dorsal spine of a vertebra.

Nuptial tubercle. Temporary pearl organs on head or body developed during the breeding season.

Occiput. Dorsal, rear portion of the head.

Opercular flap. Backward extension of operculum; see text, sunfishes.

Operculum. Gill cover, composed of four separate bones.

Oral valve. Membranes in anterior part of mouth which prevent backflow of water during breathing cycle.

Orbit. Bony socket in a fish skull containing the eye.

Origin of fin. Anterior edge of fin base.

Oviparous. Fishes which lay eggs to develop in the external environment.

Ovoviviparous. Eggs developing within the body of a female, but without placental formation; see text, mosquito fish.

Palatines. Paired bones in roof of mouth lateral to single median vomer.

Parr. Juvenile stage of trout or salmon lacking silvery coloration.

Parr marks. Oblong, dark pigment patches on sides of

young trout or salmon.

Pearl organs. Horny structures developed on head or scales of fishes during the breeding season.

Pelagic. Open water habitat, free-floating or swimming.

Pellucid. Translucent; see text, sand darter.

Peritoneum. Lining of the body cavity.

Pharyngeal arch. Fifth gill arch of fishes bearing teeth, in minnows and suckers.

Pharyngeal teeth. Throat teeth; see text, minnows and suckers.

Pharynx. That portion of the digestive tract between the mouth and esophagus; associated with teeth in minnows and suckers.

Physoclistous. Swim bladder with closed duct to esophagus.

Plicate. With wrinkle-like folds.

Potamodromous. Fishes migrating from lakes into streams to spawn, as salmon in Great Lakes.

Premaxillary. Median, anterior, paired bones of upper jaw of most bony fishes.

Preopercle. Cheek bone, part of the opercular series.

Prickles. Small spines in skin in place of scales; see text, sculpins.

Primary scale radius. Radius on a scale reaching from the margin to the focus.

Principal rays. All branched rays plus one unbranched ray; see text, minnows.

Protractile. Said of premaxillaries that can be extended beyond margin of upper jaw.

Proximal. Portion of a structure closest to the body.

Pseudobranch. Gill-like secretory structure on inner side of operculum.

Pyloric caecae. Blind pouches leading off from posterior portion of stomach; see text, salmon.

Pyloris. Posterior portion of stomach.

Radius. Groove on a fish scale which radiates out from the focus.

Ray. Fin support.

Redd. Nest in which trout and salmon deposit their eggs.

Retrorse. Turned backward.

Sac fry. Larval stage of a fish with visible external yolk sac.

Scale radius. A line of flexure on a scale perpendicular to the margin.

Scute. Modified scale; see text, shad and sturgeon.

Secondary scale radius. Radius on a scale not reaching to the focus.

Sensory pores. External openings to sensory canal.

Serrated. Notched or toothed.

Smolt. Juvenile stage of salmon prepared to migrate to sea.

Snout. Front of the head anterior to the eyes.

Soft dorsal fin. Portion of the dorsal fin containing only soft rays.

Soft ray. Jointed, paired, bony support for a fin.

Spatulate. Flat, depressed snout; see text, paddlefish.

Spiny dorsal. Portion of the dorsal fin containing only spiny rays.

Spiny ray. Unjointed, bony element of a fin.

Spiracles. Paired openings on upper posterior part of head of fishes, representing the first post-oral gill slit.

Splake. Hybrid between brook trout (speckled) and lake trout.

Squamation. Arrangement of scales on a fish.

Standard length. Tip of snout or lower jaw to end of hypural plate.

Sympatric. Organisms occurring in the same geographical area.

Tapetum. Reflective mechanism in eye of certain fishes; see text, walleye.

Tear-drop. Dark, drop-shaped spot below the eye; see text, pikes.

Terete. Cylindrical and tapering.

Terminal mouth. Mouth opening at tip of snout.

Tessellated. Marked with little squares.

Thoracic pelvic fins. Placement of pelvic fins far forward of anus.

Total length. Tip of snout or lower jaw to end of caudal fin.

Truncate. Abruptly cut off.

Tubercles. Horny structures developed on head or scales of fishes during the breeding season.

Tuberculate. Having pearl organs on head, body, or fins.

Unicuspid. A tooth with a single cusp on its base.

Urostyle. The last vertebral segment, often modified.

Vent. The anus.

Vermiculations. Worm-like marks; see text, brook trout.

Villiform. Small, slender structures in bands, as the teeth of catfishes.

Vomer. Single, median bone in roof of mouth.

Weberian apparatus. Series of small bones connecting inner ear with base of brain; see text, minnows and suckers.

Key to the Families

The following key is artificial, using characters that demand only a superficial knowledge of fish anatomy. General diagrams of morphology of bony fishes illustrate some of the characters used (Fig. 7). More detailed descriptions of families, genera, and species follow in later sections.

1 a. Fishes with no jaws, mouth surrounded by a sucking disc, or with an overhanging oral hood; single, median nostril; pectoral and pelvic fins absent; seven pore-like gill openings on each side of head. Jawless fishes (Class Agnatha): **Lampreys** (Petromyzontidae).

b. Fishes with jaws; nostrils bilateral; pectoral fins always present; pelvic fins usually present; gills covered by a bony operculum with a single posterior opening on each side of the head.
Bony fishes (Class Osteichthyes): **2**

2 a. Pelvic fins completely absent; Long, low dorsal fin continuous with caudal and with anal fin; caudal fin isocercal; body long and slender: **Freshwater eels** (Anguillidae).

b. Pelvic fins present; dorsal and anal fins completely separated from caudal fin (deep notches separate caudal fin from dorsal and anal fins in the burbot): **3**

3 a. Caudal fin strongly heterocercal (Fig. 8,A); main axis of vertebral column upturned and continued onto tail almost to its tip: **4**

b. Caudal fin abbreviate heterocercal (Fig. 8,B); main axis of vertebral column upturned, but extends only a short distance onto tail: **5**

c. Caudal fin homocercal (Fig. 8,C); last vertebra not dorso-ventrally symmetrical, but does not extend onto fin; outline of caudal fin rounded or forked, but dorso-ventrally symmetrical: **6**

4 a. Body without scales or bony plates; snout long and extremely depressed, spatulate, with 2 small barbels on ventral surface a short distance in front of mouth: **Paddlefishes** (Polyodontidae).

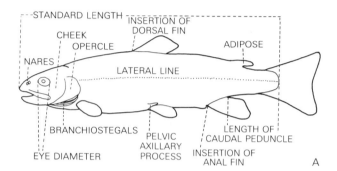

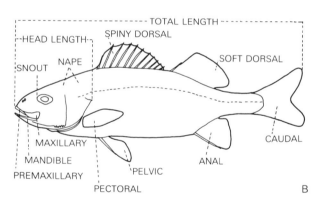

Figure 7. Morphology of a soft-rayed fish (A) and a spiny-rayed fish (B).

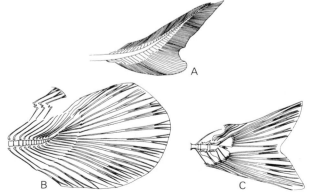

Figure 8. Types of caudal fins found in bony fishes: Heterocercal (A); Abbreviate Heterocercal (B); Homocercal (C).

b. Body with 5 rows of bony plates; snout relatively short with 4 long barbels on ventral side ahead of protrusible mouth: **Sturgeons** (Acipenseridae).

5 a. Body armored completely with closely-fitted, rhombic, ganoid scales; both upper and lower jaws extended into a long, narrow snout; no gular plate; dorsal fin short; fewer than 15 rays; located close to tail: **Gars** (Lepisosteidae).

b. Body covered with overlapping cycloid scales; head covered with bony plates, including unique gular bone on ventral side of the head between the jaws (Fig. 9); dorsal fin very long, containing more than 45 rays, but separated from caudal fin: **Bowfins** (Amiidae).

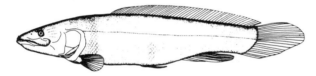

6 a. Adipose fin present on dorsal side of caudal peduncle: **7**

b. Adipose fin absent: **10**

7 a. No scales on body; eight barbels on head, 2 nasal, 2 maxillary, and 4 on chin; true spines in dorsal and pectoral fins, in cross section, a single bony element (Fig. 10): **Bullhead catfishes** (Ictaluridae).

b. Body normally covered with scales; barbels absent; no spines in pectoral fins: **8**

8 a. Body covered with ctenoid scales (Fig. 11); dorsal and anal fins contain weak spines: **Trout-perches** (Percopsidae).

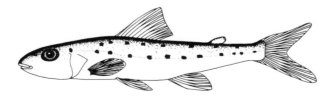

Figure 9. Ventral aspect of the head of a bowfin, showing the unique gular plate.

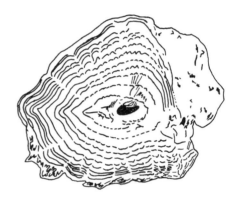

Figure 10. Cross section of the dorsal spine of a catfish.

b. Body covered with cycloid scales (Fig. 11); no spines in fins: **9**

9 a. A pointed, flap-like process present at the base of each pelvic fin (pelvic axillary process, Fig. 12,A) directed backwards: **Trouts** (Salmonidae).

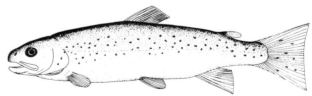

b. No pelvic axillary process (Fig. 12,B) present at base of pelvic fins: **Smelts** (Osmeridae).

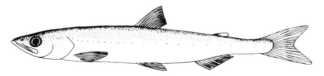

10 a. A single barbel present on tip of chin: **Codfishes** (Gadidae).

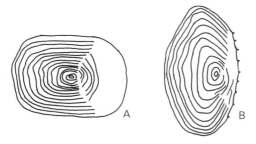

Figure 11. Cycloid scale from brook trout (A), and ctenoid scale from trout perch (B).

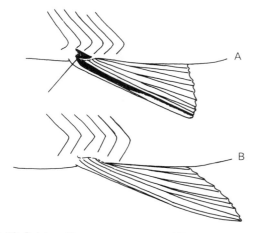

Figure 12. Pelvic axillary process present (A), and absent (B).

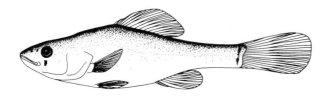

b. No single barbel present on tip of chin. Barbels may be present in other locations on head: **11**

11 a. Anus, in adult fishes, located far forward in advance of pelvic fins; juvenile forms have anus in normal posterior position: **Pirateperches** (Aphredoderidae).

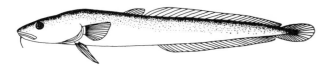

b. Anus, in adult and juvenile forms, located in normal posterior position slightly anterior to anal fin: **12**

12 a. Dorsal fin preceded by 4 to 6 isolated, stout spines not connected to each other by membranes: **Sticklebacks** (Gasterosteidae).

b. No isolated spines preceding dorsal fin; a spinous dorsal fin may precede a soft-rayed dorsal; but the spines are connected by membranes: **13**

13 a. First ray of dorsal and anal fin modified as a hard, bony element, serrated on posterior margins. [This is not a true spine; in cross section its derivation from a bi-partite soft-ray is obvious (Fig. 13)]: **Common Carp and Goldfish** (Cyprinidae; introduced).

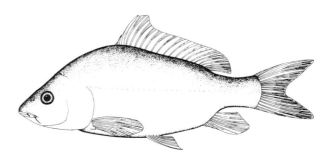

b. No modified soft rays in dorsal and anal fins; true spines present or absent in fins: **14**

14 a. Dorsal fin single; with no spines: **15**

b. Dorsal fins one or more; but always containing some true spines. (True spines may be rather soft and flexible, as in sculpins): **22**

15 a. No scales on head or operculum: **16**

b. Head at least partially scaled, at least on cheeks: **19**

16 a. Prominent pelvic axillary process present (Fig. 12); gill slits extend forward to beneath the eye: **17**

b. Pelvic axillary process absent (Fig. 12), or reduced to a small remnant; gill slits do not extend forward beyond edge of preopercle: **18**

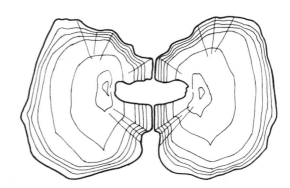

Figure 13. Modified soft ray in dorsal fin of carp or goldfish, in cross section, showing paired bony elements.

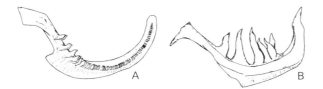

Figure 14. Pharyngeal arch of sucker (A) and minnow (B).

17 a. Lateral line well developed; gill rakers few and knobby: **Mooneyes** (Hiodontidae).

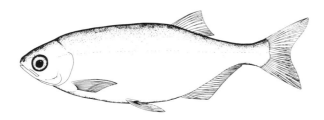

b. Lateral line absent; gill rakers long and numerous. (Note that the lateral line is identified as a series of pores or tubes passing through specialized scales; the septum dividing the body musculature into dorsal and ventral portions must not be confused with the true lateral line): **Herrings** (Clupeidae).

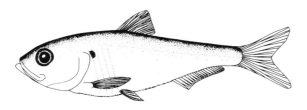

18 a. Anal fin placement more posterior than in minnows (distance from posterior edge of opercle to anterior edge of anal fin much greater than distance from anterior edge of anal fin to base of caudal fin). Pharyngeal arch with a single row of more than 15 teeth (Fig. 14,A): **Suckers** (Catostomidae).

b. Anal fin placement more anterior than in suckers (distance from posterior edge of opercle to anterior edge of anal fin only slightly greater than distance from anterior edge of anal fin to base of caudal fin). Pharyngeal arch with 1 to 3 rows of teeth, never more than 6 teeth in the principal row (Fig. 14,B): **Minnows** (Cyprinidae; native).

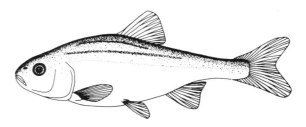

19 a. Tail forked: **Pikes** (Esocidae).

b. Tail rounded: **20**

20 a. Premaxillaries non-protractile; no groove separates upper lip from top of head; pelvic fin placement more posterior (anterior origin of pelvic fins closer to caudal base than to tip of snout): **Mudminnows** (Umbridae).

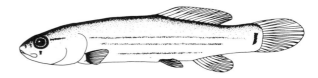

b. Premaxillaries protractile, deep groove separates upper lip from top of head; pelvic fin placement more anterior (anterior origin of pelvic fin midway between caudal base and tip of snout, or nearer to snout): **21**

21 a. Egg laying fishes; anal fin of male similar to that of female: **Killifishes** (Cyprinodontidae).

b. Viviparous; anal fin of male modified into intromittent organ, the gonopodium; adult females usually contain embryos in various stages of development: **Livebearers** (Poeciliidae).

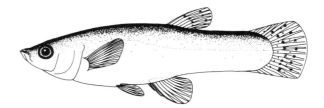

22 a. Body naked except for minute prickles: **Sculpins** (Cottidae).

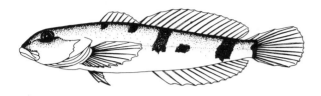

   b. Most of body covered with scales: **23**
23 a. Body covered with cycloid scales: **Silversides** (Atherinidae).

   b. Body covered with ctenoid scales: **24**
24 a. Anal spines 3 or more: **25**
   b. Anal spines 1 or 2: **26**
25 a. Spine on opercle: **Temperate basses** (Percichthyidae).

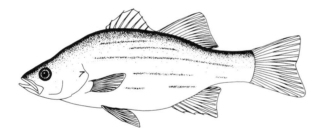

   b. No spine on opercle: **Sunfishes** (Centrarchidae).

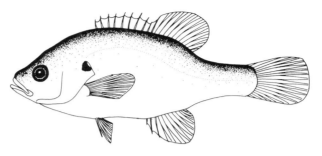

26 a. Lateral line not extending onto caudal fin: **Perches** (Percidae).

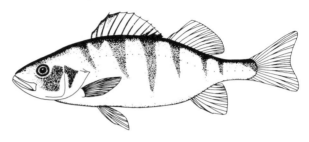

   b. Lateral line extending well onto caudal fin: **Drums** (Sciaenidae).

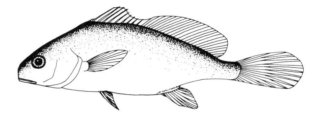

Accounts and Keys of Genera and Species

Lampreys—Petromyzontidae

Lampreys lack typical jaws of other fishes and also lack both pectoral and pelvic fins. There is a single median nostril. There are seven pairs of gills each opening separately to the outside, but also with an opening to the pharynx. The oral hood of the ammocoete is replaced at metamorphosis with a circular, sucker-like mouth armed with horny teeth in patterns that are useful in depicting phylogenetic relationships.[353,924,925]

All lampreys have a unique life cycle which involves an extended larval (ammocoete) stage, a period of resting or transformation to the adult form, further growth, sexual maturation, spawning, followed immediately by death. Non-parasitic forms have shortened this typical life cycle by becoming sexually mature during the metamorphosis period; in these species the spawning adults are frequently smaller than the ammocoetes just prior to their transformation.

Lampreys spawn in depressions constructed in gravel riffles of streams. Both males and females build the nest, and several pairs may occupy a pit at the same time. Eggs and sperm are emitted during the spawning embrace and fertilized eggs sift down among the gravel. Newly-hatched ammocoetes drift downstream and burrow into silty substrates where they will live and grow for several years apparently feeding on organic detritus and bacteria filtered from the water.[21] During metamorphosis, the oral hood changes to a sucking mouth, adult dentition appears, and eyes develop externally. After metamorphosis, parasitic forms feed actively on fish and grow for about a year before maturing sexually. Often there is an upstream migration of pre-spawning adults, even in the non-anadromous forms.

KEY TO SPECIES OF LAMPREY AMMOCOETES

Morphological characters of ammocoetes cannot be used to clearly separate some species. Of those with a single dorsal fin, habitat preference and geographic distribution are helpful in determining species. For example, *I. bdellium* and *I. greeleyi* are found only in the Ohio River tributaries with the non-parasitic form, *I. greeleyi,* preferring smaller headwater streams. *I. unicuspis* and *I. fossor* are restricted to the Great Lakes drainage in Pennsylvania, with the non-parasitic form, *I. fossor,* found in headwater streams.

1 a. Single dorsal fin (Fig. 15,A), *Ichthyomyzon:* **2**
  b. Two dorsal fins, separated at least by a notch (Fig. 15,B): **3**
2 a. Number of myomeres 49–55 (Fig. 16): Silver lamprey, *I. unicuspis,* or Northern brook lamprey, *I. fossor.*
  b. Number of myomeres 55–61: Ohio lamprey, *I. bdellium,* or Mountain brook lamprey, *I. greeleyi.*
3 a. Number of myomeres 54–60; dark pigment on caudal membrane restricted to thin area along body (Fig. 17,A): Least brook lamprey, *Lampetra aepyptera.*
  b. Number of myomeres greater than 63; dark pigment on much of caudal membrane: **4**

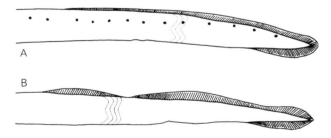

Figure 15. Dorsal fins of lamprey ammocoetes: single (A), double (B).

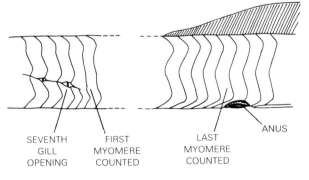

SEVENTH GILL OPENING   FIRST MYOMERE COUNTED   LAST MYOMERE COUNTED   ANUS

Figure 16. Method of counting myomeres of lampreys.

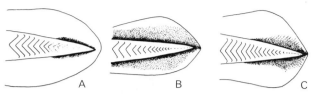

Figure 17. Pigment patterns of caudal fins of lamprey ammocoetes: *L. aepyptera* (A); *P. marinus* (B); *L. appendix* (C).

4 a. Tip of caudal fin rounded; dark pigment spread over most of caudal membrane (Fig. 17,B): Sea lamprey, *Petromyzon marinus*.

  b. Tip of caudal fin pointed; dark pigment restricted to central half of caudal fin (Fig. 17,C): American brook lamprey, *Lampetra appendix*.

KEY TO SPECIES OF ADULT LAMPREYS

1 a. Single dorsal fin (Fig. 18,A) *Ichthyomyzon:* **2**

  b. Two dorsal fins separated at least by a distinct notch (Fig. 18,B): **5**

2 a. Circumoral teeth unicuspid (Fig. 19): **3**

  b. At least one of the circumoral teeth bicuspid (Fig. 20): **4**

3 a. Parasitic; sucking disc expands wider than body: Silver lamprey, *I. unicuspis.*

  b. Non-parasitic; expanded sucking disc less than body width: Northern brook lamprey, *I. fossor.*

4 a. Parasitic; expanded sucking disc as wide as body; anterior circumoral tooth usually bicuspid, but often tricuspid: Ohio lamprey, *I. bdellium.*

  b. Non-parasitic; expanded sucking disc not as wide as body: Mountain brook lamprey, *I. greeleyi.*

5 a. Parasitic; teeth large and sharp (Fig. 21); mature adults larger than 12 inches: Sea lamprey, *Petromyzon marinus.*

  b. Non-parasitic; teeth blunt, except for circumorals, many hidden in skin; mature adults smaller than 9 inches: **6**

6 a. Number of myomeres 54–60; only small marginal teeth present on posterior field of sucking disc (Fig. 21): Least brook lamprey, *Lampetra aepyptera.*

  b. Number of myomeres 63–70; a row of teeth visible on posterior field of sucking disc in addition to marginals (Fig. 21): American brook lamprey, *Lampetra appendix.*

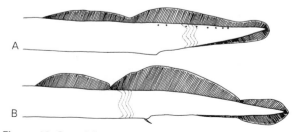

Figure 18. Dorsal fins of adult lampreys: single (A); double (B).

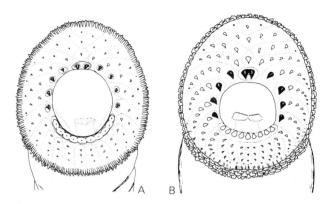

Figure 19. Unicuspid circumoral teeth of adult lampreys: *I. fossor* (A); *I. unicuspis* (B).

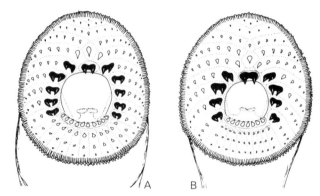

Figure 20. Bicuspid circumoral teeth of adult lampreys: *I. greeleyi* (A); *I. bdellium* (B).

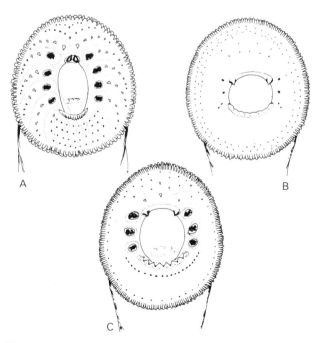

Figure 21. Tooth pattern of adult lampreys with two dorsal fins: *P. marinus* (A); *L. aepyptera* (B); *L. appendix* (C).

Genus *Ichthyomyzon*

A single dorsal fin in both ammocoetes and adults, often notched but never divided into two separate fins; dorsal fin not separated from the caudal fin by a sharp notch; myomeres 63 or fewer; Extraoral teeth in regular rows completely filling the oral disc; circumoral teeth usually 11; parasitic and non-parasitic species pairs, which are sometimes sympatric.

Ohio lamprey, *Ichthyomyzon bdellium* (Jordan)[456]

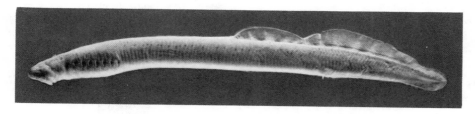

Length 241 mm. Potato Creek, McKean County, Pa. 26 May 1977

Distribution This parasitic species and its non-parasitic form, the mountain brook lamprey, are common inhabitants of the Allegheny River and much of the Ohio River drainage.[419] In Pennsylvania, populations of the Ohio lamprey fluctuate greatly, at times becoming abundant enough to be commonly observed feeding on redhorses, smallmouth bass, and walleyes. Several hundred ammocoetes and spawning adults were collected in one survey of Brokenstraw Creek, Warren County, in the spring and summer of 1965, but were rare there in 1977. Meanwhile, populations of this species remained abundant in other nearby tributaries of the Allegheny River.

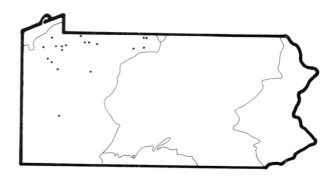

Behavior In three instances, partially spent adults of both the Ohio lamprey and the mountain brook lamprey were captured in the same spawning pit. In two of these cases, males and females of both species were involved, based on complete separation of total length range and of relative size of the oral disc of the two species. Although no interspecific pairing or spawning was observed in the few minutes prior to capture, the close proximity of this group of spawning adults leads to the possibility of hybridization between parasitic and non-parasitic forms with markedly different life cycles.

Northern brook lamprey, *Ichthyomyzon fossor* Reighard and Cummins[779]

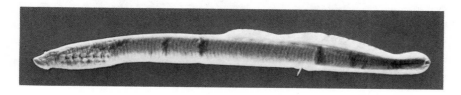

Length 132 mm. Conneaut Creek, Crawford County, Pa. 25 May 1977

Distribution This non-parasitic species has a wide and scattered distribution in the midwest.[127,681,924] In Pennsylvania, we collected three small series of individuals from the headwaters of Conneaut Creek in Crawford County in recent years, including both ammocoetes and adults. This stream also supports a large population of American brook lamprey and has a small spawning run of the sea lamprey from Lake Erie. The northern brook lamprey has been reported from the Ohio River drainage in Ohio,[902] but we have not found it in the Ohio drainage in Pennsylvania.

This non-parasitic form probably evolved from the parasitic silver lamprey and is considered to be the most degenerate of the brook lampreys.[415]

Behavior We have found one small aggregation of

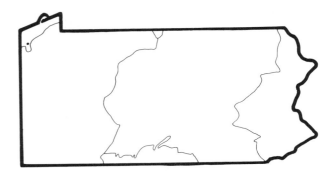

seven individuals late in May, secreted under a flat stone in moderate current of a riffle. They were spawning in a manner similar to that reported for other lampreys.[681]

Mountain brook lamprey, *Ichthyomyzon greeleyi* Hubbs and Trautman[419]

Length 141 mm. Fishing Creek, Potter County, Pa. 30 May 1975

Distribution This species, the least degenerate of the non-parasitic lampreys, has a scattered north-south distribution on the west slope of the Appalachians from New York to Tennessee.[129] It is more abundant than previous records indicate, but is seldom noticed except for brief periods in May. It is usually found further upstream in the headwaters than its parasitic counterpart, the Ohio Lamprey, but sometimes spawns in the same nest.[826] Ammocoetes of these two species cannot be distinguished morphologically.

Behavior The mountain brook lamprey spawns in the spring, somewhat later than the more common American brook lamprey. Males and females together construct a small pit-nest in a gravel riffle, and die soon after spawning.[826] In Pennsylvania, observations on spawning of this species in 1935 by Raney were repeated by us in

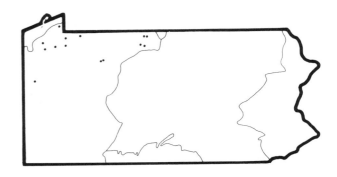

the same locality in 1975, indicating a very stable ecosystem over this time period. They are commonly associated with the striped and rosyface shiners on spawning riffles.[735]

Silver lamprey, *Ichthyomyzon unicuspis* Hubbs and Trautman[419]

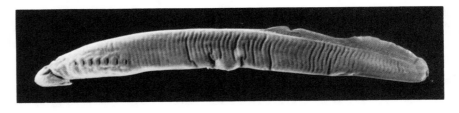

Length 238 mm. Swan Creek, Toledo, Ohio, 26 April 1935

Distribution This species is widely distributed through-out the Great Lakes and Mississippi River drainages,[286,932] but has never been reported from Pennsylvania streams. It is included here as a probable inhabitant of Lake Erie during the parasitic phase, and based on early reports of its presence there and in the Ohio River at least as far east as Portsmouth, Ohio.[419,916]

Behavior This parasitic form is considered to be the most primitive lamprey, and as in the non-parasitic form, *I. fossor,* has fewer myomeres than other species of *Ichthyomyzon.* It almost never has any bicuspid circumo-ral teeth as adults. Despite its parasitic habit, populations

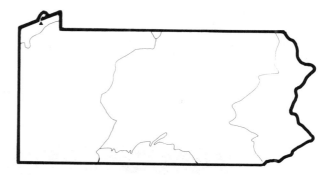

of this species seldom become numerous enough to be a nuisance to other fishes.[924]

Genus *Lampetra* *

Dorsal fin divided by a deep notch into two parts, and is also separated from the caudal fin by a distinct notch; extraoral teeth in irregular rows; lateral and posterior fields of oral disc between circumorals and marginals toothless; circumoral teeth 13 or more.

Least brook lamprey, *Lampetra aepyptera* (Abbott)[1]

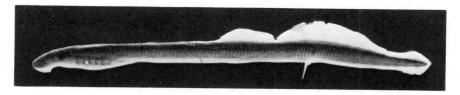

Length 127 mm. Tributary to Oostanaula River, Floyd County, Ga. 2 March 1978

Distribution This non-parasitic species is a widespread form with many documented collections from streams in Pennsylvania south to the Gulf of Mexico.[749] It occurs on both slopes of the Appalachians. On the Delmarva Penin-sula, *L. aepyptera* occurs only in streams on the western slope of the peninsula while *L. appendix* occurs only in streams draining the eastern slope.[802,803] We have found this same pattern to continue at a few localities just across the border into southeastern Pennsylvania.

Adults of the least brook lamprey are found only in headwater streams spawning in a shallow riffle. The fish is apparently too small to move stones from the nest; sand and silt are swept away from stones in the nest by swimming motions.[98,804] Extensive upstream migration for spawning has not been observed. Ammocoetes are

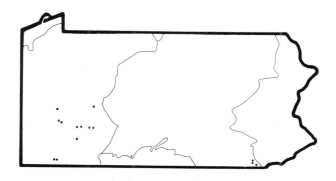

found in firm mud banks or in organic debris close to the stream current.[844]

---

*There is some disagreement about the generic assignment of the least brook lamprey and the American brook lamprey.[802,931] Following the List of Common and Scientific Names of Fishes,[798] the genus *Lampetra* as used here includes *Entosphenus, Lethenteron,* and *Okkelbergia.*

Behavior The least brook lamprey is considerably smaller than the American brook lamprey at most collection sites; 34 breeding adults of *L. aepyptera* from various localities in Pennsylvania averaged 132 mm total length; a collection of 30 spawning adults from a tributary of the Oostanaula River in Georgia averaged only 119 mm total length. Both of these mean values are higher than that of the Atlantic Coast population.[804]

American brook lamprey, *Lampetra appendix* DeKay[199]

Length 129 mm. White Clay Creek, Chester County, Pa. 12 April 1978

Distribution This non-parasitic form has a broad range throughout the midwest, and along the Atlantic coast.[415,804,924] In Pennsylvania, it is completely allopatric with the least lamprey, and both have unique disjunct distributions.

Adults are found in gravelly headwater streams in April or May spawning in small groups in a nest of stones from which fine pebbles and sand have been removed either by carrying the stones, or by swimming motion of the fish.[227,975] Ammocoetes live in burrows in mud banks, apparently feeding on diatoms and organic debris which they sieve from the water flowing over the mouth of the burrow.[644]

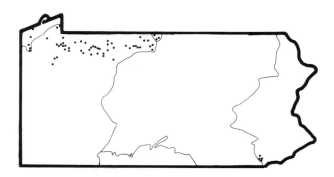

Behavior The mean total length of *L. appendix* spawning adults, based on five random collections of 61 individuals in Pennsylvania, was 168 mm, making Pennsylvania specimens intermediate in size between those reported for the Delmarva Peninsula (127 mm)[804] and the Ontario population (188 mm).[497] In this respect, and in the number of myomeres, dentition, and other morphological characters, *L. appendix* is a highly variable species. Because local populations of non-parasitic lampreys living in streams are reproductively isolated, such diversity is not unexpected.[415]

Genus *Petromyzon*

Dorsal fin divided by a deep notch; dorsal fin also separated from the caudal fin by a notch; extraoral teeth in curvilinear rows which completely fill the oral disc; circumoral teeth almost always 9.

Sea lamprey, *Petromyzon marinus* Linnaeus[558]

Bigelow and Schroeder. 1953. U.S. Fish. Bull. 53, p. 12

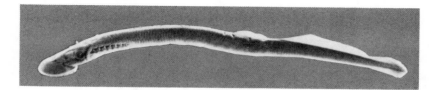

Length 138 mm. Carp Lake River, Mich.

Distribution This anadromous fish parasite is found in the North Atlantic Ocean, ascending many streams to spawn and die. Its original distribution also included land-locked forms in Lake Ontario and some of the Finger Lakes of New York. It successfully invaded the upper Great Lakes in the 1920s.[21, 414, 955]

The first specimen of *P. marinus* taken above Niagara Falls was that collected on 8 November 1921 from Lake Erie at Merlin, Ontario.[220] Populations of this fish never became abundant in Lake Erie, presumably because of the scarcity of suitable spawning habitat in streams. In Pennsylvania, spawning runs now commonly occur throughout the Delaware River drainage and in a few western tributaries of Lake Erie.

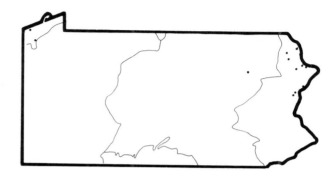

Behavior The life history of this migratory parasitic fish is the best known of all lampreys, due primarily to its impact on the commercial fishery of the Great Lakes. Adults migrate into freshwater streams in the spring to spawn and die. Ammocoetes live in mud banks for 4 to 7 years, feeding on diatoms and organic debris. After metamorphosis they return to the Great Lakes or the Atlantic Ocean to feed on fish until they become sexually mature in about 1 year.[22,539,571,644,817]

Sturgeons—Acipenseridae

This small family, considered to be the most primitive of the bony fishes, is characterized by the following: four barbels in front of a protractile mouth; body with 5 rows of bony plates, 1 dorsal row, 2 lateral rows, 2 ventral rows; no branchiostegal rays; no teeth on jaws; jaws do not articulate with skull; heterocercal tail; first ray of pectoral fin hardened into a bony spine, often used in determination of age; pelvic fins abdominal and without true spines.

Sturgeons are worldwide in distribution, represented in recent times by only a few genera and species. There are both freshwater and marine forms, with all adults spawning in the spring in fast current of large rivers on stony substrates. Sturgeons generally live longer than most species of fishes. They also spawn for the first time at a more advanced age than most fishes. They are important commercial species for both flesh and caviar in some parts of the world,[814] but in the Great Lakes of North America they have historically been considered more of a nuisance to commercial fishermen than as an important resource.[930]

KEY TO SPECIES OF STURGEONS

1 a. Snout wide and depressed (Fig. 22); caudal peduncle long and narrow; upper lobe of caudal fin extended into a large filament (Fig. 23); barbels are fringed; no spiracles between eye and upper angle of gill opening (Fig. 24): Shovelnose sturgeon, *Scaphirhynchus platorynchus*.

   b. Snout more rounded in cross section; caudal peduncle short and broad (Fig. 25); upper lobe of caudal fin not extended into a long filament; barbels are not fringed; spiracles present, about halfway between eye and upper angle of gill opening (Fig. 26), Genus *Acipenser:* **2**

2 a. Mouth small (Fig. 27), interorbital width about twice the width of the mouth; postdorsal and pre-

Figure 23. Caudal peduncle and caudal fin of *Scaphirhynchus platorynchus*.

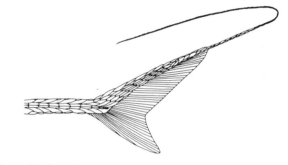

Figure 24. Lateral view of head of *Scaphirhynchus platorynchus*.

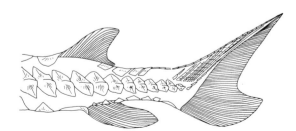

Figure 25. Lateral view of caudal fin and peduncle of *Acipenser*.

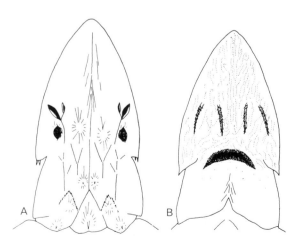

Figure 22. Dorsal (A) and ventral (B) views of snout of *Scaphirhynchus platorynchus*.

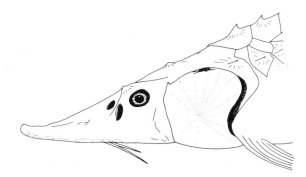

Figure 26. Lateral view of head of *Acipenser*.

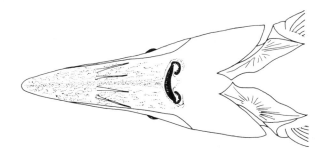

Figure 27. Ventral view of head of *Acipenser oxyrhynchus*.

anal shields in pairs (Fig. 28): Atlantic sturgeon, *Acipenser oxyrhynchus*.

b. Mouth large (Fig. 29), interorbital width about 1½ times the width of the mouth; postdorsal and pre-anal shields in a single row: **3**

3 a. Lateral scutes of the same shade as the background; anal fin rays 25–30; insertion of anal fin plainly behind insertion of dorsal fin; tip of anal fin reaching only to anterior edge of caudal fulcral plate (long caudal peduncle): Lake sturgeon, *Acipenser fulvescens*.

b. Lateral scutes much paler than the background; anal fin rays 19–22; insertion of anal fin opposite insertion of dorsal fin; tip of anal fin reaching past fulcrum to origin of caudal fin (short caudal peduncle): Shortnose sturgeon, *Acipenser brevirostrum*.

Figure 28. Dorsal view of caudal peduncle of *Acipenser oxyrhynchus*.

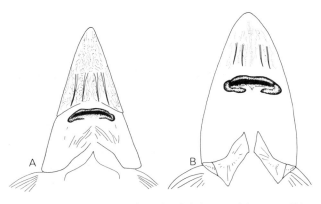

Figure 29. Ventral view of heads of *Acipenser fulvescens* (A), and *Acipenser brevirostrum* (B).

Genus *Acipenser*

Spiracles present about halfway between eye and upper corner of gill opening; snout sub-conical, not greatly flattened; gill rakers lanceolate; barbels not fringed.

Shortnose sturgeon, *Acipenser brevirostrum* Lesueur[548]

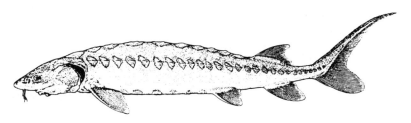

Vladykov and Greeley. 1963. Mem. Sears Found. Marine Res. 1(3): p. 37

Distribution This species is sympatric with *A. oxyrhynchus* along the Atlantic Coast from Florida to New Brunswick.[313] In recent years, specimens have been taken in the lower Delaware River, and there are four specimens in the collections of the Academy of Natural Sciences of Philadelphia recorded from freshwater at Torresdale, Pennsylvania, taken in November 1911. It is now considered as an endangered species in Pennsylvania and over most of the Atlantic Coast.[627]

Large populations of the shortnose sturgeon have been found recently in the Sheepscot River in Maine and the Saint John River in New Brunswick.[313]

Behavior The shortnose sturgeon spawns in rivers over rubble in the spring; some adults then wander out to sea for considerable distances.[930] The smallest sturgeon of the genus, the shortnose grows slowly and matures at the early age of 5 to 6 years.[326,567]

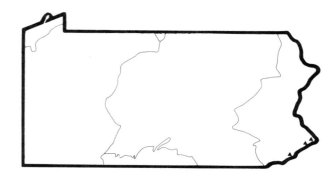

Food The diet of the few sturgeon examined consisted of benthic sludgeworms, midges and small crustaceans.[493]

Value Because of its small size and relative scarcity, the shortnose sturgeon is not of much interest to commercial fishermen.

Lake sturgeon, *Acipenser fulvescens* Rafinesque[723]

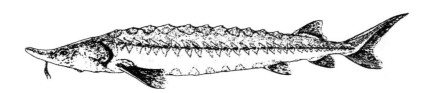

Vladykov and Greeley. 1963. Mem. Sears Found. Marine Res. 1(3): p. 42

Distribution This fish is found primarily in freshwater lakes and large rivers over a large part of eastern North America, although it is occasionally sympatric with the Atlantic sturgeon in brackish water habitats of Hudson Bay and the St. Lawrence River, where a commercial fishery for these two species still exists.[929] Once very abundant in the Great Lakes, populations in interior waters have greatly diminished in recent years, and the lake sturgeon is now only occasionally taken in Lake Erie.

Behavior The lake sturgeon ascends rivers in the spring to spawn in swift water.[930] The adhesive eggs stick to rocks and rubble, and there is no parental care of eggs or young. The young move downstream at a very early age, since very few have ever been taken near spawning sites.[716,839] Lake sturgeon mature only after an age of 10 to 15 years, and females do not spawn each year after maturity.[811]

Food Lake sturgeon are benthic feeders on a wide variety of invertebrates. Large chironomid larvae are some-

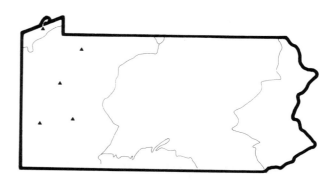

times found in tremendous numbers in the crop of a single large sturgeon. Some small fishes are occasionally taken.

Value In some areas of Canada the species is still abundant enough to be harvested commercially,[182] and in Wisconsin the lake sturgeon still supports a recreational fishery.[716]

Atlantic sturgeon, *Acipenser oxyrhynchus* Mitchill[635]

Vladykov and Greeley. 1963. Mem. Sears Found. Marine Res. 1(3): p. 47

Distribution The Atlantic sturgeon, as different sub-species, ranges along the Atlantic coast from Labrador through the Gulf of Mexico.[930] It has been confused in the past with the European sea sturgeon, but is now recognized as distinct from *A. sturio*.[568] The Atlantic sturgeon has been taken occasionally in recent years in the lower Delaware River in Pennsylvania; in other places, such as the Hudson River of New York, it is abundant enough to support a small commercial fishery.[342,929]

The Atlantic sturgeon is anadromous; the young may spend up to 4 years in freshwater before going to sea. Adults travel extensively in the ocean; one tagged individual moved as far as 900 miles in one summer.[839,926]

Behavior This sturgeon migrates into brackish or freshwater in the spring for spawning. Adhesive eggs are deposited over various hard bottoms in fast water; there is no nest preparation or care of eggs after spawning.[573]

Food The Atlantic sturgeon is a benthic feeder, digging

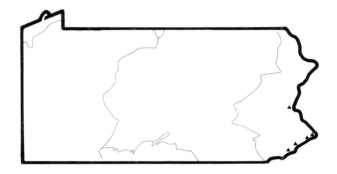

in sand or mud with its snout like a pig.[930] Its diet consists of worms, shrimps, other marine invertebrates, and fishes.[926]

Value This species is the largest of the Atlantic coast species, with a 14-foot female weighing 811 pounds reported from New Brunswick, Canada, in 1924.[538] It is valued as a smoked fish and for caviar.

Genus *Scaphirhynchus*

No spiracles present on top of head; snout long and greatly depressed; gill rakers fan-shaped; barbels fringed.

Shovelnose sturgeon, *Scaphirhynchus platorynchus* (Rafinesque)[732]

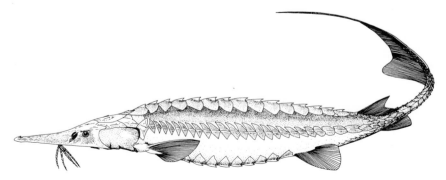

Length 425 mm. Mississippi River, Vicksburg, Miss. 1973

Distribution The shovelnose sturgeon has a wide distribution throughout much of the Mississippi River drainage.[36] It has not been collected or reported in Pennsylvania since Rafinesque[732] reported it in the Ohio River as far upstream as Pittsburgh. It is considered a lowland big-river form,[173,704] often occurring with the channel catfish and the quillback.[50]

Behavior Similar to other sturgeons, the shovelnose spawns in strong current in open channels of rivers over a rocky bottom. The adhesive eggs are deposited at random and then deserted by the parents. It is one of the smaller sturgeons, seldom exceeding 30 inches in length and maturing at an age of 5 to 7 years.[36,704]

Food The shovelnose is a benthic feeder, subsisting mainly on aquatic insects, small clams, and snails.[366,383]

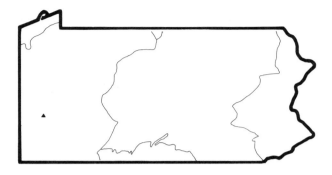

Value Despite its small size, the shovelnose sturgeon is still of commercial importance in parts of the Mississippi and Missouri rivers.[704]

Paddlefishes—Polyodontidae

Close relatives to the sturgeons, this unique family is a relic of very old fossil forms. It is represented in North America by a single species, with its closest relative, again a single species, present in China.

Genus *Polyodon*

Snout longer than remainder of head, depressed, and paddle-shaped; heterocercal tail; no scales or bony plates on trunk; caudal fulcra of moderate size, 13 to 20 in number; posterior extension of operculum long and triangular; hundreds of long, fine rakers on each gill arch.

Paddlefish, *Polyodon spathula* (Walbaum)[938]

Length 315 mm. Mississippi River, Vicksburg, Miss. 21 February 1973

Distribution The paddlefish is a unique species that is widely distributed throughout the Mississippi River drainage. Once reliably reported from Lake Erie, the Allegheny River, and Clarion River in Pennsylvania, the paddlefish is now thought to be extirpated from the Great Lakes and much of the upper Ohio River.[129,274,902] It is considered to be a threatened species in some states due to loss of its required large-river habitat.[196] It lives in large rivers and lakes, preferring large deep pools with little current.[139,173]

Behavior The paddlefish is described as a nomadic inhabitant of large rivers, migrating long distances in the spring to spawn on submerged gravel bars in swift current. The adhesive eggs are deposited at random over the bottom, and no further care is given.[173,718,877] Growth is rapid and fish up to 5 feet long are available to the fishery at an age of about 17 years.[719]

Food The paddlefish is not a bottom feeder like the sturgeons; instead it swims near the surface or in shallow water, feeding on microscopic organisms, plankton, and

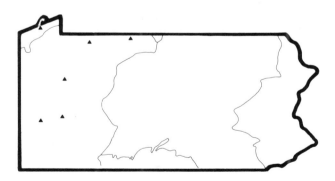

small aquatic insects. The paddle is probably a tactile organ.[256,263,877]

Value The paddlefish is a commercial species in some states. In others a recreational fishery by snagging is permitted. The eggs are often used for caviar and the flesh is considered palatable but somewhat better as smoked fish.[173,317,719]

Gars—Lepisosteidae

The gars are primitive bony fishes found principally in the Great Lakes and Mississippi drainages of North America. They inhabit sluggish streams and lakes and are tolerant of low oxygen conditions due to a highly vascularized swim bladder which is connected to the throat by an open duct.[886,956]

The largest species of this group, *L. spathula*, often exceeds 100 pounds and 6 feet,[704] but does not occur in Pennsylvania.

Genus *Lepisosteus*

Body armored with thick ganoid scales; nasal openings at end of long snout; fine canine teeth in both jaws; both dorsal and anal fins are short and placed far back on elongate body, close to the abbreviate-heterocercal tail.

KEY TO SPECIES OF *LEPISOSTEUS*

The shortnose gar has not been collected, to my knowledge, in Pennsylvania waters. It is included in the key on the possibility that a straggler might be found in the upper Ohio River. Fowler's report of *L. platostomus* in Lake Erie probably refers to *L. oculatus*.

1 a. Snout very long and narrow (Fig. 30); the distance between orbits goes 6.1 to 6.5 times in snout length; spots restricted to posterior part of body, none on head: Longnose gar, *Lepisosteus osseus*

   b. Snout shorter and broader, distance between orbits goes 3.6 to 4.8 times in snout length: **2**

2 a. Distance between orbits goes 3.6 to 3.8 times in snout length (Fig. 31); distinct spots on head, fading on preservation: Spotted gar, *Lepisosteus oculatus*

   b. Distance between orbits goes 4.4 to 4.8 times in snout length (Fig. 32); no distinct spots on head: Shortnose gar, *Lepisosteus platostomus*

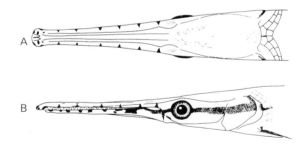

Figure 31. Dorsal (A) and lateral (B) views of *Lepisosteus oculatus*.

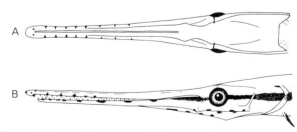

Figure 30. Dorsal (A) and lateral (B) views of *Lepisosteus osseus*.

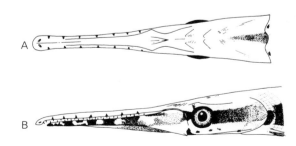

Figure 32. Dorsal (A) and lateral (B) views of *Lepisosteus platostomus*.

Spotted gar, *Lepisosteus oculatus* (Winchell)[964]

Length 218 mm. Lacassine Refuge, Cameron Parish, La. 17 October 1966

Distribution The spotted gar is broadly distributed in brackish water along the Gulf of Mexico but also extends up the Mississippi drainage and into the lower Great Lakes.[886] In Pennsylvania it occurs together with the longnose gar in bays and canals of the Presque Isle peninsula at Erie, but is rare elsewhere. It is most abundant in quiet, clear water with abundant vegetation.

Behavior Spawning occurs in the spring; large groups of males and females congregate over gravelly riffles of streams or lake shores. No nest is prepared but the gravel is cleaned by the activity of the spawning fish. In other localities it spawns in shallow water over vegetation.[764,839] This species grows more slowly than does the longnose gar.

Food In some habitats the spotted gar is more inclined to feed on crustaceans than on fishes. It feeds most actively in the morning.[312,521,689]

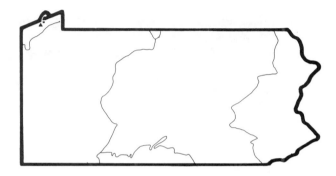

Value Along with other gars, this species is considered as undesirable by some fishery managers and is not protected by regulations. Other managers think that it is beneficial in helping to control overabundant panfishes by predation.[75] It is classed as threatened in many places due to loss of suitable swampy habitat.

Longnose gar, *Lepisosteus osseus* (Linnaeus)[558]

Length 235 mm. Lake Apopka, Orange County, Fla. 10 July 1959

Distribution The longnose gar ranges widely throughout the Mississippi River drainage and the lower Great Lakes, and north along the Atlantic Coast at least to New Jersey. It has been reported from widely scattered localities in Pennsylvania but has never been abundant anywhere.[274] The young spend the first summer in the stream, but adults typically inhabit lakes or sluggish pools, backwaters or impoundments.[704,904]

Behavior The longnose gar spawns in the spring, often migrating into gravelly streams for this purpose.[573] Fe-

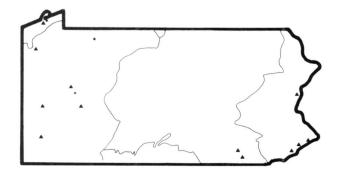

males spawn promiscuously with more than one male, releasing as many as 30,000 eggs over an extended spawning period. There is no nest building or parental care of eggs following spawning.

Branchiostegal rays can be used to estimate the growth and longevity of gars.[665] Based on this technique, the longevity of the longnose gar is at least 22 years, reaching a total length of about 50 inches in that time. Females live longer than males do.

Food The diet of the longnose gar is predominantly other fishes, with gar as small as 2.5 inches eating large numbers of fish along with crustacean zooplankton.[312,381,520,664]

Value The predatory habit of the gars has led some managers to control populations by netting, poisoning, or electrofishing, in the belief that better survival and production of game fishes would occur.[521]

Shortnose gar, *Lepisosteus platostomus* Rafinesque[732]

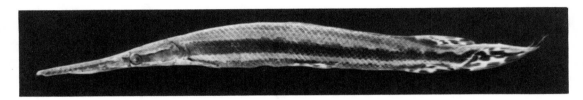

Length 216 mm. Alabama 1965

Distribution The range of the shortnose gar is restricted to the larger and more sluggish habitats of the Mississippi River drainage. This species was reported as occurring in the Ohio River as far as Pittsburgh,[732] and in Lake Erie,[274] but it has not been collected in Pennsylvania for many years. There are doubts that these early reports were based on correct indentifications; a similar species, the spotted gar, is known to be present in this area.

Behavior The shortnose gar spawns in spring or early summer, two or more males attending a single female as they swim over shallow weed beds. The eggs are deposited in small masses, held together by a clear gelatinous substance which attaches to the weeds or to the lake bottom.[139,706]

Food The diet of the shortnose gar, like other species, consists of small crustaceans when gar are small, but

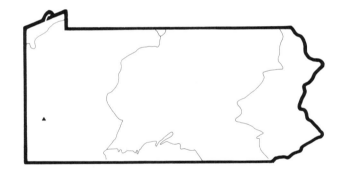

quickly changes to a fish diet as the gar grows.[521,705]

Value Because of its predatory nature and its poor value as a sport fish or food fish, the shortnose gar has a widespread reputation as a worthless nuisance.[706]

Bowfins—Amiidae

This family of primitive fishes is represented by a single living species in North America and many fossil forms both here and in Europe. This fish combines some characters typical of ganoid ancestors, such as a heterocercal tail and a gular bone, with other characters, such as cycloid scales and a physostomous swim bladder, which are typical of more advanced soft-rayed fishes.

Genus *Amia*

A large gular bone on the ventral side of the head between the broad jaws, anterior to the branchiostegals; entire head covered with bony plates; a single, low dorsal fin extends over posterior two-thirds of the body, but is clearly separated from the abbreviate-heterocercal tail.

Bowfin, *Amia calva* Linnaeus[559]

Length 192 mm. Huron River, Washtenaw County, Mich. 15 September 1976

Distribution The bowfin is widely distributed over the eastern half of North America, but becomes abundant only in heavily vegetated warm lakes and rivers.[68,264,655] It is a rare fish in Pennsylvania, found only in the Presque Isle region of Lake Erie or a few other places. The sporadic reports of large bowfin taken by anglers in different locations in Pennsylvania are probably due to occasional introductions.

Behavior The bowfin is a spring spawner with the adhesive eggs deposited on vegetation. The male prepares a nest and guards the eggs and school of fry for some time after hatching.[210,466,774] The gills and swimbladder are specialized for living in water of low oxygen content, or even using atmospheric oxygen.[68,655] The bowfin

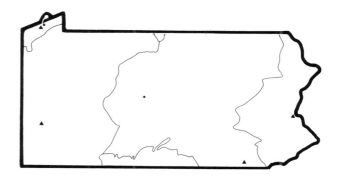

grows to a large size of several pounds, leading one to believe that it is an important predator.[122]

43

Food The diet of the bowfin consists mostly of aquatic insects, molluscs, shrimp, and earthworms. Its reputation as a voracious predator on fish has been questioned.[63,87,517,520]

Value Historically, the bowfin was considered an unwanted predator, and was removed as undesirable in rough fish control programs, along with carp and gars. More recently, it has been stocked by fish managers to help control overabundant panfishes.[63] There is little evidence in favor of either of these management programs.

Freshwater eels—Anguillidae

The only catadromous family of fishes in North America is represented by a single species. This fish has been studied for many years to find its spawning locality in the Atlantic Ocean, [67,928] and to firmly distinguish it from its close European relative.[198]

Genus *Anguilla*

Body very long and slender, covered with embedded, cycloid scales which are easily overlooked; long, low dorsal fin extends over posterior two-thirds of body and is continuous with caudal and anal fins; pectoral fins well developed; pelvic fins missing; lateral line well developed; head rather long; tapering to small mouth with low jaw protruding slightly.

American eel, *Anguilla rostrata* (Lesueur)[542]

Length 172 mm. Mill Creek, Carteret County, N.C. 29 October 1978

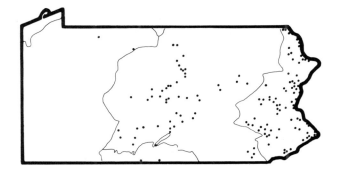

Distribution The American eel ranges widely along Atlantic and Gulf coasts of North America, with the young moving far upstream into small tributaries.[67,928] In Pennsylvania it is very abundant in the Delaware River where no obstructions are present to restrict the upstream migration of young. Continued stocking of elvers above existing dams in the Susquehanna has maintained adult populations in this system also. It was more widespread and common around 1900 than it is today.[274] The American eel is common in streams or lakes in a wide variety of habitats. It is especially abundant in heavy cover under logs, rocks, or undercut banks.

Behavior Adults migrate to the Sargasso Sea in the Atlantic Ocean for spawning, but no one has observed them spawning. After spawning, the larval leptocephali drift with the ocean currents. Transforming young enter estuaries and the females migrate to the headwaters of coastal streams, where they will live for ten years or more. Seaward migration of adult "silver" eels for spawning occurs in the fall, at which time large numbers were taken by commercial fishermen in specially de-

signed eel racks placed across the riffles of large rivers.

Food The American eel eats a wide variety of insects, worms, crustaceans, frogs, and fishes.[69,309,927] Although it appears to be a strong competitor for food with trout and other game fishes, the control of eels in North America has been largely ignored. This predatory behavior of eels has been extensively studied in New Zealand.[109]

Value In Pennsylvania, eels were taken under license by the Fish Commission. The licensees operated eel-racks and baskets in the Susquehanna and Delaware Rivers, usually at the time of peak migration downstream of adult eels. The remains of these eel racks are still visible in some places as long wing dams which led the eels through a narrow opening into an inclined series of baskets. These were designed to fish at different water levels as the stream rose and fell with the frequent spring floods.[225] The catch for 1912, which was judged a poor year because of extensive flooding, exceeded 50 thousand fish and weighed more than 44 thousand pounds.

Herrings—Clupeidae

The herrings are a numerous group of primitive bony fishes, readily distinguished from other freshwater fishes by the scales along the midbelly being specialized into sharp scutes, thus the common name "sawbelly" given to several species in this group. Most species are pelagic, marine forms, some are anadromous, and a few are strictly freshwater. Many are important as human food or for processing into fish meal and oil; others, such as the American shad, have become important sport fishes in North America. The taxonomy of this group has been treated in detail.[65,372]

The spawning behavior of herrings is consistent with the very large number of eggs produced. Females commonly pair with one or more males and broadcast their demersal, adhesive eggs over stony riffles of streams or gravelly shoals in lakes. A 12-inch, 1-pound gizzard shad contained more than 250,000 eggs at maturity[73] and there is a record of 156,000 eggs being stripped from a single American shad.[373]

KEY TO SPECIES OF HERRINGS

Two species, the skipjack herring and the hickory shad, are included in this key on a basis of their possible or rare occurrence in Pennsylvania waters. The skipjack herring was reported by Rafinesque (1820) in the Ohio River a short distance below Pittsburgh; it is very similar in appearance to the hickory shad, which is taken on spawning runs in the lower Delaware River. The menhaden is omitted although it occasionally reaches the Pennsylvania area in brackish water.

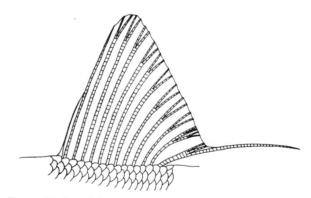

Figure 33. Dorsal fin of gizzard shad.

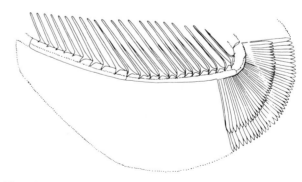

Figure 34. Counting gill rakers (22) on lower limb of left arch of shad.

1 a. Last ray of dorsal fin greatly elongated (Fig. 33); mouth inferior, lower jaw closes behind upper jaw: Gizzard shad, *Dorosoma cepedianum*

b. Last ray of dorsal fin not elongated; mouth terminal, or lower jaw slightly projecting: **2**

2 a. Gill rakers more than 60 (in adults over 16 inches in length, but less than 30 in fish smaller than 3 inches); cheeks deeper than long; jaws with no teeth in adults: American shad, *Alosa sapidissima*

b. Gill rakers less than 50 (Fig. 34) (in adults larger than 9 inches, fewer in young); cheeks as long as or longer than deep; jaws with minute teeth in adults: **3**

3 a. Gill rakers 40 to 50 in adults; lower jaw projects only slightly beyond upper jaw when mouth is closed; no median notch in upper jaw; single spot behind opercle: **4**

b. Gill rakers less than 30 in adults; lower jaw strongly projecting, entering into profile of upper jaw; definite median notch in upper jaw; a series of spots behind opercle: **5**

4 a. Peritoneum black: Blueback herring, *Alosa aestivalis*

b. Peritoneum pale: Alewife, *Alosa pseudoharengus*

5 a. Occasional straggler in upper Ohio River: Skipjack herring, *Alosa chrysochloris*

b. Taken on spawning runs in Delaware River: Hickory shad, *Alosa mediocris*

Genus *Alosa*

Silvery fishes with thin cycloid scales; no adipose fin; lateral line short, present on a few anterior scales; teeth on jaws absent or weakly developed; dorsal fin short, placed about midway on body; tail homocercal, strongly forked; distinguished from the genus Dorosoma by lacking a gizzard-like stomach, and the last ray of the dorsal fin not developed as a long filament.

Blueback herring, *Alosa aestivalis* (Mitchill)[635]

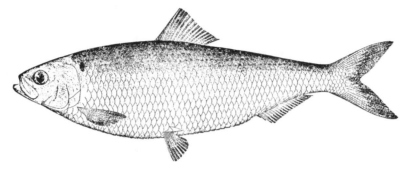

Bigelow and Schroeder. 1953. USFWS Fish. Bull. 53, p. 106

Length 282 mm. Delaware River, Lambertville, Pa. Spring 1962

Distribution The blueback herring is anadromous along the Atlantic Coast of North America from Nova Scotia to Florida. The young remain in freshwater for most of their first summer, but do not penetrate far upstream.[69,146,373] In Pennsylvania this species is restricted to the lower Delaware River. In streams further south, it is exceedingly abundant, hence the name glut herring. Adults inhabit a narrow band of coastal water, and never migrate much above tidewater.

Behavior The blueback herring is one of the first of the clupeids to migrate up the Delaware estuary in the spring. They spawn in brackish water and soon return to the ocean. Eggs are demersal and somewhat adhesive, and are broadcast over firm bottoms.[573]

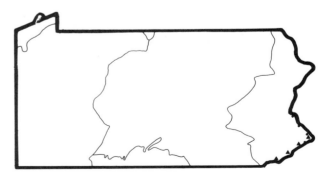

Food The diet of both young and adult bluebacks is chiefly small planktonic crustacea. This is consistent with their large number of fine gill rakers.[372]

Value The blueback was usually marketed together with the more abundant alewife, principally as whitebait or sprats for fishing,[311] although in the early 1900s it was salted and canned for human use. In 1920, the Chesapeake Bay fishery alone produced more than 22 million pounds of these mixed herring.[373]

Skipjack herring, *Alosa chrysochloris* (Rafinesque)[732]

Length 157 mm. Kentucky Lake, Tennessee River, Tenn. August 1965

Distribution The skipjack herring is a Mississippi River and Gulf Coast species, ranging from Minnesota to Texas. It is now believed to be extirpated from Pennsylvania portions of the Ohio River drainage; early reports in the Conemaugh River and in the Ohio River as far upstream as Pittsburgh[274,732] have not been confirmed by specimens. The skipjack herring is a highly migratory form in large rivers, concentrating below dams in the spring, presumably for spawning. It does not enter small creeks. In the Mississippi River drainage it is frequently confused with the sympatric Alabama shad, and is also very similar to the east coast hickory shad.[129,139]

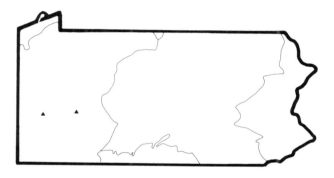

Behavior The details of its spawning are unknown, but may be related to its common habit of leaping from the water.[139] It apparently avoids turbid water, but occasionally enters brackish water along the Gulf Coast.

Food The diet of this shad consists of insects, small crustaceans, and worms. An occasional small fish is also taken.[311,372]

Value It has no importance as a food fish since it is very bony and of poor flavor. However, it is valuable as a host for the glochidia of commercially important mussels in the Mississippi River.[460]

Hickory shad, *Alosa mediocris* (Mitchill)[634]

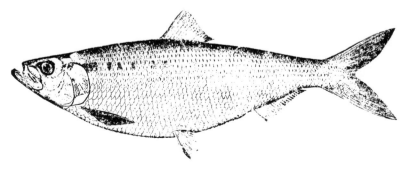

Bigelow and Schroeder. 1953. USFWS Fish. Bull. 53, p. 100.

Length 410 mm. Atlantic Ocean, off Virginia. July 1975

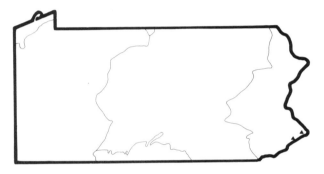

Distribution This shad is the least abundant of the Atlantic Coast clupeids, ranging from Florida to Maine with its center of abundance in the Chesapeake Bay.[588] It has been reported in the lower Delaware River as a fall migrant,[274] although a spring spawning migration is now documented in Maryland.[575,577] The young migrate to brackish estuaries during their first summer. Adults are coastal marine forms, probably never going far from land.[573]

Behavior The hickory shad spawns in tidal freshwater, broadcasting slightly adhesive eggs over gravel bars in moderate current. The eggs become semi-buoyant after water hardening and develop as they drift along the bottom.[575,577]

Food This species is considered to be more of a fish eater than other shads, although crustaceans and squid

are also important. Coastal marine fishes are prominent in the diet of adult shad.[55,69,373]

Value The hickory shad is harvested commercially along with alewife, principally as bait. In the South it is gaining in popularity as a sport fish.[575,577]

Alewife, *Alosa pseudoharengus* (Wilson)[962]

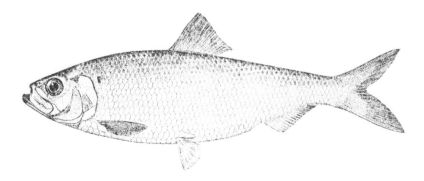

Bigelow and Schroeder. 1953. USFWS Fish. Bull. 53, p. 102

Length 116 mm. Colyer Lake, Centre County, Pa. 28 June 1978

Distribution The original distribution of this anadromous clupeid was restricted to the Atlantic coast from South Carolina northward.[222,373] More recently it has invaded the Great Lakes, where it has spread rapidly and become very abundant.[624] The alewife readily adapts its normal anadromous life history to a resident, freshwater habitat in small lakes, too.[316] The Pennsylvania Fish Commission has introduced it into several inland lakes, and in at least one instance, that of Colyer Lake in Centre County, it is reproducing successfully.

Behavior The alewife spawns chiefly in lakes or quiet stretches of stream, with little preference shown for bottom type. The eggs are adhesive and stick to the bottom or on debris.[679,810] Large natural mortalities occur in early summer; this may be associated with spawning stress, or with other causes.[328]

Food The diet of the alewife is mainly zooplankton, although plant fragments, insects, fish eggs, and small crustaceans are also found in stomachs. It is a pelagic,

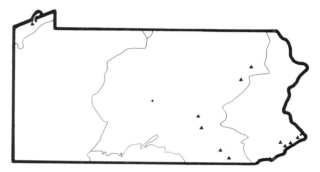

schooling fish feeding in midwater or along the surface.[679]

Value The alewife, together with other clupeids, comprised the bulk of the food fishery in the early days of settlement of the Atlantic Coast by the English. This fishery continued through the 1800s, although at reduced productivity. The alewife now forms a large part of the diet of the Pacific salmon stocks introduced into the Great Lakes.[865]

American shad, *Alosa sapidissima* (Wilson)[962]

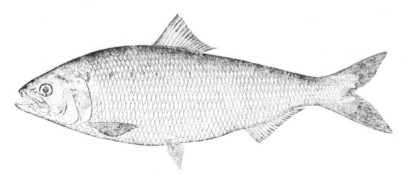

Bigelow and Schroeder. 1953. USFWS Fish. Bull. 53, p. 108

Length 130 mm. National Fish Hatchery, Lamar, Pa.

Distribution Broadly distributed along the Atlantic Coast, this fish has been a highly prized food fish in Pennsylvania and elsewhere ever since colonization by the white man.[586] It has been stocked into many new watersheds, but has become well established outside its original range only along the Pacific Coast.[579] Large anadromous populations in the Delaware River and many other coastal streams now support commercial and sport fisheries, and locally, efforts are being made to reestablish anadromous populations formerly abundant in the Susquehanna River.

The American shad move extensively along the coast as adults, with several discrete breeding populations identified as they ascend individual rivers in the spring to spawn.[890,933,940] The young spend their first summer in fresh water streams, and move downstream to brackish water in the fall.

Behavior The American shad spawns in the spring, broadcasting eggs loosely in the water. Favorite spawning grounds are on sand bars in freshwater, sometimes at long distances from tidewater. The non-adhesive, semi-buoyant eggs drift along the bottom until they hatch.[890]

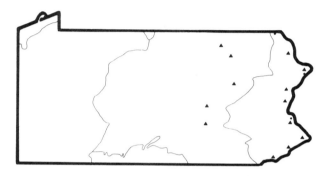

Food The American shad's diet consists largely of micro-crustaceans, but also includes plankton, insects, crustaceans, worms, and small fishes.[579,889]

Value A very important commercial fishery in the Chesapeake Bay declined over 90% from the early 1900s. It still remains an important sport fishery in the Delaware River and elsewhere along the coast.[889,940]

Genus *Dorosoma*

Readily distinguished from Alosa by the presence of a gizzard-like stomach, and the last ray of the dorsal fin developed as a long filament; silvery fishes with thin cycloid scales; no adipose fin; no lateral line; mouth small, inferior; tail strongly forked; dorsal fin short, placed about midway on body.

Gizzard shad, *Dorosoma cepedianum* (Lesueur)[546]

Length 150 mm. Ryerson State Park Lake, Greene County, Pa. 2 June 1977

Distribution The original range of the gizzard shad covered most of the southeastern United States except for the Appalachian Mountains. It appears to be spreading northward as warming climate permits, and is now spreading through the Great Lakes. There is some question about whether or not it was native to Lake Erie; presumably it invaded from the upper Mississippi River by way of the glacial Lake Maumee connection.[624] It is a pelagic schooling fish in large lakes and impoundments and appears to become more abundant as lakes become more eutrophic. Gizzard shad are usually confined to freshwater, but sometimes are found in brackish water.[73,338,622]

Behavior The gizzard shad spawns in large schools, the adhesive eggs deposited on roots, fibers, and debris along shore.[64,625] Growth is rapid, reaching maximum sizes in excess of 10 inches. Large populations often interfere with commercial fishing for other species, and culminate in massive mortalities.

Food The gizzard shad is described as a filter feeder, with its diet representing a concentrated random sample

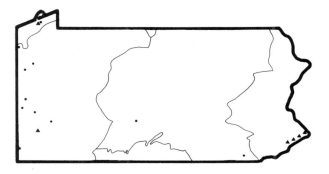

of the plankton available to it.[73,242,897]

Value Populations of the gizzard shad are considered a mixed blessing to fish managers. They constitute an important forage for many game fishes in fertile impoundments but rapidly grow out of suitable size for forage.[518] Moreover, massive mortalities following spawning and their common impingement on screens of water-cooled electric generating stations are often considered severe nuisances.[73]

Mooneyes—Hiodontidae

There is a single genus with two species now recognized in this family, confined to freshwaters of central North America. Early descriptions of these fishes are confusing; Rafinesque[732] distinguished between five species of "false herring" which apparently moved upstream into smaller tributaries of the Ohio River in the spring.

The flesh of mooneyes, because of the large number of small bones, was considered inferior to that of skipjack herring which also was taken commercially by seines on upstream spawning runs.

Genus *Hiodon*

Silvery, herringlike fishes; lateral line complete, but easily overlooked; no adipose fin; long, prominent pelvic axillary process; no scales on head; large eye with bright guanine tapetum, and short eyelid; gill rakers flat, blunt knobs, about 12 on lower limb of first arch (Fig. 35).

KEY TO SPECIES

1 a. Origin of short dorsal fin opposite or behind origin of long anal fin; maxillary long, reaching to beyond middle of eye; tapetum remains golden even after preservation: Goldeye, *Hiodon alosoides*

   b. Origin of short dorsal fin slightly anterior to origin of long anal fin; maxillary short, barely reaching middle of eye; tapetum with slight golden hues, fading in preservative: Mooneye, *Hiodon tergisus*

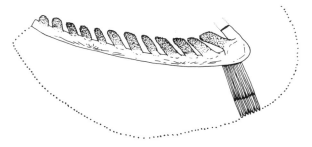

Figure 35. Stubby gill rakers on lower limb of left arch of mooneye.

Goldeye, *Hiodon alosoides* (Rafinesque)[728]

Length 207 mm. Missouri River, Charles Mix and Gregory Counties, S. D. 29 August 1952

Distribution The goldeye has a range covering most of the Mississippi River drainage and extending northwest into the Northwest Territory of Canada. It has not been taken in Pennsylvania in recent years, and is probably known here only from its reported occurrence in the Beaver and Youghiogheny Rivers of western Pennsylvania.[274] The goldeye is very tolerant of turbidity and consequently does well in the Missouri River and other muddy rivers and impoundments of the Great Plains.[335]

Behavior Spawning occurs in the spring in quiet, turbid water of rivers or lakes, probably at night. Newly hatched larvae are pelagic, as are juveniles and adults.[52]

Food Goldeyes are nocturnal in feeding; their eyes, with a reflecting tapetum, are well adapted to dim light conditions, a trait they share with the mooneye and the sauger.[642] Their food is varied, consisting of almost any

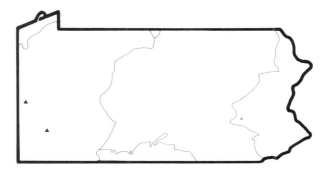

insect, crustacean, or small fish of suitable size.[139,223,606]

Value The goldeye is still a common species in the Great Plains, where it is smoked, dyed a bright red color, and sold commercially for the gourmet diner.[477]

Mooneye, *Hiodon tergisus* Lesueur[546]

Length 225 mm. Kentucky Lake, Tennessee River, Tenn. August 1965

Distribution The mooneye is common throughout the Mississippi River and some of the Great Lakes.[921] The probable northern limit of this species in the Great Lakes area is Lake St. Clair, with one good record in Lake Huron. It was originally described from specimens taken from the Ohio River at Pittsburgh as two separate species, *H. tergisus* and *H. clodalus*.[546] As the Ohio River tributaries became more turbid, populations of the mooneye declined to the point where it is now quite rare, although it is still quite abundant in the Ohio portion of Lake Erie.[902] We have no recent records of its occurrence in Pennsylvania, although it was collected in Lake Erie near Erie, Pennsylvania, on 25 October 1920 (UMMZ Cat. No. 55667). Reports of large mortalities of mooneyes in the harbor at Erie, Pennsylvania, in recent years have usually turned out to be the result of mistaken identification of the alewife or the gizzard shad.

Behavior Spawning occurs in the spring, sometimes following a migration in large clear rivers. It prefers clearer water than the goldeye, and recent declines in popula-

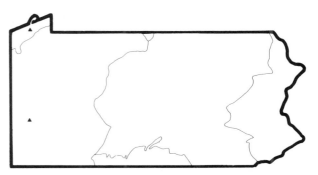

tions of mooneyes are often linked to increased silt and turbidity of large rivers in the Ohio watershed.

Food The diet of the mooneye consists of a wide variety of insects, crustaceans, and small fishes, although no extensive food study has been published.[74,852]

Value The mooneye is not considered a good quality fish for eating, although it is improved by smoking.[139]

Trouts—Salmonidae

Pelvic axillary process prominent; adipose fin present; cycloid scales; homocercal tail; pelvic fins abdominal in position; numerous pyloric caecae; vomer with a backward-projecting shaft; stomach with esophagus and pyloris not close together.

The Salmonidae, as considered here,[332] include not only trout, salmon and chars, but also whitefishes, ciscoes and graylings, often grouped in two other families, Coregonidae and Thymallidae. This is a large and diverse family of fishes originally confined to the northern hemisphere, but with many species acclimated widely now outside their original range. Various species are often ecologically dominant in cool waters, and many have both anadromous and resident life habits. They also comprise many of the most popular food and sport fishes of the world. For this reason, an extensive literature on the biology and management of most species now exists.[557]

Representatives of four genera have been reported for Pennsylvania either as native forms (*Coregonus, Salvelinus*) or as self-reproducing introduced populations (*Oncorhynchus, Salmo*). Another genus, *Prosopium,* is included here due to its presence in all of the Great Lakes except Lake Erie, and in several lakes in New England.[491]

Characters which all of these genera share, useful in separating them from other primitive families, are given above. Characters useful in distinguishing genera and species are included in the following key to species.

KEY TO SPECIES OF SALMONIDAE

1 a. Scales large, less than 100 in lateral line; no teeth on jaws, except in very young, Ciscoes and whitefishes: **2**

  b. Scales small, more than 110 in lateral line; teeth well developed on jaws: **5**

2 a. Upper and lower jaws more or less equal (mouth terminal); gill rakers on lower limb of first arch 30 or more (Fig. 36), Ciscoes: **3**

  b. Mouth inferior, obviously overhung by snout; gill rakers on lower limb of first arch usually fewer than 20 (Fig. 36), Whitefishes: **4**

3 a. Gill rakers on lower limb of first arch 30–39; tip of lower jaw often extends beyond premaxillaries; head larger, more robust, and lighter in pigmentation: Longjaw cisco, *Coregonus alpenae*

  b. Gill rakers on lower limb of first arch 42–50; tip of lower jaw usually equal to premaxillaries; head smaller, less robust, and more darkly pigmented: Lake herring, *Coregonus artedii*

4 a. Gill rakers on lower limb of first arch about 15; a single small flap of skin between nostrils: Round whitefish, *Prosopium cylindraceum*

  b. Gill rakers on lower limb of first arch about 18; two small flaps of skin between nostrils: Lake whitefish, *Coregonus clupeaformis*

5 a. Anal rays 13 to 19 (usually 14 to 16): **6**

  b. Anal rays 7 to 12 (usually 9 to 11): **9**

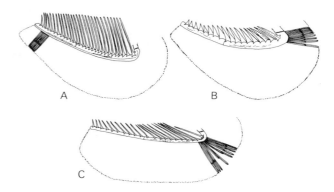

Figure 36. Gill rakers on lower limb of first arch on left side of cisco (Lake herring), *C. artedii* (A); lake whitefish, *C. clupeaformis* (B); and sockeye salmon, *O. nerka* (C).

6 a. Distinct black spots on back and caudal fin: **7**

  b. No distinct black spots on back or caudal fin, pigment restricted to fine speckling; 28–40 long, slender gill rakers; lateral line scales 125–143: Sockeye salmon, *Oncorhynchus nerka*

7 a. Spots on back and caudal fin large and oval; lateral line scales usually more than 170; gill rakers 26–34: Pink salmon, *Oncorhynchus gorbuscha*

  b. Spots on back and caudal fin small and round; lateral line scales usually less than 150: **8**

8 a. Black spots restricted to upper lobe of caudal fin; no black pigment along bases of teeth; gill rakers 19–25; lateral line scales 121–140: Coho salmon, *Oncorhynchus kisutch*

   b. Black spots on both lobes of caudal fin; black pigment along bases of teeth; gill rakers 18–30; lateral line scales 140–153: Chinook salmon, *Oncorhynchus tshawytscha*

9 a. Black spots present on head and body; scales large (fewer than 165 in lateral line) vomer with teeth extended in two rows backward along shaft (Fig. 37): **10**

   b. No black spots on head or body (spots may be light colored, pink, or red); scales small (more than 165 in lateral line); vomer with teeth restricted to head end (Fig. 38): **12**

10a. Caudal fin marked with rows of black spots; never any red spots on body: Rainbow trout, *Salmo gairdneri*

   b. Caudal fin never has rows of black spots; body often with red spots: **11**

11a. Caudal peduncle long and rounded in cross section; no red on adipose fin; branchiostegals usually 12; dorsal fin rays usually 11: Atlantic salmon, *Salmo salar*

   b. Caudal peduncle short and elevated in cross section; adipose fin usually reddish-orange; branchiostegals usually 10; dorsal fin rays usually 9: Brown trout, *Salmo trutta*

12a. Pyloric caecae more than 90; caudal fin deeply forked; no red or orange spots on body: Lake trout, *Salvelinus namaycush*

   b. Pyloric caecae less than 75; caudal fin slightly forked to squarish; red or orange spots on body: **13**

13a. Young with 8 to 10 regularly arranged parr marks on sides; lower fins with white edges contrasting

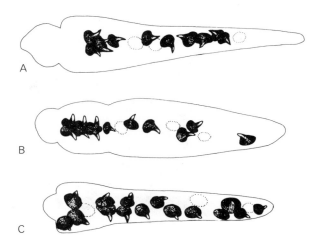

Figure 37. Teeth on vomer of rainbow trout, *S. gairdneri* (A); Atlantic salmon, *S. salar* (B); and brown trout, *S. trutta* (C).

Figure 38. Teeth on vomer of brook trout, *S. fontinalis* (A); lake trout, *S. namaycush* (B); and Arctic char, *S. alpinus* (C).

with black stripe; dorsal and caudal fins with distinct dark, wavy lines or blotches: Brook trout, *Salvelinus fontinalis*

   b. Parr marks not well defined; lower fins with white edges, but without contrasting black stripe; dorsal and caudal fins without dark, wavy lines or blotches: Arctic char, *Salvelinus alpinus*

Genus *Coregonus*

Silvery fishes with large scales, less than 100 in lateral line; teeth weakly developed or absent in adults; caudal fin distinctly forked; adipose fin present; no parr marks in young; two small flaps of skin between anterior and posterior nares.

Despite the extensive literature available on this group, the taxonomy remains confused. This is due in no small part to the environmentally induced variation of many characters used to describe species.[887] The coregonids are a variable group; in many cases intraspecific differences within subspecies of *Coregonus artedii* may be greater than those which separate one species from another.[490] No less than 24 groups of *C. artedii* were once recognized in a study of many lakes in northeastern America.[491]

Only three species of *Coregonus* are found in Pennsylvania waters, including Lake Erie. For these three species, a few notes on distribution and life history are given. Several other ciscoes and deep-water chubs are found in the other Great Lakes.[839]

Longjaw cisco, *Coregonus alpenae* (Koelz)[489]

Koelz, W. 1929. U. S. Bur. Fish. Doc. 1048, p. 364

Distribution The discovery of this species in the deep hole of eastern Lake Erie was validated from specimens taken between 1946 and 1957.[840] The gross similarity of *C. alpenae* to the only other cisco present in Lake Erie, *C. artedii,* and its occurrence only in deep water that is seldom fished by commercial fishermen, prevented its discovery until this late date. It was known previously as one of the deep-water chubs from only Lakes Huron and Michigan. This species now is very rare, and possibly extirpated, from Lake Erie.

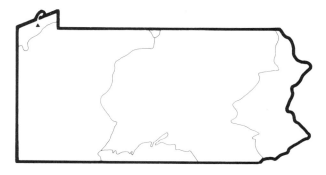

Behavior Spawning occurs in late fall, similar to other ciscoes, judging by the presence of pearl organs on ripe males. Spawning presumably occurs in water deeper than 60 feet, although no actual spawning has been observed.[443,490]

Food The food of the longjaw is predominantly the large

zooplankter, *Mysis relicta,* although many other items are eaten as available.[66]

Value This commercial species was one of the largest chubs taken in the Great Lakes, well flavored, moderately fat and in great demand by fish smokers.[839]

Cisco or lake herring, *Coregonus artedii* Lesueur[546]

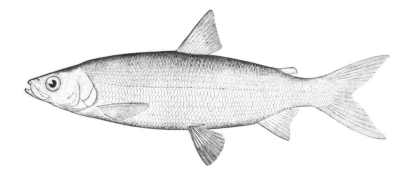

Brice.1898. Manual of Fish Culture, U. S. Comm. Fish and Fisheries, p. 181

Distribution Widely distributed in North America, and highly variable from one inland lake to another,[491,492] *C. artedii* was an important commercial species in the Great Lakes until about 1950. The species is now very rare in Lake Erie, judging by a lack of reports by commercial fisherman and test netting by investigators. We have no records other than the specimens taken in 1957 from Lake Erie near Erie, Pennsylvania, now in the collections of UMMZ. This species was introduced into Harvey's Lake, tributary to the Susquehanna River, from 1969 to 1972 by the Pennsylvania Fish Commission.

Behavior The cisco spawns in late fall both in the Great Lakes and in a number of inland lakes as the temperature drops to near freezing.[374,864,917] Large aggregations occur at this time, making it easy to exploit these populations by netting. The eggs usually do not hatch until the following spring.[444]

Food The cisco is a pelagic schooling species feeding

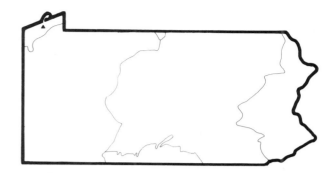

primarily on zooplankton. Surface insects and small fishes often occur in the diet when available.[218]

Value The cisco is not only an important food fish for man, especially smoked or pickled, but forms an important food source for large piscivores such as the lake trout.[839]

Lake whitefish, *Coregonus clupeaformis* (Mitchill)[638·]

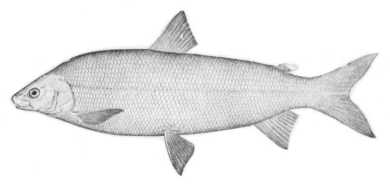

Brice. 1898. Manual of Fish Culture, U. S. Comm. Fish and Fisheries, p. 119

Distribution The widespread distribution of this form from the Great Lakes to Alaska, closely adhering to the glaciated area of North America, is now thought to be due to the combination of several species;[555,557] Dwarf and normal forms have been found living together in a few lakes.[252,474] The lake whitefish is also found in Otsego Lake, New York, at the head of the Susquehanna River, although it has never been recorded from the few deep, headwater lakes of the Susquehanna River in Pennsylvania.[325]

Behavior Like other coregonids, the lake whitefish spawns in late fall in aggregations over clean sand or stony shoals of lakes. Eggs hatch the following spring and the young remain for a short time in small schools along lake shores, soon moving to deep water.[243,763]

Food Whitefish are principally bottom feeders, but sometimes feed on zooplankton. Occasionally they can

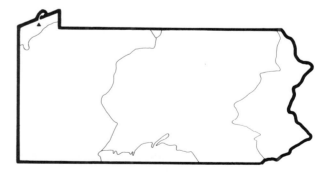

be caught on hook and line when feeding at the surface in quiet water.

Value Because of its large size and excellent flavor, both fresh and smoked, the lake whitefish was one of the mainstays of the commercial fisheries in the Great Lakes for many years. In Lake Erie, commercial production of this fish fluctuated widely, reaching a peak of more than 7 million pounds in 1949.[535] There has been a precipitous decline since then which has been correlated with eu-trophication, unfavorable water temperatures, and abundant smelt populations in the lake.

Where large populations exist in inland lakes they are often taken by sport fishermen.[565]

Genus *Oncorhynchus*

Terete, silvery fishes with small scales (more than 100 in lateral line); teeth well developed on jaws and on vomer; caudal fin well forked; anal rays usually more than 13; young with conspicuous parr marks; adults with black spots on caudal fin.

Four species of Pacific salmons have been successfully transplanted to eastern United States and Canada, either as landlocked forms in small lakes (*O. nerka,* the kokanee) or as potamodromous forms in the Great Lakes (*O. gorbuscha, O. kisutch,* and *O. tshawytscha).* These transplantations are used to broaden the recreational fishing opportunities in Pennsylvania waters.

The Pacific salmons, as a group, have few rivals in their importance to man for both food and recreation. Consequently a bibliography was published of the literature available on these fishes.[54]

Pink salmon, *Oncorhynchus gorbuscha* (Walbaum)[938]

Length 83 mm. Pacific Ocean, Fougner Bay, Bella Coola Inlet, British Columbia, 29 May 1966

Distribution This salmon is typically anadromous in the North Pacific and Arctic Oceans, with young and spawning adults found in tributary streams.[361] Introductions have been tried in many places with varied success. In the Great Lakes, the first natural reproduction of introduced stocks was noticed in 1958 in Lake Superior, and by 1979 the species had successfully colonized all of the Great Lakes.[506] In Pennsylvania, spawning adults were reported in 1979 in four tributaries of Lake Erie.[231] These reports have not been verified however; two supposed pink salmon taken in 1981 from a trap operated by the Pennsylvania Fish Commission on Godfrey Run were identified as malformed chinook salmon.

Behavior Spawning occurs very near brackish water in late summer and early fall, with the female preparing a gravel redd in typical salmonid fashion. Spawned-out adults die in a few weeks. The young stay in spawning streams such a short time that they often do not feed in fresh water. Pink salmon usually have a 2-year life cycle, but occasional 3-year fish have been taken on spawning runs.[16,937] Such individuals have given rise to off-year runs of spawning adults.

Food Young pink salmon reaching the ocean feed on plankton. As they grow, larger items such as squid and other fishes are included in the diet.[28]

Value The pink salmon historically was not considered as choice a food fish as the sockeye, chinook or coho.[376] However, with declines of salmon stocks in recent years, the pink salmon is now utilized to a greater extent by commercial fisherman. And, with the realization that pink salmon could be taken by trolling an artificial bait, the sport catch by anglers has been increasing considerably.[423]

Coho salmon, *Oncorhynchus kisutch* (Walbaum)[938]

Length 165 mm. Spring Creek, Centre County, Pa. 25 January 1977

Brice. 1898. Manual of Fish Culture, U. S. Comm. Fish and Fisheries, p. 13

Distribution The coho salmon is found throughout most of the North Pacific ascending streams to spawn in the fall. Young spend about 2 years in streams before smolting and running downstream.[847] In recent years millions of coho have been reared and released into the Great Lakes and other areas in eastern North America to support an important recreational fishery. Some natural reproduction occurs in Pennsylvania streams tributary to Lake Erie, but most of the fish returning to these streams in the fall as mature fish come from large annual plants of smolts.[839]

Behavior When necessary, the coho salmon migrates long distances to spawn in very small headwater streams. Females cut a redd in gravel riffles and bury the eggs after courtship and fertilization by the male. The young usually spend 2 years before smolting and another 2 years in the ocean or large lake before they mature, spawn, and die. The propensity for the coho to migrate into very small streams puts their juveniles into competition with other resident salmonids.[362] When important resident fisheries for brown trout or brook trout are affected, managers have found the introduction of the coho into eastern waters to be a mixed blessing.

Food The diet of juvenile coho is consistent with their stream habitat in that a wide variety of aquatic and terrestrial invertebrates are taken.[125,708,806,855] Adults feed pelagically in small loose schools on fish or large marine plankton. In the Great Lakes, large schools of alewife and smelt probably contribute to the fast growth and good condition of coho stocks.

Value It is hard to overestimate the value of this salmon to the commercial and sport fisheries which they support. A major problem posed to the managers of the Great Lakes populations is to increase the exploitation of these maturing fish in deep, offshore waters before they arrive in large numbers at the mouth of tributary streams.

Sockeye salmon, *Oncorhynchus nerka* (Walbaum)[938]

Length 105 mm. Benner Springs Hatchery, Centre County, Pa.

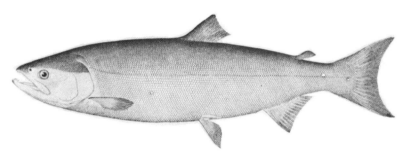

Brice. 1898. Manual of Fish Culture, U. S. Comm. Fish and Fisheries, p. 11

Distribution Both landlocked and anadromous forms of the sockeye occur naturally over a large part of the North Pacific watershed in Asia and North America.[258] It is the most important commercial salmon in the Pacific.[606] A landlocked form of this species, the kokanee, has been successfully stocked into Pennsylvania at least twice: an early introduction into Lake Winola west of Scranton in 1923,[86] and a more recent introduction with successful reproduction in Upper Woods Pond northeast of Scranton.[15,112]

Behavior Fry are found in small spawning streams for only a few days; juveniles take up a lake existence for about 2 years prior to smolting. Adults spend about 2 years in the ocean before they mature, spawn, and die. For kokanee, the overall silvery appearance of juveniles and adults, occasionally taken by anglers who know

how, changes to a brilliant red, green, and black coloration during spawning in the fall.

Food The kokanee and juvenile sockeye are pelagic zooplankton feeders, with the larger and most abundant food items usually selected. They also consume small insects both from the bottom of the lake and at the surface.[677] In view of these reports that planktonic crustacea are most important as food,[385,792] it is somewhat unusual to find that these fish can be easily taken by angling with small flashing artificial baits in lakes.

Value Although very little suitable lake environment for the growth and maturation of this species exists in Pennsylvania, it offers unique and diverse recreation to a few anglers.

Chinook salmon, *Oncorhynchus tshawytscha* (Walbaum)[938]

Length 145 mm. Pacific Ocean, Yaquina Bay, Oregon, Spring 1968

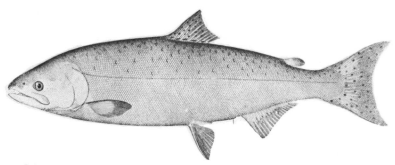

Brice. 1898. Manual of Fish Culture, U. S. Comm. Fish and Fisheries, p. 7

Distribution The chinook salmon has a broad distribution throughout the North Pacific and has been acclimated to New Zealand waters.[13] The largest salmonid in North America, the chinook has recently been reintroduced into the Great Lakes including Lake Erie, where it is being maintained by stocking juveniles. Early attempts at transplantation of this species included such places as the Delaware and Susquehanna Rivers,[277] but most early plantings into apparently suitable habitats such as the Great Lakes[839] or several of the large, oligotrophic lakes of New Hampshire[384] failed to become self-supporting.

Behavior The life cycle of the chinook is the longest and most varied of all the Pacific salmon. The young spend a few months to several years in streams,[606] and the anadromous adults may spend several years in the ocean before migrating into streams to spawn and die. The extended adult life before reaching sexual maturity ac-

counts for the large size of spawning adults.

Food The food of young chinook in freshwater streams is mostly insects taken from all water levels. Marine or large lake adults feed principally on a wide variety of fishes or large pelagic invertebrates available to them.[708,715,855]

Value Because of its large size and favorable reputation both as a sport and commercial fish, the chinook has great management potential in large oligotrophic lakes. Its failure to establish self-sustaining populations, and the feasibility of controlling upstream migration of spawning populations, are considered as advantages. There is little danger of competition with other stream salmonids while utilizing large populations of forage fishes in lakes.

Genus *Prosopium*

Silvery fishes with large scales, less than 100 in lateral line; young with parr marks resembling those in trouts and salmons; single flap of skin between anterior and posterior nares; body more rounded than in whitefishes and ciscoes.

Of the six species recognized in this genus,[674] two are present in eastern North America, with neither having been recorded from Lake Erie or other waters in Pennsylvania. The mountain whitefish, *P. williamsoni,* is rather widespread and abundant throughout western North America, where it often becomes locally important as a sport fish. A relict, deep water population of the pigmy whitefish, *P. coulteri,* was recently described from Lake Superior.[235] The round whitefish, *P. cylindraceum,* is included in the key to species because of its greater abundance and wider dispersal in the Great Lakes and northeastern North America.

Round whitefish, *Prosopium cylindraceum* (Pallas)[686]

Mud Lake, Hamilton River drainage, Labrador, 24 August 1950

Distribution The round whitefish has a northern distribution extending from Labrador to Alaska and including all of the Great Lakes except Lake Erie.[490] In the southern part of its range it is limited to deep lakes; further north it is found in clean rivers or streams. It has never been reported from Pennsylvania.

Behavior The round whitefish spawns in late fall over gravel bars in lakes sometimes as deep as 48 feet. Adults swim in pairs and broadcast their eggs over the bar. No care of eggs or young ensues.[490,675] Round whitefish grow slowly to sizes of 20 inches and live at least 14 years, especially in northern waters such as Great Slave Lake, Canada.[759]

Food The diet of round whitefish is mostly benthic organisms, putting them in direct competition with the lake whitefish when present. Mayflies, caddisflies, midges, and small molluscs are also important, and small fish are occasionally found in round whitefish stomachs.[761]

Value This species has never been as important to the commercial fishery as other ciscoes and whitefishes, primarily because of lesser abundance. It is taken occasionally by anglers from streams in northwestern New Brunswick.

Genus *Salmo*

Black-spotted trouts with usually fewer than 12 anal rays; scales easily seen, fewer than 165 in lateral line; vomer with two rows of teeth extending along shaft; pelvic and anal fins not conspicuously edged in white.

Pennsylvania lies outside the original range of all species of this genus, although both the rainbow trout and the brown trout now are well established. Other species such as the cutthroat trout and the Atlantic salmon have been introduced from time to time,[277] but so far have failed to maintain natural populations.

Because of the extensive fish culture program in Pennsylvania, the distribution maps for individual species of trouts probably include some localities where only recently stocked fish were collected. It was not always feasible to distinguish between stocked individuals and those recruited from natural spawning.

Rainbow trout, *Salmo gairdneri* Richardson[786]

Length 111 mm. Sinking Creek, Craig County, Va. 16 June 1976

Distribution The original distribution of the rainbow was restricted to resident and anadromous stocks on the Pacific Coast of North America. Both life history forms have now been successfully acclimated to suitable habitats around the world.[13,654,847]

In Pennsylvania, documentation of natural reproduction of this spring-spawner is rare except for the anadromous steelhead population in Lake Erie and tributary streams. Attempts have been made to establish anadromous runs in the Delaware River drainage, but no success has been observed. Two unique forms of the rainbow, the golden trout of West Virginia and the palomino trout of Pennsylvania, have been developed as fish cultural oddities. There is no evidence of these forms be-

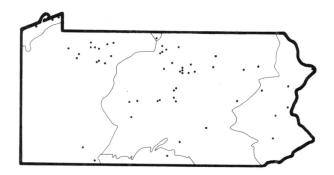

coming established as natural populations, but they are well accepted by anglers as adding some diversity to their fishing experience.

The rainbow trout is a variable species within its natural range, and this environmental variabiltiy has given rise to a jumble of scientific and common names.[654] Closely related species such as the cutthroat trout are presently recognized, but the status of others remains questionable.[621]

Behavior All forms of the rainbow trout are spring spawners in nature, with typical trout spawning behavior. The female cuts the redd, and after suitable courtship by a male, deposits the eggs in pockets covered with fine gravel. There is no care of eggs or young.[556,323] Growth is variable and depends upon the habitat and food available. Sexual maturation at 3 years of age and a size of 12 inches is common for stream resident forms. Steelhead stocks often exceed 30 inches and 15 pounds at an age of 8 or 10 years.[846]

Food The rainbow has been called a generalized carnivore, eating zooplankton, insects, crustacea, and fishes as they are available in proper sizes.[180]

Value The rainbow trout is one of the most valuable of the sport fishes in North America as natural populations. It is also a favorite among fish culturists because of its resistance to parasites and diseases, and its fast growth under crowded conditions in hatcheries.

Atlantic salmon, *Salmo salar* Linnaeus[558]

Length 166 mm. Fish Hatchery, Mass. May 1976

Distribution The original distribution of the Atlantic salmon extended throughout the Atlantic Ocean from Europe, Iceland, Greenland, and the North American coast south to the Connecticut River. It was landlocked in a few lakes in Maine and New York,[839] and is occasionally stocked in suitable waters in Pennsylvania as eggs or stocks of fingerlings become available.

Behavior The Atlantic salmon is anadromous, running into streams to spawn in the fall. Adults do not die following spawning, but may return to and from the ocean to spawn again. The young spend 1 to 3 years in freshwater streams before smolting and running to the sea. Eggs are deposited in gravel redds by the female after courtship and fertilization by the male. There is no care of eggs or young after hatching.[450,707] Growth is slow in freshwater streams but increases greatly at sea. Maximum sizes in excess of 80 pounds have been reported, although a fish of 15 to 20 pounds is now considered large.[839]

Food The Atlantic salmon is a generalized carnivore whose diet reflects the environment at all stages of its life history. Young eat a variety of freshwater invertebrates from streams or lakes; adults at sea consume fish, as well as shrimp and other marine invertebrates.

Value The best known of all salmonids, the Atlantic salmon has been prized by anglers and commercial fishermen for many centuries. Attempts to restore populations of this species to their former abundance in North America have recently shown some success.[663]

Brown trout, *Salmo trutta* Linnaeus[558]

Length 126 mm. Pennsylvania

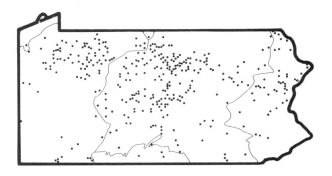

Distribution Originally widely distributed throughout Europe and Asia, where the taxonomy is still confusing, the brown trout has been acclimated to all major continents of the world.[13,564] Introduced into Pennsylvania in 1886, it is probably the most successful trout in the commonwealth, replacing the native brook trout in many localities.

Behavior The brown trout is a fall spawner, with the female constructing a redd in gravel and depositing eggs in pockets after courtship and fertilization by one or more males. There is no care of eggs or young.[323] Some migratory populations exist; these run either from the ocean (in which case they are called sea trout) or from the Great Lakes into tributary streams for spawning.[106] Resident populations also are numerous in Pennsylvania streams, where their home range is very limited.[12]

Juvenile brown trout eat mostly insects and small crustaceans; adult trout are generalized carnivores preferring crayfish and fish, but taking almost anything of

suitable size that moves within their feeding range.[106,566]

Value The brown trout is preferred by managers in situations where fishing pressure is high because of its difficulty in capture by anglers. Special angling regulations are often used to increase recreation from this source.[148,849]

Genus *Salvelinus*

Scales very small, often unnoticed, more than 165 in lateral line; pelvic and anal fins edged in white, often with additional contrasting black stripe; vomer with teeth restricted to anterior portion; fishes often highly colored with bright red spots; worm-like markings on back.

Several species of this genus, known as chars, have a more northerly distribution than most other salmonids. They have been important for food and recreation for many human populations in the Northern Hemisphere, although some species are often considered as detrimental to more preferred salmonids.

In the northeast, several chars have sometimes been considered as separate species. We follow the American Fisheries Society list of fishes[798] in regarding the Sunapee trout, and blueback trout, and the Quebec red trout as being synonymous with the Arctic char.

Arctic char, *Salvelinus alpinus* (Linnaeus)[558]

Length 158 mm. USNM Cat. No. 177650, Labrador

Distribution As its name implies, this char has a circumpolar distribution in Europe, Asia, and North America, with a few relict populations in New England.[26,605] We have no records of this char ever being found in Pennsylvania.

Populations of the Arctic char are frequently anadromous and grow to large sizes, rivalling the lake trout. Others are lacustrine and seldom exceed 2 or 3 pounds. Coloration and body shape are variable, as illustrated by the several named species in the monograph on the trout or chars of New England.[468]

Behavior The Arctic char is a late summer or fall spawner, depending on latitude. The female prepares a redd in suitable gravel and spawns with one or more males. The eggs are deposited in pockets in the gravel, covered by the female, and then deserted. Adults do not die following spawning, but return to spawn again in following years.[244]

Growth rates and maximum sizes vary with habitat, food supply, and longevity. There is difficulty in determining the age of far northern populations, but char up to 40 years of age and a size of 26 pounds have been reported.[426,606]

Food The Arctic char is a generalized carnivore, utilizing many invertebrates and fishes at different sizes.[318]

Value This species is very important food for dogs and humans in polar regions. It is also becoming an important sport fish in many places.[809]

Brook trout, *Salvelinus fontinalis* (Mitchill)[635]

Length 85 mm. Indiantown Creek, Dauphin County, Pa. 29 September 1973

Distribution The original distribution of the brook trout was northeastern North America, extending through the Great Lakes and south along the Appalachians to Georgia. It has been acclimated to numerous other areas. It is the only stream salmonid native to Pennsylvania.[97] It readily adapts to small ponds and lakes, if suitable spawning habitat is provided, and it is found in small creeks far upstream in the headwaters.

Behavior The brook trout is a fall spawner, with the female cutting the redd and burying fertilized eggs in pockets in the gravel riffle.[323,950] Migratory forms are common along the Atlantic Coast and in the Great Lakes area; these are variously known as sea-run or coaster trout.

The natural distribution of this char appears to be correlated with the mean annual temperature and the amount of surplus precipitation. This provides for proper temperature and oxygen control, which are necessary for good development of eggs and alevins in the gravel redd throughout the winter.[61,842] Growth is variable with habitat and with migratory form. Fish of 14 pounds from the Nipigon River, Ontario, bear little resemblance to the 4-inch pigmy adults of many Appalachian streams.

Food The brook trout diet is variable. It will eat any living creature its mouth can handle, including aquatic and terrestrial invertebrates, fishes, and small mammals.[653,790]

Value The brook trout is one of the most important sport fishes in eastern North America. It is considered less desirable in the west because of its small size in comparison to the anadromous salmonids. Not only is the

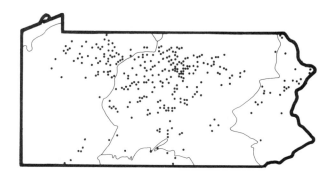

brook trout a favorite of fish culturists for stocking, but many streams in Pennsylvania support abundant wild populations as well.

Lake trout, *Salvelinus namaycush* (Walbaum)[938]

Length 104 mm. Kinzua National Fish Hatchery, Warren County, Pa. April 1976

Distribution The lake trout was originally found over most of the northern half of North America, from Quebec to Alaska, including all of the Great Lakes. It was also native to several lakes in the Susquehanna River drainage of New York and in Silver Lake, Susquehanna County, Pennsylvania.[325] It has been planted repeatedly in Harvey's Lake and is occasionally caught there by anglers. It is recognized as a cold-water benthic form in oligotrophic lakes.[234,606]

Behavior The lake trout is a fall spawner in lakes on rocky shoals in deep water, but some populations run into large tributary streams to spawn at night.[234,561,600] It grows more slowly than many other salmonids, but reaches large sizes because of its great maximum age. Under low levels of exploitation in northern lakes, the lake trout has a life span exceeding 20 years, and has been reported exceeding 100 pounds in weight.[476,839]

Food The lake trout as adults eat mostly fish when available, but readily change to the most common foods present. Zooplankton are used when other foods are not

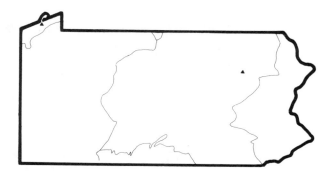

present, but slower growth usually results.[132,133,492,583]

Value The lake trout seldom is considered as good a sport fish as many other salmonids, but remains a favored commercial species in many large northern lakes because of its fine flavor and catchability in a gill net. The close affinity between the lake trout and the brook trout has led to the culture of a fertile hybrid, the splake, which has been used by fish managers in some situations.[584]

Smelts—Osmeridae

The few species included in this family are cold water fishes of the Northern Hemisphere. Only one species is present in our area, an anadromous form introduced from the East Coast. There is some controversy, however, about the taxonomy of the genus *Osmerus*. Some investigators choose to refer several populations of North American and European smelts to the *"Osmerus eperlanus"* complex until there is more information available.[606]

Genus *Osmerus*

Small, slender, silvery fishes with large mouths and strong teeth; adipose fin present; cycloid scales; homocercal tail, strongly forked; pelvic fins abdominal in position, no pelvic axillary process; upper jaw extends beyond eye; vomer without a backward-projecting shaft; stomach with esophagus and pylorus close together at anterior end; pyloric caecae few or absent.

Rainbow smelt, *Osmerus mordax* (Mitchill)[634]

Length 130 mm. Lake Erie, Wheatley, Ontario, Canada, September 1965

Description As now recognized, the rainbow smelt has disjunct centers of distribution in the North Pacific and in the North Atlantic. The Atlantic form was introduced into Lake Michigan via Torch Lake, Michigan, in 1912 and has subsequently spread throughout the Great Lakes.[171] In Pennsylvania, the smelt was reported on a spawning run in the Schuylkill River below Fairmount Dam,[676] but has not been taken this far south along the coast in recent years.

Smelt are abundant in Lake Erie, having been reported as early as 1935 by commercial fishermen.[918] They are also reproducing in Harvey's Lake, Luzerne County, where a remnant population persists from a planting made in 1952.[207] Smelt have also been recently introduced by the Pennsylvania Fish Commision in several

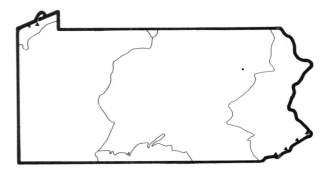

other inland lakes, but their success as naturally reproducing populations is unknown.

Behavior An anadromous spring spawner, the smelt runs into the mouths of small streams and broadcasts its adhesive eggs over clean bottom. Smelt have also been observed spawning along shores of lakes on clean sand and gravel.[69,812] Young fish are found in lake shallows in summer, but move to deeper water in the fall. Adults occur in tremendous midwater schools in Lake Erie, moving closer to the surface at night.[253]

Food Juvenile smelt are plankton feeders, changing to a wide variety of invertebrates and fishes as they grow larger. They are heavy predators on young lake trout and whitefish in the Great Lakes.[44,330]

Value Smelt offer the unique recreational opportunity of dipping them on spawning runs in addition to angling for them through the ice. They are an important commercial fish in many places, used both for human food and for animal food. They are considered to be excellent eating, but have a distinctive odor and flavor. The smelt is also an excellent forage for cold-water predators such as trout and salmon.[471,920]

Mudminnows—Umbridae

The mudminnows are a small group of freshwater fishes closely related to the pikes, and similarly restricted in their distribution to the Northern Hemisphere. They are found in extremely shallow habitats, such as marshes, stagnant streams, or weedy shores of lakes. The physostomous swim bladder apparently has a respiratory function which helps them to survive under very low dissolved oxygen conditions.

Genus *Umbra*

Snout short and rounded; scales on some parts of head; origin of dorsal fin only slightly posterior to pelvics; no adipose fin; caudal fin rounded; no lateral line.

Two species of mudminnows occur in Pennsylvania with discrete geographic separation. However, early references to mudminnows may be confusing because the two species were not recognized as distinct, and the collecting locality was not always identified.

KEYS TO SPECIES

1 a. Body with about 14 vertical bars. Found only in streams to the west of the Appalachian divide: Central mudminnow, *Umbra limi*

b. Body without vertical bars, about 12 longitudinal streaks. Restricted to Atlantic slope: Eastern mudminnow, *Umbra pygmaea*

Central mudminnow, *Umbra limi* (Kirtland)[481]

Length 72 mm. Cusic Lake, Macomb County, Mich. 13 September 1976

Distribution The central mudminnow is restricted mostly to the upper Mississippi River and Great Lakes drainages west of the Appalachians. In Pennsylvania, it is found only in a few swampy or marshy places in the northwest; it is often overlooked because of its typical shallow water habitat close to shore, and to its secretive behavior.[20,694]

Behavior It apparently spawns in the spring, judging by the presence of gravid females. There is no nest building; adhesive eggs are attached to submerged vegetation. Breeding males become brighter in color, with bluish-green iridescence on the pelvic and anal fins.

Although the mudminnow usually hides under debris and vegetation, there is no evidence of extensive burrowing in the mud, as reported in early accounts of the eastern mudminnow.[694] The mudminnow is tolerant of low oxygen, surviving in stagnant pools after other fish have died.[413] It is a common associate of the grass pickerel and the brook stickleback.

Food Young mudminnows prefer small crustacea, but many other small invertebrates are taken. Adults more often eat snails and aquatic insects, sometimes leaping from the water in feeding. It is described as a stalker of its food, seizing it by a sudden strike from short dis-

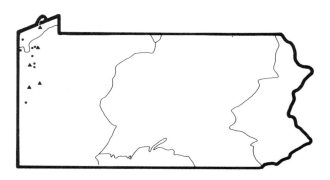

tances much like a miniature pike.[464,692]

Value It is considered of some importance as a forage fish, but chiefly as bait for game species because of its hardiness.[413]

Eastern mudminnow, *Umbra pygmaea* (DeKay)[199]

Length 72 mm. Butler Mill Branch, Nanticoke River, Sussex County, Del. 14 October 1979

Distribution The eastern mudminnow is a lowland form restricted to Atlantic coastal streams from Long Island to Florida. It was common in the Delaware watershed in the late 1800s,[3] but we have found it to be rare and scattered today. Much of its apparent scarcity may be due to its secretive behavior, and its preferred habitat in very shallow water under vegetation and debris. It is very difficult to find, even when quite abundant.[320,378]

Behavior It is a spring spawner, depositing its adhesive eggs singly on aquatic plants,[813] or in hollowed out nests in algae.[573] Common associates in these swampy brown waters are the redfin pickerel and the creek chubsucker.[176] It is able to withstand very low oxygen levels and hides by burrowing beneath debris.

Food The diet of the eastern mudminnow consists of small aquatic and terrestrial invertebrates; the fish occa-

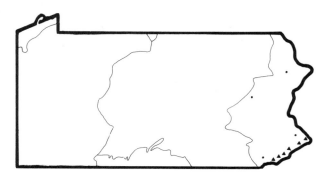

sionally leaps from the water in feeding.[4]

Value Due to its scarcity and secretive habits, it is seldom seen by anglers. It has little value as a forage fish because of its restricted habitat.

Pikes—Esocidae

A small family, consisting of 5 species in the genus *Esox,* the pikes are well known for their predatory food habits. This feature, and their large size (except for *E. americanus)* account for their importance in fishery management and their high status as sport fishes. The culture of pikes, consequently, has a long history, with many attempts to also use some of the hybrids in management of fish populations. Natural hybrids are not uncommon in North America where sympatry among species occurs, and 16 of the possible 20 hybrid crosses have been reared.[179] All pikes are spring spawners, broadcasting their eggs over vegetation or bottom debris in shallow, marshy areas.

Pikes are distributed throughout the Northern Hemisphere as cool-water fishes, with only *E. lucius* occurring on all three continents; *E. reicherti* is endemic to Siberia; the other three species are endemic to North America.

Genus *Esox*

Snout rather extended and flattened, like a duck's bill; scales on some parts of the head; complete lateral line; origin of dorsal fin about halfway between pelvics and base of tail; no adipose fin; tail deeply forked.

With the recent culture and introduction of *E. reicherti* into Glendale Lake, Cambria County, all five species of pikes can now be found in Pennsylvania. It is difficult to establish the original distribution of some of these species because of both the confusion that existed in the early taxonomy, and the successful introduction of species outside their native range. However, because the distribution of the two subspecies of *E. americanus* has been so well established,[177] and because they are completely allopatric in Pennsylvania, we diverge from our normal custom in describing both of these two forms.

KEY TO SPECIES

1 a. Sensory pores on lower jaws 9 or fewer (both jaws combined) (Fig. 39) cheeks and opercula fully scaled: **2**

  b. Sensory pores on lower jaws 10 or more (both jaws combined); lower half of cheeks scaleless: **4**

2 a. Branchiostegal rays 14–17 on each side (Fig. 40); snout length (front of orbit to tip of upper jaw) about 2.3 times in head length (posterior edge of opercle to tip of lower jaw): Chain pickerel, *Esox niger*

  b. Branchiostegal rays 11–13 on each side (Fig. 40); snout length 2.4–2.6 times in head length, *Esox americanus:* **3**

3 a. Cardioid scales between pelvics fewer than 5, and fewer than 5 in rows from anal fin to dorsal midline (Fig. 41); restricted to watersheds draining Atlantic slope: Redfin pickerel, *Esox americanus americanus*

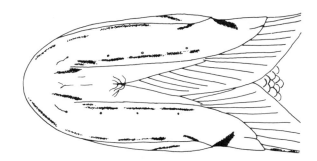

Figure 39. Sensory pores on lower jaw of a pike.

  b. Cardioid scales between pelvics more than 5, and more than 5 in rows from anal fin to dorsal midline (Fig. 41); restricted to Ohio River and Great Lakes drainages on the west slope of the Allegheny Mountains: Grass pickerel, *Esox americanus vermiculatus*

Figure 40. Branchiostegal rays on left side of a pike.

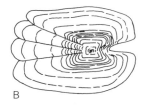

Figure 41. Normal scale (A) and cardioid scale (B) of a pike.

4 a. Sensory pores on lower jaws 10 or 11 (both jaws included) (Fig. 39); cheek fully scaled; lower portion of opercle scaleless; branchiostegal rays 13–16 on each side (Fig. 40): Northern pike, *Esox lucius*

   b. Sensory pores on lower jaws 12–20 (both jaws included); lower portions of both cheek and opercle scaleless; branchiostegal rays 16–19 on each side: Muskellunge, *Esox masquinongy*
   Note: The introduced Amur pike, *Esox reicherti,* is very similar to the northern pike in most morphological characters examined.

Redfin pickerel, *Esox americanus americanus* Gmelin[308]

Length 177 mm. Martin's Creek, Northampton County, Pa. 4 October 1978

Distribution The smallest of the pikes, the redfin pickerel ranges along the Atlantic Coast from Massachusetts to Florida, where it intergrades with the grass pickerel. In Pennsylvania it is common in the Delaware but rarely found in the Susquehanna drainage. It inhabits sluggish streams and shallow, weedy areas of lakes and ponds.[177,373,469]

Behavior The redfin spawns in the spring; adults pair in shallow water and broadcast adhesive eggs over vegetation or debris. There is no care of eggs and young.[573] This species is sometimes found in brackish water along the coast in swampy areas, often associated with the eastern mudminnow and the creek chubsucker. It is very tolerant of low-oxygen conditions found in these swampy areas.[175,176,469]

Food This small pike seldom eats fish, probably due to its very restricted shallow water habitat. Stomach analyses indicate that small crustacea, crayfish, aquatic in-

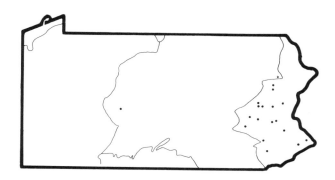

sects, and other invertebrates are most important items of its diet.[175] The utilization of a broad invertebrate food base may explain why this species is often very abundant in one locality.

Value Due to its small size, secretive habitat, and similarity to the chain pickerel, very few anglers are even aware of this species of pike.

Grass pickerel, *Esox americanus vermiculatus* Lesueur[550]

Length 142 mm. Sandy Creek, Mercer County, Pa. 8 August 1968

Distribution Quite similar to the redfin pickerel, the grass pickerel is completely allopatric in Pennsylvania; it ranges throughout the Mississippi River drainage and intergrades with the redfin along the Gulf Coast from Louisiana to Florida.[177] Its preferred habitat is marshes, pools, oxbows, and low-gradient clear streams with aquatic vegetation.

Behavior The grass pickerel broadcasts its adhesive eggs over vegetation in the spring,[487] with occasional hybrids occurring with the northern pike.[597] Fall spawning has been reported but survival was probably very low.[519] The grass pickerel is often associated with the central mudminnow and the green sunfish, probably because of its preferred habitat in shallow weedy areas.[633]

Food The food of the grass pickerel is similar to that of the redfin; few fish are eaten in contrast to the variety of invertebrates found in their stomachs. The small size of the pickerel may account for some of this food selection.[487]

Value The grass pickerel is often mistaken for the young of other pikes, and is considered a nuisance because of its small size.[469]

Northern pike, *Esox lucius* Linnaeus[558]

Length 292 mm. Lake Erie, Erie County, Pa. 28 July 1981

Distribution The northern pike is circumpolar in its distribution in the Northern Hemisphere.[245,281] The northern pike and a similar Amur pike are the only esocids to occur outside North America.

Because of its wide distribution, it is not surprising that scientists have recognized several different forms of this species in North America and Asia.[645] A mutant form, "silver pike," has also appeared in different areas, apparently breeding true.[227,533] However, all of these forms are presently considered to be *E. lucius*.

In Pennsylvania, the northern pike was native only to the Lake Erie and the Ohio River drainages,[277] but it continues to be stocked outside this original range to develop important sport fisheries.

Behavior The northern pike spawns in the spring, migrating into flooded marshes to deposit adhesive eggs over vegetation or debris in shallow water. No care of eggs and young is given.[117] Large individuals have rather vague feeding territories and are likely to be solitary and sedentary in their restricted home range.[227] They are most active in the middle of the day.[119] The northern pike lives many years and grows to more than 50 pounds, facts which have been exaggerated in numerous fanciful accounts of its large size and extreme age covering several centuries.[839]

Food The northern pike and the muskellunge are the largest predators in Pennsylvania, eating fish and many different small animals.[589] However, their reputation as a serious predator on young ducks is probably exaggerated.[516]

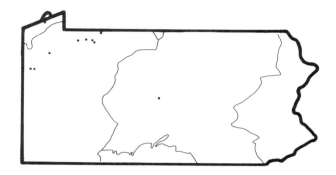

Value The northern pike is prized as a sport fish due to its large size and scarcity. However, it is not always considered beneficial in Canada, where a parasitic tapeworm, common as the adult form in the northern pike, is responsible for a serious larval infestation of grubby whitefish. Attempts to control this parasite of an important commercial fish through the elimination of northern pike populations was deemed impractical,[617] and infested whitefish are not marketed.

Muskellunge, *Esox masquinongy* Mitchill[199]

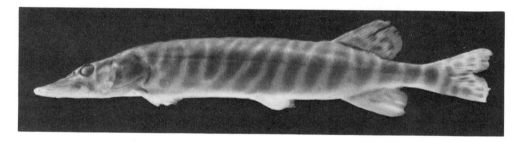

Length 242 mm. Spring Creek, Centre County, Pa. 11 March 1966

Distribution The original distribution of the muskellunge was centered in the midwest around the Great Lakes, with some populations found as far south as Tennessee.[690] In Pennsylvania it was originally described from Lake Erie and is regularly found in the Allegheny River and large natural glacial lakes in the northwest. It is regularly stocked in many new impoundments and river systems outside its natural range, but there is little documentation of natural reproduction in these new localities.[274,469]

The preferred habitat of this solitary fish is cool-water bays of lakes or slow rivers, often at the edge of dense vegetation or other cover. It has a very restricted home range for a large predator, seldom moving more than 2 miles from its summer feeding range.[174]

Behavior The muskellunge spawns in the spring, moving into shallow areas to broadcast adhesive eggs over

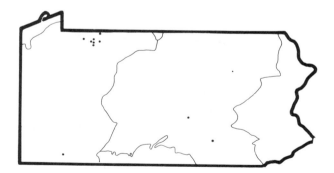

submerged vegetation or debris. There is no care of eggs or young.[446,680] Except for the lake sturgeon, the musky is undoubtedly the largest of our Pennsylvania fishes, often exceeding 40 pounds in weight.

Food The muskellunge is a generalized predator, and under culture conditions is cannibalistic.[446] Its diet changes rapidly from zooplankton to fishes as the musky grows, but it will take almost any small animal,[17] including ducks and muskrats.[386]

Value The musky is prized by anglers for its large size and rarity. The culture and stocking of this species as a part of a recreational fishery, and for the predatory control of stunted panfishes, has been pursued by many states, notably Wisconsin, New York, and Pennsylvania.[680] The tiger musky hybrid (*E. lucius* X *E. masquinongy*), easily reared and stocked, also has added to the diversity of angling in many states.[179]

Chain pickerel, *Esox niger* Lesueur[547]

Length 372 mm. Little Flatbrook, Sussex County, N.J. 17 February 1960

Distribution The original distribution of the chain pickerel was probably limited to the Atlantic and Gulf Coast tributaries west to Arkansas, but it has been widely introduced outside this range.[178] It is by far the most abundant and widely distributed of all pikes in Pennsylvania. It is found in clear sluggish streams or lakes with vegetation, and tolerates a wide temperature range.

Behavior Like other pikes, the chain pickerel broadcasts adhesive eggs randomly over vegetation, and the newly hatched young attach to the vegetation for a short while after hatching.[573,911] As reported for the grass pickerel, this species also occasionally spawns in the fall.[616] It is a solitary, sedentary fish with a very restricted home range. It hybridizes readily with other esocids under culture conditions[179] and natural hybrids with the redfin pickerel are not rare.[750]

Food The chain pickerel feeds on different invertebrates and small fishes, showing peak feeding activity at dawn

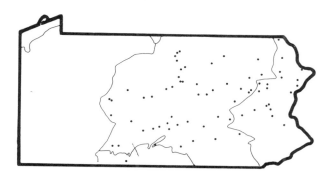

and dusk.[261,743,954] It is a solitary feeder, stalking its prey.

Value Smaller in adult size than both the northern pike and the muskellunge, but reaching a size in excess of 25 inches, the chain pickerel is still a favored sport fish in Pennsylvania and northeastern states, especially for the ice-fisherman.[954]

Amur pike, *Esox reicherti* Dybowski[219]

Length 200 mm. Benner Springs Experiment Station, Pennsylvania Fish Commission, February 1975

Distribution This exotic pike, native only to the Amur Valley of Siberia,[672] was cultured and planted in Glendale Lake, a man-made reservoir near Altoona, Pennsylvania, in 1968, where it has added diversity to the recreational angling.[18,607] Severe acid-mine drainage to the outlet stream is thought to be an adequate barrier to dispersal of this exotic from its planting site. It is too early to determine whether or not this species will maintain a natural population here. A mature individual of 15 pounds was taken from Glendale Lake recently.[18]

Distinguished from the northern pike in the adult form by its prominent, small, black spots over a silvery body, the Amur pike closely resembles the northern pike in most other morphometric and meristic characters.

Minnows—Cyprinidae

No adipose fin; cycloid scales; pharyngeal teeth in one to three rows, but with not more than 8 teeth in a row; fins without spines, except for introduced carp and goldfish with anterior hardened rays in dorsal and anal fins; dorsal fin short, usually less than 10 rays; anal fin placed farther forward than in suckers, distance from anterior insertion of anal fin to base of caudal fin less than 1.8 times the distance from anterior insertion of anal fin to the posterior edge of the opercle.

There are more species of minnows than any other family of fishes; in Pennsylvania alone we have recorded in recent years 39 species of minnows arranged in 13 genera, not including the introduced forms. They vary in size from less than 3 inches for the bridle shiner to more than 50 pounds for the introduced carp, although most species reach maximum sizes of less than 12 inches. It is not unusual to find 15 species in one collection, especially in streams tributary to the Allegheny River.

Minnows constitute an important forage base for predatory fishes, and are often cultured as bait fishes for sport fishing. Only a few species are important in themselves, either as human food or as sport fishes, even though minnows often comprise the majority of the biomass of fish present in streams.

Most minnows feed on invertebrates and thus are direct competitors with the young of most sport fishes such as trout, smallmouth bass, and sunfishes. A few minnows, such as the stoneroller, with its greatly elongated intestine wound around the swimbladder, have apparent adaptations for eating plants, but this is unusual.

This family contains taxonomic groups which are evolving rapidly, and are therefore difficult to classify. However, discrete geographic separation is often helpful, along with morphometric differences, in identifying these fishes that look alike to the beginner.

KEY TO GENERA OF CYPRINIDAE

1. a. Dorsal and anal fins with a bony, serrated spine (Fig. 42); dorsal fin with more than 11 soft rays:**2**
   b. Dorsal fin with fewer than 11 soft rays; no spines in dorsal or anal fins:**3**
2. a. Two pairs of slender barbels on upper jaw (Fig. 43,A); pharyngeal teeth molar-like (1,1,3-3,1,1) (Fig. 44); gill rakers 21 to 27 on entire first arch: *Cyprinus*
   b. No barbels on upper jaw (Fig. 43,B); pharyngeal teeth molar-like (4-4); gill rakers 37 to 43 on entire first arch: *Carassius*
3. a. Lower jaw with a separate cartilaginous ridge (Fig. 45); intestine wound around swimbladder: *Campostoma*
   b. Lower jaw without a separate cartilaginous ridge; intestine not wound around swimbladder:**4**
4. a. Premaxillaries non-protractile; a fleshy frenum connects premaxillaries to snout:**5**
   b. Premaxillaries protractile; a deep groove continuous across midline of snout (Fig. 46):**6**
5. a. Scales in lateral line fewer than 55; lower jaw more or less modified into separate lobes: *Exoglossum*
   b. Scales in lateral line more than 55; lower jaw not modified into separate lobes: *Rhinichthys*

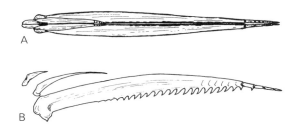

Figure 42. Dorsal view (A) and lateral view (B) of serrated spine in dorsal fin of carp or goldfish.

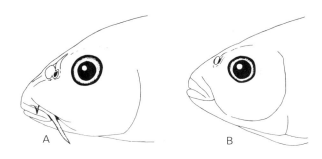

Figure 43. Head of carp (A) and goldfish (B).

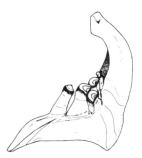

Figure 44. Pharyngeal teeth on left arch of carp.

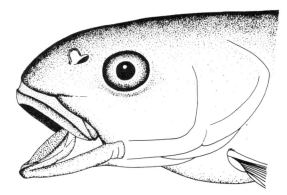

Figure 46. Deep groove across snout of creek chub.

6 a. A small barbel present at junction of upper and lower jaws; visible when mouth is closed (Fig. 47,A):**7**
   b. No barbel present at junction of upper and lower jaws; in *Semotilus* a small barbel is sometimes present, located some distance anterior to junction of jaws (Fig. 47,B): **9**

7 a. Lateral line scales more than 52: *Couesius*
   b. Lateral line scales less than 50: **8**

8 a. Breeding males colored pink-rosy, orange, and/or bluish; males build a mound nest of small stones: *Nocomis*
   b. No elaborate breeding coloration; males do not build nests: *Hybopsis*

9 a. Abdomen behind pelvic fins with a fleshy keel which is not covered with scales (Fig. 48); lateral line curved downward; anal fin falcate: *Notemigonus*
   b. Abdomen behind pelvic fins without a fleshy keel: **10**

10 a. Lower surface of head flattened, with large cavernous chambers in bones (Fig. 49): *Ericymba*
   b. Lower surface of head bones normal, without large cavernous chambers: **11**

11 a. First dorsal ray thickened and separated by a membrane from second ray (Fig. 50,A): *Pimephales*
   b. First dorsal ray a thin splint, closely attached to second ray (Fig. 50,B): **12**

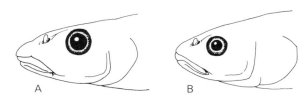

Figure 47. Terminal barbel of river chub (A) vs. flap-like barbel of creek chub (B).

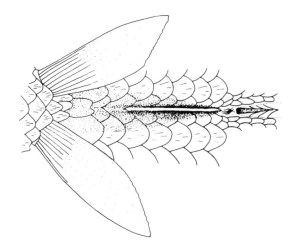

Figure 48. Fleshy keel on abdomen behind pelvic fins in the golden shiner.

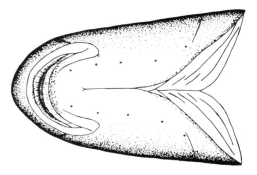

Figure 45. Cartilaginous ridges in mouth of central stoneroller.

12 a. Scales very small, transparent, very difficult to distinguish even under magnification; usually more than 75 in lateral series: *Phoxinus*
   b. Scales larger, thicker, usually less than 75 in lateral series: **13**

13 a. Intestine long, distinctly coiled on right side: *Hybognathus*
   b. Intestine short, S-shaped; not coiled on right side: **14**

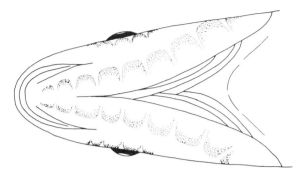

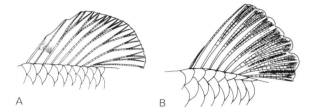

Figure 50. First dorsal ray thickened and separated from second ray in bluntnose minnow (A); first dorsal ray a thin splint attached to second ray in spotfin shiner (B).

Figure 49. Cavernous chambers in lower jaws of the silverjaw minnow.

14 a. Small, flap-like barbel located in groove of upper jaw some distance anterior to junction of both jaws (barbel not terminal) (Fig. 47,B)
[Note: This barbel is frequently absent from both

sides in *S. margarita;* the examination of 10 or more specimens is frequently necessary to confirm this character]: *Semotilus*
     b. No flap-like barbel in groove of upper jaw: **15**
15 a. Lateral line scales 48 or more: *Clinostomus*
     b. Lateral line scales 45 or fewer: *Notropis*

Genus *Campostoma*

Intestine greatly elongated, usually wound around the swimbladder; lower jaw appears double with a separate ridge of cartilage; breeding males with prominent pearl organs on head and body, and with a dark, crescent-shaped bar through the orange dorsal fin; breeding females do not develop pearl organs.

Central stoneroller, *Campostoma anomalum* (Rafinesque)[732]

Length 100 mm. Saline River, Washtenaw County, Mich. 15 September 1976

Distribution This is a highly variable and widespread minnow in much of central and eastern United States, with several subspecies recognized.[413,807,808] Our collections extend its known distribution to the upper Delaware drainage of Pennsylvania; it was previously recorded as common in the Susquehanna River, but not present in the Delaware drainage of New York.[325]

Behavior Males dig out one or more pits in shallow,

gravel-bottomed areas where currents are slow to moderate. These often merge with pits of other males when nest sites are limited, creating large cleared areas. Females enter these pits and spawn with one or more males, but the nests are then deserted by both sexes.[619] Hybrids between this species and several other minnows have been reported.[400,902]

Food The diet of the stoneroller is largely plant material and small invertebrates presumably associated with the periphyton found on the stones of riffles.[498] This is in keeping with the absence of a stomach and the elongation of the intestine, although apparently no one has demonstrated the presence of special intestinal enzymes to utilize this plant material.[499]

Value Possibly as a consequence of their herbivorous food habits, populations of the stoneroller often reach high densities in clean, eutrophic streams. More than 7,000 fish per acre were reported in the headwater streams of the Tennessee River,[540] and we have estimated densities of this species of more than 400 pounds

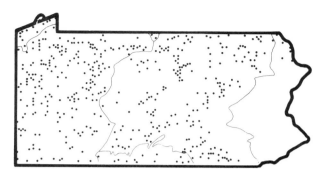

per acre in tributaries of the Ohio River in southwestern Pennsylvania.

Genus *Carassius*

Dorsal fin elongate, with about 18 soft rays; anterior rays of both dorsal and anal fins modified into a hard, serrated spine; pharyngeal teeth 4-4 with definite flattened, grinding surfaces on distal edges; no barbels about the mouth.

Goldfish, *Carassius auratus* (Linnaeus)[558]

Length 130 mm. Codorus Creek, York County, Pa. 2 November 1969

Distribution This exotic, originally from Asia, was introduced into North America in the 1800s and was cultured and stocked in natural environments as a forage species.[277,432] It is common now in all states except Alaska. In Pennsylvania it is largely confined to the warm waters of the southeast, but occurs sporadically in small ponds or sluggish streams in other places. Much of its present distribution is probably due to the disposal of unwanted

aquarium specimens. In western Lake Erie it is especially abundant, and there it hybridizes readily with the common carp.[916]

Behavior Adhesive eggs are deposited on floating or submerged plants in warm weedy shallows of streams or lakes in the spring. There is no care of eggs or young after spawning.[51,215] The solid, olive-green wild color pat-

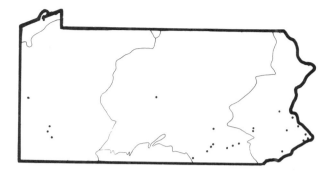

tern is most often seen, but individuals with multi-colored bodies and veil-tails are also found in natural populations.[370]

Food The goldfish is an omnivore, consuming a wide variety of plant and animal foods of suitable sizes.[215,432]

Value In addition to the large ornamental trade, the goldfish is an important bait fish in some states. In others it is considered as an undesirable competitor with game fishes and is prohibited as a bait fish to prevent additional introductions.

Genus *Clinostomus*

Small fishes with moderately compressed bodies; mouth large and terminal, no barbels; breeding adults with red or rosy lateral band, iridescent sides mottled with dark scales; scales intermediate in size between most dace and shiners.

KEY TO SPECIES OF *CLINOSTOMUS*

1 a. Lateral line scales 59 to 70; body long and slender (body depth about 4.5 times in standard length); snout longer than eye diameter (Fig. 51,A): Redside dace, *C. elongatus*

   b. Lateral line scales 48 to 57; body shorter and stouter (body depth about 4.0 times in standard length); length of snout about equal to eye diameter (Fig. 51,B): Rosyside dace, *C. funduloides*

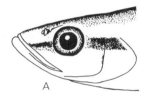 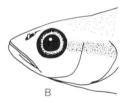

Figure 51. Lateral view of head of redside dace (A) and rosyside dace (B).

Redside dace, *Clinostomus elongatus* (Kirtland)[480]

Length 76 mm. West Branch of Caldwell Creek, Warren County, Pa. 29 May 1966

Distribution This minnow is one of several species which invaded the upper Susquehanna from the Missis-sippi drainage by way of the Horseheads Outlet during glaciation.[31] In the midwest it has a disjunct distribution in the Mississippi River and Great Lakes drainages. In Pennsylvania, it is found in a few localities in the Susquehanna drainage but is apparently absent from the Delaware and Potomac, where the rosyside dace is found. It prefers small creeks with much pool and riffle habitat over bottoms of sand and gravel.[496,722]

Behavior The redside dace scatters its non-adhesive eggs in late spring on gravelly riffles in close proximity to common shiners and creek chubs, often using gravel redds of other species. Hybrids between these several minnows are not rare. Populations appear to be declining due to the loss of clean streams with pools and riffles.[496]

Food The large mouth and preference for midwater habitat is correlated with many kinds of terrestrial and aquatic organisms eaten by the redside dace. During the summer, the diet is largely terrestrial, taken from the surface.[832]

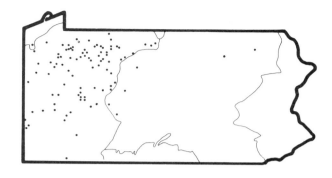

Value This minnow is probably harvested as bait along with other unidentified minnows, but it is not cultured for this purpose. It seldom becomes abundant enough locally to be important as natural forage for game fishes.

Rosyside dace, *Clinostomus funduloides* Girard[305]

Length 77 mm. Northeast Creek, Chester County, Pa. 7 April 1978

Distribution This species reaches its northern limit along the Atlantic Coast in small stream tributaries of the Delaware and Susquehanna Rivers in southeastern Pennsylvania.[194] It is present west of the Appalachians in Kentucky and Tennessee, but is allopatric with the less robust redside dace in Pennsylvania.

Behavior The rosyside dace spawns in late spring on gravelly riffles with several shiners, sometimes using nests of chubs; hybrids between these species are therefore to be expected. No nest is built and there is no parental care of the eggs, which are broadcast in midwater over suitable substrates.[84,85]

Food The food of the rosyside dace consists of small invertebrates usually taken in the drift.[92,257]

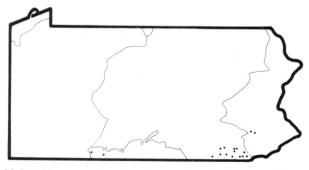

Value The rosyside dace is occasionally harvested from natural populations and used as bait for game fishes, but is seldom cultured for this purpose. It is not an abundant species at any locality but populations do not appear to be declining.

Genus *Couesius*

A monotypic genus of uncertain relationship; slender fish with a short head and slightly subterminal mouth; a slender, well-developed barbel located just anterior to the end of the upper jaw; origin of the dorsal fin posterior to the origin of the pelvic fin.

Lake chub, *Couesius plumbeus* (Agassiz)[8]

Length 84 mm. Lamoille River, Morrisville, Vt. 26 August 1970

Distribution The lake chub is a far-ranging northern species with more or less distinct forms on the East Coast, the upper Great Lakes, and the West Coast.[554] It reaches its southern limit along the East Coast in New York tributaries of the Delaware River.[325] It has not been taken or reported in Pennsylvania.

Although the lake chub is sometimes included in the genus *Hybopsis,* no close morphological relationship with other chubs has been shown. Over its broad range it tolerates a wide variety of habitats, from lakes to streams with considerable current.

Behavior The lake chub spawns over stony substrates during the spring and summer. No nest is constructed and the parents do not guard the eggs after spawning.[606]

Food Stomach contents include terrestrial and aquatic insects, zooplankton, algae, and an occasional small fish.

Value The lake chub probably serves as an important forage species in some northern lakes where other forage fish are scarce.[606]

Genus *Cyprinus*

Dorsal fin elongate, with about 20 soft rays; anterior rays in both dorsal and anal fins modified into a hardened, serrated spine; pharyngeal teeth 1,1,3-3,1,1 and molar-like; two pairs of slender barbels on upper jaw.

Common carp, *Cyprinus carpio* Linnaeus[558]

Length 220 mm. Elk Creek, Erie County, Pa. 27 August 1968

Distribution Originally introduced from Europe, the common carp now is spread over most of the United States, with the center of abundance in the fertile waters of the Mississippi River drainage.[114] It is uncertain when this species was first introduced into the United States, as many early references by European settlers to carp on the East Coast were probably misidentifications of quillback. In 1872, the common carp was successfully introduced into California, and in 1879 more than 12,000 were distributed by the U.S. Fish Commission to persons in 25 states and territories.[142] The common carp prefers shallow, marshy habitat with abundant vegetation, but adapts readily to many habitats.[601]

Behavior In the spring, the common carp migrates into shallow weedy bays to spawn. A female is pursued by one or more males over beds of vegetation and the adhesive eggs are broadcast over the bottom.[142,573] There is no care of eggs or young.

Food The common carp is an omnivorous feeder on many different plants and animals. It roils the water in its feeding activity, but is rather particular in selecting indi-

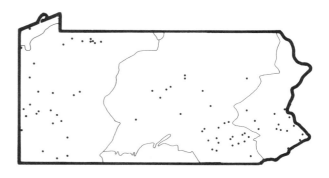

vidual insects or invertebrates from soft bottoms.[242]

Value Presently the common carp is considered to be a serious competitor to native warm-water game species in natural environments.[858] It quickly grows beyond the size suitable for forage for predatory fishes; it is also very tolerant of highly eutrophic conditions.[7] In shallow, fertile lakes it is considered incompatible with production of waterfowl because of the destruction of aquatic plants by its feeding activities.[601]

Genus *Ericymba*

Suborbital and interopercular bones with separated mucous cavities; mouth inferior; eye large; scales on body large, about 33 in lateral series; dorsal fin origin about opposite origin of pelvic fins; small silvery fishes superficially similar to many shiners.

Silverjaw minnow, *Ericymba buccata* Cope[159]

Length 71 mm. Loyalhanna Creek, Westmoreland County, Pa. 15 August 1967

Distribution The silverjaw minnow has a unique, disjunct distribution with two centers, one in the Ohio River drainage, and the other in Gulf Coast tributaries of Mississippi.[943] It was originally described from the Kiskiminitas River in Pennsylvania, a stream drainage

that is now badly affected by acid-mine pollution. It prefers small, slow-moving headwater streams with clean sand or gravel bottoms.[942] Common associates in these streams are the stoneroller and the bluntnose minnow.

Behavior The silverjaw migrates short distances in the spring to spawn over sand or gravel on a riffle. There is no sexual dimorphism at spawning time. Non-adhesive eggs are broadcast over the bottom and there is no care after spawning.[346,393] It is often found in mixed schools of other minnows, apparently competing well with them for food. It is one of the smaller minnows, seldom exceeding 3 inches.[392]

Food The silverjaw minnow is a generalist in its food habits with some preference for midges, mayflies, and detritus. It is mostly a benthic feeder, although the young consume large numbers of pelagic zooplankton.[129,391,704]

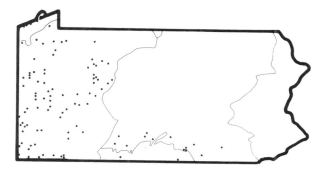

Value It is probably an important forage fish for smallmouth bass or large rock bass when abundant. It is used occasionally as bait along with other unidentified shiners.

Genus *Exoglossum*

Mouth peculiar, dentary bones parallel, united throughout their length; lower lip represented by a broad fleshy lobe on outer side of mandible; upper jaw non-protractile; branchiostegal membranes broadly connected across isthmus.

KEY TO SPECIES OF EXOGLOSSUM

1 a. Lower jaw slightly modified into three portions (Fig. 52,A); an inconspicuous barbel present near junction of upper and lower jaws: Tonguetied minnow, *E. laurae*
   b. Lower jaw markedly modified into three portions (Fig. 52,B); no barbels present on jaws: Cutlips minnow, *E. maxillingua*

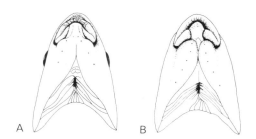

Figure 52. Lower jaws of tonguetied minnow (A) and cutlips minnow (B).

Tonguetied minnow, *Exoglossum laurae* (Hubbs)[398]

Length 122 mm. Fishing Creek, Potter County, Pa. 10 August 1978

Distribution Prior to 1931, the distribution of the tonguetied minnow was confused with that of the cutlips minnow because the two were not recognized as distinct species.[398] It is now clear that the tonguetied minnow is found only in the Ohio River drainage and as far east as the upper Genesee River in the Lake Ontario drainage.[741,900] It apparently did not invade the Susquehanna drainage via the Horseheads Outlet, as many other western forms did, and is not present in Atlantic slope streams where the cutlips minnow is abundant.

The tonguetied minnow prefers clear, warm, gravelly streams with a moderate current.[321] It is most likely to be found at the deeper edges of quiet pools near cover.

Behavior Males prepare mound-like nests of pebbles in slow to moderate current, usually near shelter. They defend the nest from egg predators during construction, but desert the nest soon after broadcasting the adhesive eggs.[736] A moderate-sized minnow, this species seldom exceeds 5 inches in length.

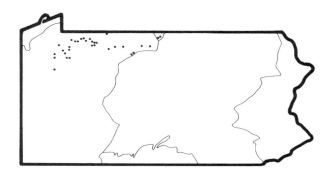

Food The diet of the tonguetied minnow consists of small crustaceans and insects, based on an examination of a few stomachs.[321]

Value This minnow is seldom abundant enough to be important either as bait or as natural forage for game species.

Cutlips minnow, *Exoglossum maxillingua* (Lesueur)[543]

Length 84 mm. Red Clay Creek, Chester County, Pa. 24 March 1977

Distribution One of the most common minnows on the Atlantic slope, the cutlips often becomes extremely abundant in fertile, limestone valley streams. Records of its occurrence in the Allegheny River of New York and Pennsylvania, and in the Genesee River above the falls at Portageville, New York, are in error; they are really records of the tonguetied minnow.[741] The cutlips minnow prefers the moderate current of clear warm streams near rocks.[161,914] It is commonly associated with the margined madtom and the tesselated darter, but in somewhat less current.

Behavior The male cutlips minnow builds a nest of small pebbles similar to that of the tonguetied minnow and several chubs.[914] Semi-adhesive eggs are broadcast over the upstream slope of the nest and are subsequently buried by the addition of stones to the nest.

Food The greatly modified mouth and lower jaw were found to be associated with food items of small size,

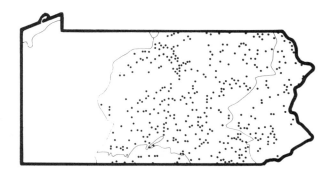

consisting largely of snails, fingernail clams, vegetation, and debris.[92]

Value It is often abundant enough to be important as forage for game fishes in warm streams. It is not used by anglers now, despite an 1892 report by Bean,[53] who mentioned that this fish readily takes a hook and is highly prized by boys.

Genus *Hybognathus*

Body elongate, somewhat compressed; dorsal fin inserted slightly in advance of pelvic fins; premaxillaries protractile; no barbels on jaws; scales large, less than 40 in lateral series; peritoneum black, intestine about 4 times the length of the body, distinctly coiled on the right side, but not wound around the swimbladder.

Of the six recognized species of *Hybognathus* only one, the eastern silvery minnow, now occurs in Atlantic slope rivers of Pennsylvania. In the Mississippi River drainage, similar species are often sympatric, which has contributed to difficulties in identification.[35,254,703]

The Mississippi silvery minnow, as presently recognized,[798] was reported in the Kiskiminitas River.[269] These specimens, catalogued in the Academy of Natural Sciences of Philadelphia (ANSP), have been identified as the bluntnose minnow.[570]

KEY TO SPECIES OF *HYBOGNATHUS*

1 a. Dorsal fin rounded, definitely not falcate (Fig. 53,A); radii in posterior field of scales often more than 20, the number increasing with size of the fish; color brassy: Brassy minnow, *H. hankinsoni*

   b. Dorsal fin somewhat falcate, not rounded (Fig. 53,B); radii in posterior field of scales about 10, the number increasing with size of fish; color more silvery: Eastern silvery minnow, *H. regius*

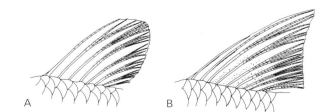

Figure 53. Dorsal fins of brassy minnow (A) and eastern silvery minnow (B).

Brassy minnow, *Hybognathus hankinsoni* Hubbs and Greene[410]

Length 80 mm. Goose Creek, Kalkaska County, Mich. 17 September 1976

Distribution The brassy minnow has a northern distribution across the United States and Canada from New York to British Columbia, but it is most abundant in the Great Plains.[33] It has never been reported in Pennsylvania. A common inhabitant in bog waters, it is also found in small, weedy, sluggish streams or over silt bottoms.[606]

Behavior The spawning behavior of the brassy minnow has not been reported, but adhesive eggs are probably scattered over bottom sand, mud, or debris in the spring. Mature females have been taken in small ponds with no inlet or outlet streams, indicating no need for running water.[216,606] It is one of the smaller minnows, adults seldom exceeding 3 inches at an age of 2 to 3 years.

Food As might be expected from its elongated intestine, this minnow has been characterized as a bottom-ooze feeder. However, aquatic and terrestrial invertebrates taken from surface drift have also been found in stomachs.[216,872]

Value It is one of the common bait fishes of the Great Lakes region, especially away from the Great Lakes proper where the emerald shiner is so abundant and available.[216]

Eastern silvery minnow, *Hybognathus regius* Agassiz[10]

Length 90 mm. Delaware River, Bucks County, Pa. 12 May 1972

Distribution The eastern silvery minnow as now recognized[703] is found only east of the Appalachians from Quebec to Georgia. It is common only in the Delaware River and some large tributaries.[270] It prefers the shallow water of quiet bays or stream pools.[7]

Behavior This minnow spawns in April and May in New York, concentrating in large schools in quiet coves off large streams. Groups of males spawn with a single female; the non-adhesive eggs are broadcast in shallow water over a substrate of decaying vegetation with no nest preparation or subsequent care of eggs.[734]

Food The food of the eastern silvery minnow consists of a variety of plants and animals, ranging from diatoms to small insects and characterized by one author as bottom ooze and algae.[257]

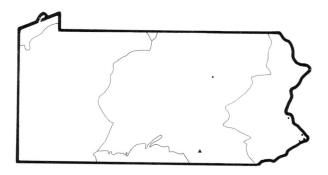

Value This minnow is easily cultured in shallow earthen ponds with no need for running water or specialized habitat. It could be an important bait minnow for this reason.[742,828] Although there is little interest in this fish now for food, an old report[53] stated that the silvery minnow was esteemed by anglers when deep fried in oil.

Genus *Hybopsis*

A widely diversified group of fishes having maxillary barbels, protractile premaxillaries, scale radii restricted to the posterior field, and subterminal mouths. Nuptial males do not develop the prominent pearl organs and bright colors so common to the genus Nocomis.

From the earliest accounts, the identity and phylogeny of several groups of North American minnows with barbels have been confused. Studies to the present time have not resolved all of the controversial issues, and additional revisions are to be expected when more comprehensive studies are available.

Several genera, such as *Couesius, Exoglossum, Hybopsis, Nocomis,* and *Semotilus,* show affinities on the basis of mound-building spawning behavior,[437] but there is little support for a consolidation of this varied group into one genus. Detailed studies of the cephalic lateral line system,[783] brain patterns,[191] and arrangement of pearl organs[82] have not shed much light on the phylogeny of this assemblage of minnows.

KEY TO SPECIES OF *HYBOPSIS* AND *NOCOMIS*

1 a. Anal rays usually 7: **2**
   b. Anal rays usually 8: **5**
2 a. Primary radii* in posterior field of scales less than 10: **3**
   b. Primary radii* more than 12: **4**
3 a. Body elongate (greatest depth of body more than 5 times in standard length); dark mid-lateral stripe extends forward through eye and around snout, usually broken along sides into a series of dark spots; caudal peduncle does not taper abruptly toward tail: Streamline chub, *Hybopsis dissimilis*
   b. Body not greatly elongate (greatest depth of body less than 5 times in standard length); no prominent mid-lateral stripe, but body is mottled with a few to many X-shaped pigment spots; caudal peduncle tapering abruptly toward tail: Gravel chub, *Hybopsis x-punctata*
4 a. Dark spot at base of tail; snout length shorter than post-orbital length of head: Hornyhead chub, *Nocomis biguttatus*
   b. No dark spot at base of tail; snout length about equal to post-orbital length of head: River chub, *Nocomis micropogon*
5 a. Head short, more than 4 times in standard length: Silver chub, *Hybopsis storeriana*
   b. Head long, less than 4 times in standard length: Bigeye chub, *Hybopsis amblops*

Bigeye chub, *Hybopsis amblops* (Rafinesque)[732]

Length 85 mm. Tionesta Creek, Forest County, Pa. 26 July 1974

Distribution The bigeye chub ranges through the central Mississippi River and Ohio River drainages and into some tributaries of Lake Erie. It is not found in Atlantic Coast streams. It is usually found in moderate-sized, hard-bottomed streams with little vegetation.[191,289] It is often confused with several shiners, but is easily distinguished by the presence of terminal maxillary barbels. Common associates in Pennsylvania streams are the silver shiner and the variegate darter.

Behavior The bigeye chub probably spawns in the spring, but there are no published observations.[704]

Food Although there are no published studies, it is likely that aquatic insects and small invertebrates form the diet of this chub.[264]

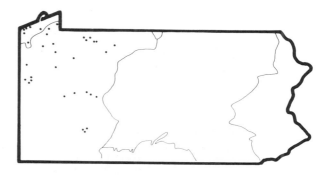

Value The bigeye chub is never very abundant, but is probably harvested from streams as bait for game fishes along with other unidentified minnows.[129]

---

*A primary radius is one which extends from the margin of the scale to more than half way to the focus. Numbers of primary radii also increase with increase in length of the fish. This key is based on counts of radii from individual specimens ranging from 68 to 76 mm standard length.

Streamline chub, *Hybopsis dissimilis* (Kirtland)[482]

Length 85 mm. French Creek, Venango County, Pa. 5 August 1968

Distribution The streamline chub has two centers of distribution in the Mississippi River drainage. It is sparingly scattered throughout the Ohio River tributaries and is present in several streams in Arkansas and Missouri.[129,902] It prefers moderate-sized streams with clean gravel and little vegetation.[191,289] It is often found in collections with the smallmouth bass and the variegate darter. Although this species was only recently recognized as distinct from the gravel chub, hybrids now have been identified.[902]

Behavior Spawning of the streamline chub has not been observed, but may be similar to that of other chubs which spawn in the spring, broadcasting their eggs over gravel riffles. Males with well-developed testes were taken in Illinois in the middle of June.[264]

Food No food studies have been published, but stream invertebrates probably are an important part of the diet.

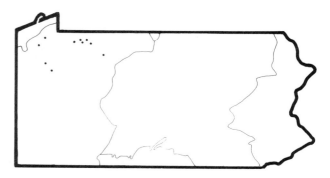

Streamline chub have been observed feeding on clean gravel riffles in streams.[704]

Value The streamline chub is seldom abundant enough to have much value either as bait or as forage for game fishes.

Silver chub, *Hybopsis storeriana* (Kirtland)[483]

Length 85 mm. Lake Erie, Sandusky, Ohio. Summer 1965

Distribution The silver chub is found throughout much of the Mississippi River drainage and in the Lake Erie watershed.[289,704,916] In Pennsylvania it is known only from early reports in the Monongahela River[239] and recent records in Lake Erie. It prefers deep pools in slow-moving streams, but is an open-water species in Lake Erie.[191,479] It is often associated with the spottail shiner and the log perch.[322]

Behavior The silver chub probably spawns in June in open water,[322,479] but no actual spawning has been observed. It is one of the larger chubs, reaching a size of about 9 inches in 4 years.[479]

Food The young silver chubs prefer zooplankton and midges. The diet changes as the fish grow, and aquatic insects and amphipods appear to be most important for the adults.[74,852]

Value This species is rather uncommon except for Lake Erie. It is unlikely that it is very important as a forage fish since other species, such as the emerald shiner and the spottail, are so abundant there.

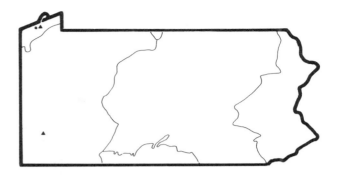

Gravel chub, *Hybopsis x-punctata* Hubbs and Crowe[409]

Length 72 mm. Bull Creek, Allegheny County, Pa. 13 August 1981

Distribution This species was only recently recognized as distinct from the streamline chub, with scattered populations throughout the central Mississippi and upper Ohio River drainages.[409] Its habitat has been reported as clear, slow-moving, deep streams with gravel bottom and little vegetation[191,643] or shallow riffles over pea-sized gravel.[227] It is rare and widely scattered in Pennsylvania, sometimes found with the quillback and black redhorse.

Behavior This species has not been observed spawning. It is likely to spawn in the spring over fine gravel, since a few young were taken in early summer in such localities.[227]

Food No studies of its diet have been published. Aquatic invertebrates found in streams are probably important.[173]

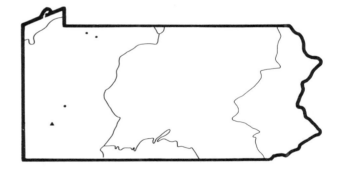

Value The species is rarely found in very restricted habitats; it may be useful as an indicator of clean-stream environment.

Genus *Nocomis**

Nuptial males develop large pearl organs on the head, become brightly colored with pink, orange, and blue hues, and construct a mound nest by carrying stones in their mouth; mouth is moderately large, subterminal, with a small terminal maxillary barbel; scales large, with radii on posterior field only.

*See *Hybopsis* for keys to species, and account of phylogeny of several genera of North American chubs.

Hornyhead chub, *Nocomis biguttatus* (Kirtland)[482]

Length 98 mm. Lamb Creek, Saginaw County, Mich. 16 September 1976

Distribution The hornyhead chub has a broad midwestern distribution, reaching western Pennsylvania only in glaciated tributaries of the upper Ohio River. It is present eastward across central New York as far as the Mohawk River.[513] It is found most abundantly in clear, gravelly streams of moderate to large size.[191,212] Common associates are the white sucker and the bigmouth shiner.[530]

Behavior Spawning males construct and guard large mound-nests in early summer in gravel riffles. They develop prominent pearl organs on the snout and posterior part of the head.[408] These convenient piles of gravel are also used by other minnows as spawning sites, probably contributing to the prevalence of hybrids found in streams where spawning sites are limited.[347,348,510] Males guard territories around these nests and spawn with one or more females. Following spawning the nests are deserted. The hornyhead chub is one of the larger chubs, reaching a length of 10 inches.[216]

Food The food of the hornyhead consists mostly of in-

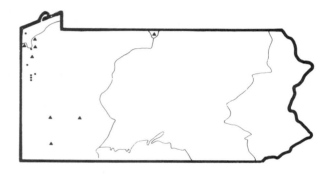

vertebrates with small amounts of plant material taken incidentally to the principal food items.[212,408,509]

Value The hornyhead chub may be cultured under stream conditions, but is usually harvested for bait from natural populations. It is an excellent bait fish for large predators because of its large size and hardiness in handling.[216]

River chub, *Nocomis micropogon* (Cope)[158]

Length 92 mm. First Fork of Sinnemahoning Creek, Potter County, Pa. 17 October 1980

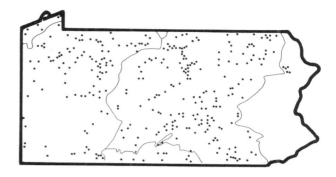

Distribution The river chub is perhaps the best known of the nest-building chubs with barbels. It is widely distributed throughout the Ohio and Great Lakes drainages[514] and, in Pennsylvania, has very recently established large populations in several streams tributary to Lake Wallenpaupack in the Delaware River drainage. Its preferred habitat is high gradient streams of moderate size with clean gravelly riffles.

The hybrid between the river chub and the longnose dace was originally described as a separate species, the Cheat minnow, *Rhinichthys bowersi,*[310] but the true nature of the hybrid was soon recognized.[740]

Behavior Male river chubs develop bright blue and green colors, a large nuptial crest, and prominent pearl organs only on the snout. They carry stones singly to construct on a riffle a mound-shaped nest often 2 feet in diameter. They defend the nest, spawning with one or more females. Several other minnows use this nest for spawning and are tolerated by the river chubs, often leading to hybrids between these species.[510,512,778]

Food The diet of the river chub consists of many different invertebrates, particularly aquatic insects and fingernail clams.[215]

Value Because of its widespread distribution and large populations, the river chub is one of the important bait fishes in eastern North America. Large individuals are occasionally eaten; the flesh is white and of good flavor, but very bony. It may be cultured under controlled stream conditions, but is usually harvested from wild populations.[215]

Genus *Notemigonus*

Body deep and greatly compressed; sharp fleshy keel present on the belly behind the pelvic fins; lateral line greatly decurved, dipping downward; anal fin with 8 to 17 anal rays, distinctly falcate; head small, sharply pointed, mouth terminal.

Golden shiner, *Notemigonus crysoleucas* (Mitchill)[634]

Length 165 mm. Allegheny Creek, Berks County, Pa. 8 July 1969

Distribution The original distribution of the golden shiner included the eastern half of the United States and southern Canada; it has been introduced widely elsewhere. This species shows a decided preference for weedy lakes, but is found in quiet portions and oxbows of large streams.[7,161,408] The number of anal rays in this species varies,[395] high temperature during embryological development being correlated with a higher number of anal rays.[825]

Behavior The golden shiner spawns in spring and summer, scattering adhesive eggs over beds of filamentous algae or other vegetation in quiet water. It sometimes uses nests of largemouth bass.[408,501] It reaches a maximum length of about 12 inches, but the usual growth is about 8 inches in 7 years.[152]

Food The golden shiner, with its small terminal mouth and great mobility, is described as a middle-water and surface feeder. Its diet consists mostly of waterfleas, flying insects, and midge pupae.[464]

Value This is probably the most popular forage fish in North America and is propagated extensively as bait for anglers, and as forage for rearing game fishes.[266]

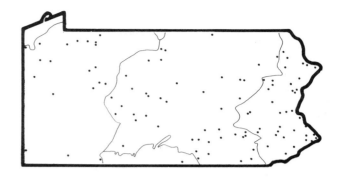

Genus *Notropis*

No barbels about mouth, which is usually terminal or subterminal; premaxillaries protractile, no frenum; scales large, 45 or fewer rows in lateral series; dorsal fin with fewer than 11 soft rays, first ray a thin splint closely attached to second ray; no spines or hardened soft rays in fins; no fleshy keel on abdomen behind pelvics; intestine short, usually with a single S-curve.

This large group of similar species contains several closely related lines, plus others which are difficult to place phylogenetically. Recent studies on subgenera such as *Cyprinella*,[292] *Luxilus*,[297] and *Lythrurus*[867] have been helpful in determining lineages. The shiners are well represented in Pennsylvania, with 17 species collected during the past 20 years. Included are several pairs of species which are superficially very similar, and consequently difficult for the beginner to identify.

KEY TO SPECIES OF *NOTROPIS*

The similarity of species in this genus of shiners presents a problem in constructing an easy key to their identification. The number of anal rays have proven to be a useful character, but only when counted in a standard manner, as indicated in the following figure (Fig. 54). And, it is advisable to count several specimens to obtain the modal number of rays indicated in the key.

1 a. Anal rays usually 7: **2**
   b. Anal rays usually 8 or more: **5**
2 a. A prominent, black, mid-lateral band present from opercle to caudal fin: **3**
   b. Mid-lateral band present only on posterior half of body, or entirely absent: **4**
3 a. Snout shorter than eye width; mid-lateral band wider than pupil of eye and extending forward through eye and across snout (Fig. 55,A): Bridle shiner, *Notropis bifrenatus*
   b. Snout as long as eye width; mid-lateral band prominent on sides, but fades across opercles and is missing on tip of snout (Fig. 55,B): Swallowtail shiner, *Notropis procne*
4 a. Lateral band absent; mid-dorsal stripe surrounds dorsal fin and continues to caudal fin (Fig. 56,A): River shiner, *Notropis blennius*
   b. Lateral band present on posterior half of body; mid-dorsal stripe expands to a wedge-shaped spot

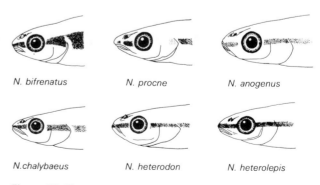

Figure 54. Method of counting anal rays in minnows.

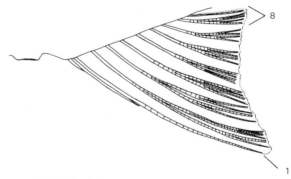

N. bifrenatus   N. procne   N. anogenus

N.chalybaeus   N. heterodon   N. heterolepis

Figure 55. Pigment patterns of heads of shiners.

at insertion of dorsal fin, but does not surround fin (Fig. 56,B); anterior lateral line scales normal (Fig. 57,A): Sand shiner, *Notropis stramineus*

5 a. Anal rays usually 8: **6**

b. Anal rays usually 9 or more: **14**

6 a. A dark-pigmented blotch present on membranes of posterior part of dorsal fin (see also 15a) (Fig. 58): Spotfin shiner, *Notropis spilopterus*

b. No blotch on posterior part of dorsal fin: **7**

7 a. A prominent mid-lateral black stripe on body, continued across head and around snout (Fig. 55,C; 55,D): **8**

b. No black stripe on sides: **11**

8 a. Mouth extremely small and oblique, gape extending backward only to anterior edge of nostril (Fig. 55,C): Pugnose shiner, *Notropis anogenus*

b. Mouth larger and less oblique, gape extending backward beyond middle of nostril: **9**

9 a. Body deepest just anterior to dorsal fin, tapering abruptly toward tail; lateral line depressed below insertion of dorsal fin (Fig. 55,D): Ironcolor shiner, *Notropis chalybaeus*

b. Body nearly uniform in thickness from head to posterior part of dorsal fin; lateral line not greatly depressed below insertion of dorsal fin: **10**

10 a. Black pigment on snout and on chin (Fig. 55,E): Blackchin shiner, *Notropis heterodon*

b. Black pigment on snout, no pigment on chin (Fig. 55,F): Blacknose shiner, *Notropis heterolepis*

11 a. Dorsal fin insertion distinctly anterior to insertion of pelvic fins: Spottail shiner, *Notropis hudsonius*

b. Dorsal fin insertion not anterior to insertion of pelvic fins: **12**

12 a. Exposed portions of anterior lateral line scales not greatly elevated (Fig. 57,A): Bigmouth shiner, *Notropis dorsalis*

b. Exposed portions of anterior lateral line scales greatly elevated (Fig. 57,B): **13**

13 a. Infraorbital canal missing; other pores in cephalic lateral line system inconspicuous; pigment on body usually lacking (Fig. 59,A): Ghost shiner, *Notropis buchanani*

b. Infraorbital canal complete, cephalic lateral line system conspicuous (Fig. 59,B); pigment on body

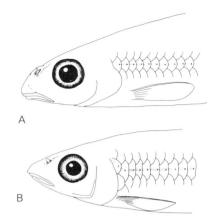

Figure 57. Anterior lateral line scales normal in sand shiner (A), or greatly elevated in mimic shiner (B).

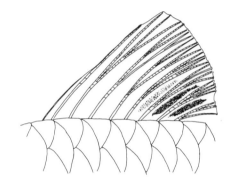

Figure 58. Pigment blotch between posterior rays of dorsal fin in spotfin and satinfin shiners.

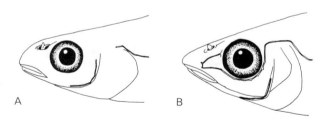

Figure 59. Infraorbital canal missing in ghost shiner (A), or complete in mimic shiner (B).

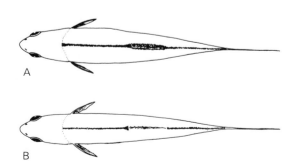

Figure 56. Mid-dorsal stripe of river shiner (A) and sand shiner (B).

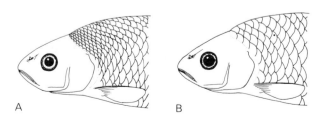

Figure 60. Anterior scale rows small and crowded in common shiner (A), or large and regularly spaced in striped shiner (B).

prominent, anterior lateral line scales greatly elevated (Fig. 57,B): Mimic shiner, *Notropis volucellus*

14 a. Anal rays usually 9: **15**

   b. Anal rays usually 10 or more: **17**

15 a. A dark-pigmented blotch present on membranes of posterior part of dorsal fin (Fig. 58): Satinfin shiner, *Notropis analostanus*

   b. No dark blotch on posterior part of dorsal fin: **16**

16 a. Scales anterior to dorsal fin small, and arranged in many irregular rows above the lateral line (Fig. 60,A): Common shiner, *Notropis cornutus*

   b. Scales anterior to dorsal fin large, and arranged in few regular rows above the lateral line (Fig. 60,B): Striped shiner, *Notropis chrysocephalus*

17 a. A black blotch present at insertion of dorsal fin; body deepest just anterior to dorsal fin (Fig. 61): Redfin shiner, *Notropis umbratilis*

   b. No black blotch at insertion of dorsal fin: **18**

18 a. Pelvic rays 9: Silver shiner, *Notropis photogenis*

   b. Pelvic rays 8: **19**

19 a. Snout long and pointed: Rosyface shiner, *Notropis rubellus*

   b. Snout shorter and blunter: **20**

20 a. Found only in Ohio River and Great Lakes drainages of Pennsylvania: Emerald shiner, *Notropis atherinoides*

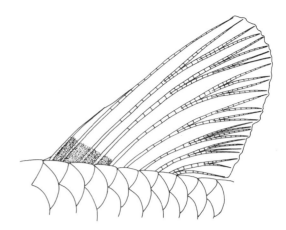

Figure 61. Black pigment blotch at insertion of dorsal fin in redfin shiner.

20 b. Found only in Atlantic slope drainages: Comely shiner, *Notropis amoenus*

The emerald shiner and comely shiner are very similar in appearance although the emerald shiner has a shorter head and a shorter snout than the comely shiner. In Pennsylvania, their distributions do not overlap.

Comely shiner, *Notropis amoenus* (Abbott)[5]

Length 77 mm. Muddy Creek, Lancaster County, Pa. 24 October 1968

Distribution The comely shiner is restricted to Atlantic Coast streams from the Hudson River in New York south to North Carolina.[866] This species is similar to the emerald shiner, but in Pennsylvania the two species are not found together in the same watershed.[270] The comely shiner is an open-water species, usually in small schools, found in moderate to large streams. It usually avoids the very fast water of riffles.[478,747]

Behavior Tuberculate males and ripe females have been taken during the summer, but no spawning has been observed. Close relatives such as the emerald shiner and

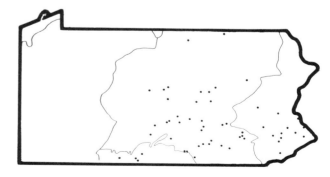

the rosyface shiner spawn in open water over gravel riffles.

Food The comely shiner has been described as a mid-water feeder[755] but no detailed stomach analyses have been published.

Value There is little information available on this species. It probably is used for bait in harvesting many kinds of minnows from streams.

Satinfin shiner, *Notropis analostanus* (Girard)[307]

Length 79 mm. Pequea Creek, Lancaster County, Pa. 25 October 1968

Distribution The satinfin shiner is an Atlantic Coast species, mostly found in clear headwater streams from New York to the Carolinas, but sometimes tolerating some brackish water.[573] It is similar to the steelcolor shiner of the Midwest, from which it is distinguished with extreme difficulty.[294] In Pennsylvania the satinfin occurs sympatrically with the spotfin shiner, another similar species.[270]

Behavior The satinfin shiner spawns by depositing eggs in crevices of bark or cracks in rocks.[573] Males actively defend territories and engage in elaborate courtship behavior[324,881] while producing a variety of sounds described as knocks or purring.[969]

Food The food of this shiner is mostly small mayfly naiads and caddisfly larvae, although other small invertebrates are taken.[257]

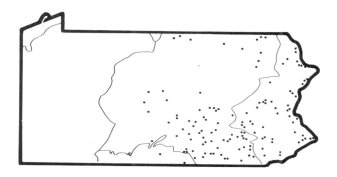

Value Because this minnow is so widespread and common in small warmwater streams along the Atlantic Coast, it is undoubtedly an important forage fish for the rock bass and the smallmouth bass. It is harvested as bait with several other unidentified minnows.

Pugnose shiner, *Notropis anogenus* Forbes[262]

Length 54 mm. Saddle Lake, Mich. 15 July 1952

Distribution The pugnose shiner has a narrow zone of distribution extending from Minnesota eastward through Michigan to a few tributaries of Lake Ontario. It has been reported from the western part of Lake Erie but, so far, not from Pennsylvania.[34] It apparently prefers clear water streams with much vegetation.

Behavior This species probably spawns in the spring, although no studies have been published. It is a small species seldom exceeding 2 inches.

Food No food studies have been published. The small and upturned mouth would prevent feeding on anything but small items.

Value This species is so rare that it probably has little value either as a forage fish or as a bait species.

Popeye shiner, *Notropis ariommus* (Cope)[161]

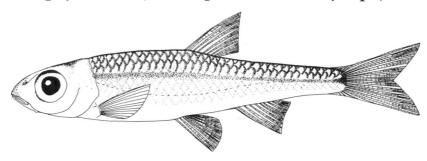

Length 74 mm. Redbird Creek, Ky. 25 June 1949

Distribution The popeye shiner has a restricted range centered in Kentucky and Tennessee with a few reports north to Indiana. Its range appears to be shrinking in recent years. The only collection of this species in Pennsylvania is that of Baird in 1853 taken in the mouth of the Clarion River. Specimens of this collection were recently discovered in the Museum of Comparative Zoology, Harvard University.[300]

The report of the bigeye shiner at the same locality[271] probably can be attributed also to the popeye shiner, because of the similarity of these two species. The bigeye shiner is a more western species in its distribution, and does not reach Pennsylvania. The popeye shiner is found in clear large steams and rivers, free of vegetation. It is usually confined to localities with gravel bottom.[298]

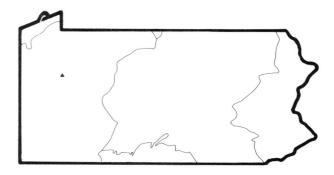

Food Judging from its large eye and preference for clear water over a gravel bottom, it is likely that the popeye shiner is a sight feeder on stream insects and invertebrates.[298]

Behavior The spawning habits of the popeye shiner have not been published. It is a medium-sized shiner, reaching adult sizes of little more than 3 inches.

Value This rare species is probably extirpated in Pennsylvania. Elsewhere it is seldom abundant enough to be of value as a forage species.

Emerald shiner, *Notropis atherinoides* Rafinesque[725]

Length 50 mm. Lake Erie, Erie County, Pa. 4 October 1975

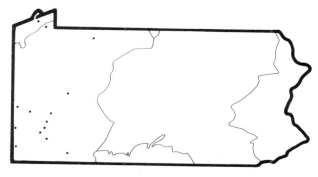

Distribution The emerald shiner ranges widely from freshwater tributaries of the Gulf of Mexico to the Northwest Territories of Canada, and is very abundant in the Great Lakes. In Pennsylvania, it is found only in the Lake Erie and Ohio River drainages, completely allopatric from the similar comely shiner.[866] The emerald shiner prefers a lake habitat but is very abundant in larger streams and rivers. In the Great Lakes it is commonly associated with the spottail shiner and the rainbow smelt.

Behavior The emerald shiner spawns in open water, broadcasting eggs over gravel shoals in May and June. It forms large schools in open water, and grows to a maximum size of about 3 inches.

Food In large lakes, impoundments, and slow water of rivers the emerald shiner often becomes the dominant pelagic species.[7] Its diet changes from algae and zooplankton when small to larger pelagic insects as the fish grows.[241,284,319]

Value In fall and early winter, tremendous schools congregate in quiet bays and are easily harvested for bait. It is an important bait minnow, especially around the Great Lakes, and is also considered important natural forage for lake trout, burbot, and other piscivores.[215,922]

Bridle shiner, *Notropis bifrenatus* (Cope)[161]

Length 53 mm. Aquashicola Creek, Carbon County, Pa. 25 July 1967

Distribution The bridle shiner is mostly an east coast form, ranging from Maine to the Neuse River in North Carolina, but is also found in the St. Lawrence drainage from the Finger Lakes in New York to Quebec. Once abundant in eastern Pennsylvania, it is now taken only rarely in the Delaware drainage.[354] Its habitat is slow swampy streams, sometimes entering tidewater.[440] It is often confused with the sympatric swallowtail shiner.[7]

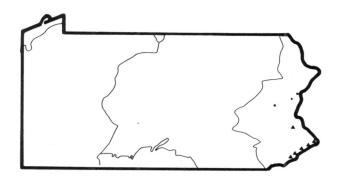

Behavior In New Hampshire, the bridle shiner spawns from May to July, the males turning bright yellow-gold with a black stripe. There is no extensive spawning migration, but pairs of adults select cleared areas and scatter their semi-adhesive eggs over submerged vegetation. There is no nest building or care of eggs after spawning.[356] The bridle shiner is a small and short-lived species seldom exceeding 2 inches at the end of 3 summers.[355]

Food This shiner, like many others, feeds mostly on zooplankton and aquatic insects, searching along the bottom or among vegetation.[356]

Value Although its small adult size would make the bridle shiner a good forage species, it seldom is abundant enough to be important.

River shiner, *Notropis blennius* (Girard)[305]

Length 53 mm. Ohio River near Gallipolis, Ohio. 12 September 1975

Distribution The river shiner ranges throughout the Mississippi River and Hudson Bay watersheds. It is found only in the main stem of large rivers in deep water; it does not enter small creeks.[129,871] The river shiner has been reported in the Monongahela and Ohio rivers in Pennsylvania sporadically since 1886,[239,504] but we have seen no specimens.

Behavior The river shiner spawns in July or August, broadcasting eggs over sand and gravel shoals. There is no care of eggs after spawning.[873,902] It is a moderate-sized minnow, reaching a maximum size of about 5 inches. Common associates are the emerald shiner and the spottail shiner.

Food No food studies have been reported. It is likely to be a mid-water pelagic feeder on drifting insects and

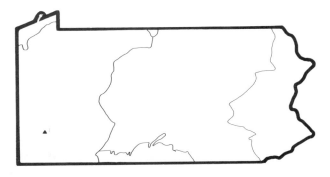

other invertebrates.[704,873]

Value The river shiner is not an abundant minnow like the sympatric emerald shiner. Hence it is unlikely that it is an important bait minnow or forage species.[129]

Ghost shiner, *Notropis buchanani* Meek[608]

Length 37 mm. Monongahela River, Washington County, Pa. 3 April 1978

Distribution The ghost shiner ranges throughout the Mississippi River drainage and some Texas tributaries of the Gulf of Mexico. It prefers gentle eddies alongside the main current in large rivers.[173,612] During the winter and spring of 1978, two specimens were taken in the Monongahela River near Elizabeth as a part of a very intensive environmental survey; this is the first validated record of its occurrence in Pennsylvania, although it was reported in the Ohio River in the 1950s.[504] Superficially similar to the mimic shiner, the ghost shiner lacks completely the infraorbital canal and its associated pores.[32,782]

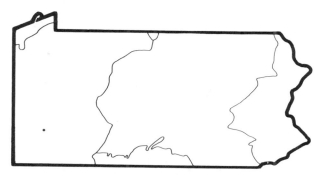

Behavior The ghost shiner spawns in early summer over sluggish riffles of sand and gravel, and reaches its maximum size of slightly more than 2 inches during its third summer.[195,612,704]

Food Although no food studies have been reported, it is likely that this schooling, mid-water feeder eats. zooplankton and other small invertebrates found in the drift.

Value The ghost shiner is rare, compared to sympatric species such as the mimic shiner and the emerald shiner. It is unlikely to be important as a forage species.

Ironcolor shiner, *Notropis chalybaeus* (Cope)[161]

Length 44 mm. Francis Marion National Park, Berkeley County, S.C. ANSP 143514

Distribution The ironcolor shiner has a peculiar lowland distribution along the Atlantic Coast from New York to Texas, and up the Mississippi River drainage to Michigan and Wisconsin.[278,290,704] It was originally described from the Schuylkill River[161] but is now believed to be extirpated from Pennsylvania. It prefers slow-moving creeks, marshes, and ditches with abundant vegetation, sometimes entering brackish water.[290,573,828] It is most similar to the bridle shiner in appearance and life history.

Behavior Spawning takes place in sand-bottomed pools or over vegetation over a prolonged period in spring and summer. No nests are built. An orange-colored male pursues and spawns with a single female as they dash across the cleared area. Adhesive eggs are broadcast over the bottom with no care of the eggs after spawning.[582] It is a small species, seldom exceeding 2 inches. Common associates in these lowland weedy streams are the creek chubsucker and the golden shiner.

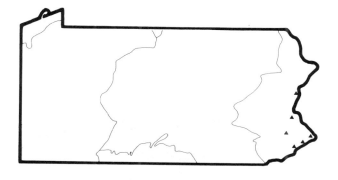

Food The ironcolor shiner feeds by sight on small crustacea and insects in slowly moving water.[582]

Value Due to its infrequent occurrence, it is unlikely to be an important bait minnow or forage for game fishes.

Striped shiner, *Notropis chrysocephalus* (Rafinesque)[732]

Length 125 mm. French Creek, Crawford County, Pa. 1 June 1966

Distribution As presently recognized, the two subspecies of the striped shiner range over most of the eastern part of the Mississippi River drainage and into the lower Great Lakes. The striped shiner and the common shiner are sympatric in western Pennsylvania and over much of the midwest. In these areas, many intergrading populations exist. Most investigators, but not all, regard these two forms as separate species.[296,620,785]

The striped shiner is commonly found in small to medium-sized streams having moderate current and a clean gravelly bottom. It is slightly more tolerant of turbid conditions than its close relative, the common shiner.[530]

Behavior The striped shiner spawns over gravelly riffles, frequently congregating with other minnows over the mound nests of the river chub or the hornyhead chub for spawning.[348] Hybrids among many of these riffle-spawning minnows are therefore rather common[510] and lead to difficult problems of identification for the beginner. Non-adhesive eggs are broadcast over suitable bottom. There is no nest building or parental care.

Common associates of the striped shiner in turbid, gravelly streams are the bigmouth shiner and the silver-

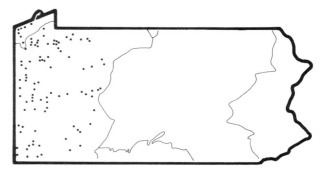

jaw minnow. The striped shiner is one of the largest *Notropis,* commonly exceeding 6 inches.[530]

Food Although the striped shiner eats some algae, small insects and crustaceans are its chief diet.[129]

Value The striped shiner is one of the important bait minnows harvested from wild populations along with several other unidentified minnows. Large populations which occur also provide important forage for game fishes in streams.

Common shiner, *Notropis cornutus* (Mitchill)[637]

Length 87 mm. North East Branch of Perkiomen Creek, Montgomery County, Pa. 1 April 1971

Distribution The common shiner is widely distributed throughout North America from Missouri to the Canadian Maritimes, and historically has been considered as con-specific with the striped shiner.[297,785] It frequents streams with moderate current, preferring clean substrates.

Behavior The common shiner broadcasts its eggs in the spring over gravelly riffles,[348,737] often congregating with other stream minnows over the mound nests of river chubs. Hybrids between the common shiner and the rosyface shiner are rather common, since both species use river chub nests to deposit their eggs. First generation hybrid males of this cross have been observed spawning with female common shiners, but there is no definite proof that the hybrids were fertile.[738]

The common shiner is a large minnow, sometimes exceeding 10 inches. It is an associate of the river chub and the rosyface shiner.

Food The common shiner eats diatoms and other algae,

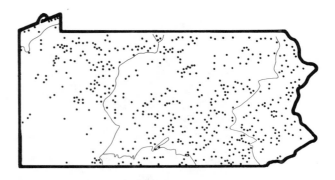

but most of its food is insects. It often feeds at the surface and readily takes small artificial flies.[92,408,872]

Value It is a common bait minnow when harvested from natural populations, but is difficult to culture because of spawning requirements.[215,408]

Bigmouth shiner, *Notropis dorsalis* (Agassiz)[9]

Length 63 mm. Potato Creek, McKean County, Pa. 25 May 1978

Distribution The bigmouth shiner has an unusual disjunct distribution, with the main center in the prairie states, but small foci in Michigan, Ohio, Pennsylvania, and New York. In Pennsylvania it is only present in the upper Allegheny drainage.[280] The fish occurs in small streams with clean sand or gravel bottoms, or in the sandy shallows of lakes.[7,687,871]

Behavior Breeding adults have been collected in June and July, but spawning has not been observed.[704] It is often taken together with the sand shiner and the silver-jaw minnow.[530,872] It is a small minnow, seldom exceeding 2 inches in length.

Food The diet of the bigmouth shiner consists of small invertebrates and algae picked off the bottom.[333,871]

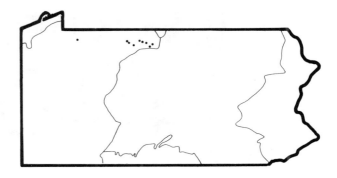

Value This species probably is harvested from streams as a bait minnow, but it is seldom recognized because of its similarity to other shiners taken at the same time.

Blackchin shiner, *Notropis heterodon* (Cope)[158]

Length 46 mm. Cusic Lake, Macomb County, Mich. 13 September 1976

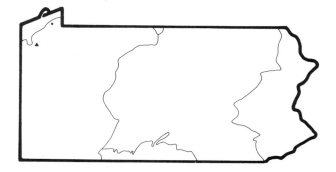

Distribution Reported from glacial lake districts from North Dakota east to New York, a small population of the blackchin shiner was found in Pleasant Lake, Pennsylvania, as recently as 1977.[733] It has also been reported from other parts of the Allegheny River[327] and the Genesee River[321] drainage in New York. The blackchin shiner prefers clear weedy areas of lakes, but is found sometimes in quiet streams.[7,733]

Behavior It probably spawns in spring or early summer, although no breeding observations have been reported. It is a small minnow, seldom exceeding 2 inches in length. Fishes often found with the blackchin shiner are the bluntnose minnow and juvenile bluegills.

Food This shiner eats many different organisms, including algae, zooplankton, small snails, and insects.[463,464,692] There is a progression of food from young to adult; the young eat algae and zooplankton while the adults seem to be specialized feeders on water fleas and surface midges.

Value It may be an important forage fish or bait minnow where abundant, but due to its similarity to the blacknose shiner and the mimic shiner it is seldom recognized by anglers as a separate species.[839]

Blacknose shiner, *Notropis heterolepis* Eigenmann and Eigenmann[229]

Length 62 mm. Beaver Dam on Goose Creek, Kalkaska County, Mich. 17 September 1976

Distribution Although it was reported in scattered localities throughout the glaciated area of western Pennsylvania in 1938,[733] I have been unable to find the blacknose shiner there in recent years. It is widely distributed from Iowa east through the New England states, and south in the midwest as scattered populations to Missouri and Tennessee.[327] The blacknose shiner is found in weedy shore areas of lakes and streams.[7,240,264]

Behavior Although gravid females have been taken in spring and in early sumer, actual spawning has not been observed.[839] It is a small minnow, seldom exceeding 2 inches, and is commonly associated with the lake chub-sucker and the grass pickerel. A hybrid between the blacknose shiner and the brassy minnow was originally described as a separate species, *Notropis germanus,* but was later correctly identified as a hybrid.[399]

Food The diet of the blacknose shiner changes from zooplankton and algae in juveniles to predominantly worms and small insects as the fish grows. This shiner often feeds at the surface in quiet water.[214,692]

Value It may be an important bait species where locally

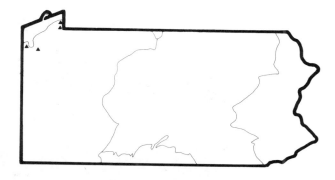

abundant, but it is seldom distinguished from other small shiners.[839]

Spottail shiner, *Notropis hudsonius* (Clinton)[135]

Length 58 mm. Octaroro Creek, Lancaster County, Pa. 26 October 1967

Distribution The spottail shiner occurs as several recognized subspecies from western Canada to the Hudson River in New York[324] and south along the Atlantic Coast to Georgia. It has been introduced recently into the Allegheny Reservoir and is common in the Allegheny River below the dam near Warren, Pennsylvania. The spottail occurs in large benthic schools in lakes, moving over long distances, but also exists as small localized populations in streams.[324] The juveniles are often found in shallow water with abundant vegetation; adults prefer clean bottoms.[573]

Behavior Spawning takes place in large aggregations over sandy shoals or algal mats in spring or summer. No care of eggs ensues.[527,596] Females grow faster than males and reach a total length in excess of 4 inches at the end of 4 years.[861] The yellow perch is often found with the spottail shiner in lakes.

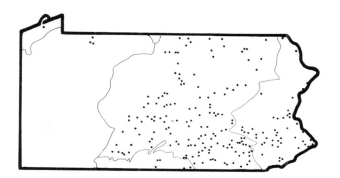

Food The diet of the spottail shiner is varied, but algae, cladocera, and insects are chief food items.[596,951] Young shiners prefer microcrustacea, while adults often take terrestrial insects from the surface.[74]

Silver shiner, *Notropis photogenis* (Cope)[158]

Length 98 mm. Allegheny River, Warren County, Pa. 1 August 1975

Distribution The silver shiner is common in clear streams of the Upper Ohio and Tennessee River systems.[129,289] It is also found in a few tributaries of Lake Erie.[336,902] It is completely allopatric from the similar comely shiner found only in Atlantic Coast tributaries.

The silver shiner has often been confused with the comely shiner, the rosyface shiner, and the emerald shiner, but the 9 pelvic rays and a jet-black mid-dorsal stripe of the silver shiner easily separates it from all similar forms.[866] The silver shiner is a moderate-sized minnow, preferring moderate current in deep runs of gravel bottomed streams.[289,515]

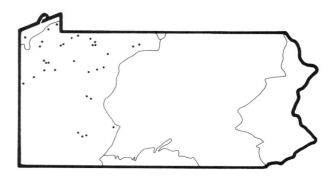

Behavior The spawning of this species has not been observed, but it probably spawns in the spring like many other pelagic shiners. It is often found with the rosyface shiner and the striped shiner.[515] It is one of the larger shiners, often exceeding 4 inches.

Food Published food studies are limited, but the silver shiner frequently jumps into the air to capture flying insects,[902] and stomachs contain mostly aquatic insect larvae.[336]

Value Although the silver shiner is not a rare species, it seldom occurs in large populations. For this reason it probably is not an important forage species in a stream ecosystem.

Swallowtail shiner, *Notropis procne* (Cope)[158]

Length 53 mm. West Branch of Codorus Creek, York County, Pa. 2 November 1969

Distribution The swallowtail shiner is an Atlantic coastal species found from New York to South Carolina. It is abundant in moderate-sized, clean streams[161] but occasionally taken in lakes.[325] Superficially resembling the bridle shiner, it differs by having a complete lateral line, a more diffuse streak across the head, and the caudal spot disconnected from the lateral band.[418]

Behavior There is no spawning migration, the adults moving to the nearest suitable riffle in the spring. Males defend small territories and spawn repeatedly with different females over a period of several days. Eggs are broadcast over sand and fine gravel and the area is then deserted by the parents.

The swallowtail shiner is a small species, seldom exceeding 2 inches. It is quite tolerant of turbidity, which may explain its continued abundance in many streams where the bridle shiner is disappearing. It schools with other minnows, often associated with the satinfin shiner and the rosyside dace.[745]

Food The diet of the swallowtail changes from filamen-

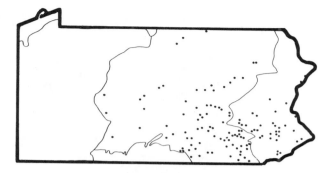

tous algae and diatoms in juveniles to a selection for small aquatic insects as the fish grows.[92]

Value It is undoubtedly an important forage fish, because of its abundance and size. It is often harvested as bait from natural populations in streams.[53]

Rosyface shiner, *Notropis rubellus* (Agassiz)[8]

Length 64 mm. Pine Creek, Lycoming County, Pa. 22 July 1971

Distribution The rosyface shiner is one of many fishes with a large midwestern distribution. It probably gained access to the Susquehanna drainage and thence to Atlantic coastal streams by way of the postglacial Horseheads Outlet.[31] We have found it in one location in the Delaware drainage in Pennsylvania, a new record for this drainage.

Behavior The rosyface shiner spawns over a prolonged period in summer,[767] often associated with other shiners over the mound nests of the river chub or hornyhead chub. Spawning occurs in small groups some distance above the bottom, scattering their eggs over the gravel, sometimes coincident with spawning striped shiners.[700] Adults reach a maximum size of about 3 inches in their third year.[768]

The hybrids between this species and either the striped shiner or the common shiner are the most abundant hybrid minnows found in Pennsylvania. Hybrid individuals were observed spawning together, but there was no evidence of success in reproduction.[738]

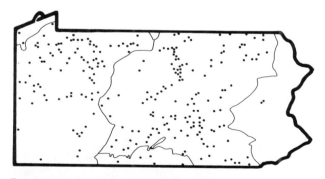

Food The rosyface shiner, when young, is a bottom feeder on algae and invertebrates. As it grows, it becomes a semi-specialized feeder on aquatic insects, with many terrestrial forms taken from the surface.[700,768]

Value This shiner is undoubtedly an important forage fish for game fishes found in warm-water streams. It becomes very abundant locally, and has a wide distribution. It is harvested from small streams together with other minnows.

Spotfin shiner, *Notropis spilopterus* (Cope)[161]

Length 102 mm. Cussewago Creek, Crawford County, Pa. 26 June 1975

Distribution The spotfin shiner is one of several species that has extended its distribution from the Mississippi drainage through the glacial lake outlets to Atlantic coastal streams, where it is now common from the Hudson River to headwaters of the Potomac. It occurs sympatrically with both the steelcolor shiner in the west and the satinfin shiner in the east, and has historically been confused with both of these recognized species.[293] It is found in various habitats from rapid streams to clear weedy lakes.[408]

Behavior The spotfin shiner spawns throughout the summer, males defending territories around submerged logs, and producing various sounds which may serve to identify species and prevent hybridization.[969] Eggs are invariably deposited in crevices or beneath loose pieces of bark.[701]

The spotfin shiner is a medium-sized minnow occasionally reaching 4 inches. In large warm-water streams such as the Susquehanna River, it becomes very abundant.

Food The diet of the spotfin shiner changes from algae

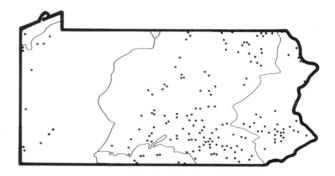

and small aquatic insects for juveniles, to a concentration on insects, both aquatic and terrestrial forms taken from surface drift, for the adults.[215,408,871]

Value The tolerance to different habitats, widespread distribution, and dense populations of this minnow undoubtedly make it an important forage species. It has some value as a bait minnow, but it is difficult to culture.[227,408]

Sand shiner, *Notropis stramineus* (Cope)[158]

Length 63 mm. North Fork of Ten Mile Creek, Washington County, Pa. 2 June 1977

Distribution The sand shiner ranges throughout the midwest and southcentral United States as two subspecies. Intergrades and hybrids also make identification of this shiner difficult and have led to a confused nomenclature.[410,629,885] In Pennsylvania it is often collected with the similar mimic shiner. They are found in localized populations along lake shores or moderate-sized streams and have a strong affinity for sandy shoals.[408,884]

Behavior Gravid females have been found from June through August, but no spawning observations have been published.[891] It is a small minnow, with large spawning adults occasionally reaching 2.5 inches in length.

Food The diet of this small minnow consists mostly of zooplankton and small aquatic insects, with an apparent

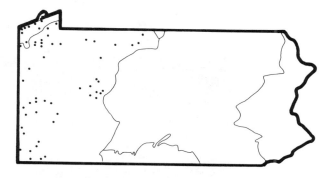

preference for water fleas and midges.[74,173]

Value It is an important forage fish because of its small size and abundant populations. It is not used much as a bait minnow because it is difficult to keep alive in containers.[408]

Redfin shiner, *Notropis umbratilis* (Girard)[305]

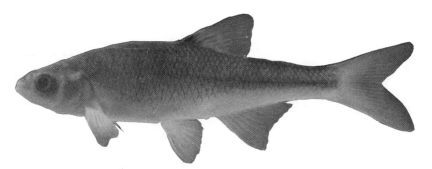

Length 65 mm. Cussewago Creek, Crawford County, Pa. 25 May 1977

Distribution The redfin shiner is a midwestern species of broad north-south distribution.[868] I have found it only in two isolated populations in Pennsylvania. Although the redfin is reported to prefer clear water in weedy areas, I have taken it from extremely turbid streams.

Behavior During spawning, dense aggregations of tuberculate males occur over cleared areas, spawning with females as they move through these dense swarms.[429] They sometimes pick a spawning site above the occupied nests of green sunfish, apparently in preference to unoccupied nests or to other sites. Male green sunfish only rarely chased shiners that held territories over their nests.[428]

The redfin shiner is a small minnow, seldom exceeding 3 inches. It is often found with the superficially similar golden shiner and the striped shiner.[530]

Food Although no food habits have been reported, it is

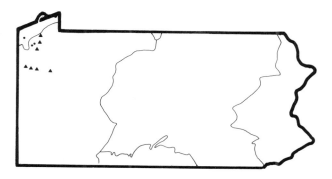

likely that zooplankton and small invertebrates are important items of its diet.[264,408]

Value This species is uncommon in Pennsylvania. In the central Mississippi River drainage it is probably an important forage species.

Mimic shiner, *Notropis volucellus* (Cope)[158]

Length 53 mm. Brown's Run, Warren County, Pa. 2 August 1973

Distribution The mimic shiner has an extensive north-south distribution in the midwest, but is missing from most of the Atlantic coastal streams, except for an isolated area in the Roanoke and the Neuse River systems. It was first reported in 1977 by Robert W. Malick, Jr., in the Susquehanna River near Harrisburg, where its population is spreading rapidly. This is the first record of its occurrence outside the Ohio River drainage in Pennsylvania.

The mimic shiner and the sand shiner are perhaps the most difficult pair of minnows for the beginner to identify, because of their close similarity and their frequent occurrence in the same collection.[410,885] Until recently it was considered conspecific with the ghost shiner.[32] The mimic shiner becomes very abundant in some lakes and in clean, gravelly streams, but is quite adaptable to different habitats.

Behavior The mimic shiner probably spawns in the summer, but its breeding behavior has not been reported. It is a small minnow, reaching an adult size of about 2.5 inches in three summers of growth.[71] It is a common associate

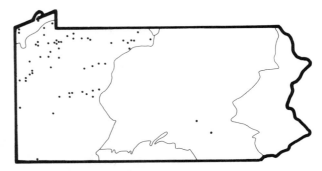

of the bluntnose minnow and small white suckers.

Food The mimic shiner is an omnivorous small minnow, but algae and microcrustacea are most important food items.[71,74]

Value Because of its small size and wide distribution it is an important forage species, and is often used as a bait minnow, harvested from natural populations.[71]

Genus *Phoxinus*

Scales small and transparent, usually more than 75 in lateral series; first dorsal ray a thin splint, closely attached to second ray; no barbels about mouth.

The three species in this group are closely allied, with some hybrids producing fertile offspring. They are similar to the Old World genus *Phoxinus* in which they are currently placed. However, some workers prefer to use the genus *Pfrille* for the finescale dace, and the genus *Chrosomus* for the two redbelly daces, while other workers use the genus *Chrosomus* for all three species.

KEY TO SPECIES OF *PHOXINUS*

1 a. Body with a single, dusky lateral band, intestine short, with a single main loop: Finescale dace, *P. neogaeus*
  b. Body with two black, lateral bands; intestine with two coils in addition to main loop: **2**

2 a. Mouth strongly oblique; distance from tip of snout to posterior margin of eye scarcely longer than rest of head: Northern redbelly dace, *P. eos*
  b. Mouth less oblique; distance from tip of snout to posterior margin of eye noticeably longer than rest of head: Southern redbelly dace, *P. erythrogaster*

Northern redbelly dace, *Phoxinus eos* (Cope)[156]

Length 59 mm. Beaver Dam on Goose Creek, Kalkaska County, Mich. 17 September 1976

Distribution Widely distributed in the north from British Columbia to Nova Scotia, the northern redbelly dace was reported only in the Susquehanna drainage of Pennsylvania (Meshoppen Creek) by Cope in 1862.[156] It was not found in the 1935 New York survey of the Susquehanna or Delaware watersheds,[325] nor has it been taken recently anywhere in Pennsylvania.

This small minnow lives in boggy water or in sluggish, mud-bottomed creeks.

Behavior The northern redbelly dace spawns throughout most of the summer in Michigan, a single female pairing with one or more males and depositing non-adhesive eggs in masses of filamentous algae.[153] Maturity is reached in the second summer of life and some individuals live at least 3 years. It is often found with the brassy minnow and the brook stickleback. It also commonly hybridizes with the finescale dace, making identification of these two species difficult.[536,666]

Food This species is one of only a few fishes which eat

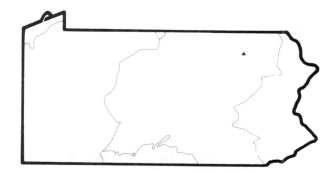

large amounts of plant material; filamentous algae are very important, with a few zooplankton and small aquatic insects found in the stomach.[408,606]

Value Redbelly dace are easy to culture in small ponds and could be an important forage for game fishes.[215] In its natural habitat it may be used as forage for northern pike or brook trout.

Southern redbelly dace, *Phoxinus erythrogaster* (Rafinesque)[732]

Length 55 mm. Service Creek, Beaver County, Pa. 29 July 1968

Distribution The southern redbelly dace ranges from southern Michigan south to Tennessee and Arkansas[408] and is present in western Pennsylvania in scattered populations in lakes and clear cold brooks.

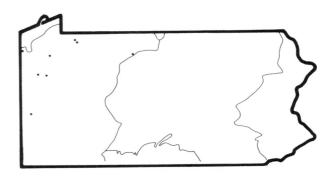

Behavior Breeding males have a brilliant scarlet stripe along their lower sides during the spawning season, which occurs in late May or early June in Illinois. A single female spawns with a pair of males on sandy or pebbly riffles in contact with the bottom, often using the nest of the hornyhead chub.[348] In large congregations of spawning adults, four or more adults were observed spawning in one group.[859]

The southern redbelly dace is often found with the creek chub and the white sucker. A hybrid, originally described as a new species *Oxygeneum pulverulentum*, between the southern redbelly dace and the stoneroller has been reported.[402] Other hybrids are known.[902]

Food This species eats less plant material and more small aquatic insects than its relative, the northern redbelly dace.[212,408]

Value It is an important bait minnow for culture and is harvested excessively from natural populations because of its habit of living in tight schools.[212,408]

Finescale dace, *Phoxinus neogaeus* Cope[161]

Length 57 mm. Goose Creek, Kalkaska County, Mich. 17 September 1976

Distribution The finescale dace occurs in boggy waters from Wyoming to Maine, reaching as far south as northern New York and Michigan. It has never been reported in Pennsylvania, but it possibly is present in some boggy waters in the Pocono Mountains area.

Behavior Details of breeding behavior or place of spawning have not been documented. Commonly sympatric with the northern redbelly dace and the brook stickleback in boggy waters, the finescale dace is presumed to spawn in late spring.

Hybrids between the finescale dace and the northern redbelly dace[405,666] have caused difficulty in identifying these two species, because of their frequency and intergradation of many morphological characters. The finescale dace is the larger of the three species of *Phoxinus,* reaching an adult size of about 3 inches.

Food Its diet is mostly small insects, with some algae occurring in the stomachs.[215]

Value It is commonly used as a bait minnow in Canada because of its abundance and hardiness; it is very tolerant to low levels of dissolved oxygen.

Genus *Pimephales*

Dorsal fin with a dark blotch on anterior edge, but well above the base of the fin; first ray of dorsal fin thickened, and separated from second ray by a membrane; a deep groove present across midline of snout, no frenum; no barbels about mouth.

KEY TO SPECIES OF *PIMEPHALES*

1 **a.** Body depth less than 4.0 times in standard length; incomplete lateral line (Fig. 62,A); wide, prominent lateral band; faint caudal spot; terminal mouth; peritoneum brown; intestine looped or coiled; no dark crescent on side of snout: Fathead minnow, *P. promelas*

b. Body depth more than 4.5 times in standard length; complete lateral line (Fig. 62,B); prominent lateral band; caudal spot prominent in young, fading in adults; mouth subterminal; peritoneum brown; intestine looped or coiled; no dark crescent on side of snout: Bluntnose minnow, *P. notatus*

c. Body depth more than 4.5 times in standard length; complete lateral line; lateral band faint; caudal spot prominent; mouth nearly terminal;

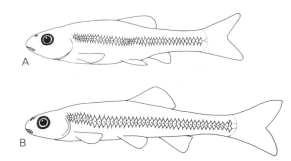

Figure 62. Incomplete lateral line of fathead minnow (A), and complete lateral line of bluntnose minnow (B).

peritoneum silvery; intestine with single S-shaped fold; dark crescent on side of snout: Bullhead minnow, *P. vigilax*

Bluntnose minnow, *Pimephales notatus* (Rafinesque)[732]

Length 90 mm. Lake St. Clair, St. Clair County, Mich. 14 September 1976

Distribution The bluntnose minnow was found originally over much of eastern United States and Canada, and has been widely established elsewhere as a forage species.[7,946] It is one of the most common minnows in Pennsylvania, tolerating many different habitats and water quality conditions.

Behavior Sexual dimorphism is striking, the males developing large pearl organs about the blackened head, and guarding territories around excavated depressions beneath flat objects. The adhesive eggs are plastered in one or more layers on the underside of these submerged objects. Males grow to larger sizes than females, reaching a maximum size of about 4 inches.[912,953]

Food The food of the bluntnose minnow is primarily bottom invertebrates, although much organic debris or plant material is also ingested.[242,464,500]

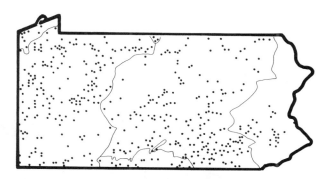

Value The bluntnose minnow is one of the most important bait minnows sold. It is harvested from natural populations and is cultured commercially in small ponds.[215,408]

Fathead minnow, *Pimephales promelas* Rafinesque[732]

Length 72 mm. Goose Creek, Kalkaska County, Mich. 17 September 1976

Distribution The native distribution of the fathead minnow covered most of North America between the Rocky Mountains and the Appalachians; it has been introduced widely elsewhere.[913] Populations are usually restricted to sluggish creeks and small ponds.[839]

Behavior The fathead is often called the blackhead minnow because of the striking appearance of mature spawning males. They prepare and guard nests under submerged flat objects and guard and aerate the adhesive layers of eggs until they hatch.[408,581,973] Spawning occurs repeatedly in the same nest, with the period extending from May to July.

The maximum length attained by mature males is about 3.5 inches, somewhat shorter than the bluntnose minnow. It is a common associate of the golden shiner and the brown bullhead. The fathead minnow is very tolerant to low oxygen and other unfavorable water quality and often thrives after winter kill wipes out competing species. It is not as common as the bluntnose minnow in Pennsylvania, and appears to disappear under

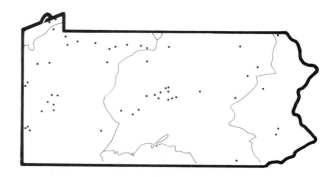

heavy predation by game fishes.

Food The fathead minnow feeds on many different kinds of organisms, but is somewhat unique in also eating large amounts of algae.[166]

Value The fathead minnow is commonly reared as a hardy and prolific bait minnow.

Bullhead minnow, *Pimephales vigilax* (Baird and Girard)[41]

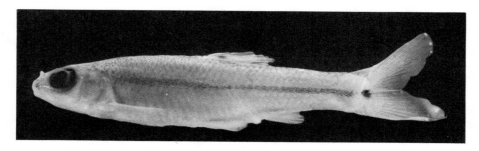

Length 56 mm. Ala. 1965

Distribution The bullhead minnow ranges throughout most of the Mississippi River drainage. Despite the early report of its abundance in the Monongahela River in Pennsylvania,[239] recent records show its northern limit to be in the Ohio drainage some distance below the Pennsylvania-Ohio boundary.

The bullhead minnow prefers sluggish bayous of large streams.[404,871] Several subspecies of the bullhead minnow are presently recognized, and the taxonomy is confused.[404]

Behavior The bullhead minnow is most similar to the bluntnose minnow. Males prepare a nest under submerged flat objects, and guard and aerate the layers of adhesive eggs. Males develop pearl organs on the head, and spawn repeatedly with females over a long period in May and June.[688] It is often found with the yellow bullhead.

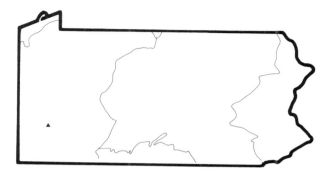

Food The diet of the bullhead minnow is mostly algae and bottom ooze, with some insects also found in stomachs.[227,872]

Value The bullhead minnow is a common bait minnow in the midwest, usually harvested from natural populations.

Genus *Rhinichthys*

Dorsal fin with fewer than 11 soft rays; premaxillaries non-protractile, a fleshy frenum connects upper lip to snout; scales in lateral series more than 55; lower jaw not modified into separate lobes; a slender barbel present at junction of upper and lower jaws.

KEY TO SPECIES OF *RHINICHTHYS*

1 a. Mouth almost terminal and oblique; eye large, contained about 4 times in head length; lateral band usually prominent: Blacknose dace, *R. atratulus*

  b. Snout projecting beyond the horizontal mouth (Fig. 63,B); eye small, contained about 5 times in head length. Lateral band often faint or missing: Longnose dace, *R. cataractae*

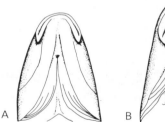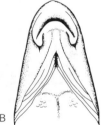

Figure 63. Terminal mouth of blacknose dace (A), and snout projecting beyond the inferior mouth of the longnose dace (B).

Blacknose dace, *Rhinichthys atratulus* (Hermann)[369]

Length 64 mm. Isers Run, Somerset County, Pa. 31 May 1979

Distribution The blacknose dace has a broad north-south distribution throughout the midwest and south along the Atlantic coast to North Carolina. Several sub-species are recognized, two of which are present in Pennsylvania: *R. a. meleagris* in the west and *R. a. atratulus* in the east. Nearly every small stream in Pennsylvania contains this fish. It requires running water, but not the very fast riffle habitat of the longnose dace. It is tolerant to many different environmental conditions, but apparently avoids ponds and lakes.

Behavior The blacknose dace spawns during May and June, selecting a shallow riffle over sand or small pebbles. Males guard territories[739] for several days, and spawn with one or more females in the same nest, or nearby suitable areas.[903] Sexual dimorphism is prominent, with breeding males having orange fins and a bright red-orange band along the sides. Blacknose dace seldom live as long as 3 years, reaching a maximum size of about 3 inches.[673] Common associates in these small streams are the Johnny darter and the tesselated darter.

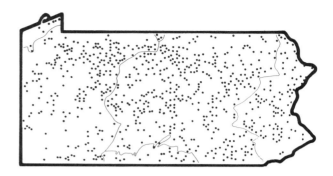

Food Stomach analyses indicate a diet mostly of bottom invertebrates, with some diatoms and filamentous algae also consumed.[903]

Value This species is widely harvested as a bait minnow in Pennsylvania, but it is seldom cultured or sold commercially. Its abundance offers an important forage base for stream game species from trout to smallmouth bass.

Longnose dace, *Rhinichthys cataractae* (Valenciennes)[183]

Length 81 mm. Spring Creek, Centre County, Pa. 13 April 1981

Distribution The longnose dace is distributed from coast to coast in much of North America, occurring in rapid streams and the inshore waters of the Great Lakes. It is noted for its restriction to the fast riffles of streams, almost completely segregated from the slow-current habitat of the blacknose dace.

Behavior Virtually nothing has been published on their spawning habits, except that spawning occurs during June and July in most places. Nests may be guarded by one parent, but observations are quite indefinite.[215] Occasional hybrids between longnose dace and the river chub have been reported (improperly identified as *Rhinichthys bowersi*),[310] indicating that longnose dace sometimes spawn in close proximity to the river chub.[740] The longnose dace is one of the longer-lived stream minnows in Pennsylvania, reaching a size of about 5 inches in about 5

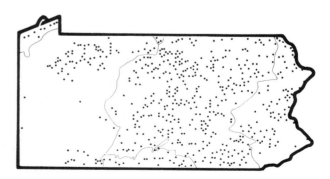

years. Females appear to grow somewhat faster and live longer than males.[769] A common associate of the longnose dace on fast riffles is the northern hog sucker.

Food The diet of the longnose dace is principally aquatic insects, with some algae eaten by the smaller dace.[288]

Value This minnow is not often used for bait because it

is difficult to keep alive in containers. The demand for fast current makes it impractical to culture this species commercially.

Genus *Semotilus*

Dorsal fin with fewer than 11 soft rays; premaxillaries protractile, no fleshy frenum connecting upper lip with snout; no barbel present at junction of upper and lower jaws, but often with a small flap-like barbel some distance anterior to junction, hidden in groove between upper jaw and head; first dorsal ray a thin splint, attached to second ray: intestine short, S-shaped.

This genus now contains three species once thought to be in three separate genera, indicating the rather diverse external appearance of these three species. Similarities in several characters such as pharyngeal teeth, flap-like barbel, 8 anal rays, and a complete lateral line, were used to place the three species in a single genus.[35]

KEY TO SPECIES OF *SEMOTILUS*

1 a. Black spot on anterior base of dorsal fin: Creek chub, *S. atromaculatus*
  b. No black spot on anterior base of dorsal fin: 2
2 a. Sides of body mottled with irregular pattern of pigmented scales; head short (more than 4 times in standard length): Pearl dace, *S. margarita*
  b. Sides of body not marked with dark scales; scales regularly outlined with dark pigment; head long (less than 4 times in standard length): Fallfish, *S. corporalis*

Creek chub, *Semotilus atromaculatus* (Mitchill)[638]

Length 113 mm. Little Bull Creek, Allegheny County, Pa. 20 August 1980

Distribution The creek chub is one of the commonest stream fishes in central and eastern North America, preferring moderate current in small streams.[7]

Behavior The creek chub is a nest-building minnow, with males constructing and guarding a long mound of gravel for several days of spawning with several females.[776,856] Sexual dimorphism is prominent, with males developing large pearl organs on the head. Other minnows such as the common shiner and the rosyface shiner use the nest for a spawning site; several hybrid combinations have been reported, probably resulting

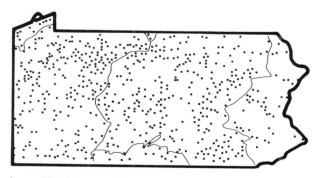

from this close spawning association.

The creek chub is very tolerant to low oxygen concentrations. It is frequently the last species to die due to organic pollution or acid water from coal-mining operations. It is a large minnow, commonly growing to 10 inches or more in 3 or 4 years.

Food The diet of the creek chub consists primarily of aquatic insects, but almost any invertebrate or small fish of suitable size will be taken. It is an aggressive surface feeder often taken by fly fishermen fishing for trout or smallmouth bass.[237,541]

Value The creek chub is a favorite bait minnow for large game fishes such as the northern pike and muskellunge because of its large size and hardiness. Special culture methods of running water raceways have been shown to be effective in rearing this bait fish.[215]

Fallfish, *Semotilus corporalis* (Mitchill)[637]

Length 160 mm. Pine Creek, Lycoming County, Pa. 22 July 1971

Distribution The fallfish is a common inhabitant of East Coast streams from New Brunswick to Virginia, and extending west to the Lake Ontario and Hudson Bay drainages. In Pennsylvania it apparently avoids small streams and is more often taken in clean gravelly pools and slow runs of large streams and small rivers.[7]

Behavior The mound nests built by large males are very striking piles of gravel and stones, often left above water as the stream level drops during the summer.[473,746,963] These nests, guarded by the tuberculate male, are used by other fishes such as the common shiner for spawning. Hybrids involving the fallfish are therefore not uncommon.[327]

The fallfish is by far the largest native minnow in East Coast streams and clear lakes, growing to more than 18 inches in 10 years.[770]

Food Young fallfish prefer algae and zooplankton as food, but large adults are aggressive feeders on a wide

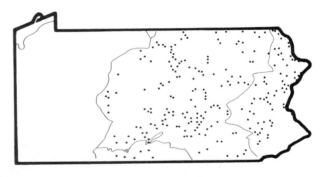

variety of aquatic and terrestrial insects drifting in the stream.[92,257]

Value The fallfish is often called the silver chub by eastern fly fishermen. Less discriminating anglers consider this as an acceptable sport fish, although it is rather bony.[7]

Pearl dace, *Semotilus margarita* (Cope)[161]

Length 99 mm. Little Antietam Creek, Franklin County, Pa. 28 August 1972

Distribution The pearl dace is found in scattered locations, but seldom in abundant numbers, across Canada and the upper midwest, and south along the Atlantic Coast to Virginia.[35] In the north it is commonly found in boggy waters; along the Atlantic Coast it prefers moderate current of cool streams. In Pennsylvania, it is much less abundant than the creek chub or fallfish, but is occasionally sympatric with both species.

Behavior The pearl dace differs from other species of *Semotilus* in that no mound nest is built. Males defend territories and spawn with single females over a variety of bottom types.[526] Both sexes develop fine pearl organs on head, body, and fins, with more extensive coverage on the males.[251]

Adult pearl dace seldom exceed 5 inches, remaining smaller than either the creek chub or the fallfish. The maximum age appears to be about 4 years.[250] Common associates of the pearl dace in Pennsylvania are the blacknose dace and the mottled or slimy sculpins. In the north it is most often found with the brassy minnow and northern redbelly dace.

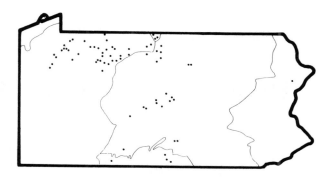

Food The diet of the pearl dace changes from algae, plant debris, and zooplankton in small fish to larger items such as insects, molluscs, and some small fishes as the dace grows.[215,606]

Value This species is seldom cultured for bait, but it is an important forage fish where locally abundant in the midwest.[215]

Suckers—Catostomidae

No adipose fin; no barbels; cycloid scales; pharyngeal teeth in a single series of more than 16 teeth, sometimes molar-like; fins without spines; anal fin placed farther back than in minnows.

The suckers are a large family of freshwater fishes in North America, with a few representatives in Siberia and China. Twelve species in seven genera have been taken recently in Pennsylvania waters. Most species occur in running water, but the white sucker and a few others adapt readily to lake habitats. Except for the dwarfed forms of a few species, suckers generally grow to much larger sizes than the native minnows, often reaching a weight of several pounds. A few species are used by anglers for sport fishing and for food, although the fine bones embedded in the musculature discourage some people.

KEY TO GENERA OF CATOSTOMIDAE

1. a. Dorsal fin long, more than 20 principal rays: **2**
   b. Dorsal fin of 18 or fewer principal rays: **4**
2. a. Body long, slender and terete, standard length more than 4 times the maximum body depth; lateral line scales more than 50: *Cycleptus*
   b. Body short, robust and compressed, standard length less than 4 times the maximum body depth; lateral line scales less than 50: **3**
3. a. Anterior portion of dorsal fin extended into a moderate lobe with first ray about three times as long as shortest dorsal ray (Fig. 64,A); mouth larger, maxillary twice eye diameter; caudal fin with a shallow fork; intestine arranged in elongate, S-shaped loops: *Ictiobus*
   b. Anterior portion of dorsal fin extended into a long, pointed lobe with first ray about 5 times as long as shortest dorsal ray (Fig. 64,B); mouth smaller, maxillary about equal to eye diameter; caudal fin with deep fork; intestine arranged in long coil or convolutions: *Carpiodes*
4. a. Lateral line incomplete or absent in adult: **5**
   b. Lateral line well developed in adult: **6**
5. a. Lateral line incomplete; mouth horizontal and inferior; each scale with a black spot: *Minytrema*
   b. Lateral line absent; mouth oblique; no regular pattern of spotted scales, but may have bars or blotches on body: *Erimyzon*
6. a. Lateral line scales 55 or more: *Catostomus*
   b. Lateral line scales 50 or fewer: **7**
7. a. Head strongly depressed between the eyes (Fig. 65,A); air bladder divided into two parts: *Hypentelium*
   b. Head concave between the eyes (Fig. 65,B); air bladder divided into three parts: *Moxostoma*

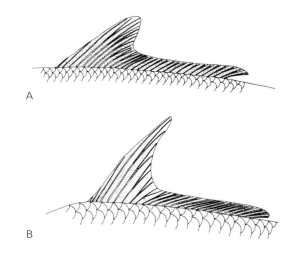

Figure 64. Anterior portion of dorsal fin moderately extended (A), or long and pointed (B).

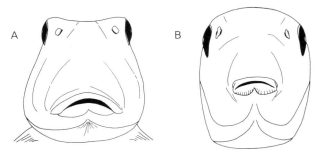

Figure 65. Head strongly depressed between the eyes (A), or concave between the eyes (B).

Genus *Carpiodes*

Body very deep and laterally compressed; single dorsal fin with more than 20 rays, anterior ones elongated; mouth horizontal, small, with maxillary reaching only to anterior edge of eye; caudal fin deeply forked; intestine arranged in a long coil.[62]

Early records of the carpsuckers in Pennsylvania are very confusing. Of the six species listed by Fowler in 1919, only three are considered as valid species, and only the quillback has been collected in recent years. All of the specimens originally identified as either the river carpsucker or the highfin carpsucker and deposited in the collections of the Academy of Natural Sciences of Philadelphia have been recently identified by Smith-Vaniz (*personal communication*) as the quillback. Thus, although it is possible that the river and highfin carpsuckers once were present in Pennsylvania, we have no museum specimens to verify this.

KEY TO SPECIES OF *CARPIODES*

1 **a.** Small protuberance present on tip of lower jaw; tip of lower jaw scarcely in advance of anterior nostril; lateral line scales usually 33–37: **2**

   b. Small protuberance absent on tip of lower jaw; tip of lower jaw definitely in advance of anterior nostril; lateral line scales usually 36–40: Quillback, *C. cyprinus*

2 **a.** Longest ray in dorsal fin in adults longer than fin base; body in adult more elongate, depth about ⅓ standard length; young difficult to separate from river carpsucker: Highfin carpsucker, *C. velifer*

   b. Longest ray in dorsal fin in adults less than ⅔ the length of the fin base; body in adult deep and compressed, depth about ½ standard length; young difficult to separate from highfin carpsucker: River carpsucker, *C. carpio*

River carpsucker, *Carpiodes carpio* (Rafinesque)[732]

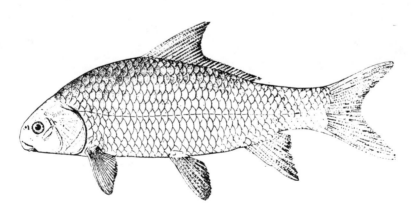

Forbes and Richardson. 1920. Fishes of Illinois, Ill. Natur. Hist. Surv., p. 76

Distribution This species was reported as late as 1913 in the Beaver River near Pittsburgh[274] but is now thought to be extirpated. Museum specimens identified originally as the river carpsucker are actually the quillback (Smith-Vaniz, *personal communication*). The species is still fairly abundant in Ohio and elsewhere throughout the Mississippi River drainage.[704,902] The preferred habitat of this sucker is the quiet backwaters of large rivers. It appears to tolerate more silt and turbidity than the quillback.

Behavior Gravid females and tuberculate males have

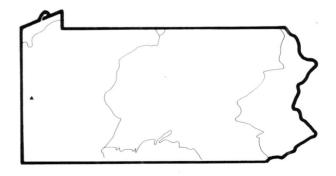

been taken from June through August,[58] although no observations of spawning have been reported.

Food The river carpsucker is a schooling form which feeds from the bottom on attached algae and associated

animals, including insects, crustaceans, and worms.[96,107]

Value Carpsuckers are seldom taken by anglers, but sometimes occur in commercial catches. They are generally considered rather tasteless and of little value.[139,264]

Quillback, *Carpiodes cyprinus* (Lesueur)[544]

Length 90 mm. Conewango Creek, Warren County, Pa. 8 October 1971

Distribution One of the three carpsuckers widely distributed throughout central United States, the quillback also extends its distribution along the Atlantic coastal streams from the St. Lawrence River to Virginia.[839] Early records are confused because of problems of identification. In Pennsylvania, the species is widespread but seldom abundant locally, and is the only carpsucker now present in our waters.

The quillback is found in lakes or large streams in pools with gravel bottoms, tolerating less silt and turbidity than the river carpsucker.[704]

Behavior There is often a migration to gravelly riffles in summer for spawning. Gravid females and tuberculate males have been taken in summer, but no spawning has been observed.[430]

Food Early studies of stomach contents indicate that fingernail clams and aquatic insects are the most impor-

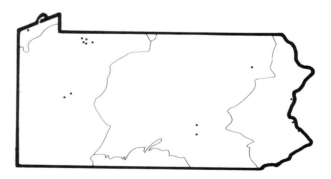

tant foods, although some vegetation and detritus was also taken.[263]

Value Because they live for 10 years or more and grow to large sizes[915] they are occasionally taken commercially in the midwest or by angling, but are considered of less value as food than the channel catfish or buffalofishes.

Highfin carpsucker, *Carpiodes velifer* (Rafinesque)[732]

Forbes and Richardson. 1920. Fishes of Illinois, Ill. Natur. Hist. Surv., p. 76

Distribution Another carpsucker, now thought to be extirpated from Pennsylvania waters, the highfin is still present in portions of the Mississippi River drainage. Due to its low tolerance to silt and turbidity, populations appear to be declining.[195,704] In 1886 it was reported as common in the Monongahela River south of Pittsburgh.[239] Museum specimens originally identified as the highfin carpsucker are actually the quillback (Smith-Vaniz, *personal communication*). The habitat of this carpsucker is large rivers, reservoirs, and quiet sloughs in clear water.

Behavior Adults in breeding condition were collected over deep riffles, presumably spawning, but no actual observations of spawning have been published.[430]

Food No food studies have been published. Other carpsuckers are bottom feeders on a variety of organisms.

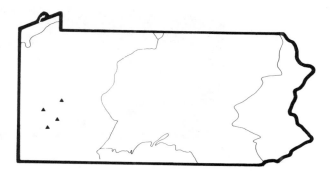

Value Highfin carpsuckers in Iowa grew more slowly than the quillback, reaching about 12 inches in 8 years.[915] As a consequence, this species is not an important sport or commercial fish.

Genus *Catostomus*

Dorsal fin with 18 or fewer principal rays; complete lateral line; cycloid scales; scales small, crowded anteriorly, more than 55 rows in lateral line; head concave between the eyes.

KEY TO SPECIES OF *CATOSTOMUS*

1 a. Snout projecting far beyond upper lip (Fig. 66,A); lower lips broad and extending posteriorly beyond a vertical line drawn through the nostrils; more than 85 scales in lateral line: Longnose sucker, *C. catostomus*

b. Snout scarcely projecting beyond upper lip (Fig. 66,B); lower lips thinner and do not reach a vertical line drawn through nostrils. Less than 85 scales in lateral line: White sucker, *C. commersoni*

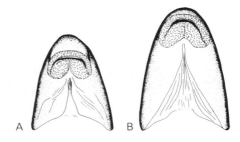

Figure 66. Snout projecting far beyond upper lip in longnose sucker (A), or scarcely projecting in white sucker (B).

Longnose sucker, *Catostomus catostomus* (Forster)[268]

Length 88 mm. Flaugherty Creek, Somerset County, Pa. 18 July 1968

Distribution The most widespread sucker in North America and Asia, only a relict population of this species remains in the headwaters of the Youghiogheny River in Pennsylvania and Maryland. It inhabits clear, cold streams and lakes, with lake populations usually running into tributary streams for spawning.[287,470,472] Dwarf forms of this species have been reported from Canada[42] and from the Adirondacks of New York,[472] but their genetic distinctness has been questioned.[762]

Behavior Longnose suckers were observed over gravel riffles in May, with two or more males spawning with a single female.[287] There was no nest preparation or guarding of the eggs after spawning. This species is very long-lived. Although scale-reading of this species is questionably accurate, northern populations appear to grow slowly, reaching a size of about 4 pounds in not less than 20 years.[359]

Food Despite the common belief that suckers feed on

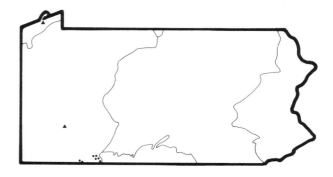

bottom silt and ooze, studies have shown that crustacea, molluscs, and aquatic insects are dominant food items.[132,133]

Value Because the flesh is so full of bones, the longnose sucker is not a favored food fish. It is used for animal food in the north and is occasionally marketed commercially.

White sucker, *Catostomus commersoni* (Lacepede)[508]

Length 115 mm. Brodhead Creek, Monroe County, Pa. 20 July 1977

Distribution One of the most abundant and best-known fishes in Pennsylvania, and widespread throughout North America, the white sucker is tolerant to many different habitats,[876] ranging from cool mountain streams to warm-water lakes and ponds.[272]

Behavior The white sucker spawns in stream riffles or stony beaches of lakes in the spring. Two or more males spawn with each female as she invades the spawning riffle. The larger pelvic fins and pearl organs on the enlarged anal fin easily distinguish the male during spawning.[870] There is no nest preparation or guarding of the eggs after spawning.[744,777] Lake populations usually migrate to inlet streams for spawning.[287,757]

Dwarf populations of the white sucker have been studied in the Adirondacks of New York. Spawning runs of the dwarf form occurred at a different time than that of the larger form living in the same lake,[201] leading some persons to view these as separate subspecies.

Food The diet of the white sucker is mostly zooplankton

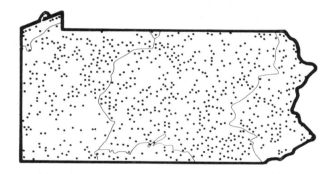

and aquatic insects, depending on size of the fish and the habitat. Despite the common opinion that suckers are important predators on the eggs of trout, there is little evidence for this view.[876]

Value The white sucker is an important sport fish in the spring and is considered excellent eating as fresh fish or pickled or smoked. It is easily cultured in small ponds, and consequently is an important part of the fish-bait industry.[215]

Genus *Cycleptus*

Body long, slender, and terete, caudal peduncle very long; head small, short, and slender; mouth small, inferior; lips papillose; dorsal rays about 30, the first rays somewhat elongated; complete lateral line of 53–59 pored scales; color dark blue.

Blue sucker, *Cycleptus elongatus (Lesueur)*[544]

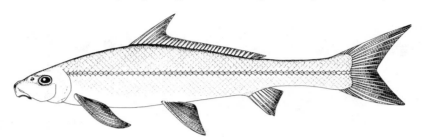

Length 203 mm. Mississippi River, Vicksburg, Miss. 2 August 1973

Distribution The blue sucker ranges widely throughout central United States and probably reached its northeastern limit in the lower Allegheny River in Pennsylvania. A specimen was collected from the Kiskiminetas River by Cope during the 1860s[279,299] and several others were taken in the Ohio River near the Pennsylvania line between 1925 and 1950.[902] It is now believed to be extirpated, but with the recent improvement in water quality of the Ohio River, it is possible that it will again move upstream into Pennsylvania waters.

The blue sucker prefers channels and pools with some current in large rivers, but is found in some impoundments.[641,850]

Behavior Judging from the condition of the gonads, the blue sucker probably spawns in the spring. Although spawning has not been observed, the sucker probably scatters its eggs over rocky bottom in the current. Common associates in large river habitats are the shovelnose

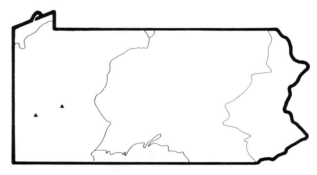

sturgeon and the paddlefish.[139,173]

Food The diet of the blue sucker is mostly aquatic insects, other invertebrates, and some plant material.[100]

Value It is one of the larger suckers, reaching a length of 3 feet, and sometimes occurs in commercial catches.[441]

Genus *Erimyzon*

Body oblong, more or less compressed; mouth sub-inferior; dorsal rays 11 or 12; no lateral line; young with conspicuous dark, lateral stripe, fading to lateral blotches in adults.

KEY TO SPECIES OF *ERIMYZON*

1 a. Lateral scale rows about 43; crowded anteriorly (Fig 67,A): Creek chubsucker, *E. oblongus*
   b. Lateral scale rows about 38; not crowded anteriorly (Fig. 67,B): Lake chubsucker, *E. sucetta*

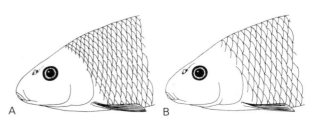

Figure 67. Scale rows crowded anteriorly in creek chubsucker (A), or not crowded anteriorly in lake chubsucker (B).

Creek chubsucker, *Erimyzon oblongus* (Mitchill)[635]

Length 161 mm. Swans Gut Creek, Worcester County, Md. 15 May 1976

Distribution The creek chubsucker ranges widely throughout the eastern United States, although it is seldom abundant in any locality.[936] It is found most often in weedy areas of sluggish streams or small lakes.[552] Along the Atlantic Coast it is found in boggy situations, sometimes entering brackish water.

Behavior The chubsucker spawns in early spring, moving short distances onto gravelly riffles of streams.[121] Males develop a few large pearl organs on the head and on the anal fin.[264,910] Growth is rapid for the first two years, and a maximum size of about 14 inches is reached in 6 to 8 years.[936] Common associates in sluggish waters are the chain pickerel and the brown bullhead.

Food The creek chubsucker is a benthic feeder on many different invertebrates; zooplankton and algae are most important for the small fish.[257,264]

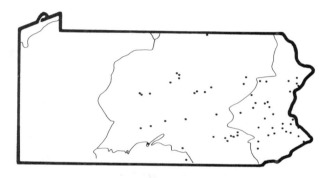

Value Young of this species are considered to be excellent forage for game fishes, but the adults are seldom taken by anglers and have little potential for management.[910]

Lake chubsucker, *Erimyzon sucetta* (Lacepede)[508]

Length 132 mm. Walnut Lake, Oakland County, Mich. 15 September 1976

Distribution This species was reported from the Erie Basin in Pennsylvania,[274] but it has not been taken recently. Its presence in Lake St. Clair, tributaries of western Lake Erie, and nearby localities in Ohio merits its inclusion here.[836] It is common in the midwest in small, weedy lakes or backwaters of sluggish streams. It seldom is an abundant species in any locality.

Behavior The lake chubsucker reproduces successfully in small weedy ponds, spawning in the spring over different types of bottom.[60,151,346] The young grow rapidly to a size of about 3 inches in one year; adults are mature during their third summer at a size of 6 inches, with a few fish getting larger than 12 inches at an age of about 8 years. An unusual Florida population grew to a maximum length of about 15 inches and a weight of over 2 pounds.[640]

Food The food of the lake chubsucker is primarily benthic invertebrates, with zooplankton and midges important for the young stages.[242,263]

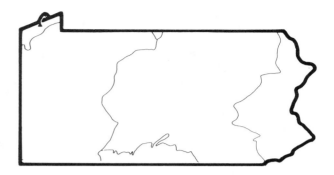

Value It is an ideal forage fish for game species, with adults seldom becoming abundant enough to be considered nuisance competitors.[60] It is seldom taken by anglers and offers little opportunity for managing as a fishery.

Genus Hypentelium

Single dorsal fin with 11 rays; lateral line well developed in adult; scales large, not crowded anteriorly, fewer than 50 rows in lateral series; air bladder divided into two parts; head strongly depressed (concave) between the eyes.

Northern hog sucker, *Hypentelium nigricans* (Lesueur)[544]

Length 113 mm. Saline River, Washtenaw County, Mich. 15 September 1976

Distribution The northern hog sucker is common over the eastern half of the United States and southern Canada. In Pennsylvania it is curiously missing from most of the Delaware drainage, but very common elsewhere. It rests on the bottom of the stream in shallow riffles, where its camouflaged body pattern makes it difficult to observe.[754]

Behavior Like other suckers, it spawns in the spring over riffles, several males attending a single female. Enlarged pelvic and anal fins and greater development

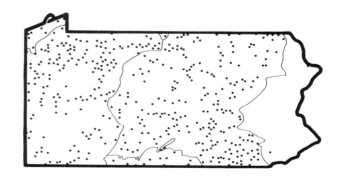

of pearl organs over most of the fins and body easily distinguish mature, spawning males.[777] Age determination by scale reading indicates a longevity of about 11 years; adults commonly reach a size of about 12 to 14 inches.[717,754] The northern hog sucker is a common associate of smallmouth bass in clean, gravelly or stony streams. It has a very restricted home range, limited in small streams to a few hundred feet.[291]

Food The diet of the hog sucker is mostly algae and bottom invertebrates taken from very shallow riffles.[630]

Value It is seldom taken by anglers, but it is a good clean-stream indicator. It is rarely found where siltation or other pollutants are common.[291,902]

Genus *Ictiobus*

Single dorsal fin with about 26 rays, the anterior portion somewhat elevated into a short lobe; caudal fin with a shallow fork; mouth large for suckers, subinferior, maxillary about twice the diameter of the eye; body deep, somewhat compressed, with large uniform scales; intestine arranged in elongate, S-shaped loops.[62]

KEY TO SPECIES OF *ICTIOBUS*

1 a. Mouth small, inferior; tip of upper lip definitely below lower edge of eye; upper jaw shorter than snout; lips full, well striated: Smallmouth buffalo, *I. bubalus*

b. Mouth large, terminal; tip of upper lip horizontal with lower edge of eye; upper jaw as long as snout; lips thin, faintly striated: Bigmouth buffalo, *I. cyprinellus*

Smallmouth buffalo, *Ictiobus bubalus* (Rafinesque)[728]

Length 403 mm. Monongahela River, Allegheny County, Pa. 3 May 1978

Distribution Throughout the midwest, the smallmouth buffalo is a common inhabitant of the Mississippi River and larger tributaries. In Pennsylvania, it has been taken in the Beaver River and in Lake Erie many years ago, and in 1978 one specimen was found in the Monongahela River near Elizabeth. It is a large river fish, preferring clear waters with only moderate current.[704]

Behavior Although no observations of spawning have been published, the smallmouth buffalo probably spawns

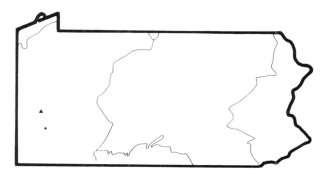

in the spring or summer.[195,704] For a species feeding mainly on zooplankton, the fast growth and large size attained is somewhat unusual. A population in Reelfoot Lake, Tennessee, averaged about 33 inches and 25 pounds by their 13th growing season.[823]

Food The diet of the smallmouth buffalo consists largely of zooplankton, changing only slightly to chironomids as the fish grow larger.[263,598,632]

Value Historically, this species and other buffalofishes were important commercial species in the Mississippi River drainage. Populations appear to be declining due to pollution.[264] Its recent appearance in Pennsylvania is some indication that water quality in the Ohio River drainage is improving.

Bigmouth buffalo, *Ictiobus cyprinellus* (Valenciennes)[183]

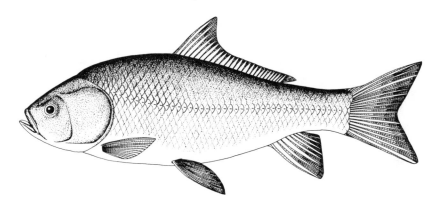

Redrawn from several sources.

Distribution The bigmouth buffalo is common throughout the Mississippi River drainage from the Dakotas to Louisiana and is present in part of the Great Lakes drainage. In Pennsylvania, it was collected at Erie in 1925, the only validated record in the commonwealth. It usually prefers large, sluggish rivers, oxbows, and flood plain lakes.

Behavior The bigmouth buffalo often migrates long distances to spawn in flooded marshes.[449] The adhesive eggs are broadcast over flooded vegetation in shallow water. The sudden rise in water level appears to be necessary to elicit these spawning migrations.[115]

Food Zooplankton and midges, important items of its diet, are taken from the bottom or often in open water.[598,632,639]

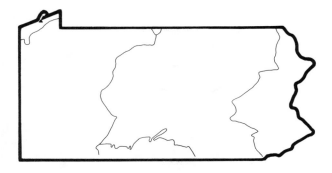

Value Although it is an important commercial fish in some areas, it is controlled as a rough fish in inland lakes of Iowa.[639]

Genus *Minytrema*

Single dorsal fin with 10–13 rays; lateral line incomplete or absent; mouth horizontal and inferior; body not deep or compressed; a black spot at base of each scale, appearing in 48 to 50 scale rows along sides of body.

Spotted sucker, *Minytrema melanops* (Rafinesque)[731]

Length 280 mm. North Fork of Dunkard Fork, Wheeling Creek, Greene County, Pa. 20 July 1976

Distribution Recent records for this species in Pymatuning Lake and in Wheeling Creek indicate that the spotted sucker is a rare species in Pennsylvania. Elsewhere in the midwest and the south it is rather common in clear, warm waters with low gradient and aquatic vegetation.[630]

Behavior In Oklahoma the species spawns in the spring, broadcasting the eggs over riffles,[434] the males developing pearl organs on the head and some of the fins.[81] The spotted sucker has a life span of about 5 years, reaching a size of about 18 inches. It is often taken with the channel catfish and the striped shiner.[902]

Food Limited analyses of stomach contents of the spotted sucker indicate that fingernail clams, midges, and zooplankton are eaten.[263] It is likely that other aquatic insects are taken when available.

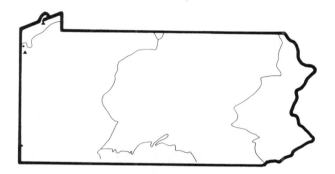

Value For the angler it offers very little recreation and its eating quality has been described by one author[455] as "pretty good for a sucker, which is not saying much."

Genus *Moxostoma*

Single dorsal fin with 10 to 17 rays; complete lateral line of 50 or fewer scale rows; air bladder divided into 3 parts; head concave (not depressed) between the eyes.

A large genus of 18 recognized species mostly distributed in the midwest and south, redhorses are difficult to identify for the beginner. Most of the characters used are weakly distinctive when considered individually, but are adequate for identification when taken in combination.[412] Recent publications on the systematics of redhorses and their allies[436,800] should be consulted for many additional details.

KEY TO SPECIES OF *MOXOSTOMA*

1 a. Scale rows around caudal peduncle usually 15 or 16: Greater redhorse, *M. valenciennesi*
  b. Scale rows around caudal peduncle usually 12 or 13: **2**

2 a. Lower surfaces of lips with fine ridges, deeply dissected into irregularly sized papillae; posterior margins of lower lip meet in an acute angle (Fig. 68,A): Silver redhorse, *M. anisurum*
  b. Lower surfaces of lips basically plicate, not papillose (Fig. 68,B) posterior margins of lower lip meet in an obtuse angle: **3**

3 a. Pharyngeal arch stout, with squarish, molariform teeth (Fig. 69): River redhorse, *M. carinatum*
  b. Pharyngeal arch light, with a comb-like series of

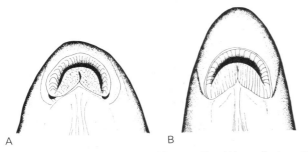

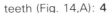

Figure 68. Lower lips dissected into papillae (A), or plicate, not papillose (B).

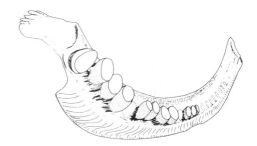

Figure 69. Stout pharyngeal arch with molariform teeth in river redhorse.

teeth (Fig. 14,A): **4**

4 a. Head small and short, about 5 times in standard length:*Shorthead redhorse, *M. macrolepidotum*

 b. Head longer, about 4 times in standard length: **5**

5 a. Lateral line scales usually 44 to 47; body relatively long and slender (depth about 3.8 times in stan-

dard length);*pelvic rays most often 10 in one or both fins: Black redhorse, *M. duquesnei*

 b. Lateral line scales usually 40 to 42; body relatively robust (depth about 3.4 times in standard length);* pelvic rays most often 9 in both fins: Golden redhorse, *M. erythrurum*

Silver redhorse, *Moxostoma anisurum* (Rafinesque)[731]

Length 93 mm. Muddy Creek, Crawford County, Pa. 9 August 1967

Distribution This species is not found along the Atlantic Coast south of the St. Lawrence River to Virginia, but has apparently colonized the Atlantic slope from the Carolinas to Georgia. It is widespread throughout much of the Mississippi and Great Lakes drainages.[436] In Pennsylvania it is most common in the Allegheny and its larger tributaries. Its preferred habitat is long, deep pools of large streams with moderate gradient.

Behavior Although no spawning has been observed, ripe males congregate in the spring, and spawning presumably takes place over gravel and rubble bottom. They occasionally migrate short distances to suitable spawning substrate.[436] This species is fairly tolerant to

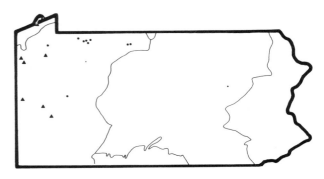

turbid water, more so than other redhorses.[289,902]

The silver redhorse is one of the larger species in this

*Body proportions change as the fish increases in length; characters compared in key refer to specimens larger than 6 inches.

genus, sometimes reaching a weight of 10 pounds in the Ohio River.[902] A more usual rate of growth would be about 20 inches in 10 years.[613] It is often taken in the same habitat with the quillback and the common carp.

Food The diet of this benthic feeder is variable, changing from attached algae and zooplankton for the young to a diet of mostly aquatic insects and molluscs as the fish grows.[613,852]

Value Despite the many small free bones in the flesh, the silver redhorse is marketed by commercial fishermen from large rivers in the midwest, and is favored among suckers by anglers because of its large size and firm, white flesh.

River redhorse, *Moxostoma carinatum* (Cope)[162]

Length 132 mm. Hatchery Pond, Greene County, Ala. 13 September 1967

Distribution The river redhorse is a Mississippi River fish with a few disjunct populations in the Great Lakes and Gulf Coast drainages.[436] It appears to be declining in abundance throughout most of its range, apparently as a result of loss of the large river habitat by impoundments.[340] Only a few large individuals of this species have been taken in Pennsylvania, and these were only from the Allegheny River.

Behavior The river redhorse sometimes migrates long distances to spawn on suitable riffles. The male prepares and defends a redd in the gravel, but one or two males spawn with a single female as she invades the riffle from deeper water.[340] There is no care of eggs following spawning. The river redhorse is one of the largest of this genus, reaching lengths of over 30 inches and weights of more than 10 pounds.[902]

Food The food of young river redhorse is unknown because small individuals are seldom collected, even

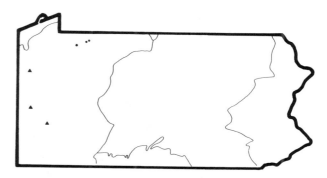

where the species is abundant.[340] Larger individuals eat mostly aquatic insects and molluscs along with some bryozoans and aquatic plants.[263,340]

Value It is considered an excellent sport fish in Alabama because of its large size and good eating qualities. It is taken by bowfishing, spearing, and snaring, but seldom by angling.[340]

Black redhorse, *Moxostoma duquesnei* (Lesueur)[544]

Length 142 mm. Conewango Creek, Warren County, Pa. 8 October 1971

Distribution Widespread through the upper Ohio River drainage and much of the midwest, this species is locally abundant in the Allegheny River with other redhorses. It is a moderate- to small-stream species, preferring some current over a gravel bottom. The black redhorse was not recognized as a separate species until 1930; the systematics of this group was recently revised and clarified.[436,902]

Behavior The black redhorse is a spring spawner, utilizing shallow gravel or rubble shoals. There is no extensive migration prior to spawning. Males establish territories on the riffles, but several males spawn with a single female as she swims over the riffle from deeper water.[80] The black redhorse is one of the smaller of this group. It seldom exceeded 13 inches in length at an age of about 10 years in the Missouri streams studied,[80] although larger specimens are found in the Allegheny River. The golden and the shorthead redhorses are often found with this species in the Allegheny River, posing a problem in identification, especially for the juveniles.

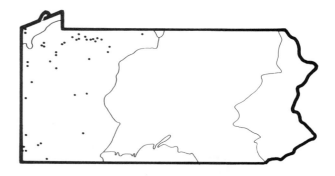

Food The diet of young redhorses consists of attached algae, zooplankton, and small insects found in slack water areas among vegetation;[585] the diet changes to mostly aquatic insects as the fish grows.[80,852]

Value It is frequently taken by angling in the spring, and is marketed commercially as mullet in other states.[839]

Golden redhorse, *Moxostoma erythrurum* (Rafinesque)[726]

Length 224 mm. Mahoning Creek, Armstrong County, Pa. 18 July 1967

Distribution The golden redhorse is a common species in portions of the Great Lakes drainages and in much of the Mississippi River system.[413] Locally it is abundant in the Allegheny River. Our records of it in the Potomac

River drainage in Pennsylvania apparently reflect a new range extension for this species, since it is absent from most Atlantic Coast streams. Golden redhorse juveniles can be found on riffle margins in moderate current, but adults inhabit slow deep runs. They seem to prefer moderate-sized streams, but have no apparent preference for bottom type.[173,331,585]

Behavior As is true for other redhorses, this species moves only short distances to spawn in the spring, broadcasting non-adhesive eggs over gravel riffles of moderate-sized streams.[291,777] The golden redhorse is one of the smaller species; a maximum length of 26 inches and weight of 4.5 pounds was reported from Lake Erie.[902] A population in the Des Moines River, Iowa, grew to a size of about 19 inches in 7 years.[613] The golden redhorse is often found with both the black and the shorthead. This creates a problem in identification, especially for the juveniles.

Food This species is a benthic feeder and eats most

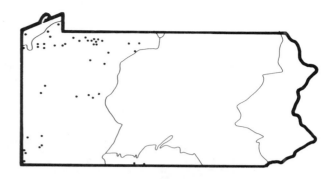

small aquatic insects and molluscs.[291,436,613]

Value Because of its widespread distribution and local abundance, it is often taken by anglers and sometimes preferred over the other suckers for food. Large specimens are excellent when baked and the many small bones removed.

Shorthead redhorse, *Moxostoma macrolepidotum* (Lesueur)[544]

Length 190 mm. Susquehanna River, Dauphin County, Pa. 27 October 1972

Distribution The most widespread of all redhorses throughout central North America, both the common name and scientific name of this species have been confused. Some investigators prefer to distinguish the east coast populations from those which are abundant in the Mississippi River drainage. Although this species is common in the Ohio and Susquehanna drainages in Pennsylvania, it is apparently absent from the Delaware.[325] The shorthead differs from most redhorses in adapting to lake habitats, at least in some northern areas.[613,630]

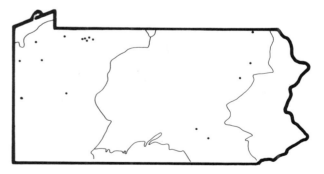

Behavior It is a spring spawner using riffles in streams. It is one of the larger redhorses. The population of the Des Moines River, Iowa, grew to a size of about 26 inches in 8 years;[630] by contrast, a population from the Saskatchewan River, Canada, took 12 years to grow to about 17 inches.[765] The shorthead is often taken with the black and golden redhorses in the Allegheny River, making identification of juveniles difficult.

Food The food of this species is highly variable. Small fish prefer midges, while larger individuals eat mostly snails and fingernail clams when present.[263,563,852]

Value The shorthead redhorse is often caught by anglers in the spring, and is considered as a good food fish once it is prepared properly to remove most of the small bones.[563]

Greater redhorse, *Moxostoma valenciennesi* Jordan[457]

Length 490 mm. Irondequoit Bay, Lake Ontario, Monroe County, N.Y. 12 May 1977

Distribution This redhorse is confined mainly to the upper Mississippi River and the St. Lawrence-Great Lakes drainages. It has never been reported from Pennsylvania waters of Lake Erie, the only logical choice for its occurrence here.[436] It is found in large streams with clear water and gravel or rubble bottom.[839,902]

Behavior It is probably a spring to summer spawner in moderately rapid streams, although no fish have been observed spawning. There is confusion over its maximum size because of possible misidentification, but individuals as large as 10 pounds have been reported.[224,397,837]

Food No food studies are available, but it is likely that many different invertebrates make up its diet.[839]

Value The scarcity of this fish and its poor flavor make this species of little importance to anglers or managers.

Bullhead catfishes—Ictaluridae

Adipose fin present, may be free or apparently connected to caudal fin; no scales, body is covered with a tough skin; barbels 8, consisting of 2 nasal, 2 maxillary, and 4 on chin; dorsal and pectoral fins armed with strong spines; teeth in villiform bands, present only on premaxillaries and dentaries.

This family consists of a large number of catfishes that range in size from the miniature madtoms to the blue catfish, which is one of the largest fishes in North America, sometimes exceeding 100 pounds. Adults are generally most active at night, or in very turbid waters in the daytime. The madtoms are seldom encountered, but are well known for the poison glands associated with the pectoral spines, which can produce a painful sting. Other catfishes also have poison glands associated with their pectoral spines.[70] Most of the larger species are favored by sport fishermen and are important in commercial fisheries. The channel catfish, especially, is cultured widely for human food. Some of the smaller catfishes are frequently used as bait for sport fishing. Several of the economically important species have been introduced into suitable waters throughout the world.

For all of the species investigated, catfishes are spring spawners. Males and females pair and construct nests in depressions, hollows, or bank burrows. Usually the male tends the nest, aerates the sticky egg masses, and guards the newly hatched fry.[273] The young aggregate in tight schools, separating and hiding individually for a short time only when frightened.[78,79] Both thigmotactic and chemosensory clues are used by many catfishes to modify many aspects of their behavior, presumably because of their poor vision.[45,899]

Several specimens of a blind catfish (*Gronias nigrilabris*) were reported many years ago from Conestoga Creek in Lancaster County,[157] supposedly originating from a subterranean stream in Silurian limestone formations. We have been unable to learn more about these specimens; presumably the population is now extinct.

The walking catfish, *Clarias batrachus*, now common in southern Florida, is an exotic from southeast Asia, and a member of the family Clariidae. Because of its intolerance to cold, it is very unlikely that this species would survive in Pennsylvania. Nevertheless, it is illegal to introduce this species into our waters.

KEY TO GENERA OF ICTALURIDAE

1 a. Adipose fin adnate to back: *Noturus*
   b. Posterior end of adipose fin free from back: **2**
2 a. Premaxillary band of teeth with lateral posterior processes (Fig. 70, *P. olivaris*): *Pylodictis*
   b. Premaxillary band of teeth nearly straight; no lateral posterior processes (Fig. 70, *I. nebulosus*): *Ictalurus*

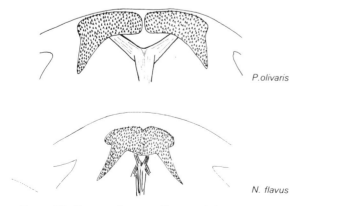

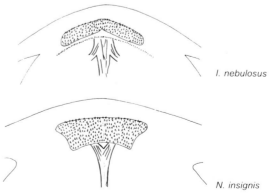

Figure 70. Pattern of premaxillary teeth in some catfishes, showing lateral backward extension in some species.

Genus *Ictalurus*

Adipose fin free from back; premaxillary band of teeth nearly straight with no lateral posterior processes; 10 preoperculo-mandibular pores on each side; 8 pelvic rays; skull not greatly depressed.

KEY TO SPECIES OF *ICTALURUS*

(In counting anal rays for this key it is necessary to remove the skin and adipose tissue from the base of the fin to count all of the rudimentary rays visible [Fig. 71]; in counting gill rakers, include all rudimentary rakers.)

1 a. Caudal fin deeply forked: 2
   b. Caudal fin straight or rounded: 4
2 a. Anal rays 25 or fewer; tail lobes not greatly pointed; pectoral spine with strong teeth on posterior margin (Fig. 72): White catfish, *I. catus*
   b. Anal rays 26 or more; tail lobes sharply pointed: 3
3 a. Anal rays 30 to 36; distal margin of anal fin nearly straight; pectoral spine with very strong teeth on posterior margin (Fig. 72): Blue catfish, *I. furcatus*
   b. Anal rays 24 to 30; distal margin of anal fin rounded; pectoral spine with strong teeth on posterior margin (Fig. 72): Channel catfish, *I. punctatus*
4 a. Chin barbels whitish, without melanophores; anal rays usually more than 24; pectoral spine with strong teeth on posterior margin (Fig. 72): Yellow bullhead, *I. natalis*
   b. Chin barbels dusky or black, with melanophores; anal rays usually less than 24: 5
5 a. Gill rakers on first arch usually 14 or 15;* pectoral spine with strong teeth on posterior margin, eroding on larger specimens (Fig. 72); body usually mottled, no light bar on caudal base; anal rays usually 22 or 23, membranes dusky: Brown bullhead, *I. nebulosus*
   b. Gill rakers on first arch usually 18 or 19;* pectoral spine with weak teeth on posterior margin (Fig. 72); body usually bicolored with a line of demarka-

I. catus

I. punctatus

I. nebulosus

I. furcatus

I. natalis

I. melas

P. olivaris

Figure 72. Pectoral spines of some catfishes, showing variation in serrae.

Figure 71. Method of counting anal rays of catfishes, including all rudimentary rays. Shown is a fin with 20 anal rays.

tion between belly and sides; light vertical bar on base of caudal fin; anal rays usually 18 to 20; membranes jet black: Black bullhead, *I. melas*

*A recent report[108] adds confusion to the present difficulty of separating brown and black bullheads. These authors report that the number of gill rakers on the first arch is the best distinguishing character, and that other characters customarily employed (pectoral serrae, and number of anal rays) are not very useful in separating these two species in Virginia.

White catfish, *Ictalurus catus* (Linnaeus)[558]

Length 133 mm. Ohio River, Allegheny County, Pa. 13 September 1976

Distribution This catfish was originally restricted to the Atlantic Coast drainage from New York to Florida, but has been introduced widely outside its native range. Populations in California and Nevada are thriving.[77,614] In Pennsylvania, early introductions into Lake Erie presumably failed to establish permanent populations.[902] More recently, the white catfish is taken in increasing numbers in the Ohio River drainage. It is most often found in river channels and streams in sluggish current. It also frequents lakes, ponds, and bayous.[573,580,709]

Behavior The white catfish seldom migrates very far to spawn. The male excavates or selects a cavity and guards the mass of eggs and young for a short time after hatching.[273,573,614] It is a medium-sized species reaching a length of more than 20 inches in 10 to 12 years.[831] It is perhaps the most tolerant of all bullhead catfishes to high salinity, inhabiting brackish waters up to 8 ppt.[580]

Food The white catfish eats some plant material, but is

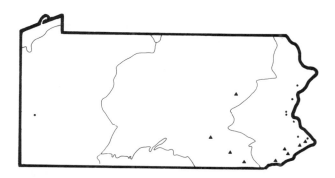

mostly a carnivore. Midge larvae are most important for the young, with larger aquatic insects, crustacea, and fish more often found in stomachs of the adults.[609,709,875]

Value The white catfish is a valuable part of the sport fishery in many places and is an important commercial species in Virginia.[77,609]

Blue catfish, *Ictalurus furcatus* (Lesueur)[183]

Length 131 mm. Tennessee River, Tishimingo County, Miss. 25 March 1976

Distribution The blue catfish is restricted to large rivers tributary to the Mississippi and the Gulf of Mexico. It was reported in the Monongahela River in 1886,[239] but has not been taken in Pennsylvania in recent years. This catfish is found in deep channels of large rivers or tidal canals. It apparently is highly mobile since populations decline rapidly in impoundments.[524,939]

Behavior Like other bullhead catfishes, the male guards eggs and young in a hollow excavated in the bank of the river. It readily uses artificial nesting kegs or boxes under pond culture for spawning. It is quite tolerant to brackish water, spawning successfully at a salinity of up to 10 ppt.[696] They grow very fast, reaching 44 inches and 46 pounds in about 11 years. It is the largest of the catfishes, with reports of specimens weighing 150 pounds.[442,704]

Food Adults of this species feed mostly on crayfishes and fishes; young also take aquatic insects and other invertebrates. Under culture conditions they grow well on pelleted diets.[99,189,524]

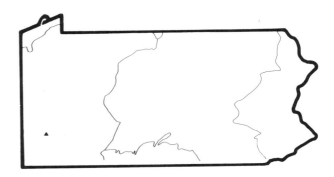

Value This is an excellent game and food fish, and is cultured widely for introduction into natural habitats and for the market. The production of hybrids between blue and channel catfish now appears to be superior to either species under pond culture.[974] The need for large free-flowing rivers makes management of natural populations incompatible with impoundment of many reservoirs on a river system.[704,939]

Black bullhead, *Ictalurus melas* (Rafinesque)[729]

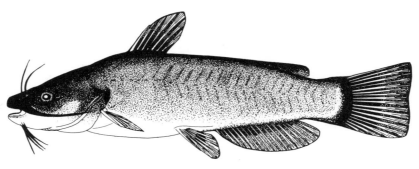

Length 205 mm. Tributary to Oostanaula River, Ga. 2 March 1978

Distribution The black bullhead is a common fish throughout the Great Plains and Midwest, reaching into western Pennsylvania. Although we have no recent records of this species, it was collected in a few localities in northwestern counties in the 1930s.[733] The black bullhead prefers quiet water in weedy ponds, or backwaters of large rivers over a mud bottom. It apparently is more restricted in its habitat preference than the ubiquitous brown bullhead.

Behavior The nocturnal activity patterns of adult fish and the nest building by the male are typical of other bullheads.[190,941] Growth is variable; 5-year-old fish in different populations in Oklahoma ranged from 8 inches to 17 inches, close to the maximum size reported for this species.[387] A population from Clear Lake, Iowa, grew to 12 inches in 8 years.[265] The black bullhead is often found with largemouth bass and bluegills.

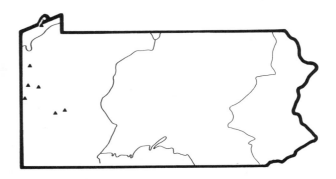

Food Studies of its feeding behavior show an interesting selection for large zooplankton and chironomids among a wide variety of foods eaten.[784] Bullfrog tadpoles were completely rejected as food items in discrimination tests, although tadpoles of other frogs were readily accepted.[505]

Value In addition to being popular as panfish, young bullheads are excellent forage for largemouth bass when grown together.[793]

Yellow bullhead, *Ictalurus natalis* (Lesueur)[549]

Length 160 mm. Jacobs Creek, Fayette County, Pa. 6 July 1976

Distribution This species ranged originally over most of the Mississippi, Great Lakes, and Atlantic Coast drainages, and has been introduced outside this area. In Pennsylvania it is found in all watersheds, but is much less abundant than the brown bullhead. The yellow bullhead has a strong preference for muddy water of small, weedy ponds and streams.[264]

Behavior There is no directed spawning migration. In the spring, males excavate a hollow in the bottom or the bank and guard the sticky mass of eggs and newly hatched young.[273,573] The yellow bullhead has a keen sense of smell which it uses to discriminate between different individuals of its own school, apparently by pheromones released by the other fishes.[899] This species is another intermediate-sized catfish, growing to a size of 15 to 19 inches in 5 years in Reelfoot Lake, Tennessee.[824] It is often found with the largemouth bass and the bluegill. This bullhead is very tolerant to low oxygen, often surviving when other species die.[264,902]

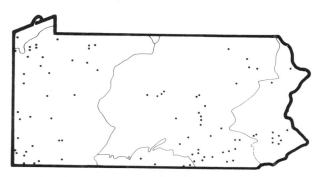

Food The yellow bullhead is an omnivore, consuming many different foods.[263] It apparently searches for food primarily by taste or smell, which explains its success in tolerating very high turbidity.

Value The yellow bullhead is considered to be one of the best flavored of all catfishes. It is smaller than the channel catfish or blue catfish, but is readily accepted as a panfish in many areas.

Brown bullhead, *Ictalurus nebulosus* (Lesueur)[549]

Length 118 mm. Goose Pond Run, Monroe County, Pa. 21 July 1977

Distribution The brown bullhead is widely distributed over the eastern half of North America and is the common species in New England and northeastern Canada. It occurs most often in warm-water ponds or sluggish streams, but tolerates a wide variety of habitats.

Behavior The brown bullhead spawns in the spring. Males pair with females and create depressions in the bottom, or utilize cavities of many kinds for nests.[88,273] The egg masses are aerated by swimming motions of the parents, and newly hatched schools of fry are guarded for some time.[90] Adults are more active at night, as are most catfishes.[170] Like other catfishes, the brown bullhead is sometimes found in brackish water up to a salinity of 15 ppt.[232] One of the intermediate-sized catfishes, the brown bullhead reaches a size of 18 inches or 3 pounds.

Food Brown bullheads are omnivores. Young feed largely on crustaceans, dipterans, and oligochaetes,[485,756] while older fish are less selective. Filamentous and bluegreen algae are readily eaten and efficiently assimilated.[337]

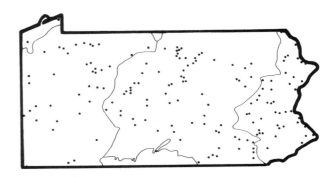

Value The brown bullhead is an important panfish to anglers in some areas.[595,883] This panfish has an unfavorable reputation as a predator on lake trout eggs on shallow reefs of lakes,[24] and because of its tendency to overpopulate and compete with other fishes, it is removed as a rough fish in other areas.[647] Young bullheads are considered to be excellent forage, especially for largemouth bass.

Channel catfish, *Ictalurus punctatus* (Rafinesque)[726]

Length 165 mm. Beaver River, Beaver County, Pa. July 1981

Distribution The original distribution of the channel cat covered most of the eastern half of the United States, excluding the Atlantic Coast north of Florida. It has been introduced widely outside its original range.[615] It survives well in a variety of habitats, from small ponds to large reservoirs and flowing streams, and apparently avoids salinities greater than 2 parts per thousand.[580,696]

Behavior Observations in aquaria indicate that the spawning behavior of pairs of channel catfish is similar to all other catfishes studied,[131] with courtship and clasping of the female by the male necessary to stimulate oviposition. In natural habitats, there is no directed migration to the spawning grounds. Males excavate a burrow in the bank or bottom and guard the sticky mass of eggs and newly hatched fry for some time. The growth of natural

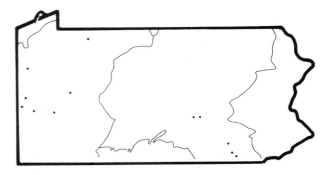

populations of channel catfish varies; at 10 years of age in Oklahoma, different populations ranged from 13 to 35 inches in length. Some fish lived as long as 14 years.[255]

Food Channel catfish are omnivores, with many plants and animals eaten.[334,383] A dead rat, pieces of ham, and other animal debris attest to its easy-going appetite.[263] Pelleted foods are extensively used in pond culture for this species.

Value The channel cat is the most important catfish in North America for both sport and food. Its large size, ease of culture, and adaptability to different habitats makes it a favorite of both the angler and the fish manager. Commercial production of this catfish is big business, especially in the southwest. More recently, the production of hybrid blue X channel catfish appears to be superior to channel catfish under culture conditions.[974]

Genus *Noturus*

Adipose fin adnate (attached to back); 10 or 11 preoperculo-mandibular pores on each side; 8 or 9 pelvic rays; skull not greatly depressed.

There are 23 species of *Noturus* now recognized in North America.[892] These madtoms are not well known because of their secretive and nocturnal habits, and because most species receive little human use. Some are rare and erratically distributed; others, like the margined madtom in eastern Pennsylvania, are widespread and exceedingly abundant.

The madtoms are well equipped with pectoral spines and axillary poison glands which are capable of inflicting wounds and toxic symptoms equivalent to the sting of a bee. There appears to be no muscular apparatus for injecting the poison directly into the wound, but the secretions from the axillary gland were shown to produce the stinging sensations. The tadpole madtom is probably the least toxic, with other species said to produce more virulent sensations.[766]

KEY TO SPECIES OF *NOTURUS*

1 a. Pectoral spine usually curved, with teeth on both anterior and posterior edges (Fig. 73, *N. stigmosus*); color pattern usually of dark saddles on back of body and fins: **2**

   b. Pectoral spine nearly straight, without teeth on anterior edge (Fig. 73, *N. insignis*); color pattern usually dark without blotches or saddles on body: **4**

2 a. A dark blotch present on upper margin of dorsal fin; adipose fin firmly adnate to back; the dark blotch on the adipose fin extends to dorsal margin; one internasal pore; strong teeth on both edges of pectoral spine (Fig. 73): Brindled madtom, *N. miurus*

   b. The dark blotch, if present on dorsal fin, does not extend to the upper margin; adipose fin nearly free from back; the dark blotch on adipose fin does not extend to dorsal margin; two internasal pores: **3**

3 a. Adipose fin blotch present only on basal half of fin; caudal rays usually 43 to 49; ten preoperculo-mandibular pores; strong teeth on posterior margin of pectoral spine, weak teeth on anterior edge (Fig. 73): Mountain madtom, *N. eleutherus*

   b. Adipose fin blotch covers basal half to four-fifths of fin but does not reach dorsal margin; caudal rays usually 49 to 53; eleven preoperculo-mandibular pores; strong teeth on both edges of pectoral spine (Fig. 73): Northern madtom, *N. stigmosus*

4 a. Premaxillary tooth patch with lateral posterior extensions (Fig. 70, *N. flavus*); no strong teeth on either edge of pectoral spine (Fig. 73): Stonecat, *N. flavus*

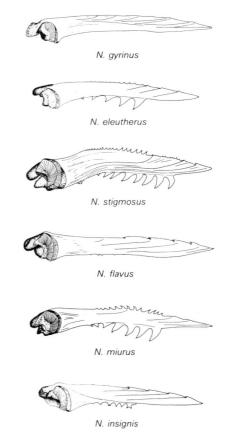

Figure 73. Pectoral spines of some madtoms showing variation in serrae.

b. Premaxillary tooth patch rectangular, with posterior corners rounded or angulate, but with no posterior extensions (Fig. 70, *N. insignis*): **5**

5 a. Mouth terminal, jaws about equal; no visible teeth on either edge of pectoral spine (Fig. 73): Tadpole madtom, *N. gyrinus*

b. Mouth inferior, lower jaw included· in upper jaw; moderate teeth on posterior edge of pectoral spine, no teeth on anterior edge (Fig. 73): Margined madtom, *N. insignis*

Mountain madtom, *Noturus eleutherus* Jordan[452]

Length 58 mm. French Creek, Erie County, Pa. 14 May 1977

Distribution The mountain madtom is known from scattered localities throughout the midwest, including French Creek and the Shenango River in western Pennsylvania.[515,733,753] It is chiefly a resident of large streams containing clear water and rocky or stony riffles, often sympatric with other madtoms.[129,892] We have found it only in the deeper and faster parts of riffles with large rubble.

Behavior Spawning of this fish has not been observed. Since most madtoms have similar habits, it is likely that it spawns in early summer, with males guarding a nest under a flat rock in the current. Also, it is probable that it is nocturnal, being active during the day only in very turbid water.[902] It is· often found with the northern hog sucker and the spotted darter in fast riffles.

Food No food studies have been published. Its small

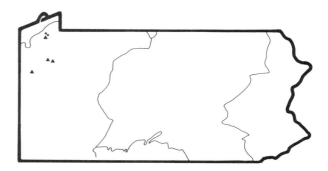

size and restricted habitat would indicate a diet of small aquatic insects or other invertebrates.[892]

Value This rare species has no value as a forage species or as a bait species. However, it is a good indicator of a very restricted, clean, fast riffle habitat.

Stonecat, *Noturus flavus* Rafinesque[727]

Length 107 mm. Wheeling Creek, Marshall County, W. Va. 11 August 1976

Distribution This madtom is widely distributed through-out the Mississippi River and Great Lakes drainages, but is absent from Atlantic Coast streams south of the Mohawk-Hudson drainage.[892] It is the commonest madtom in western Pennsylvania and Ontario, often being locally abundant.[447] It prefers riffles or rapids of large streams with stony or rocky bottom, but is sometimes found in large lakes with much wave action.[527]

Behavior The stonecat is known to spawn in early summer, attaching the sticky egg mass to the underside of stones in running water.[527] The nest is guarded by the parents, similar to other catfishes.[322] It is the largest of the madtoms, growing to a length of about 8 inches in 7 years.[120] The largest specimen in our collection is 8.9 inches. The stonecat apparently avoids cold water and is more often found together with rock bass and smallmouth bass than with trout or sculpins.[344]

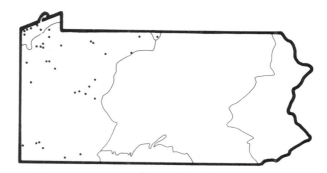

Food The diet of the stonecat in Lake Erie is mayflies to a large extent, but little else is known of its food habits.[295]

Value It is not often taken by anglers, but is reported to be excellent eating.[322]

Tadpole madtom, *Noturus gyrinus* (Mitchill)[637]

Length 79 mm. Canadohta Lake, Crawford County, Pa. 10 June 1977

Distribution One of the best known of the madtoms, this species is found throughout the eastern half of North America, including many Atlantic Coast drainages.[892] There are many records of the tadpole madtom for Pennsylvania streams below the Fall Line years ago,[274] but we have found no specimens there in recent years. It is most often found in quiet or slow-running waters such as weedy, shallow bays or sloughs of streams,[240] sometimes being very abundant.[333]

Behavior The tadpole madtom spawns in natural cavities, or in hollow objects such as tin cans or crockery.[29,345] Egg masses and young are guarded by the parents.[573] This madtom is a short-lived, small species. A population in Demming Lake, Minnesota, seldom exceeded 4 inches in length or an age of more than 3 summers.[382]

Although catfish hybrids are rare, there are good records of hybrids between the tadpole and brindled madtoms in Lake Erie and other Ohio waters.[892,901]

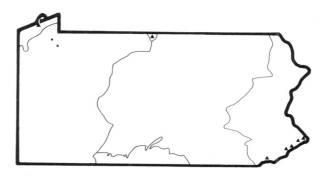

Food The tadpole madtom eats many different foods, changing from zooplankton and midges when young to larger items such as freshwater shrimp as it grows.[242,263]

Value This is a rare species in Pennsylvania, seldom seen by anglers. Elsewhere it may have some use for game fishes as forage.[892]

Margined madtom, *Noturus insignis* (Richardson)[786]

Length 117 mm. Little Elk Creek, Chester County, Pa. 16 April 1977

Distribution This common eastern madtom is largely confined to Atlantic Coast streams, with a few introductions outside its original range.[892] Its widespread use as a bait fish presumably has been responsible for some of these introductions. It is very abundant in all warm-water streams in eastern Pennsylvania, where it favors stony or rocky riffles.

Behavior Nests of this species with eggs or young were observed in Tohickon Creek, tributary to the Delaware River near Trenton. Numerous nests were found under flat rocks in moderate current; each nest was guarded by a single male. In all respects the behavior was similar to numerous other accounts of spawning catfishes.[273]

The margined madtom does not get as large as the stonecat. A population in central Pennsylvania reached a length of nearly 6 inches during their fifth summer, but the species is reported to reach a size of nearly 12 inches.[417] Both males and females matured sexually during their third summer.[138] The margined madtom is a common associate of the northern hog sucker and the stoneroller on stony riffles.

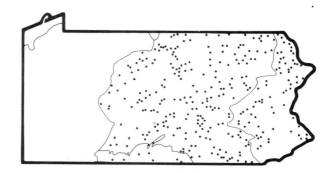

Food The diet of this fish is reported to be insects and small fishes, but this is based on stomach contents of only three individuals.[257]

Value The margined madtom is used extensively as bait for smallmouth bass. It is easily harvested from large natural populations by lifting flat stones from the bottom of the stream and chasing the fish into a small net.[325]

Brindled madtom, *Noturus miurus* Jordan[452]

Length 88 mm. Wheeling Creek, Marshall County, W. Va. 11 August 1976

Distribution This madtom is largely confined to the lower Mississippi, the Ohio, and the lower Great Lakes drainages.[892] In Pennsylvania it has been found in the warmer waters of the Allegheny, Lake Erie, and Wheeling Creek drainages. Several hundred specimens were taken from one flat, rocky run in Wheeling Creek recently. It apparently avoids the fast current and rocky riffles preferred by the mountain madtom and the northern madtom, favoring a bottom type of sand or gravel.[14]

Behavior The brindled madtom nests in cavities in July and August in Michigan, somewhat earlier in Ohio. The egg clusters are deposited under rocks or boards in running water. Under unfavorable conditions it may spawn in quiet water in close proximity to spawning tadpole madtoms. This sometimes results in hybrids between the two species.[901] This species is one of the smaller madtoms, seldom growing larger than 4 inches. Like some other small madtoms, it can inflict a painful wound with its poison spines.[766] It is very secretive and probably active only at night. Associated on the riffle with the

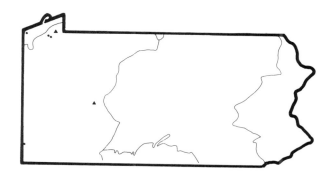

madtom are the stoneroller and the northern hog sucker.

Food Algae and mud were found in the stomach of one specimen, but little else is known of its food habits.[43]

Value The local abundance of a few scattered populations makes it unlikely that this madtom is an important forage species.

Northern madtom, *Noturus stigmosus* Taylor[892]

Length 95 mm. Spring Creek, Hardeman County, Tenn. 1 September 1959

Distribution This little-known madtom is restricted to the upper Ohio River drainage and a few localities in southern Michigan,[129,733,892] and the western end of Lake Erie. It is a fish of large streams with swift rocky riffles, commonly taken with the stonecat and the mountain madtom. We have found it to be very rare in Pennsylvania. This species has been commonly misidentified as the Carolina madtom in this area.[902]

Behavior The northern madtom spawns in the spring. Males guard a sticky mass of eggs and newly hatched young in a cavity beneath a flat stone in the current. It is one of the smaller madtoms, seldom exceeding 3 inches, and is probably nocturnal.[892]

Food No stomachs have been examined, but small insects and invertebrates probably are included in its diet.

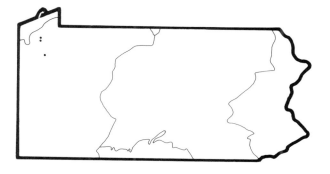

Value This rare, secretive fish is valuable in identifying very restricted habitats of clean water and fast riffles in warm-water streams.

Genus *Pylodictis*

Adipose fin free from back; premaxillary band of teeth with lateral posterior processes; 12 preoperculo-mandibular pores on each side, anterior ends of this canal joined, anterior pore common to both sides; 9 or 10 pelvic rays; skull greatly depressed.

Flathead catfish, *Pylodictis olivaris* (Rafinesque)[726]

Length 145 mm. South Fork of Ten Mile Creek, Greene County, Pa. 1 September 1976

Distribution The flathead catfish is a large-river, solitary species found throughout the Mississippi River and Gulf Coast drainages, but absent from Atlantic Coast streams. It is a mobile fish in the adult stage, and dams and reservoirs are thought to be detrimental to this species.[285,704] The young are found in riffles together with madtoms, but adults prefer pools with submerged cover.[173,704]

Behavior This species spawns in early summer, somewhat later than the channel catfish. The spawning behavior is similar to other catfishes; adults pair, build nests in depressions or natural cavities, and guard eggs and young.[260] Adults mature sexually at a size of about 15 inches and an age of about 5 years.[631] Growth is fairly rapid: a Salt River, Missouri population grew to 20 inches in about 8 years,[717] and large individuals in excess of 50 pounds have been reported.[50]

Food The flathead catfish is omnivorous, with a notice-

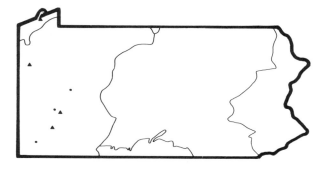

able change in diet from aquatic insects to crayfish and fishes as the catfish grow in size.[99,631]

Value In large warm-water rivers it is an important commercial food fish, and is commonly taken by anglers on trot lines or by jug fishing.[50] It is one of the largest game fishes in the Ohio River drainage.

Pirate perches—Aphredoderidae

Only a single living species and genus remain of this family in North America; a few related fossil forms are also known. In many respects, such as ctenoid scales and spines in the pelvic fins, the pirate perch is similar to other percoids, but the forward placement of the anus near the isthmus marks this species as somewhat unique.[572]

Genus *Aphredoderus*

Ctenoid scales with some scales on head; no adipose fin; anus in young in normal position, but shifts far forward in adults; small, robust fish with deep and thick caudal peduncle.

Pirate perch, *Aphredoderus sayanus* (Gilliams)[301]

Length 62 mm. Selby Mill Branch, Swan's Gut Creek, Accomac County, Va. 9 May 1981

Distribution The pirate perch has an extended distribution in lowland streams and ponds south along the Atlantic Coast from Long Island to Florida, and up the Mississippi River drainage to Minnesota, including parts of the lower Great Lakes.[264] It was formerly found below the Fall Line in southeastern Pennsylvania[274] but we have been unable to collect any specimens there in the past 20 years. It is usually found in bottomland lakes and quiet backwaters of low gradient streams with abundant vegetation or debris.[343]

Behavior There are no published observations on spawning, which is said to occur in the spring. In its natural environment it probably builds a nest which is guarded by both parents.[2,264] A population of pirate perch in Oklahoma grew to a maximum size of about 5 inches in 4 years.[343] The pirate perch is often collected with the creek chubsucker and the warmouth in boggy waters on the coastal plain.

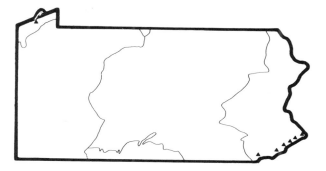

Food Although it was named pirate perch because of its strictly piscivorous habits in aquaria,[2] its natural food consists primarily of aquatic insects.[227,257]

Value This small secretive fish has no apparent value to anglers. Its unique morphology makes it a good example of development for embryologists.[572]

151

Trout-perches—Percopsidae

A small family of two species in freshwaters of North America, this group is morphologically intermediate between the soft-rayed and spiny-rayed fishes.

Genus *Percopsis*

Adipose fin present; pelvic fins in abdominal position; no scales on head; ctenoid scales; spines in dorsal, anal, and pelvic fins; premaxillae non-protractile forming margin of upper jaw; lateral line canals on head very large.

Trout-perch, *Percopsis omiscomaycus* (Walbaum)[938]

Length 72 mm. Bull Creek, Allegheny County, Pa. June 1979

Distribution The trout-perch is a distinctly northern form widely distributed throughout the Nearctic regions. It becomes very abundant in large, shallow, prairie lakes of the midwest. It is present, but not abundant, in clear streams in Pennsylvania, close to its southern limit of distribution.

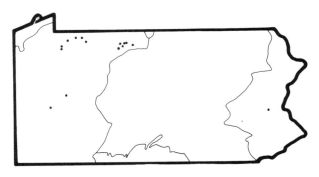

Behavior Trout-perch are late-spring and summer spawners, often running into streams from large lakes, or spawning along wave-washed beaches of large lakes.[533] There is no nest building or guarding of eggs and young. Two or more males cluster around a single female in open water, simultaneously releasing eggs and sperm. The adhesive eggs drift to the bottom and attach to the substrate.[569]

Trout-perch are small fishes seldom exceeding 5 inches after 4 years of growth, according to a detailed study of a population in lower Red Lake, Minnesota.[569]

Food Items of food eaten by trout-perch, indicated by small samples, are primarily restricted to small insects and crustaceans.[479,711]

Value The trout-perch is a valuable forage species in large shallow lakes of the midwest, where it is often the only forage present in large numbers for the walleye.[533] It is seldom abundant enough in Pennsylvania to be important either as bait or as forage.

Codfishes—Gadidae

The codfishes are primarily marine, bottom-dwelling fishes occurring in cool seas in northern latitudes. Only one species, the burbot, is a truly freshwater form, although at least one other, the Atlantic tomcod, enters freshwater occasionally.

Genus *Lota*

Unique in having a single barbel on tip of chin; no spines, but physoclistous; cycloid scales; pelvic fins in jugular position.

Burbot, *Lota lota* (Linnaeus)[558]

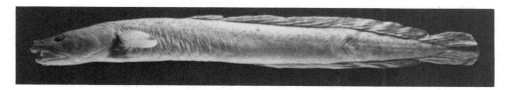

Length 445 mm. Reed Run, Potter County, Pa. 10 August 1978

Distribution The burbot is widely distributed in freshwaters of North America southward to the Great Lakes.[809] Relict populations occur in cold headwaters of the Susquehanna River in New York, and in the headwaters of the Allegheny River in Pennsylvania.[651,799]

Behavior The burbot is one of a very few fishes in North America to spawn in midwinter, often running into streams under the ice.[799] No nest is built, the non-adhesive eggs are scattered over gravel and stony bottoms. No care is given to the young.

Adults are reported to reach a weight of 75 pounds, although a weight of about 10 pounds and an age of 10 to 15 years are the maxima most often reported.

The burbot is considered to be an important competitor with lake trout and whitefishes, based on its food habits and similar preferred habitat in deep water of large lakes.[214,492]

Food The burbot is a generalized carnivore. Young select

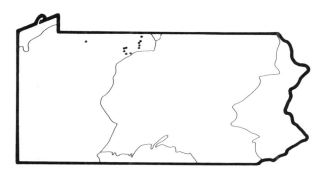

for zooplankton and midge larvae, and the adults eat mostly crayfish and fish. Worms, molluscs, and frogs have also been found in stomachs.[214,492,602]

Value Although the flesh is white and flaky, it is not considered to be equal to other northern commercial species for human food.

Killifishes—Cyprinodontidae

No spines; but physoclistous; single dorsal fin; lateral line absent; pectoral fins high on sides; anal fin in male not modified as an intromittent organ; egg laying; cycloid scales; mouth small, terminal, and protractile; head scaly.

The killifishes comprise a large family of small fishes, primarily inhabiting very shallow waters.[652] This preferred habitat has often led to another common name for this group, the topminnows. Many species are euryhaline, commonly occuring in freshwater to brackish water, and some even entering sea water. Most species show sexual dimorphism; in similar species it is often necessary to distinguish the sex of adult specimens for positive identification. Only three killifishes are present in Pennsylvania waters, making identification somewhat simpler.

KEY TO SPECIES OF CYPRINODONTIDAE

1 a. Jaw teeth tricuspid (Fig. 74, *C. variegatus*): Sheepshead minnow, *Cyprinodon variegatus*
   b. Jaw teeth conical (Fig. 74, *F. diaphanus* and *F. heteroclitus*): **2**

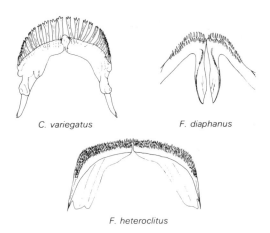

C. variegatus   *F. diaphanus*

F. heteroclitus

Figure 74. Teeth on lower jaws of some killifishes.

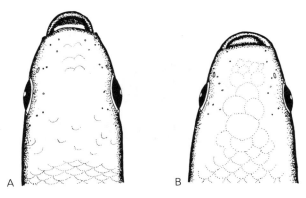

Figure 75. Head and snout of banded killifish (A), and the mummichog (B).

2 a. Body elongate (body depth more than 4 times in standard length); snout long and pointed (Fig. 75,A); scales in lateral series usually 43 to 46: Banded killifish, *Fundulus diaphanus*
   b. Body short and robust (body depth less than 4 times in standard length); snout short and blunt (Fig. 75,B); scales in lateral series usually less than 38: Mummichog, *Fundulus heteroclitus*

Genus *Cyprinodon*

Teeth tricuspid; mouth very small, not reaching anterior edge of eye; body very deep and compressed; dorsal profile greatly arched; origin of dorsal fin far in advance of anus.

Sheepshead minnow, *Cyprinodon variegatus* (Lacepede)[508]

Length 62 mm. Gulf of Mexico, off coast of Alabama. 19 June 1966

Distribution Closely allied to many species of desert pupfishes, the sheepshead minnow occasionally enters brackish water and even survives in freshwater. It is an abundant species along the Atlantic Coast from Cape Cod to Mexico.[69] It might be expected as an occasional stray in the freshwaters of the Delaware River drainage near Philadelphia, although we have no specimens from that vicinity.

Behavior During the spawning season in the spring, males become brilliantly colored with steel-blue back and an orange belly. Females are more subdued in coloration. Display, courtship, and defense of territory by the males occurs with release of eggs and sperm during the clasping act.[669] No nest building or care of eggs ensues. Males are somewhat larger than females, reaching a maximum size of about 3 inches.

Food The diet of the sheepshead minnow is largely plant material, but it readily consumes disabled invertebrates or small fishes by nibbling away the scales and flesh with its sharp teeth.[373]

Value It is too small to be commercially important, but it is a good forage species for shallow water game fishes.

Genus *Fundulus*

Teeth conical; mouth very small, not reaching anterior edge of eye; body stout; dorsal profile nearly horizontal, not greatly arched; origin of dorsal fin only slightly in advance of anus.

This is a large group of fishes in which the species are superficially similar, but adequately separated by many different characters.[102,314,623] Sexual dimorphism is common, also leading to problems of identification, since juveniles of several species are similar. Despite the common sympatric occurrence, natural hybrids between species of killifishes are extremely rare,[420] although some species are easily hybridized under laboratory conditions.[670] One specimen of the banded killifish X mummichog natural hybrid was reported from a large collection of killifishes from Prince Edward Island, Canada.[420]

Banded killifish, *Fundulus diaphanus* (Lesueur)[545]

Length 58 mm. Lake Erie, Presque Isle, Pa. 4 October 1975

Distribution The banded killifish occurs as two recognized subspecies in freshwaters of North America. One subspecies extends along the Atlantic Coast from the Canadian Maritimes to South Carolina, the other in a narrow northern band from New York and Pennsylvania west to Montana.[839] Both subspecies are present in Pennsylvania. This killifish is found in very shallow water along quiet edges of pools or ponds. It is most common in sluggish waters with much vegetation.[153]

Behavior The spawning habits are similar to all other killifishes studied, with males defending territories and spawning individually with females.[669,787] There is no nest building or care of the eggs or young. No good growth studies have been reported; a length-frequency analysis of a population from Gibson Lake, New Brunswick, indicates only a possible maximum size of about 4 inches reached in 3 years.[862]

Food The banded killifish has been described as a versatile feeder, selecting a wide variety of aquatic insects

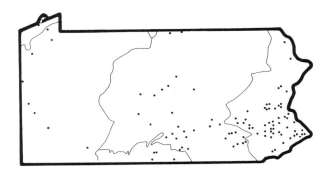

and plankton. It feeds effectively at all strata in shallow waters of lakes, despite the obvious adaptation of the small dorsal-terminal position of its mouth for surface feeding.[464]

Value The killifishes are excellent bait fishes, tolerating low oxygen and crowded conditions very well. They can be cultured easily and productively in small weedy ponds.[153]

Mummichog, *Fundulus heteroclitus* (Linnaeus)[559]

Length 69 mm. Swan's Gut Creek, Accomac County, Va. 5 May 1977

Length 66 mm. Swan's Gut Creek, Accomac County, Va. 5 May 1977

Distribution The mummichog is an abundant killifish found in shallow waters along the Atlantic Coast from the Gulf of St. Lawrence to Texas.[69,373] It is most common in brackish water, although it tolerates ocean salinities, and has been found reproducing successfully in fresh water in Pennsylvania and in Nova Scotia.[486]

Behavior The spawning habits have been described in detail in aquaria, as part of extensive experimental work done on the behavior and physiology of this species.[104,669] Males are larger and more strikingly marked than are females. They defend territories, court, and spawn with single females in secluded areas. Eggs stick together by adhesive fibrils which attach the eggs to vegetation. No nest building or subsequent care of eggs and young occurs. No good studies of growth have been reported. Maximum size appears to be 5 or 6 inches, making this one of the largest of the killifishes in North America.

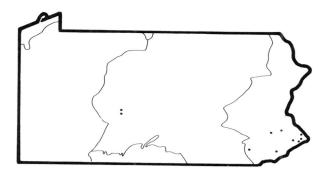

Food The mummichog is omnivorous, feeding on algae, various invertebrates and small fishes.[69,373]

Value The mummichog is a common bait fish in saltwater angling. It is very tolerant to low oxygen and hardy in containers and on the hook. It is easily harvested with small seines from abundant populations in shallow marshes.

Livebearers—Poeciliidae

This family contains several common aquarium fishes, such as guppies, mollies, and swordtails, which were either native or introduced into North America. Because most of these are tropical forms, it is unlikely that they would survive the cold winters in Pennsylvania. The mosquitofish is the only species of this group that apparently adapts to cool waters of northern states. On the other hand, southern Florida, with its warm climate, interconnected waterways, and commercial production facilities for exotic fishes, has experienced a flood of these fishes into the native fish fauna.[165]

Genus *Gambusia*

Viviparous; single dorsal fin; pectoral fins high on sides; anal fin in males modified as a gonopodium; no spines in fins; lateral line absent; similar in other characters to killifishes.

The name owes its etymology to the provincial Cuban word *gambusino*, which denotes 'nothing' in the jocular or scoffing sense; so it is said to fish for *Gambusinos* is to catch nothing.[503]

Mosquitofish, *Gambusia affinis* (Baird and Girard)[40]

Length 30 mm. Summerland Key, Fla. 29 October 1979

Length 44 mm. Summerland Key, Fla. 29 October 1979

Distribution This species occurs as two subspecies, one in the Mississippi and Gulf Coast drainages as far north as southern Illinois, the other along the Atlantic Coast to southern New Jersey. It has been introduced world-wide in suitable environments as a mosquito control measure. No records of this fish are available for Pennsylvania, except for an introduced population in Delaware County.[277] The low winter temperatures may limit the success of populations in Pennsylvania.[101,503]

Behavior In nature mosquito fish start breeding in early spring to late summer, depending on growth of the females and the seasonal warming of the water.[503,843] Four or more broods of young are produced each season, again dependent on the local climate. Females born early in the season commonly breed during the same season.

With this high reproductive potential it is possible to saturate a habitat with mosquitofish in a single season. This high production of young results in a high degree of cannibalism.[129] It is also a factor in the use of this species as a forage fish in southern climates. The mosquitofish is a small species, with the larger female seldom being more than 2 inches in length. It is quite tolerant to low oxygen and salinity.

Food Although mosquitofish readily take mosquito larvae, many other aquatic plants and animals are important as food.[49,358]

Value In most natural environments, killifishes and other fishes are also important in maintaining control of mosquitos.

Silversides—Atherinidae

Long, slender, and silvery fishes with two dorsal fins, elongate anal fin, and a prominent mid-lateral stripe; lateral line poorly developed, few pored scales on body; upper jaw protractile; single anal spine; dorsal spines slender and flexible; pelvic fins abdominal in position; body scales cycloid.

This is a large family containing mostly marine fishes; only two species occur as strictly freshwater forms in North America. One of these, the brook silverside, is present in western Pennsylvania. Another, the inland silverside is usually found in brackish water, but is occasionally found in fresh water tributaries of the lower Delaware River.

KEY TO SPECIES OF ATHERINIDAE

1 a. Upper jaw quite protrusible, projected into a short beak; snout about two times the diameter of the eye; anal rays 20 to 25; body scale rows 75 to 79:

Brook silverside, *Labidesthes sicculus*

   b. Upper jaw protractile, but not projected into a short beak; snout about equal to eye diameter; anal rays 15 to 19; body scale rows 37 to 41: Inland silverside, *Menidia beryllina*

Genus *Labidesthes*

Scales small, more than 50 lateral rows; predorsal scales crowded, more than 23 rows; premaxillae produced into a short beak when viewed from above; snout longer than eye diameter; anal soft rays 22 to 24.

Brook silverside, *Labidesthes sicculus* (Cope)[159]

Length 78 mm. Lake Erie, Presque Isle, Pa. 4 October 1975

Distribution This species is restricted to the Great Lakes, the Mississippi, and the Gulf Coast drainages from Michigan to Texas and Florida. It is absent from Atlantic Coastal streams of eastern United States. Although it formerly was present in the Youghiogheny River in Pennsylvania,[274] its distribution now appears to be extremely limited to the northwestern parts of the commonwealth. It is more common in lakes than in streams.

Behavior The brook silverside spawns in the spring on

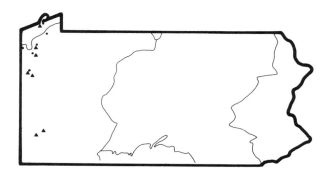

lake shoals or in moderate current of streams, with pairs spawning over gravel bottoms. No nest building or care of eggs ensues. The eggs have a conspicuous filament which attaches the egg to the substrate.[657] Younger silversides are one of the few fresh-water fishes to adopt a pelagic, surface habitat in large lakes soon after hatching. They move to the typical surface-water shore zone as they become larger.[394] Growth is rapid, with a maximum size of about 3.5 inches reached at the end of 2 years. Few individuals live as long as 3 years.

Food The brook silverside is characterized as a specialized feeder, highly selective for water fleas, dipteran larvae, and small flying insects.[463,650] Feeding occurs mostly at the surface, with the fish occasionally leaping from the water to catch a hovering insect.[74,464,976]

Value Brook silversides sometimes occur in schools, which renders them vulnerable for harvesting as bait, but they are very sensitive to low oxygen and die very quickly when confined in a bait bucket.

Genus *Menidia*

Scales large, less than 45 lateral rows; predorsal scales not crowded, usually less than 18 rows; premaxillae rounded when viewed from above; snout about equal to eye diameter; anal soft rays 15 to 17.

Inland silverside, *Menidia beryllina* (Cope)[161]

Length 73 mm. Wallop's Island, Accomac County, Va. 12 May 1978

Distribution The inland silverside is a coastal atherinid reported from Massachusetts to northern Mexico[448] tending to inhabit waters of lower salinity than most other marine silversides.[467] Strictly freshwater populations are known from lakes and large rivers in South Carolina and Texas.[421,801,898] In Pennsylvania it has been collected only once in a tributary of the lower Delaware River.

Behavior The spawning season extends from April to September. Eggs are broadcast over the bottom and adhere to vegetation or debris by sticky fibrils.[560] Females grow larger than do the males, with a maximum size reported at about 3 inches.[373]

Food The diet of the inland silverside is varied; small crustaceans, small molluscs, insects, and worms found in its stomach are consistent with the small mouth of

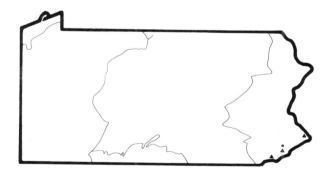

this fish. Some algae are taken also.

Value The chief value of this silverside is as forage for game fishes. It is often harvested locally for bait, but is difficult to keep alive in small containers.[373]

Sticklebacks—Gasterosteidae

Small laterally compressed fishes with a slender caudal peduncle; no scales; body sometimes bears oblong dorsal-ventral bony plates; several free spines preceding dorsal fin; all fin spines can be locked in an erect position.

The sticklebacks are closely allied to the pipefishes, sea horses, and tube-snouts. They are principally marine or brackish-water fishes, although a few species have adapted to fresh water. Among some genera, there is a high degree of variability, with occasional loss of the complete pelvic skeleton. This has led to insecurity of nomenclature and the recognition of species complexes in some genera.[660,661] The elaborate spawning behavior and other life history features of sticklebacks have been studied extensively for all species.[839] Not only do these fish guard their eggs, but the males secrete a sticky thread from their kidneys which binds together bits of vegetation into a hollow, ball-shaped or tunnel-shaped nest with two small openings. Eggs are deposited in this nest, fertilized, and then guarded by the male. The females are then chased away from the nest.[95]

KEY TO SPECIES OF GASTEROSTEIDAE

1 a. Dorsal spines usually 3; pelvic skeleton with a large, wide median posterior process (Fig. 76, *G. aculeatus*): **2**
  b. Dorsal spines usually more than 3: **3**
2 a. Pelvic fins with two soft rays; the pelvic spine with a strong basal tooth on both dorsal and ventral sides of the spine (Fig. 76); dorsal soft rays usually 10: Blackspotted stickleback, *Gasterosteus wheatlandi*
  b. Pelvic fins with one soft ray, pelvic spine with only minute denticulations along the side of the spine (Fig. 76); dorsal soft rays usually 12: Threespine stickleback, *Gasterosteus aculeatus*
3 a. Dorsal spines usually 9, inclined alternately to left and right from the midline; pelvic spine long and slender (Fig. 76): Ninespine stickleback, *Pungitius pungitius*
  b. Dorsal spines 4, 5, or 6: **4**
4 a. Pelvic skeleton with lateral posterior processes (Fig. 76); dorsal spines inclined alternately to left and right: Fourspine stickleback, *Apeltes quadracus*

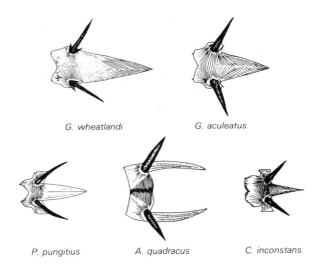

G. wheatlandi   G. aculeatus

P. pungitius   A. quadracus   C. inconstans

Figure 76. Pelvic skeleton and spines of sticklebacks.

  b. Pelvic skeleton without lateral posterior processes (Fig. 76); dorsal spines in median plane, not inclined to left or right: Brook stickleback, *Culaea inconstans*

Genus *Apeltes*

Dorsal fin usually with 4 spines, inclined alternately to left and right; pelvic skeleton without median posterior process, but with paired lateral posterior processes; caudal peduncle without a lateral keel, skin naked, without scales or bony plates.

Fourspine stickleback, *Apeltes quadracus* (Mitchill)[636]

Length 46 mm. Big Spring, Cumberland County, Pa. 23 July 1965

Distribution The fourspine stickleback ranges along the eastern coast of North America from Newfoundland to North Carolina.[658] It is very tolerant of salinity, but populations adapt readily to freshwater habitats. Breeding populations in Pennsylvania have been present in Big Spring, Cumberland County, and in Harvey's Lake, Luzerne County, for many years.[502] They are common in quiet water among vegetation and appear to avoid wave-washed sandy shores.

Behavior Nest building, courtship, and spawning of this species is typical of other sticklebacks. Males build an elaborate hollow nest, and guard eggs and young for some time after hatching.[780] This is a small species, males sometimes exceeding 2.5 inches. Common associates in these brackish waters are the mummichog and the sheepshead minnow.

Vertebrae were used for age determination, indicating a maximum size and age for females in a Chesapeake Bay population of about 58 mm total length, attained during their third summer. No males older than 2 summers were found.[830] An interesting cleaning-symbiosis, similar to that described for many groups of marine fishes and invertebrates, was reported: by appropriate behavior, a rainwater killifish encouraged the fourspine

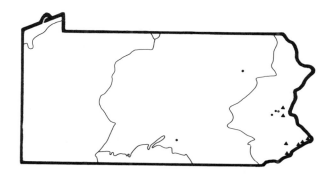

stickleback to remove external trematode parasites, *Gyrodactylus,* from its body.[909]

Food This stickleback is usually carnivorous, preferring small stages of crustaceans such as amphipods. They probably eat small insects and other invertebrates in freshwater.[69,373]

Value The small size and secretive nature of this stickleback make it of little value, except as occasional forage for some shallow-water predators. The large spines may also inhibit predation by larger fishes.[69]

Genus *Culaea*

Dorsal fin with 4 to 7 (usually 5) isolated spines, not inclined from midline; pelvic skeleton without posterior lateral processes, but with short, pointed median posterior process; caudal peduncle without lateral keel; body smooth, scaleless with small bony plates around lateral line pores.

Brook stickleback, *Culaea inconstans* (Kirtland)[481]

Length 44 mm. Goose Creek, Kalkaska County, Mich. 17 September 1976

Distribution The brook stickleback occurs in freshwater lakes and streams across North America from British Columbia to Pennsylvania.[618,659] It is the least tolerant species of the sticklebacks to salinity, although laboratory studies indicated that it could survive salinities up to 22 parts per thousand.[658] It is a rare, though locally abundant, species in Pennsylvania.

Behavior Typical nest-building and spawning behavior of the sticklebacks have been reported also for this species.[46,894,968] Males construct hollow nests of bits of vegetation plastered with mucous, and guard eggs and fry for some time after hatching. Very little is known of its growth rate or longevity. The largest specimen examined in an extensive study on geographic variation was 66 mm standard length,[658] although a maximum total length of of 87 mm has also been reported.[839]

Brook sticklebacks occasionally move downstream into Lake Huron in large numbers in late spring or early summer from tributaries. There is apparently no return migration of similar magnitude. No explanation was given for the purpose of such a mass movement.[23,525]

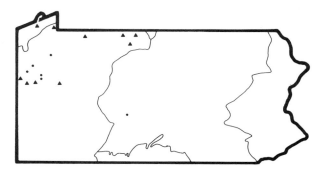

Food The diet of this stickleback is quite varied, consisting of nearly any organism small enough to be captured and swallowed.[221,678,968]

Value The brook stickleback is seldom noticed by anglers due to its secretive habits and small size, but it is often an important forage species in cold, spring-fed ponds.[618] Brook trout have no trouble ingesting them despite their formidable spines.

Genus *Gasterosteus*

Dorsal fin usually with three isolated spines anterior to soft rays; pelvic skeleton with a broad median posterior process, but no lateral posterior processes; body with variable number of dorsal-ventral bony plates; caudal peduncle usually with a lateral keel.

Threespine stickleback, *Gasterosteus aculeatus* Linnaeus[558]

Length 57 mm. Pennypack Creek, Philadelphia County, Pa. 18 March 1969

Distribution The threespine stickleback is a coastal and brackish-water form, nearly circumpolar in the Northern Hemisphere.[329] Populations sometimes recognized as separate species[341] are present in freshwater, but except for Lake Ontario and the St. Lawrence River, seldom occur far from the ocean. We have only a single specimen, which was found in Pennypack Creek, a tributary of the Delaware River near Philadelphia. It has occasionally been reported in this area as a stray from saltwater.

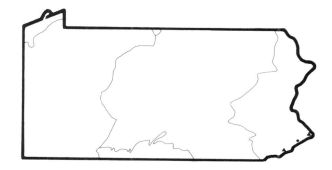

Behavior The threespine stickleback spawns over a wide period of spring and summer in different parts of its extensive range. Nest building, courtship, and care of eggs and young by the males, typical of all sticklebacks, have been reported by numerous authors.[341,935] Growth of populations in different localities in England was quite variable: four-summer fish ranged from 40 to 80 mm total length, based on analyses of otoliths.[451]

Food A detailed study of food selection in different seasons of the year indicates that crustaceans and insects are the chief components of its diet.[431]

Value This stickleback may be locally important as forage for game fishes, but its chief use has been that of a laboratory animal for studies in physiology and behavior.[839]

Blackspotted stickleback, *Gasterosteus wheatlandi* Putnam[721]

Length 39 mm. Sam Orr's Pond, Chamcook, New Brunswick, Canada 3 May 1977

Distribution The blackspotted stickleback occurs only along the Atlantic Coast from Newfoundland south to Long Island. Thus Pennsylvania is outside its range of distribution.[396,695] Its habitat is almost strictly marine, penetrating only a short distance into brackish waters of sloughs or bays, and seldom occurring in freshwater.[590]

Behavior The blackspotted stickleback spawns somewhat later than the threespine stickleback with which it is frequently collected, although the extended spawning season in the spring and early summer often overlaps between the two species. Detailed observations of nest building, courtship, and other aspects of the spawning behavior of this species differ only in minor details from published accounts of other sticklebacks.[603,781] The maximum size reported from the Atlantic Coast is 3 inches.

Food No detailed food studies are available. It is likely that small crustaceans and other invertebrates are chief items of the diet.

Value The lesser abundance of this stickleback than the threespine probably means that it is not very important as a forage species.

Genus *Pungitius*

Dorsal fin with 8 to 11 (usually 9) isolated spines, alternating to right and left, preceding soft rays; pelvic skeleton without lateral posterior processes, but with a median posterior process; slender caudal penduncle with a well-developed lateral keel; no true scales on body, but dorsal-ventral bony plates usually present along anterior part of the body.

Ninespine stickleback, *Pungitius pungitius* (Linnaus)[558]

Length 60 mm. Devils Track River, Minn. 18 July 1922

Distribution The ninespine stickleback is found throughout fresh and brackish waters of the northern part of our hemisphere, but does not reach Pennsylvania waters. It is present in all of the Great Lakes except Lake Erie, and south along the Atlantic Coast to New Jersey.[839] It is somewhat intermediate in tolerance to salinity among the several sticklebacks tested.[658]

Behavior The breeding habitat, nest building, courtship, spawning behavior, and care of eggs and young for this species are similar to all other sticklebacks studied, differing only in minor details among North American and European populations.[604] Populations of the ninespine stickleback in England exhibited a much slower growth rate than did populations of the threespine stickleback living in the same localities. Ninespine sticklebacks seldom exceed 50 mm total length during their 4th summer, as determined by examing otoliths.[451]

Food A study of populations in England indicated that the principal food items consisted primarily of crustaceans and insects.[431]

Value The low general abundance of this species means that it is not a very important forage fish.

Temperate basses— Percichthyidae

This group of percoid fishes is now recognized as distinct from the serranids on a basis of several osteological and morphological characters that show it to be more primitive. However, temperate basses have a highly specialized gas bladder, extending both backward into a hollow interhemal bone, and forward as two prongs to the wall of the inner ear.[315] An extensive literature is available on this small group of marine and freshwater forms,[839] because of their importance to sport and commercial fisheries.

Genus *Morone*

Spiny-rayed, physoclistous fishes with ctenoid scales; lateral line complete and continuous; premaxillary with two ascending processes; maxillary expanded posteriorly; opercle with two rounded spines, the main one below; no scaly process in the axil of the pelvics; pelvics thoracic, of a spine and five soft rays, the outer the longest; cheeks and opercles scaly, preopercle serrate; anal spines 3 or more; pseudobranchiae well developed.

KEY TO SPECIES OF *MORONE*

1 **a.** Second anal spine stout, almost as long as third spine (Fig. 77); dorsal fins joined by a membrane (Fig. 78); no teeth on base of tongue: White perch, *M. americana*

   b. Second anal spine rather thin, definitely shorter than third spine (Fig. 77, *M. saxatilis* and *M. chrysops*); dorsal fins not connected with a membrane (Fig. 78, *M. saxatilis* and *M. chrysops*); teeth present on base of tongue: **2**

2 **a.** Second anal spine contained more than 4 times in head length (Fig. 77): Striped bass, *M. saxatilis*

   b. Second anal spine contained about 3 times in head (Fig. 77): White bass, *M. chrysops*

M. americana   M. saxatilis

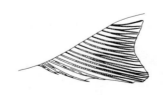

M. chrysops

Figure 77. Anal fins of temperate basses.

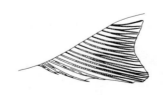

M. americana   M. saxatilis

M. chrysops

Figure 78. Dorsal fins of temperate basses.

White perch, *Morone americana* (Gmelin)[308]

Length 166 mm. Brandywine Creek, Chester County, Pa. 1967

Distribution The white perch is indigenous to the Atlantic Coast of North America and tolerates a wide range of salinity, from strictly landlocked, freshwater lakes to the more usual brackish estuarine habitats.[838,893] It is now common in Lake Ontario.[848] It has also been reported as strays from Pennsylvania waters of Lake Erie[531] and in the lower Susquehanna River.

Behavior The white perch is a schooling, gregarious species, undertaking marked seasonal movements. From estuaries, there is an upstream migration in the spring to spawn in fresh water, and back to deeper, brackish water for fall and winter. Observations on actual spawning are rare, but it was described as similar to other related species. A single female is chased by several males in open water, with much milling about and splashing at the surface. No nest building or parental care ensues.[576]

Food The summer diet of the white perch in freshwater consists primarily of aquatic insects, small forage fishes, and crustaceans.[154] In brackish water, this species occasionally grows to a size of 15 inches or 2 pounds;[69] in a

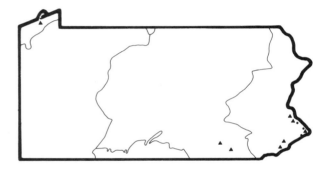

freshwater lake in Maine, the largest fish was about 12 inches long and in its 17th summer of life.[154]

Value In addition to its value as a commercial food fish in large estuaries, the white perch is considered a good pan fish along the coast in brackish water. However, because they overpopulate lake environments and grow slowly, the white perch often becomes a fish management problem in the northeast.

White bass, *Morone chrysops* (Rafinesque)[730]

Length 120 mm. Lake Erie, Presque Isle, Pa. 22 May 1959

Distribution The white bass is a freshwater species found as a native or introduced into reservoirs in much of the eastern half of North America,[939,945] but is most abundant in the lower Great Lakes and the Mississippi River drainages.[919] It has been recently introduced into Allegheny Reservoir, presumably from Lake Erie stocks.

Behavior White bass are gregarious during spawning, often migrating upstream from reservoirs in the spring.[948] The males outnumber the females on the spawning reef. Several males chase a single female erratically near the surface and the demersal eggs are scattered over the rocky shoals.[794] In Lake Mendota, Wisconsin, white bass congregate on specific spawning reefs. Displaced from these areas experimentally, they were able to orient and return faithfully to these spawning sites, presumably by a sun-compass mechanism.[363]

The white bass is intermediate in size between white perch and striped bass, commonly growing to 17 inches in about 9 years.[267,919]

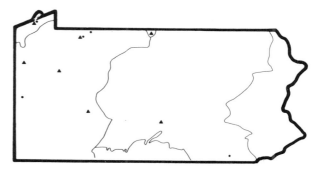

Food Their food consists principally of crustaceans, insects, and fishes, a common observation of most species in this group.[76,383,854]

Value The white bass is an important sport fish in a few localities. Spawning aggregations are easy to exploit and the flesh is considered flavorful and of fine quality. Since it is often the dominant predator in large, turbid reservoirs, heavy exploitation is recommended to control the population and to prevent stunting.[854,939,945]

Striped bass, *Morone saxatilis* (Walbaum)[938]

Length 331 mm. Delaware River, Bucks County, Pa. 19 July 1961

Distribution The striped bass, or "rock" of Chesapeake Bay, is common along the Atlantic Coast from the St. Lawrence River to the St. John's River in Florida, and in some tributaries of the Gulf of Mexico.[748] Two groups of fingerlings were planted in San Francisco Bay, California, in 1879 and 1882 which soon established a thriving sport and commercial fishery.[833] It is predominately an anadromous form, but landlocked freshwater populations exist.[69,587,933] In Pennsylvania, it has been recently introduced into Walker Lake, Snyder County, and repeated plantings have been made in Raystown Reservoir, Huntingdon County, but there is no evidence of natural reproduction.

Behavior Striped bass migrate upstream in the spring to spawn near the mouths of large freshwater rivers.[610] Several males chase a single female in erratic

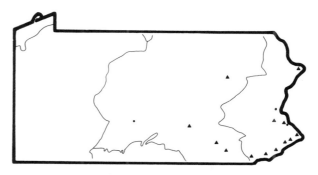

"rock fights" over stony riffles. The semi-buoyant eggs drift downstream with the current during the incubation period.

Growth of striped bass is rapid, estuaries being used extensively by young and juveniles as nursery areas.[758] After a few years, adults become more pelagic along the Atlantic Coast. Sizes in excess of 100 pounds have been reported in the literature; a 65-pound female was estimated to be about 30 years of age.

Food The striped bass appears to be omnivorous, utilizing fishes, crustaceans, and molluscs as they are available.[380,905]

Value It is difficult to overestimate the value of the striped bass to the sport and commercial fishery. It appears to have great promise as an exotic in large reservoirs where a pelagic predator would help to control overabundant species such as the alewife or gizzard shad.

Sunfishes—Centrarchidae

Pelvic fins thoracic in position, composed of 1 spine and 5 branched rays; anal fin with 2 to 8 spines; anterior portion of dorsal fin with 5 to 14 spines, connected with soft rays behind (deeply divided only in the largemouth bass); body and cheeks covered with ctenoid scales, top of head is scaleless; mouth terminal; maxillae not lying under preorbitals when mouth is closed; no opercular spines; preopercle not serrate; gill membranes separate, not united to isthmus; pseudobranchiae, if present, small and concealed by a membrane; physoclistous.

The sunfishes are a primitive group of perciform fishes, closely allied to the temperate basses and sea basses. Except for the Sacramento perch, a sunfish which is endemic to the Pacific Coast, all sunfishes originally were confined to the freshwaters of North America east of the Rocky Mountains.[83]

Many species of sunfishes have been introduced into various countries around the world.[400] None of the species are capable of surviving in sea water, although the largemouth bass is often found in brackish water. Species of this family usually are the dominant fishes in warm waters of North America.

The spawning behavior of all of the sunfishes is remarkably similar. Males prepare a nest over clean, hard substrates, spawn singly with one or more females in the nest, and then drive away all fishes. The adhesive eggs in the nests are aerated by swimming motions of the male, and eggs and young are guarded against all predators.[89,95]

The frequent occurrence of hybrids among sunfishes, and the fertility among some interspecific hybrids, often results in some odd-looking, second-generation individuals which are difficult to identify. Many of these hybrids have been verified experimentally,[126,411] with several intergeneric crosses much less successful than interspecific crosses.[371]

KEY TO GENERA OF CENTRARCHIDAE

1 a. Anal spines usually 3: **2**
   b. Anal spines usually 5 or more: **4**
2 a. Lateral scale rows more than 55; body elongate (depth of body more than 3 times in standard length): *Micropterus*
   b. Lateral scale rows less than 55; body deep (depth of body less than 3 times in standard length): **3**
3 a. Opercular bone with a notch or indentation on upper posterior margin (Fig. 79, *A. rupestris*): *Enneacanthus*
   b. Opercular bone entire, lacking a notch or indenta-

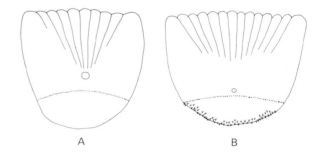

Figure 80. Cycloid scale of mud sunfish (A), and ctenoid scale of rock bass (B).

tion (Fig. 79, *L. gibbosus*): *Lepomis*
4 a. Gill rakers on lower limb of first arch more than 18: *Pomoxis*
   b. Gill rakers on lower limb of first arch fewer than 13: **5**
5 a. Scales cycloid (Fig. 80,A); caudal fin rounded: *Acantharchus*
   b. Scales ctenoid (Fig. 80,B); caudal fin slightly forked: *Ambloplites*

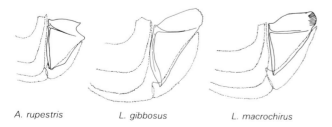

A. rupestris   *L. gibbosus*   *L. macrochirus*

Figure 79. Opercular bones of some centrarchids.

Genus *Acantharchus*

Shape oblong, not much compressed; scales cycloid, unusual for centrarchids; 6 anal spines; lower jaw projecting past upper jaw; teeth on vomer, palatines, and tongue; opercle with a broad notch on postero-dorsal angle; gill rakers in graded series from long to short on lower limb of first arch; complete lateral line; caudal fin rounded.

Mud sunfish, *Acantharchus pomotis* (Baird)[39]

Length 134 mm. Swift Creek, near Blykin, S. C. 8 June 1955

Distribution The mud sunfish is a secretive fish found along the Atlantic coastal plain from New York to Florida.[89] In Pennsylvania, it was formerly reported below the Fall Line in the Delaware drainage,[276] but it is now probably extirpated. It is found only in sluggish streams or small ponds.

Behavior The male prepares a nest and its reproductive behavior is assumed to be similar to other sun-fishes,[94,751] but no actual spawning has been observed. It is often found with the pirate perch, swamp darter, and creek chubsucker. It seldom appears to be abundant, possibly because of its nocturnal activity pattern.[89,751]

A small population of this species was found upon draining a small millpond in Maryland. It contained individuals up to 8 years of age and a maximum size of about 7.5 inches.[578]

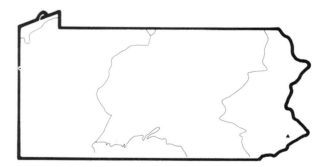

Food No food studies have been reported,[578] but it is probable that a variety of small invertebrates form the bulk of its diet, as with other related sunfishes.

Value It is seldom seen by anglers and has little or no sport fishery potential.

Genus *Ambloplites*

Anal fin with 5 to 7 short spines; gill rakers on entire first arch about 16, some of which are knob-like rudiments; scales with many, very fine ctenii; mouth very large; pelvic fins thoracic in position; caudal fin slightly forked.

Rock bass, *Ambloplites rupestris* (Rafinesque)[724]

Length 140 mm. North Branch of Casselman River, Garrett County, Md. 24 April 1977

Distribution The original distribution of the rock bass included most of the east central part of North America from the St. Lawrence and Lake Champlain drainages south, west of the Appalachians to the Gulf of Mexico. It is believed to have invaded the Atlantic slope through the canal systems, since it is now very common there.[72] It is also now well established in lakes of the Puget Sound basin of Washington.[857] It is very common in warm-water lakes and streams with rocky pools.

Behavior Spawning occurs in lakes or streams in the spring or early summer with males preparing and guarding solitary nests usually close to a log or large rock.[116,291] Growth of the rock bass varies considerably. The Nebish Lake, Wisconsin, population took 13 years to reach a total length of about 8 inches;[375] in Missouri streams this length was attained in 6 years.[717] It is often the dominant predator together with the smallmouth bass in moderate-sized streams.[344,834]

Food The rock bass is characterized as a bottom feed-

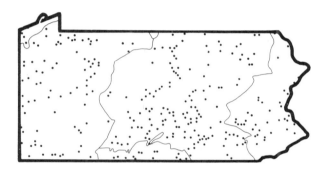

er;[463] its large mouth and secretive feeding behavior makes it adept at specializing on large aquatic insects and crayfish.[214,464]

Value The rock bass is a good panfish for anglers. Its wide range of habitat in both lakes and warm-water streams makes it available to anglers fishing with many types of gear.

Genus *Enneacanthus*

Anal spines usually 3; lateral scale rows less than 55; depth of body less than 3 times in standard length; opercular bone with a notch or indentation on upper posterior margin; small sunfishes with rounded tails.

KEY TO SPECIES OF *ENNEACANTHUS*

1 a. Soft rays in anal fin usually 12: Blackbanded sunfish, *E. chaetodon*
   b. Soft rays in anal fin usually 10: 2
2 a. Body marked with dark vertical bars; opercular

spot larger than pupil of eye: Banded sunfish, *E. obesus*
   b. Body marked with horizontal light stripes; opercular spot smaller than pupil of eye: Bluespotted sunfish, *E. gloriosus*

Blackbanded sunfish, *Enneacanthus chaetodon* (Baird)[39]

Length 84 mm. Lakehurst Naval Air Station, Ocean County, N. J. 20 May 1964

Distribution The blackbanded sunfish occurs as two recognized subspecies along the Atlantic Coast from New Jersey to Florida.[30] It is largely restricted to acid water in weedy ponds and sluggish streams along the coastal plain.[439] In Pennsylvania, there are old records of its occurrence in the lower Delaware Valley below the Fall Line,[6,275] but we have been unable to collect this fish recently from these localities.

Behavior This sunfish is a small species, reaching a maximum size of about 3 inches in 5 years.[827] Its spawning behavior, observed in an aquarium, is very similar to other centrarchids except for a site preference for weed beds in which the nest is prepared by the male.[433]

Food The food of the blackbanded sunfish includes a wide variety of zooplankton, aquatic insects and crusta-

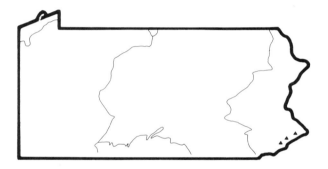

ceans depending on their size and availability. Midge larvae are predominant food items in most localities.[773,827]

Value This species is an interesting aquarium fish but it is too small and scarce to be valuable as a sport fish.

Bluespotted sunfish, *Enneacanthus gloriosus* (Holbrook)[379]

Distribution The bluespotted sunfish ranges along the Atlantic Coast from New York to Florida[373] occurring most often in weedy, bog-stained ponds or sluggish streams. It is not uncommon in brackish waters along the coast. In New York[325,326] it was locally common in the Delaware and Hudson drainages but absent from the headwaters of the Susquehanna River; in Pennsylvania, we have found it rather widespread in both of these drainages. It has recently established a substantial population in Jamesville Reservoir, New York, part of the Great Lakes drainage.[952]

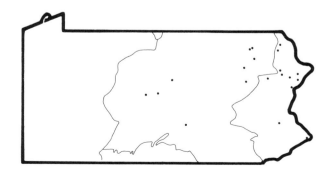

Length 74 mm. Swan's Gut Creek, Accomac County, Va. 11 May 1978

Behavior The males become brightly colored during the spawning season, defending a small territory around a solitary nest.[94,751] They are quite sedentary with a limited home range.

Food A few analyses of stomach contents reveal that micro-crustaceans and midge larvae are important food items, with a variety of insects, clams, snails, and water mites sometimes eaten.[6,373] These feeding observations are consistent with the very small mouth of this sunfish.[257]

Value This sunfish is of small size, seldom exceeding 4 inches. They have little value to anglers but the brightly colored males have been often prized as aquarium fishes.

Banded sunfish, *Enneacanthus obesus* (Girard)[304]

Length 72 mm. Lakehurst Naval Air Station, Ocean County N. J. 20 May 1964

Distribution The banded sunfish is a little known species, despite its early description[304] from specimens collected from freshwaters about Hingham, Massachusetts. It has been reported from several Atlantic Coast drainages in boggy brooks from New York to Florida.[278] In 1977, three specimens were taken on impingment screens at the Eddystone Generating Station on the Delaware River near Philadelphia, close to the site of an early record in 1850 by R. H. Richard (UMMZ 86801).

Behavior The reproductive behavior of the banded sunfish is probably similar to other sunfishes, with males preparing and guarding a small nest. No actual spawning has been reported.[751] It has a very restricted home range.

Food The food habits of this sunfish are assumed to be similar to other sympatric sunfishes such as the bluespotted and blackbanded. No food studies have been published.

Value The banded sunfish is a small species, seldom exceeding 4 inches in length, with its dark vertical bands

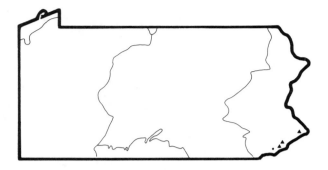

not nearly as prominent as in the blackbanded sunfish. It is probably more abundant than indicated by the few specimens available in collections, its small size and secretive habits contributing to its apparent scarcity.[357]

Genus *Lepomis*

Anal spines usually 3; body depth less than 3 times in standard length; lateral scale rows less than 55; caudal fin somewhat forked, not rounded; upper posterior margin of opercular bone entire, lacking a notch or indentation.

KEY TO SPECIES OF *LEPOMIS*

1 a. Opercle stiff to its bony margin, not flexible on its posterior edge (Fig. 79, *L. gibbosus*): **2**
   b. Opercle extended backward as a thin, flexible flap (Fig. 79, *L. macrochirus*): **5**
2 a. Teeth on base of tongue (Fig. 81,A): Warmouth, *L. gulosus*
   b. No teeth on tongue (Fig. 81,B): **3**
3 a. Pectoral fin short, rounded, more than 4 times in standard length; prominent black spot on posterior base of soft dorsal fin; gill rakers long (longest raker exceeds the width of the bony arch): Green sunfish, *L. cyanellus*
   b. Pectoral fin long and pointed, less than 4 times in standard length; no prominent black spot on base of soft dorsal; gill rakers short (longest raker less than width of the bony arch): **4**
4 a. Soft dorsal fin without definite spots; bony opercular margin slightly flexible, but much less than in *L. macrochirus* or *L. auritus:* Redear sunfish, *L. microlophus*
   b. Soft dorsal fin with definite spotted markings; bony opercular flap very stiff (Fig. 79): Pumpkinseed, *L. gibbosus*
5 a. Most gill rakers on lower first arch as long as width of gill arch; pectoral fins long and pointed, reach beyond eye when reflected forward: Bluegill, *L. macrochirus*
   b. Most gill rakers on lower first arch shorter than

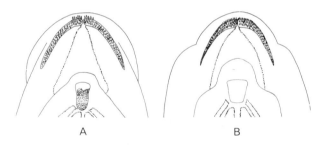

Figure 81. Lower jaw of centrarchids showing tongue with teeth (A), or without teeth (B).

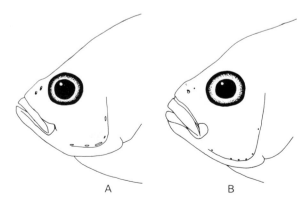

Figure 82. Heads of sunfishes showing preopercular pores lengthened (A), or rounded (B).

width of gill arch; pectorals short and rounded, do not reach beyond eye when reflected forward: **6**

6 a. Scales in lateral line usually more than 42: Redbreast sunfish, *L. auritus*

b. Scales in lateral line usually less than 38: **7**

7 a. Sensory openings along free edges of preopercle greatly lengthened (Fig. 82,A); orange spots on cheeks and body: Orangespotted sunfish, *L. humilis*

b. Sensory openings along free edges of preopercle small and circular (Fig. 82,B); no orange spots on cheeks or body: Longear sunfish, *L. megalotis*

Redbreast sunfish, *Lepomis auritus* (Linnaeus)[558]

Length 123 mm. Frankstown Branch of Juniata River, Huntingdon County, Pa. 29 August 1967

Distribution The redbreast sunfish is widely distributed in Atlantic Coast drainages from New Brunswick to Florida. It has also been introduced into Texas and Oklahoma.[751,839] It is widespread, but does not become as locally abundant as other sunfishes such as the pumpkinseed or green sunfish.

Behavior This sunfish spawns in spring and early summer, the male usually constructing and guarding a solitary nest. However, where suitable substrate is scarce, nests may be closely packed together like the bluegill.[193,751] The habitat of the redbreast is variable in shallow waters of lakes and streams, often in quite turbid water.[845] It also tolerates brackish water to some extent, reproducing successfully in tidal waters of the Chickahominy River in Virginia.[789] The redbreast is normally a solitary fish during warm weather, but aggregates in tight inactive schools when the water temperature drops below 40°F.[93]

Food Stomachs of the redbreast sunfish contain a vari-

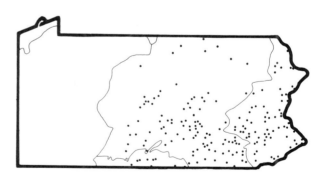

ety of aquatic and terrestrial foods, ranging from worms and molluscs, through insects, to small fishes. This is in keeping with the shallow water habitat and large mouth of this sunfish.[257]

Value One of the larger sunfishes, the redbreast is an important game and panfish throughout its range. It readily takes a surface fly, small lures, or live bait.[193,751,845]

Green sunfish, *Lepomis cyanellus* Rafinesque[728]

Length 110 mm. Meadow Brook, Montgomery County, Pa. 23 July 1979

Distribution The distribution of the green sunfish is usually cited as west of the Appalachians throughout the Mississippi Basin west to New Mexico and North Dakota.[839] Although it is not present in Atlantic Coast drainages of New York,[325] it is now known to be abundant, perhaps as introductions, in many Atlantic coastal drainages to the south.[438] It has also been successfully introduced into California.[648]

Behavior The green sunfish has an extended spawning period from June to August in which a single male will construct several nests.[427] Redfin shiners also spawn above occupied nests of the green sunfish, apparently attracted to the nests by organic substances released by spawning sunfish. Male sunfish rarely chased the shiners which held territories over the sunfish nests.[428] The green sunfish has a very restricted home range and quickly returns to its home territory when replaced. This has been demonstrated in small ponds[365] and in warm-water streams.[291] Its preferred habitat is sluggish pools of creeks or shores of ponds and lakes among cover.[648]

The green sunfish grows slowly, reaching a length of about 8 inches in 8 years.[407,717] In small ponds, it hybridizes frequently with the pumpkinseed and the bluegill, and often overpopulates and dominates the shallow water areas of the pond to the exclusion of young largemouth bass.

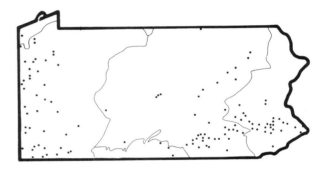

Food The food of the green sunfish consists of insects, small fishes, and crayfish.[407,751] Because of its large mouth, it is able to eat larger food items than other sunfishes; there is even a report of a short-tailed shrew found in the stomach of a 6.75 inch green sunfish.[425]

Value In Pennsylvania and colder climates to the north, the green sunfish rarely reaches a size favorable to anglers and is therefore not considered an important panfish. However, in warmer habitats to the south, where growth rates are more rapid, it is well accepted as a sport and food fish.[407,751]

Pumpkinseed, *Lepomis gibbosus* (Linnaeus)[558]

Distribution The pumpkinseed is the common sunfish to much of northeastern United States and Canada, occurring from New Brunswick to Georgia. In the midwest, its distribution is limited to the northern states, largely allopatric with the similar redear sunfish common in the southern states. It has been introduced elsewhere in North America and to several countries in Europe.[839]

Behavior The spawning of the pumpkinseed is similar to other sunfishes, with nests occurring singly or in groups

Length 140 mm. Frankstown Branch of Juniata River, Huntingdon County, Pa. 29 August 1967

of two or three, never in large colonies like the bluegill.[91] Egg predation by other sunfishes or golden shiners may be severe at times, but production from single nests sometimes exceeds 14,000 fry.[116] Chain pickerel sometimes are attracted to large concentrations of shiners surrounding a pumpkinseed nest, and inadvertently assist the male sunfish in protecting fry from minnow predation by the pike predation on the minnows.[851]

The pumpkinseed is found in a variety of habitats in shallow water among weeds or cover. It tolerates turbidity, low oxygen, low pH, and other poor environmental conditions such as winter kill that would be detrimental to many other species.[155,751,841]

Food Pumpkinseeds are diurnal in their feeding activity, with a morning and an evening peak of activity.[465] Many different invertebrates occur in their stomachs, with snails often being dominant.[242,257] This is in marked contrast to the food of the bluegill, which seldom eats snails.[841]

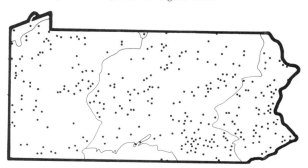

Value The pumpkinseed will exceed a length of 10 inches under good growing conditions, but usually grows more slowly, reaching a length of about 7.5 inches in 8 years.[56] Small ponds often become overpopulated with this species, resulting in very slow growth. But its widespread distribution, abundant populations, and aggressive feeding on almost any small bait makes this sunfish popular among many beginning anglers.[751]

Warmouth, *Lepomis gulosus* (Cuvier)[183]

Length 126 mm. Lackawannock Creek, Mercer County, Pa. 22 October 1981

Distribution The warmouth is widely distributed throughout the eastern half of the United States from southern Michigan to the Gulf Coast.[529] We have found it rarely in several localities in Pennsylvania, but it was apparently overlooked in earlier surveys.

Behavior The warmouth prefers rubble or loose sticks as a nesting site, apparently avoiding sand or gravel which are the usual sites for other sunfishes. Spawning occurs during spring and summer, with peak activity early in June in Illinois. Males construct and guard nests in typical sunfish fashion. An examination of the gonads indicated that a female may spawn several times in the same season.[529,751,788] It hybridizes successfully with other sunfishes.[611]

The usual habitat of the warmouth is the deeper, open water of sluggish streams or ponds. Along the Gulf Coast it tolerates brackish water to some degree.[124]

This sunfish usually does not overpopulate and dominate fish populations like the bluegill. It grows to a size of about 9 inches in 6 to 8 years[821] with large variation due to local conditions. Some populations in Illinois reached 6 inches in their first 13 months, while others averaged only 5.4 inches at the end of 6 years.[529]

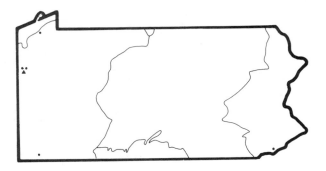

Food Fish, crayfish, and aquatic insects comprise the bulk of the food eaten by the warmouth.[257,553] There is a gradual shift from zooplankton and midge larvae for small individuals to a diet of fish and crayfish as the warmouth grows in size. This is possible partly because of the large mouth of this species.

Value The warmouth is not generally considered to be an important panfish because of its small size and secretive behavior. It is seldom taken by anglers even under exceptional conditions when populations are high.[553]

Orangespotted sunfish, *Lepomis humilis* (Girard)[306]

Length 72 mm. Wilson Creek, Ind. 5 July 1941

Distribution This small sunfish is widely distributed throughout the Mississippi River drainage in turbid, silty streams and ponds.[704] It has never been reported for Pennsylvania, or any Atlantic Coast drainages, but is included here because of its superficial resemblance to several hybrid sunfishes involving the green sunfish or longear sunfish as one of the parent species.

Behavior In Iowa, the orangespotted sunfish spawns during most of the spring and summer. Its nest is somewhat smaller than most sunfishes, but grouped together in dense colonies, similar to those of bluegills.[48] It is one

of the smallest of *Lepomis*, reaching a size of about 5 inches in 7 years, maturing during its second year at lengths of less than 2 inches.

Food The food of this species is primarily small crustaceans and insect larvae, in keeping with its small size. In some areas it is considered an important control of mosquito larvae and pupae.[48]

Value It is occasionally taken by angling, but it is too small to be an important sport fish.

Bluegill, *Lepomis macrochirus* Rafinesque[728]

Length 100 mm. Donegal Lake, Westmoreland County, Pa. 7 June 1978

Distribution The natural distribution of the bluegill included most of the eastern half of the United States and Canada, but excluded the northern part of the Atlantic Coast drainage. However, it has been widely introduced elsewhere, along with the largemouth bass, into most of North America[839] and into South Africa.[169]

Behavior The bluegill spawns over an extended time period depending on latitude and water temperature, nesting close together in colonies. Fry production per nest sometimes exceeds 60,000,[116] often leading to overpopulation of young and juveniles and subsequent slow growth.[150] Under good growing conditions maximum lengths of 13 inches and 2 pounds are reached in 8 to 10 years.[56] It is most abundant in lakes and ponds, but also inhabits sluggish portions of stream systems.[257]

Food The food of the bluegill ranges from algae and zooplankton through many different invertebrates to fish and fish scales.[424,841] Although this species is known to consume large quantities of plant material along with animal foods, the nutritional value of the plants is not sufficient to meet all its metabolic needs.[484] In nature, it

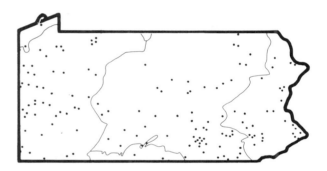

is described as a generalized feeder, with up to nine types of organisms commonly found in the stomach at one time.[464]

Value The bluegill and largemouth bass have been managed as an important prey-predator combination in much of the United States because of their excellence as sport and food fishes. Many investigators have shown the necessity of controlling recruitment of the bluegill population to maintain a balanced population which will provide good angling.[59,869,888]

Longear sunfish, *Lepomis megalotis* (Rafinesque)[731]

Distribution The longear sunfish is widely distributed in central United States from the upper midwest to Texas. It has been previously reported from two sites in northwestern Pennsylvania,[733] but recent attempts to obtain specimens there have not been successful. It is commonly found in clear, weedy streams and small ponds, preferring quiet water areas, but is also found in pools of streams with a hard bottom and moderate current.[195]

Behavior This species is a colonial nester like the bluegill where suitable substrate is scarce,[7] but males also construct and defend solitary nests.[346,972] Longears have a very restricted home range and return very quickly to their original location when displaced.[291] In warmer climates, the longear sunfish reaches a length of almost 6 inches in 7 or 8 years;[717] further north, growth is even slower.[407] It has a tendency to overpopulate its habitat,

Length 110 mm. Misteaguay Creek, Saginaw County, Mich. 16 September 1976

with resulting slower growth.

Food Snails, leeches, and aquatic insects appear to be important items of diet, judging from a few stomach samples. Further study will probably show a more varied diet.[7,751]

Value The longear grows slowly and is considered to be a poor panfish because of its small size. However, its voracious feeding makes it very easy for the angler to catch.[7,407,751]

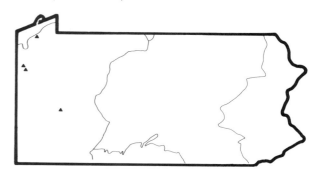

Redear sunfish, *Lepomis microlophus* (Gunther)[339]

Length 158 mm. Oostanaula River, Floyd County, Ga. 2 March 1978

Distribution The native distribution of the redear sunfish is largely south and west of that of the pumpkinseed. This includes the southern portion of the Mississippi River drainage and the Gulf Coast.[704] The redear is ecologically and morphologically very similar to the pumpkin- seed. The redear sunfish is not found in Pennsylvania waters, except for a few localities in which it has recently been introduced. It is too early to tell whether or not these introductions will succeed in establishing self-sustaining populations.

The redear is found in warm, clear lakes with much vegetation or submerged cover,[704,820] giving rise to the common name "stump-knocker". It is also found in bays, coves, and rivers and is somewhat tolerant of brackish water.[137]

Behavior The redear sunfish spawns in May or June in the midwest, nesting in tight colonies much like the bluegill.[126,818] Sometimes a second spawning occurs in August.[704] It is one of the larger sunfishes, often reaching a length of 10 inches in 7 or 8 years.[820]

Food Snails are often the dominant food of the redear sunfish, leading to the common name "shellcracker" for this species.[424] The molar-like pharyngeal teeth are suited for this type of diet.

Value The redear sunfish is one of the larger sunfishes and thus is an important panfish throughout its range.

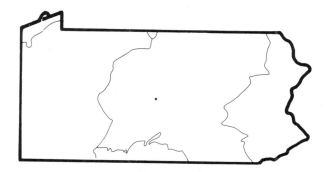

However, it does not take an artificial lure or fly as readily as other sunfishes. It makes a good combination with the largemouth bass because it seldom overpopulates its habitat and does not compete with juvenile bass for food.[103] It is a good choice for introduction into Pennsylvania for management of sport fishing.

Genus *Micropterus*

Usually three anal spines; 6 branchiostegal rays; villiform teeth on palatines; maxillary bone extending at least to center of pupil of eye; well-developed supramaxillary; 55–81 scales along lateral line; 9–11 dorsal spines; moderately compressed and elongate body.[401]

With the recent records of spotted bass in the Ohio River below Pittsburgh, three of the six recognized species of *Micropterus* are now known from Pennsylvania waters. Due to their importance as sport fishes, and the accompanying artificial culture and stocking programs, it is difficult to delineate their original ranges.

KEY TO SPECIES OF *MICROPTERUS*

1 a. Maxilla extends to beyond eye with mouth closed (Fig. 83,A); no small scales on membranes of soft dorsal and anal fins: Largemouth bass, *M. salmoides*

   b. Maxilla does not extend to posterior margin of eye with mouth closed (Fig. 83,B); small scales present on membranes of soft dorsal and anal fins: **2**

2 a. Scale rows above lateral line 12 or 13 (Fig. 84,A); basicaudal spot lacking or very faint: Smallmouth bass, *M. dolomieui*

   b. Scale rows above lateral line 7 to 10 (Fig. 84,B); basicaudal spot very prominent: Spotted bass, *M. punctulatus*

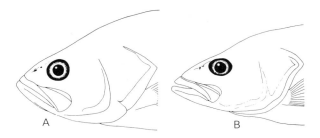

Figure 83. Heads of basses showing upper jaw extending to posterior edge of eye (A), and not reaching posterior edge of eye (B).

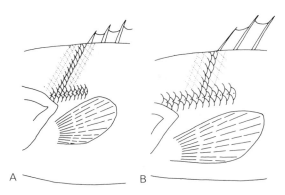

Figure 84. Method of counting scale rows above lateral line in basses; 12 rows (A), 7 rows (B).

Smallmouth bass, *Micropterus dolomieui* Lacepede[507]

Length 152 mm. Enlow Fork of Wheeling Creek, Greene County, Pa. 27 July 1976

Distribution The approximate original distribution of the smallmouth bass includes the Great Lakes drainage and the upper reaches of the Mississippi drainage.[400] It is now successfully acclimated to suitable habitats such as the Susquehanna, Delaware, and Potomac drainages, and throughout much of the world.

It is often characterized as a fish of warm, clear streams, with strong tendencies to maintain home territories.[249,291,528] It is often closely associated in rocky pools with the rock bass.[344] However, it is also abundant in large oligotrophic lakes and reservoirs.[532,949]

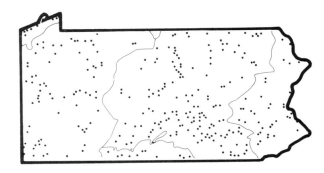

Behavior The nesting and spawning behavior of the smallmouth bass is similar to other sunfishes, with males usually selecting a nest site close to deep water or near overhead cover. More than one female may spawn in a single nest, and repeated nesting is reported over an extended spring and summer season. More than 80,000 fry may be produced per mile in suitable small streams.[702]

The growth of the smallmouth bass varies with locality and climate, often exceeding 20 inches in 10 years.[56,422] Northern populations grow more slowly; that of Big Lake, Maine, averaged only 17.1 inches at 8 years of age.[947]

Food The smallmouth bass is an opportunistic feeder, changing from zooplankton and aquatic insects for fry and juveniles to crayfish and small fishes as the fish grow larger.[400,949]

Value The smallmouth is one of North America's most prized game fishes for its fighting qualities and excellent eating.[367] It loses some of this esteem in northern climates, where slow growth results in very few large trophy fish.[947]

Spotted bass, *Micropterus punctulatus* (Rafinesque)[732]

Length 138 mm. Bells Creek, Fayette County, W. Va. 9 July 1976

Distribution The distribution of the spotted bass includes much of the southern portion of the Mississippi drainage.[704] It has been taken very recently in the Ohio River and Beaver River near Pittsburgh. Although it is common in many tributaries in Ohio,[902] we believe that this constitutes an extension of its range as the water quality of the Ohio River improves.

The spotted bass is usually found in pools of clear, warm-water streams, but adapts readily to reservoirs. It tolerates more turbidity than the smallmouth, which helps to explain its abundance in streams that are turbid most of the time.[173,195] It has a home range larger than stream sunfishes such as the green sunfish, but smaller than the smallmouth bass.[291]

Behavior The spotted bass spawns in early summer on pool edges or shores of reservoirs, selecting a gravel bottom. Males construct nests and guard eggs and fry for a short time after hatching.[704] It is easily cultured in hatchery systems for stocking fingerlings.[388,389,390]

The spotted bass does not grow as fast, or get as large as the smallmouth, but may reach a weight of 3.5 pounds under good growing conditions.[422,717]

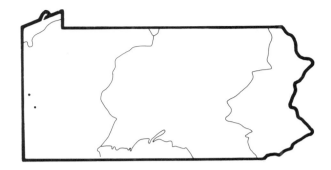

Food The diet changes normally from zooplankton and small insects to one of large crayfish and fishes as the fish grows.[19] In cool weather, feeding is likely to stop almost completely.[202,863]

Value The spotted bass is an important game fish in small streams and reservoirs in the Ozarks. However, it seldom occurs in angler's catches from mixed fish populations, even where studies have shown spotted bass to be abundant.[422,704]

Largemouth bass, *Micropterus salmoides* (Lacepede)[507]

Length 128 mm. Ryerson State Park Lake, Greene County, Pa. 2 June 1977

Distribution The native distribution of this sunfish included most of the eastern half of the United States and southern Canada, except for the Atlantic Coast north of Virginia. It is now acclimated to many temperate climates of the world.[169,839] The largemouth bass tolerates many different habitats, but is usually found in ponds and small weedy lakes.[59,134,649]

Behavior In cool climates, the largemouth bass spawns in spring and early summer, with the male aggressively defending a solitary nest and the school of newly hatched fry.[775] In southern Florida, spawning reaches a peak about the middle of February, as water temperature cools to below 70°F,[137] indicating a close relationship of maturation and spawning to seasonal changes in ambient temperature.

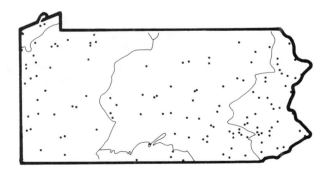

Growth of largemouth bass is also greatly dependent upon climate, population density, and food. Record growth rates are often reported from southern habitats supporting abundant forage fishes,[136] and very slow growth due to overpopulation and short growing season are not uncommon in the north.[149] Average growth for this species over most of the United States is about 20 inches in 10 years.[56,422]

Food The diet of the largemouth bass changes from cladocera and aquatic insects to crayfish and forage fishes very early in its growth history. This is due in part to its predatory behavior and large mouth size which is capable of handling large food items.[464] Fishes like gizzard shad, threadfin shad, or large pelagic schools of alewives often are associated with fast growth and high production of the largemouth bass in large reservoirs.[11,934]

Value It is hard to overemphasize the importance of the largemouth as a sport fish in view of organizations dedicated to its management and preservation. The fish is a voracious feeder, is tolerant to a wide range of habitats, and has been introduced widely.

Genus *Pomoxis*

Body deep, strongly compressed laterally; scales ctenoid, fewer than 55 rows in lateral series; anal spines usually 5 or more; opercular bone with a notch or indentation on upper posterior margin; gill rakers on lower limb of first arch more than 18.

KEY TO SPECIES OF *POMOXIS*

1 a. Dorsal spines usually 5 or 6; pectoral fin rays usually 15; length of dorsal fin base, when projected forward with dividers, extends from dorsal origin to opercle but not reaching orbital rim: White crappie, *P. annularis*

   b. Dorsal spines usually 7 or 8; pectoral fin rays usually 14; length of dorsal fin base, when projected forward with dividers, extends to eye: Black crappie, *P. nigromaculatus*

White crappie, *Pomoxis annularis* Rafinesque[727]

Length 173 mm. Maiden Creek, Berks County, Pa. 9 July 1969

Distribution The original range of the white crappie was restricted to the eastern half of North America, including the Great Lakes drainage, but it was missing from the Atlantic slope north of the Carolinas.[413] We have found it in both the Susquehanna and Delaware River drainages, possibly as introductions. It is especially abundant as pelagic schools in turbid reservoirs of all sizes.[351]

Behavior The white crappie spawns in late spring and early summer, often nesting in small colonies. Nests are often located in 2 to 10 feet of water, deeper than many other sunfishes of similar sizes.[350,352,853] Substrates used are often plant roots and submerged brush, in addition to gravel and small stones.

As is the case with most fishes, growth of the white

crappie is highly variable. Individuals of 5 or 6 pounds have been reported from Mississippi and Louisiana, with a maximum age of about 10 years. An average growth of about 15 inches in 8 years would be the usual case.[717,795,821]

Food Small white crappies eat a variety of zooplankton and aquatic insects.[242] As the fish grow, larger crustaceans and leeches are eaten, but small fishes usually dominate the diet.[383,522]

Value This species often dominates the catch by anglers in many large turbid reservoirs of the south, where it is easily caught still-fishing using small minnows around

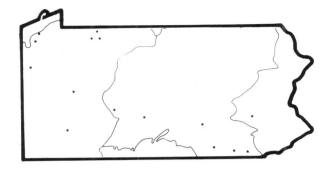

submerged brush.[351,691,939] In these habitats, black crappies are also taken, but are much less common.

Black crappie, *Pomoxis nigromaculatus* (Lesueur)[183]

Length 142 mm. Spring Creek, Floyd County, Ga. 2 March 1978

Distribution The natural range of the black crappie included most of the eastern half of the United States, with the exception of the Atlantic Slope north of the Carolinas.[413] We have found it at several localities in both the Susquehanna and Delaware drainages, perhaps as introductions. Its preferred habitat is clear, weedy lakes and ponds, and it is not as tolerant to turbidity as the white crappie.

Behavior The few observations of nesting of black crappie show many similarities to spawning behavior of all sunfishes.[89,95,693] In the spring or early summer, males prepare nests in moderately deep water, often close to overhead cover.

Growth of the black crappie is rapid, with some individuals reaching 18 to 20 inches in about 10 years; average growth of 12 to 14 inches in 10 years would be more typical.[56,717,821]

Food The diet of this species changes from midges,

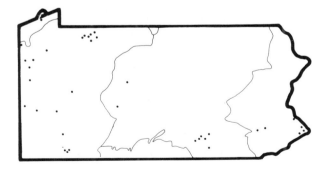

mayflies, and dragonflies to a fish diet as the fish grows.[202,424,841]

Value The black crappie often supports important sport fisheries in large clear-water impoundments. It is easy to catch and is considered one of the best eating fish in much of the midwest and south.[111] It is commonly taken on hand lines while fishing through the ice in the north.

Perches—Percidae

A diverse family of spiny-rayed, physoclistous species with small ctenoid scales. Body usually elongate-terete. Opercle usually with a flat spine. Anal spines 1 or 2, pelvic fins thoracic in position.

In North America this family is represented by the walleye, the sauger, the yellow perch, and 146 species of darters.[145] No less than 21 of these are presently found in Pennsylvania, with the largest number of species present in the Allegheny River system. Most percids prefer cool, flowing water with unsilted substrates, although some species have become adapted to lacustrine habitats.

Spawning behavior in percids varies from scattering eggs over suitable substrates (the walleye and the Iowa darter), to depositing eggs in gravel nests (the rainbow darter and the blackside darter), to guarding nests of adhesive eggs fastened to the underside of flat stones (the fantail darter and the Johnny darter). Where nest building or care of eggs occurs, the larger and more colorful male assumes these duties.

KEY TO GENERA OF PERCIDAE

1 a. Free edges of preopercle with strong teeth (Fig. 85,A); mouth large, the maxilla extending backward to middle of eye: **2**

  b. Free edges of preopercle with weak teeth (Fig. 85,B) or none; mouth small, the maxilla not reaching backward to middle of eye: **3**

2 a. Canine teeth present (Fig. 86,A); space between pelvic fins equal to length of pelvic base; pseudobranchiae well developed: *Stizostedion*

  b. Canine teeth absent (Fig. 86,B); space between pelvic fins less than length of pelvic base; pseudobranchiae not well developed: *Perca*

3 a. Body extremely elongate, its depth contained 7 to 9 times in standard length; flesh nearly transparent in life; body usually lacking scales on belly and on back: *Ammocrypta*

  b. Body depth contained less than 7 times in standard length; body normally scaled except for a naked strip on midline of belly in some species: **4**

4 a. Midline of belly with a row of enlarged, specialized scales (except for *P. shumardi* where belly in front of anus is covered with a few normal scales) (Fig. 88,B); one specialized scale between pelvic fins; pelvic fins separated by a space more than ¾ the width of the pelvic fin base; anal fin usually as large as the second dorsal fin: *Percina*

  b. Midline of belly scaleless or variously scaled with

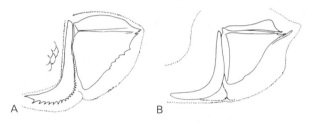

Figure 85. Preopercle of yellow perch with teeth (A), and preopercle of log perch without teeth (B).

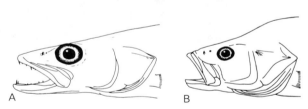

Figure 86. Canine teeth present in walleye (A), and absent in yellow perch (B).

normal scales (Fig. 88,A), but lacking a row of enlarged, specialized scales; no specialized scale between the pelvic fins; pelvic fins closer together, separated by a space less than ¾ the width of the pelvic fin base; anal fin usually much smaller than the second dorsal fin: *Etheostoma*

Genus *Ammocrypta*

Body extremely elongate, its depth contained 7 to 9 times in standard length; body usually lacking scales on belly and on back; flesh nearly transparent in life; free edges of preopercle with weak teeth, or none; mouth small, the maxilla not reaching backward to middle of eye; anal fin with a single, weak spine.

Eastern sand darter, *Ammocrypta pellucida* (Putnam)[720]

Length 66 mm. French Creek, Erie County, Pa. 14 May 1977

Distribution The eastern sand darter is found in large tributaries of the Ohio River and along sandy shores of the Great Lakes. Once common over its range, it is becoming rare due to the loss of its preferred habitat.[902] In Pennsylvania it was reported earlier from the Monongahela River,[239] but we have found it recently only in French Creek and in Lake Erie. This elongate and nearly transparent darter is usually found on sandy shoals, often burying itself with only the head exposed.[289] Its small home range, restricted habitat, and small populations have led to its description as a threatened species.[196]

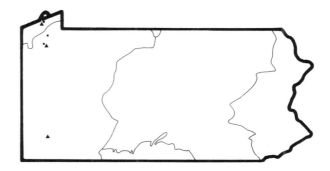

Behavior There are no observations on spawning of this darter. Analysis of the gonads indicates that it apparently spawns in June or July.[961] In streams it is often associated on the same riffle with the greenside darter and the banded darter, with some segregation of microhabitat.[515] It seldom exceeds 3 inches in length, but no age determinations have been published.

Food The diet of this sand darter is almost entirely

midge larvae, with little difference found between young and adult fish. The small mouth size and very restricted habitat is partly responsible for this lack of variability in the diet.[264,908,961]

Value The eastern sand darter is a rare, unobtrusive species of little interest to anglers. Its requirement of clean, unsilted sandy shoals makes it a useful indicator of unpolluted streams.

Genus *Etheostoma*

A highly variable group of darters, exhibiting various combinations of more specialized characters than those of Percina or Ammocrypta. The belly is covered with normal scales. The lateral line is variously incomplete. There often is a reduced number of vertebrae, ranging from 32 to 44. The spawning habits often include nest building and care of the eggs by the male.

KEY TO SPECIES OF *ETHEOSTOMA*

1 a. Deep groove separates tip of upper jaw from snout (frenum absent) (Fig. 87,A—*E. olmstedi*): **2**
  b. Tip of upper jaw connected to snout by a frenum, which may be narrow or broad (Fig. 87,B—*P. maculata*): **4**
2 a. Two anal spines; snout extends beyond upper lip: Greenside darter, *E. blennioides*
  b. One weak, flexible, anal spine: **3**
3 a. Usually 13 or more rays in soft dorsal fin: Tesselated darter, *E. olmstedi*

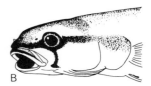

Figure 87. Deep groove across snout, no frenum (A); no deep groove across snout, frenum present (B).

  b. Usually 11 or less rays in soft dorsal fin: Johnny darter, *E. nigrum*

4 a. Gill covers broadly connected across isthmus, usually resulting in an obtuse angle (more than 90 degrees) between branchiostegal membranes when in the closed position (Fig. 89,A): **5**
   b. Gill covers free from isthmus to moderately connected, resulting in an acute angle between branchiostegal membranes (Fig. 89,B): **7**
5 a. Mouth terminal; head long and narrow; lateral line incomplete, pored scales ending beneath soft dorsal (Fig. 90,A), tail rounded: Fantail darter, *E. flabellare*
   b. Mouth subterminal; snout rounded, head triangular; lateral line complete (Fig. 90,B); tail slightly forked or squarish: **6**
6 a. Cheeks and opercles scaled (Fig. 91,A); body with 10 or more vertical bands; dorsal spines usually 10 or 11: Banded darter, *E. zonale*
   b. Cheeks and opercles scaleless (Fig. 91,B); body with 4 prominent saddles across back; dorsal spines usually 12 or 13: Variegate darter, *E. variatum*
7 a. Lateral line incomplete with posterior 10 to 20 scales lacking pores (Fig. 90,A): **8**
   b. Lateral line complete (sometimes last 3 or 4 small scales on caudal peduncle missing pores) (Fig. 90,B): **11**
8 a. Cheeks rather completely scaled (Fig. 91,A): Iowa darter, *E. exile*
   b. No visible scales on cheeks (Fig. 91,B,C): **9**
9 a. Rays in soft dorsal fin usually 8 or 9: Least darter, *E. microperca*

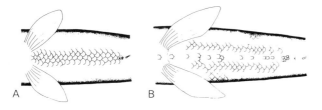

Figure 88. Scalation on belly normal (A), or with row of specialized scales (B).

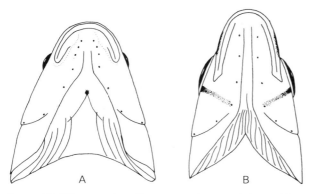

Figure 89. Gill covers broadly connected across isthmus (A), or moderately free from isthmus (B).

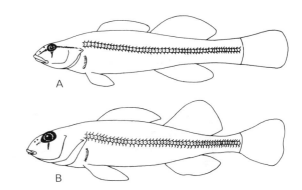

Figure 90. Lateral line incomplete in fantail darter (A), or complete as in banded darter (B).

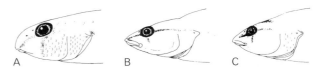

Figure 91. Cheeks and opercle scaled (A), cheeks and opercles scaleless (B), or cheeks scaleless, but scales present on opercles (C).

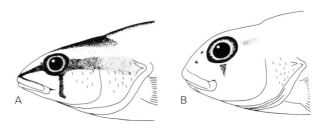

Figure 92. Snout sharply pointed, dorsal profile nearly straight in spotted darter (A); snout short and blunt, dorsal profile curved downward in bluebreast darter (B).

   b. Rays in soft dorsal fin 11 or more: **10**
10 a. Spines in anterior dorsal fin usually 12 or 13; belly behind pelvic fins scaleless or partially scaled, but not fully imbricated (Fig. 88,B) no bars or blotches on body: Tippecanoe darter, *E. tippecanoe*
   b. Spines in anterior dorsal fin usually 10 or 11; belly behind pelvics covered with imbricated scales (Fig. 88,A); body covered with bars and blotches: Rainbow darter, *E. caeruleum*
11 a. Cheeks densely scaled: Swamp darter, *E. fusiforme*
   b. No scales on cheeks (scales may be present on opercles (Fig. 91,B,C): **12**
12 a. Snout sharply pointed; dorsal profile from nape to tip of upper lip nearly straight (Fig. 92,A): Spotted darter, *E. maculatum*
   b. Snout blunt; dorsal profile from nape to tip of upper lip curved sharply downward (Fig. 92,B): Bluebreast darter, *E. camurum*

Greenside darter, *Etheostoma blennioides* Rafinesque[728]

Length 76 mm. Dunkard Fork of Wheeling Creek, Greene County, Pa. 21 July 1976

Distribution The greenside darter ranges widely throughout southern Appalachia and westward into Missouri and Arkansas.[628] It is one of the commonest darters in western Pennsylvania, apparently having reached the Potomac and Susquehanna drainages through stream capture[829] or other means. Its habitat is variable, but it is usually found in rivers or streams on fast riffles with rocks or in beds of vegetation.[246,515,966,967] It is a common associate of the fantail darter and the smallmouth bass.[344]

Behavior Spawning occurs in late spring, adhesive eggs being deposited in beds of filamentous algae in the current. There is no nest building or guarding of territory by the male, although there is an apparent upstream migration of mature fish to spawn in selected areas.[246,966,967] The greenside is one of the larger darters; bright green males up to 4 inches have been collected and determined to be about 4 years old.

Food The diet of this darter changes little from juvenile to adult; zooplankton, blackfly larvae, and small aquatic insects are the chief items found in stomachs.[246,908]

Value This darter is probably an important forage species for smallmouth bass and rock bass because of its local abundance. It is too small to be of interest to anglers.

Rainbow darter, *Etheostoma caeruleum* Storer[880]

Length 65 mm. Allegheny River, Warren County, Pa. 11 August 1975

Distribution The rainbow darter is widespread throughout the upper Mississippi River drainage and extends into the lower Great Lakes. It is absent from the Atlantic Coast drainage,[839] but is very common in western Pennsylvania. It is often found in abundance on fine gravel riffles of streams, and is almost completely absent from standing waters.[264,289]

Behavior The rainbow darter migrates to breeding riffles in the spring where the male, gaudily colored red, green, and blue, guards a small territory around a breeding female.[771,966] Adhesive eggs are deposited on a sand or gravel riffle with no nest preparation or subsequent care of eggs.

This is one of the smaller darters, seldom exceeding 2 inches. It is a common associate of several riffle fishes such as the fantail and Johnny darters.[515]

Food The diet of this darter is consistent with its small size and habitat, a few stomach samples showing small items like zooplankton, aquatic insects, and snails.[908]

Value This fish is too small to be of interest to anglers, but its local abundance makes it a good forage fish for

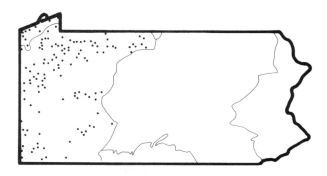

other stream fishes such as rock bass or smallmouth bass.

Bluebreast darter, *Etheostoma camurum* (Cope)[163]

Length 46 mm. Tionesta Creek, Forest County, Pa. 26 July 1974

Distribution The bluebreast darter is distributed in the Ohio River drainage from the west slope of the Appalachians in Pennsylvania and Kentucky westward to Indiana. In Pennsylvania we have found only scattered specimens in the Allegheny drainage, although one other locality has been reported in the Beaver River headwaters.[733] It shows a preference for deep, fast riffles of large streams with clear water and little silt.[902,977]

Behavior The bluebreast darter spawns in the spring, following a migration to selected riffles from deep water.[902] Males do not defend territories, but mate with individual females who select the exact spawning site. No nest preparation or guarding of the eggs occurs after spawning.[646] This darter is moderately large; adult males sometimes exceed 3 inches. It is commonly associated with the greenside and banded darters on clean rocky riffles.[515]

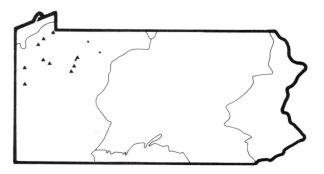

Food The diet of this darter has not been studied, although it is presumed that small invertebrates found on fast riffles are important.[753]

Value This beautiful darter is of little value to anglers because of its scarcity and small size.

Iowa darter, *Etheostoma exile* (Girard)[307]

Length 63 mm. Goose Creek, Kalkaska County, Mich. 17 September 1976

Distribution The Iowa darter ranges throughout much of north central United States and Canada. Pennsylvania is at the southeast border of its range. It was recorded rarely in the bay at Erie, Pennsylvania and in a few of the glacial lakes tributary to French Creek. I have not found it in stream riffles, although it has been reported elsewhere from weedy portions of slowly flowing streams.[289,902]

Behavior The Iowa darter migrates to shallow-water riffles for spawning. Males defend specific territories over sand or fine gravel and spawn with individual females. No care is given to the adhesive eggs deposited in the riffles.[435,966] This darter is a small fish, seldom exceeding 2 inches and not often becoming abundant at any one locality.

Food A few stomach analyses indicate that the diet

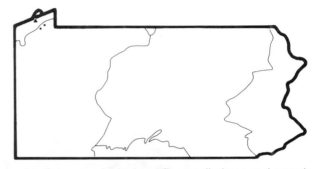

varies from zooplankton to fingernail clams and aquatic insects. The small mouth size precludes larger items from its diet.[132]

Value A small and uncommon darter in Pennsylvania, this fish has little apparent value to man.

Fantail darter, *Etheostoma flabellare* Rafinesque[728]

Length 70 mm. Dry River, Rockingham County, Va. 17 June 1976

Distribution This is one of the few darters in Pennsylvania that has extended its range from the Mississippi and Great Lakes drainage into the Atlantic Coast drainages of the Potomac and Susquehanna Rivers. We have not found it in the Delaware drainage. It adapts readily to varied habitats, but is most common in very shallow riffles or along the shallow banks in fast or quiet water where many stones and rocks afford good cover.[7,462,523]

Behavior Breeding males are unique in having fleshy knobs at the tips of the spines in the first dorsal fin, but generally lack the bright red and blue colors of other darters. The male selects a small area under a flat stone and guards the layers of adhesive eggs stuck to the

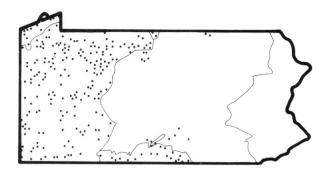

underside of the stone.[321,966,967] The fantail is more tolerant to adverse water quality than most darters, and sometimes becomes very abundant, with hundreds present in the riffles of small warm-water streams. Males of this moderate-sized darter sometimes reach 3 inches.

Food This darter feeds upon many different small invertebrates, with midges often very important.[188,908]

Value When it is locally abundant, it probably is an important forage fish for rock bass and smallmouth bass.

Swamp darter, *Etheostoma fusiforme* (Girard)[304]

Length 40 mm. Swan's Gut Creek, Worcester County, Md. 15 May 1976

Distribution The swamp darter has an extended range along the Atlantic Coast below the Fall Line from Maine to Louisiana, and extending up the Mississippi drainage to Reelfoot Lake, Tennessee.[406] Although this species was collected several times before 1920 from Mill Creek near Bristol, Pennsylvania, it has not been collected in Pennsylvania in recent years. Extensive industrial development of this area has made it difficult now to even locate the small pond and swamp habitats suitable for the swamp darter. It continues to be abundant in acid water ponds in the nearby New Jersey Pine Barrens. It is very tolerant to acid conditions in sluggish streams with little dissolved oxygen.[29,574]

Behavior The adhesive eggs are deposited singly on stems of aquatic plants after courtship, which usually takes place in dense weed beds.[143] This is a small darter that seldom exceeds 2 inches.

Food No good food studies have been reported, al-

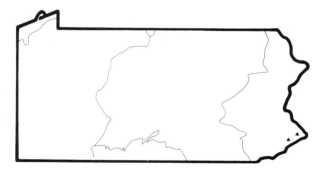

though zooplankton were found in a few stomachs.[143,238] It is likely that many small invertebrates make up the usual diet.

Value There is little apparent value to man of this secretive swamp inhabitant. It is also of little use as a forage species for chain pickerel because it is seldom abundant.

Spotted darter, *Etheostoma maculatum* Kirtland[481]

Length 55 mm. French Creek, Crawford County, Pa. 2 June 1966

Distribution The spotted darter has a restricted range in large to medium-sized streams on the western slope of the Appalachians from the Allegheny River system south to Alabama.[978] It is found only in clear-water, fast, deep riffles among large rubble or boulders.

Behavior The spotted darter is the only darter that deposits its adhesive eggs in a wedge-shaped mass under rocks guarded by the male.[733] The usual range of the spotted darter is limited, seldom extending beyond a single deep fast riffle.[753] It is a medium-sized darter, with some males reaching about 3 inches.

Food Although no detailed food study is available, some stomachs contained aquatic insects, midges being the most numerous.[753]

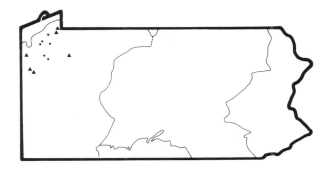

Value This very colorful darter is quite rare and thus has only limited value in scientific studies.

Least darter, *Etheostoma microperca* Jordan[458]

Length 30 mm. Misteaguay Creek, Saginaw County, Mich. 16 September 1976

Distribution The least darter has a disjunct range centered in lower Michigan and the midwest, and a small area in Missouri and Oklahoma.[839] There are no records of this species in Pennsylvania, but suitable habitat exists in the northwest glaciated area of the state close to its recorded range, making its presence possible. It is present in Lake Erie tributaries of Ontario and Ohio. It is usually found in quiet, weedy ponds and weedy backwaters of streams, preferring a lacustrine habitat more than most riffle darters.[902]

Behavior During the spring spawning season, males defend small territories around the breeding female in a weed bed. Adhesive eggs are laid singly on stems of weeds in shallow water. There is no nest building or care of the eggs.[110,697,966] The rest of the year is spent in a very restricted area near weed beds. As the name implies, this species is the smallest of all darters.[405] It is an inhabitant of warm-water streams or lakes often associated with the rock bass and the smallmouth bass.[344,697]

Food The diet of this small darter consists mostly of small crustacea and midge larvae. A few other aquatic insects are also included.[110,263]

Value This small darter is almost never seen or recognized by anglers, but it is an interesting species to ecologists because of its relationships to other fishes.

Johnny darter, *Etheostoma nigrum* Rafinesque[732]

Length 55 mm. Little Mahoning Creek, Indiana County, Pa. 11 July 1967

Distribution The Johnny darter has a wide distribution centered in the Ohio and Great Lakes drainages, but is largely absent from the Atlantic Coast drainages. The specific distinctness of the Johnny darter and the tessellated darter is not recognized by everyone; considering the two as one species would greatly increase the range of this similar species pair.[839] Although this darter tolerates a wide variety of lake and stream habitats, it is most often found in slow current over fine gravel or sand.[461,753]

Behavior Spawning is highly specialized. The male selects a site under a flat rock on the bottom, and adhesive eggs are deposited in a single layer on the underside of the rock; the male then defends this territory. At other times, the home range is restricted to a short distance within a slow riffle or backwater.[346,966] This species is one of the smaller darters, seldom exceeding 2 inches in length. It is widespread and sometimes very abundant in suitable habitat, and often occurs with the rainbow and fantail darters.

Food The diet of the Johnny darter is mostly zooplank-

ton and midge larvae, although many mayflies and other small insects, as well as worms and small snails, are taken by larger darters.[461,908]

Value This very abundant darter is probably an important forage fish for stream fishes such as rock bass and smallmouth bass. Otherwise, it is too small to have much value to anglers.[839]

Tessellated darter, *Etheostoma olmstedi* Storer[879]

Length 62 mm. Butler Mill Brook, Sussex County, Del. 14 October 1979

Distribution As presently recognized, the tessellated darter is restricted to the Atlantic coastal streams, including Lake Ontario and the St. Lawrence River. It is the most abundant darter in these streams, utilizing a wide variety of habitats, but is most often found on gravelly shoals with moderate current and some vegetation.[141] It is a common associate in warm-water streams with the blacknose dace and the bluntnose minnow. It is a close relative of the Johnny darter, but I have never found it to be sympatric in Pennsylvania. Although it is variable in morphology, it is easily separated from the Johnny darter using dorsal ray counts alone.[140]

Behavior The tessellated darter spawns in late spring, the dark-colored male selecting and guarding a small territory around a flat rock. Eggs are deposited in a single layer on the underside of the rock and are guarded until hatching. The home range is limited to a small area within a suitable riffle.[7,25,147] Males grow to nearly 3 inches in length, often larger than the similar Johnny

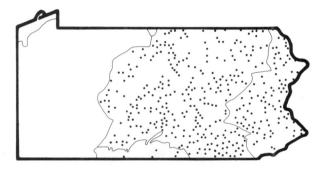

darter. It is quite tolerant to low oxygen.[906]

Food The diet of this darter consists mainly of zooplankton and midge larvae, with some algae and other small aquatic insects added as the fish grows.[7,257]

Value Large populations and the wide distribution of this fish make it quite valuable as forage for game species.

Tippecanoe darter, *Etheostoma tippecanoe* Jordan and Evermann[459]

Length 37 mm. French Creek, Crawford County, Pa. 25 June 1977

Distribution This darter is found in only a few scattered localities within the Ohio River drainage. In Pennsylvania, we have found it only in French Creek, where populations have fluctuated greatly for at least the past 40 years.[733,753] The Tippecanoe darter prefers long riffles of large streams where there is moderate current over sand and fine gravel.[129,902]

Behavior The blue and gold males are conspicuous on a breeding riffle, guarding a small territory around an egg deposition site in fine gravel. They will desert the area if the water suddenly becomes turbid during a freshet. No observations of the spawning act have been reported. It is one of the smallest and most colorful of the darters, adult males seldom reaching 2 inches in length.

Food No food studies have been published, but it is very likely that small midges and other aquatic insects are

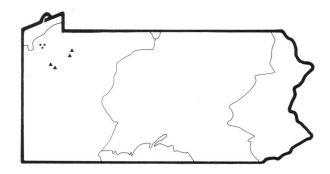

important items of diet.

Value To the ecologist, the scattered distribution, local abundance, and widely fluctuating populations of this darter raise interesting questions of factors influencing survival. It has little value as a forage species.

Variegate darter, *Etheostoma variatum* Kirtland[481]

Length 75 mm. Loyalhanna Creek, Westmoreland County, Pa. 15 August 1967

Distribution The variegate darter is common throughout stony riffles of streams of the upper Ohio River drainage and is locally abundant in French Creek and the Allegheny River in Pennsylvania.[403] It prefers high-gradient portions of large streams with a bottom of sand or fine gravel interspersed with large boulders.[515,902]

Behavior Males are larger and more brightly colored orange and green during the late spring breeding season. There is an upstream migration to the spawning riffles, and a return to deeper water for the winter. Actual spawning observations have not been reported for this species,[902] which is a common associate of the banded darter and the river chub.[753]

Food In an analysis of only four stomachs, mayflies, midges, and a few water mites were found. It is likely that other aquatic invertebrates are also used as food.[908]

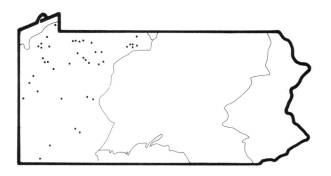

Value One of the larger and more colorful species, the variegate darter is too small to be noticed by anglers. Although common, it is seldom abundant enough to be important forage for predator fishes.[129,902]

Banded darter, *Etheostoma zonale* (Cope)[160]

Length 54 mm. Little Muncy Creek, Lycoming County, Pa. 5 October 1978

Distribution The banded darter has a wide range throughout the Mississippi River drainage from Minnesota to Louisiana, with many subspecies and races recognized.[907] It is often the most abundant species and occurs sympatrically on the same riffle with other species such as the rainbow and the greenside darters.[515] It tolerates many different habitats in streams with moderate flow.

This species has recently extended its range to the Susquehanna River by way of Pine Creek in northcentral Pennsylvania. A few collections from Pine Creek in 1964 found the tessellated darter and the shield darter to be abundant, but no banded darters were collected. An intensive survey of Pine Creek in 1971, for another purpose, showed the banded darter to be very abundant with both of the previous species. Immediately after the severe flood caused by Hurricane Agnes in June 1972, the banded darter was found in the Susquehanna River in the vicinity of Amity Hall, Pennsylvania and now is reported widespread throughout the entire watershed, including several locations in Maryland, and one in New York.[205,488]

Behavior Males are more brightly colored than females, with green and gold bodies and some fins marked with red and blue-black. They are found on spawning riffles of fine gravel in the spring, but no spawning observations

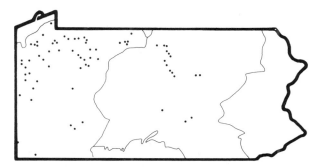

have been published.[907] Common associates on these riffles are the greenside and variegate darters. The banded darter is one of the smaller species, seldom reaching 2.5 inches in length.

Food No food studies have been published, but it is likely that aquatic insects and invertebrates form the bulk of the diet.

Value This species may be important as forage for rock bass or smallmouth bass because of its abundance. It is of high ecological interest in the Susquehanna River system because it affords an opportunity to study the interactions among other riffle fishes as the banded darter rapidly invades this new range.

Genus *Perca*

Anteriormost interhaemal bone greatly enlarged; canine teeth absent; anal spines very prominent; several vertical black blotches along sides of body; black spot at base of spiny dorsal.

Yellow perch, *Perca flavescens* (Mitchill)[634]

Length 128 mm. Walnut Lake, Oakland County, Mich. 13 September 1976

Distribution The yellow perch is widely distributed throughout North America, and its original range has been extended by many introductions.[839] It prefers the clear, cool waters of lakes, ponds, and sluggish streams, often entering brackish water. The yellow perch and European perch are now considered as distinct species, but are morphological and ecological equivalents.[896]

Behavior The spawning habits of the yellow perch are unique among the perches; males and females congregate in shallow water and eggs are deposited in long gelatinous ribbons, draped over vegetation, brush, or clean substrates. There is no breeding territory or care of eggs after spawning.[368] The yellow perch is active only during the day, moving to shoals at dusk and remaining quiescent until dawn.[364,465] This species commonly reaches a size of 12 inches, but overpopulation and slow growth are frequent in small lakes.

Food The diet of juvenile yellow perch is mostly zoo-

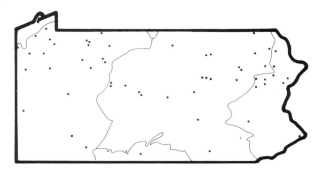

plankton and small insects, changing to a fish diet as adults. A wide range of foods are used if they are present in the habitat.[132,464,710]

Value The yellow perch is one of the most popular sport and commercial fishes in North America, largely because of its abundance and excellent food quality. It also is a valuable forage fish, especially for walleyes, in large lake and reservoir systems.

Genus *Percina*

Free edges of preopercle with weak teeth, or none; mouth small, the maxilla not reaching backward to middle of the eye; body depth contained less than 7 times in standard length; midline of belly with a single row of enlarged specialized scales; lateral line complete from the opercle at least to the hypural area.

KEY TO SPECIES OF *PERCINA*

1 a. Frenum absent or weakly developed: **2**
   b. Tip of upper jaw connected to snout by a well-developed frenum (Fig. 87,B—*P. maculata*): **3**
2 a. One or more specialized scales between pelvic fins, or on midline between pelvics and anus (Fig. 88,B): Channel darter, *P. copelandi*
   b. No specialized scales on midbelly but may have a

bridge of normal scales in front of anus; River darter, *P. shumardi*
3 a. Conical snout projecting beyond subterminal mouth; 15 or more thin vertical bars along body; lateral line scales usually more than 85: Logperch, *P. caprodes*
   b. Mouth terminal with no projecting snout; sides marked with black or dusky lateral band expanded into blotches or bars; lateral line scales usually less than 80: **4**

4 a. Head short and blunt; greatest depth of head about 1.5 times in head length: Gilt darter, *P. evides*

  b. Head not noticeably short and blunt; greatest depth of head from 1.7 to 2.1 times in head length: **5**

5 a. Opercles well scaled; few or no scales on cheeks (Fig. 91,C): **6**

  b. Opercles scaleless or with a few scattered scales; cheeks with no scales visible (Fig. 91,B): **8**

6 a. Gill covers well divided, meeting in an acute angle over isthmus (Fig. 89,B): Blackside darter, *P. maculata*

  b. Gill covers moderately joined across isthmus, resulting in an angle of almost 90 degrees between membranes: **7**

7 a. Snout noticeably longer than the anterior-posterior diameter of eye; body longer and slenderer; greatest body depth about 6 times in standard length, and more than 1.5 times in head length: Sharpnose darter, *P. oxyrhyncha*

  b. Length of snout about equal to anterior-posterior diameter of eye; body shorter and stouter; greatest body depth about 5 times in standard length, and less than 1.5 times in head length: Slenderhead darter, *P. phoxocephala*

8 a. Lateral line scales usually more than 70; midline of belly with 10 or more specialized scales anterior to anus (Fig. 88,B): Longhead darter, *P. macrocephala*

  b. Lateral line scales usually less than 60; midline of belly scaleless, or with only a few isolated specialized scales anterior to anus: Shield darter, *P. peltata*

Logperch, *Percina caprodes* (Rafinesque)[726]

Length 120 mm. West Pike Run, Washington County, Pa. 18 September 1980

Distribution The two recognized subspecies of the logperch have an extensive midwestern distribution from Hudson Bay to the Gulf of Mexico.[722] In Pennsylvania, it is restricted to the Ohio River and Great Lakes drainages. It is not only found in stream riffles but is also abundant in large lakes. I have seen dense spawning populations of logperch near the mouth of small streams tributary to Lake Erie. The young are found about dense beds of vegetation; adults are taken up to a depth of 30 feet in large lakes.[895,902] It is not a swift-water species and can tolerate quite turbid conditions.[264] Its tolerance to wide environmental conditions is accompanied by high meristic diversity.[37]

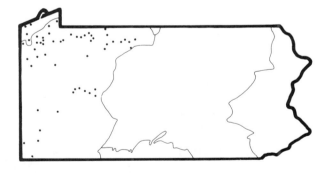

Behavior The spawning behavior consists of pairs depositing eggs and sperm at random on sandy riffles which are shared by many other individuals. There is no nest preparation or guarding of eggs or young.[966,967] It is one of the larger darters, often reaching a length of 5 inches.

Food Midges and microcrustaceans are the most important items of diet, with a change to larger organisms such as mayflies as the fish grow.[213,464,895]

Value The logperch has little potential for sport fisheries because of its small size. Where populations are abundant, it is important for large, bottom-feeding game fishes. It is sometimes mistaken for the young of walleyes.

Channel darter, *Percina copelandi* (Jordan)[454]

Length 50 mm. Allegheny River, Warren County, Pa. 14 July 1975

Distribution This species has a widespread, but disjunct, distribution throughout the upper Mississippi River drainage, and extends its range into the Great Lakes watershed. It is quite rare in Pennsylvania, with localized populations in the Allegheny River and in Lake Erie. It is most often found on wave-washed lake beaches or in pools of larger streams over a sand or gravel bottom.[173,835]

Behavior Sexual dimorphism is prominent in the channel darter. There is a short migration to spawning grounds, where males defend a small territory on a riffle. It has a primitive type of spawning. Adhesive eggs are scattered over clean, fine gravel in moderate current, but there is no care of eggs or young.[173,965] It is quite tolerant to turbidity and is often found associated with the logperch and the mimic shiner.

Food The diet of this darter is in keeping with its small

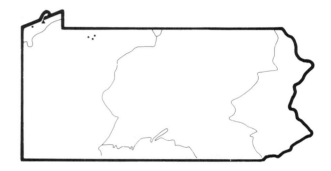

size, changing from small midges and mayfly naiads to larger aquatic insects and crustacea as the fish grows. It is a generalized benthic feeder.[908,965]

Value Due to its scarcity and small size, there is very little management interest associated with this fish. Its life history has not been studied extensively.

Gilt darter, *Percina evides* (Jordan and Copeland)[453]

Length 51 mm. South Fork of Mills River, Henderson County, N.C. 15 August 1979

Distribution The gilt darter has a scattered, midwestern distribution mostly in the upper Mississippi and Ohio River drainages, reaching its northeastern limit in the Allegheny River of Pennsylvania and New York. It is usually found in small rivers among large gravel or rocks in moderate current. It seldom is as abundant as other fishes such as the banded darter found in these localities.[203,704,733]

Behavior Sexual dimorphism is prominent, with larger and more brightly colored males found on riffles in the spring. These are assumed to be breeding males, although no spawning has been observed.[203] The gilt darter is one of the smaller darters, reaching an adult size of about 2.5 inches.

Food Aquatic insects are assumed to be important items of diet, although no food studies have been reported.[902]

Value There is little apparent interest in this small incon-

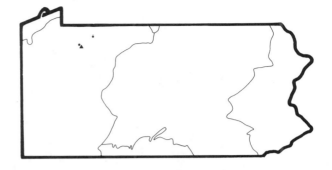

spicuous darter. Populations seldom are abundant enough to be important as a forage species.[203]

Longhead darter, *Percina macrocephala* (Cope)[161]

Length 88 mm. Allegheny River, Warren County, Pa. 13 August 1974

Distribution The longhead darter has a restricted distribution in the upper Ohio River drainage. It was originally described from three specimens collected from the Youghiogheny River in Pennsylvania, but now is probably extirpated from this system due to acid mine pollution. It remains as a rare form in several other localities in the Allegheny River.[53,196,438] This species is an upland, large-stream darter found in fast, rocky riffles, or in clean pools below these riffles. In a few localities in the Allegheny River it is quite common. It is often associated with the streamline chub and the black redhorse.

Behavior Although the spawning habits of many other darters are well known, there appears to be no published observations on spawning of this species.[129,684] It is one of the larger darters, sometimes exceeding 4 inches in length.

Food Based on the stomach analysis of very few speci-

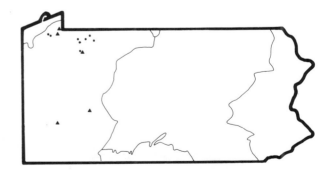

mens, mayflies and small crayfish appeared in the diet of this darter.[684]

Value This species demands large rivers with clean, rocky riffles and pools. It is valuable therefore as a clean-stream indicator species. It is rarely seen or identified by anglers.

Blackside darter, *Percina maculata* (Girard)[307]

Length 72 mm. Red Bank Creek, Jefferson County, Pa. 6 July 1967

Distribution The blackside ranges widely throughout the Mississippi River drainage, but is absent from Atlantic slope streams, where it is replaced in similar habitat by the shield darter.[698,895] It is abundant in northwestern Pennsylvania. It usually prefers the slower-moving water of streams with clean bottoms, avoiding the fast, rocky riffles inhabited by sympatric species such as the longhead and spotted darters.[321,461]

Behavior The spawning behavior is very primitive. There is an upstream migration to congregate on spawning grounds. Males do not hold territories or guard the eggs, which are deposited on sand or fine gravel in slow riffles.[895,966,967] There is very little sexual dimorphism of breeding adults, with no breeding tubercles or fin enlargement.[698] Populations may be large, but the fish is seldom seen by anglers because of its small size. Breeding adults seldom exceed 2.5 inches in length.[895] It is a common associate of smallmouth bass and rock bass.[344]

Food The diet of young blackside darters is dominated

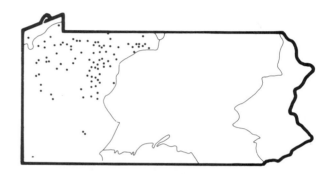

by zooplankton and small midges. This changes to larger mayflies, caddisflies, and other invertebrates as the darters grow.[461,908] Some algae and fish eggs are occasionally found in stomachs.

Value This darter may be of value as forage for game fishes when populations are abundant. Otherwise it is of very little interest to anglers.

Sharpnose darter, *Percina oxyrhyncha* (Hubbs and Raney)[416]

Length 86 mm. New River, Va. Summer 1975

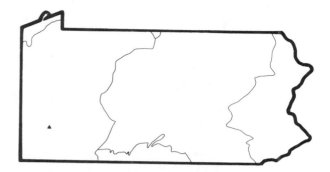

Distribution This uncommon darter has a geographical range restricted to the west slope of the central Appalachians. It was extirpated from its only reported site in Pennsylvania probably in the early 1900s when acid water from coal mining decimated almost the entire fish fauna from the main stem of the Monongahela River. The species persists in some large, clean mountain streams of Virginia and West Virginia.[206,438] It is most often found in swift water on clean, rocky riffles[377] in association with the hog sucker and longnose dace.[239,416]

Behavior This darter probably spawns in the spring, although no observations have been published. Sexual dimorphism is not prominent. It occasionally hybridizes with the Piedmont darter.[206,377] It is also similar to and was originally not recognized as distinct from the slenderhead darter in the Monongahela River, Pennsylvania.[239]

Food There are no data available on the diet of this darter, although aquatic insects are assumed to be important.[206]

Value This rare species with a restricted distribution may be of value in monitoring environmental changes in clean, large rivers.

Shield darter, *Percina peltata* (Stauffer)[874]

Length 74 mm. East Licking Creek, Juniata County, Pa. 17 July 1979

Distribution The shield darter is limited to the moderate-sized headwaters of Atlantic coastal streams from North Carolina to New York. Its close relative, the stripeback darter, with which it occasionally hybridizes, has not been found further north than the Patuxent River in Maryland.[562,752] The shield darter in Pennsylvania is abundant in the Delaware and Susquehanna drainages, but seldom is found in large numbers at one locality. This darter prefers streams with clean gravel and moderate current, but is sometimes found in vegetation when it is present.[667]

Behavior Breeding pairs of the shield darter undergo courtship leading to a spawning embrace at which time eggs are buried in the fine gravel of a riffle in moderate current. No care of eggs ensues. There is no spawning migration, but males defend small territories on the riffle used for spawning.[667] The shield darter is similar in appearance, habitat, and spawning behavior to the allopatric blackside darter. It is commonly associated with the

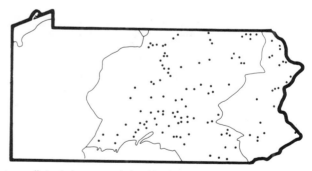

tessellated darter and the blacknose dace.

Food No food studies have been reported, but aquatic insects are presumed to be important items of diet.[667,752]

Value In the few instances when populations are moderately abundant, the shield darter may be an important forage fish; otherwise it has little value to anglers. When seen, it is often mistaken for a small walleye.

Slenderhead darter, *Percina phoxocephala* (Nelson)[656]

Length 61 mm. Neosho River, Lyon County, Kan. 13 August 1966

Distribution This darter has a wide midwestern distribution in the Mississippi, Ohio, and Great Lakes drainages.[37,172] To my knowledge, it has never been collected in Pennsylvania. Specimens reported from the Monongahela River[239] as the slenderhead darter have been re-identified and catalogued at the University of Michigan (UMMZ 196888) as the sharpnose darter. This species prefers clean sand or gravel, or rocky riffles, and is often abundant together with the hog sucker and spotted bass. The juveniles generally are found in shallow water riffles, while the adults prefer the deeper water of river channels.[685]

Behavior Males move onto a spawning riffle in late spring and presumably establish territories, although no observations were made of actual courtship or spawning. Young and juveniles were found near these shallow-water spawning bars for several weeks after hatching. The adults leave these areas soon after spawning to spend most of the year in deeper water habitats.[685] The slenderhead is one of the larger darters, often exceeding 3 inches during their third year.

Food The young darters feed mainly on midge larvae, with adults preferring the larvae of midges, mayflies, and caddisflies. Other aquatic insects such as stoneflies and beetles were not found in stomachs, although they were abundant in the feeding area.[37,461,895]

Value Large populations of slenderhead darters sometimes occur but are seldom used as forage by game fishes such as the spotted bass, which is a common associate. Segregation by microhabitat may be one reason for this lack of predation.

River darter, *Percina shumardi* (Girard)[307]

Length 69 mm. Ouachita River, Sterlington, La. USNM 172292

Distribution The river darter has an extensive north-south distribution in the midwest from the Gulf Coast to the Hudson Bay drainage in Canada. It probably does not occur in Pennsylvania but is a potential future migrant up the Ohio River as water quality improves in this area.[839] It is usually found in large rivers or major tributaries in strong currents of channels or fast deep riffles,[172] over a bottom of coarse gravel or rock.

Behavior The spawning of this darter has not been observed, but the anal fin of the breeding male is enlarged and possible has some use in courtship or breeding.

Spawning probably occurs in the spring. It is one of the commonest darters in large turbid streams, tolerating such conditions better than most darters. The limited data available suggest that a size of about 3 inches is reached during its third summer of growth.[895]

Food The diet of the river darter is mostly midge and caddisfly larvae, though various other small invertebrates are found in stomachs.[895]

Value This darter is seldom seen or recognized by anglers because of its large-river habitat and small population size. There is little possibility that it contributes much as forage for game species.

Genus *Stizostedion*

Free edges of preopercle with strong teeth; mouth large, the maxilla extending backward to middle of eye; large canine teeth present; eye silvery due to presence of reflective layer, the tapetum lucidum; pseudobranchiae well developed; space between pelvic fins equal to length of pelvic base; anterior-most interhaemal bone not greatly enlarged.

KEY TO SPECIES OF *STIZOSTEDION*

1 a. Membranes of first dorsal fin with definite spots, but no black blotch at posterior base; usually 5 pyloric caeca, each shorter than stomach: Sauger, *S. canadense*

b. Membranes of first dorsal fin without definite spots, but with black blotch at posterior base; usually 3 pyloric caeca, each about as long as stomach: Walleye, *S. vitreum**

Sauger, *Stizostedion canadense* Cuvier[184]

Length 228 mm. Mississippi River, Quincy, Ill. 6 September 1941

Distribution The range of the sauger includes much of the central part of the United States and southern Canada, but does not include Atlantic Coast drainages.[902] There are records prior to 1900 of its occurrence in the Allegheny, Beaver, and Youghiogheny rivers,[274] but it has been absent from these watersheds until very recently. It is now fairly abundant in the lower Allegheny River. The normal habitat of the sauger is silty rivers and large turbid lakes. In contrast to the walleye, the sauger is quite tolerant of turbid waters and silty bottoms, which may increase its survival in such habitats.[211,713,939]

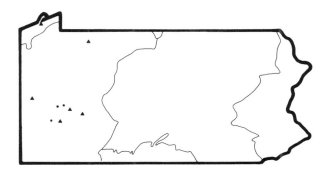

Behavior Saugers spawn in early spring along gravelly shores of lakes[713] or on rubble substrates of the tailrace of large reservoirs.[662] Spawning is initiated at temperatures of about 45°F, but no actual spawning has been

*The blue pike of Lakes Erie and Ontario is recognized by some authors[878,902] as either subspecies or distinct species. It has somewhat larger eyes, shorter bony interorbital space, and bluish body color without the brassy or yellow mottlings. It now appears to be very rare, if not extinct.

reported. The growth of the sauger is somewhat slower than the walleye. A length of 23 inches in about 7 years would be considered as good growth for female saugers;[123,923] males grow somewhat more slowly. Northern populations also grow more slowly,[118,475] as indicated by the Lake Nipigon population in which females only reached a length of 21 inches in 11 years.[360]

Food The food of young saugers consists mostly of zooplankton and midge larvae, changing gradually to forage fishes as the saugers grow. Some feeding selectivity was shown by adult saugers in that abundant young freshwater drum were avoided in preference to trout perch and emerald shiners. Saugers of all sizes used midge larvae extensively.[133,202,712]

Value In large lakes and reservoirs, the sauger is an important sport fish, contributing to a winter ice fishery as well as fishing on spawning runs and during active growing seasons.

Walleye, *Stizostedion vitreum* (Mitchill)[638]

Length 124 mm. Allegheny River, Warren County, Pa. 14 August 1975

Distribution The native range of the walleye includes most of central North America from British Columbia to the Gulf of Mexico. It has been introduced into the Susquehanna and Delaware drainages and elsewhere outside its native range as a popular food and sport fish. It is most abundant in large clear-water lakes, but adapts well to large river systems. It is often the top fish predator, occurring sympatrically with yellow perch and sauger and often giving way to the sauger as turbidity increases.[671,760,772]

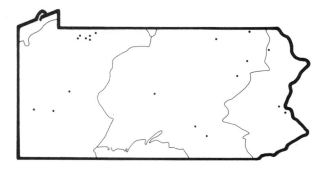

Behavior The walleye is a communal spawner along stony beaches of lakes,[233] but often migrates long distances upstream to spawn on flooded marsh grass.[714] Studies of tagged walleyes on spawning ground in large connected systems of rivers and lakes have demonstrated that walleyes return year after year to the same spawning site, which may be a long distance from their usual habitat.[181] The rarely observed spawning act consists of a series of violent synchronized acts by promiscuous groups of fish.[230] There is no nest preparation or care of the eggs after spawning.

The reported large differences in growth rate are related to climate and abundance of forage fishes, with females living longer and growing to larger sizes than males. An individual of 42 inches and 23 pounds was caught in spawn-taking operations from Georgian Bay of

Lake Huron.[839] Tagging studies have shown that some walleyes live at least 14 years.[236]

Food The diet of walleyes changes from zooplankton and midge larvae to fish, sometimes at an early age due to food shortages.[212,214,492] Adult walleyes are considered to be highly predacious, and often utilize abundant stocks of small yellow perch as food.[445]

Value The walleye is an important sport and commercial fish in North America and is widely cultured and stocked. It is the top predator in many large waters, and is sometimes considered helpful in controlling overabundant populations of yellow perch and other panfishes.[233,760]

Drums—Sciaenidae

A large family of predominantly marine species, the drums and croakers are important sport and commercial fishes over much of the shallow ocean areas of the world. Only one species occurs in fresh waters of North America.

Genus *Aplodinotus*

Spiny-rayed, physoclistous, with ctenoid scales; anal spines 2, second one long and stout; lateral line extending well onto caudal fin; in head region the canals form deep channels in cranial bones; very large otoliths present in inner ear; lower pharyngeals broad, heavy, fused, and with blunt, molar teeth; head scaly; dorsal deeply notched, but not completely separated.

Freshwater drum, *Aplodinotus grunniens* Rafinesque[728]

Length 300 mm. Lake Erie, Erie County, Pa. 5 October 1981

Distribution The range of the freshwater drum covers most of central North America, with a very extensive north to south distribution from the Hudson Bay to Central America.[47] It was once reported as common in the Allegheny and Monongahela Rivers of Pennsylvania,[239,274] but in recent years we have found it common only in Lake Erie.

The drum prefers large, shallow, fertile lakes or large river systems. It is a benthic, schooling fish preferring quiet pools or backwaters of large rivers or impoundments. It is often associated with the yellow perch or the white crappie.[186,383]

Behavior The noisy communal spawning of large

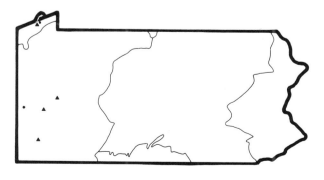

schools of the freshwater drum is similar to that of marine drums and croakers.[187,819,970] The eggs are unique

209

for a freshwater species since they are planktonic.[192] This species is also unusual in having large otoliths that are sometimes saved as lucky stones and are common artifacts found in Indian middens in the Mississippi River Valley.[283] These ancient otoliths, many of which were carbon-dated from 3600 to 3700 B.C., indicate that the drum taken by these early Indians were very similar in size to present populations.[971]

Recent studies on the growth rate of the freshwater drum show good growth to be about 18 inches in 7 years,[113,822] while the slow-growing Lake Erie population takes 13 years to reach the same size.[228]

Food Although the presence of powerful grinding pharyngeal teeth has sometimes been associated with the use of freshwater mussels as food,[139] other food studies have shown burrowing mayflies and amphipods to be important food items for all sizes of drum.[186,202,710]

Value This drum is not esteemed as a food fish, but it has become more important as a commercial species in large rivers and in Lake Erie as the stocks of more preferred species have declined.[139,228]

Sculpins—Cottidae

Second infraorbital united with preopercle; head very large in proportion to rest of body, eyes placed high; mouth large, teeth in villiform bands; premaxillae protractile; body naked except for presence of small prickles; dorsal with a spinous portion (composed of soft, flexible spines) and a soft-rayed portion; no anal spines; pelvic fins with one flexible spine incorporated with first soft ray.

Most sculpins are marine fishes of arctic and temperate seas found in the northern hemisphere, but one genus in particular (*Cottus*) has adapted to freshwater conditions and has differentiated into many forms now described as separate species. These bottom-dwelling headwater fishes are small size when compared with their many marine relatives.

KEY TO SPECIES OF COTTIDAE

1 a. Dorsal fins separated by a distinct gap; margin of gill membrane free from isthmus: Deepwater sculpin, *Myoxocephalus thompsoni*

   b. Dorsal fins touching or narrowly joined; margin of gill membrane attached to isthmus: **2**

2 a. Lateral line complete: Spoonhead sculpin, *Cottus ricei*

   b. Lateral line incomplete: **3**

3 a. Palatine teeth absent (Fig. 93); usually 3 soft pelvic rays (Fig. 94,A); caudal peduncle length greater than postorbital distance: Slimy sculpin, *Cottus cognatus*

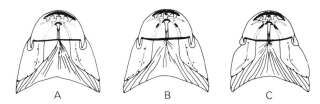

Figure 93. No teeth on palatines in *C cognatus* (A), palatine teeth present in *C. bairdi* (B) and *C. girardi* (C). (Part of lower jaw removed to show inside of upper jaw.)

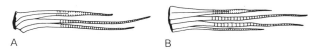

Figure 94. Pelvic fin of one spine and three soft rays (A), or one spine and four soft rays (B).

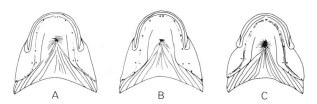

Figure 95. Sensory pores on mandible showing double median chin pore on *C. cognatus* (A) and *C. bairdi* (B), or single median chin pore on *C. girardi* (C).

   b. Palatine teeth present (Fig. 93); usually 4 soft pelvic rays (Fig. 94,B); caudal peduncle length less than postorbital distance: Mottled sculpin, *Cottus bairdi,* and Potomac sculpin, *Cottus girardi**

Genus *Cottus*

Spiny dorsal and soft dorsal fins touching or narrowly joined; margin of gill membrane attached to isthmus; second preopercular spine covered with skin, directed downwards; preopercular-mandibular pores present.

*Although all individuals of these two species can be distinguished by a combination of several morphometric and meristic characters,[882] no single character provides complete separation. Characters which favor the mottled sculpin are a uniform pigment pattern on the chin, double chin pore (Fig. 95), and variable mottling on the back anterior to the soft dorsal fin. Characters which favor the Potomac sculpin are a strongly mottled pigment pattern on the chin, single chin pore, and no pigment bars or blotches on the back anterior to the soft dorsal fin.

Mottled sculpin, *Cottus bairdi* Girard[302]

Length 71 mm. Saline River, Washtenaw County, Mich. 15 September 1976

Distribution The range of this species covers much of the central portion of the United States and Canada, where it is a common and sometimes abundant inhabitant of clear upland and mountain streams.[413,796] It is often associated with brook trout and brown trout in eastern North America,[344] but it is also found in waters too warm for trout. There is an interesting relict population of the mottled sculpin on the Maryland coastal plain of the Susquehanna River.[282] Our recent collections have extended the range of this relict population into southeastern Pennsylvania. The systematic status of several forms of this species is not completely agreed upon, but there is no doubt that the species is highly variable.[796]

Behavior The mottled sculpin spawns early in the spring. Males select a cavity beneath a rock in a stream riffle. Elaborate display and courtship of females ends with egg laying on the underside of stones, in one or more sticky egg masses.[816] Males then guard the nests during incubation.[27,349,860]

In the absence of body scales in sculpins, otoliths have been successfully used for age determination. From these studies it appears that mottled sculpins grow to maximum sizes of about 5 inches in 5 years,[27]

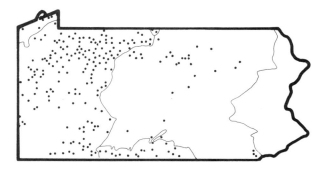

with mature males growing somewhat faster than females.

Food The diet of the mottled sculpin consists mainly of aquatic insects, amphipods, and isopods, with some selectivity toward midge larvae.[188,209,495]

Value This sculpin is occasionally used as bait while fishing for trout, and is probably important as natural forage where abundant. The effect of sculpin predation on salmonid eggs, often cited in early reports, appears to be minimal.[323,791]

Slimy sculpin, *Cottus cognatus* Richardson[786]

Length 93 mm. Sinking Run, Blair County, Pa. 17 September 1978

Distribution The slimy sculpin has an extended east to west distribution in North America from New Brunswick to Alaska, and also occurs in Siberia. On the east coast, it occurs as far south as Virginia. In Pennsylvania it is curiously missing from the headwaters of the Ohio River system, being replaced there by the mottled sculpin. It is found in streams or lakes over a clean bottom. Despite the variability of both the slimy sculpin and the mottled sculpin, a combination of several characters is usually sufficient to properly identify all specimens.[592] Hybrids between these two species were recently discovered and validated by electrophoretic study from a large collection in Pennsylvania.[882]

Behavior The slimy sculpin spawns in the spring, as early as April in Minnesota or as late as June in Alaska.[168,699] The spawning behavior is very similar to that of the mottled sculpin.[494] Males guard the sticky egg mass laid in a cavity under a stone in fast current. Very few large eggs (100 to 700) are produced, varying with the size of the female, with differences noted between stream populations and those living in deep oligotrophic lakes.[259]

Growth and longevity varies with locality; extremely slow growth of about 4 inches in 7 years has been reported for an Arctic population, while this size is commonly reached in 3 years in more southern

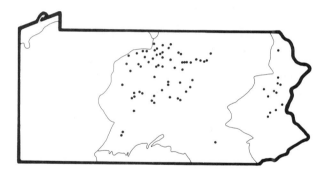

habitats.[168,699]

Food Populations of the slimy sculpin often become super-abundant in clear, stony streams, reaching at least 20 thousand per hectare, many times greater than the number of trout in the same stream section. This has led some to suggest that sculpin predation on trout eggs or fry may be serious under some conditions.[128] However, most food studies of the slimy sculpin indicate that midge larvae are favored, but many other aquatic insects are regularly consumed.[495]

Value This sculpin is often used as bait for large trout because of its ready availability in many trout streams.[699]

Potomac sculpin, *Cottus girardi* Robins[797]

Length 96 mm. Dry River, Rockingham County, Va. 17 August 1979

Distribution The present range of the Potomac sculpin appears to be mostly restricted to tributaries of the Potomac River system in Pennsylvania, Maryland, Virginia, and West Virginia, although we have discovered a population in the headwaters of the Susquehanna River nearby.[797] It has also been collected in upper tributaries of the James River in Virginia. The type locality of this species is the Conococheague Creek near Chambersburg, Pennsylvania, a site which supports a dense population of both the Potomac sculpin and the mottled sculpin. The Potomac sculpin is usually found in warm streams in rocky riffles and in quiet pools above these riffles. When the two species are sympatric, the mottled

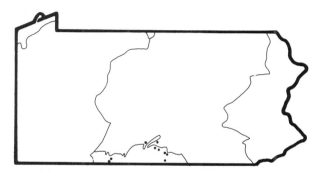

sculpin is likely to be more abundant in the riffles, and

the Potomac sculpin more abundant in the pools.

The morphometric variability of this species is similar to that of other sculpins, rendering identification very difficult for the beginner.[815] However, analyses of many morphometric and meristic characters, coupled with electrophoretic assays of several different proteins, has verified the existence of the Potomac sculpin as a distinct species.[882]

Behavior Due to the difficulty of species identification, there is little known about the life history of the Potomac sculpin. Its spawning behavior is likely to be similar to that of the mottled sculpin. This is inferred from observa-

tions of a mixed population of sculpins in aquaria.[816] The maximum size of the Potomac sculpin is often larger than the mottled sculpin in the same locality.

Food Although no food studies have been published, the diet of this sculpin is presumed to be similar to that of other stream sculpins. Midges and other small aquatic invertebrates probably form the bulk of the diet.

Value Where this species is abundant, it probably provides important forage for smallmouth bass. Otherwise, it is not often noticed by anglers.

Spoonhead sculpin, *Cottus ricei* (Nelson)[656]

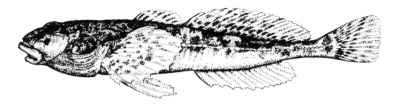

Scott and Crossman. 1973. Fish. Res. Bd. Canada Bull. 184, p. 839.

Distribution This small sculpin is the most distinctive one of its genus and exhibits remarkable stability in its meristic and morphological characters.[594] We have no records of this species from Pennsylvania, although it is present in the deep waters of Lake Erie.[916] It has a wide geographic range which includes all of the Great Lakes and an extensive northwest distribution through Canada to the Mackenzie and Peace River drainages.[606,944] The extremely flattened head, large head pores, and small eyes are apparent adaptations to turbid rivers or the deep waters of oligotrophic lakes where they are found. In the Apostle Islands area of Lake Superior, no individuals were taken at a depth of less than 20 fathoms, and the large majority were taken at depths between 40 and 50 fathoms.[217]

Behavior The spoonhead sculpin probably spawns in the summer, since ripe males were taken in August.[200] No observations have been published largely because of the deep-water or turbid habitat in which they are found.[606] It is a small sculpin, seldom exceeding 2.5 inches. Common benthic associates of this sculpin are the deep-water sculpin and the ninespine stickleback.[185]

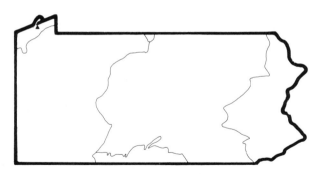

Food In the Great Lakes their food is said to consist of plankton and benthic aquatic insects, although no detailed food studies have been published.[606]

Value This species is a common forage fish found in stomachs of lake trout and burbot which occupy the deeper waters of the Great Lakes. More specimens of this sculpin have been recovered from stomachs than by other means of collecting.[197]

Genus *Myoxocephalus*

Spiny dorsal and soft dorsal fins separated by a distinct gap; margin of gill membrane free from isthmus; second preopercular spine directed backwards, conspicuous; preopercular-mandibular pores absent.

Deepwater sculpin, *Myoxocephalus thompsoni* (Girard)[303]

Scott and Crossman. 1973. Fish. Res. Bd. Canada Bull. 184, p. 842.

Distribution In adopting the common name, deepwater sculpin, for this form, we are following the suggestion to distinguish the freshwater subspecies *M. quadricornis thompsoni* from its marine relative, *M. q. quadricornis*.[606] Continuing studies strongly suggest that the deepwater sculpin is a species separate from the fourhorn sculpin. These landlocked, freshwater, glacial relict populations are known from large northern lakes in North America, and from Sweden, Finland, and European Russia.[185,944] We have no specimens from Pennsylvania, but it is probably present in the deep waters of Lake Erie. This unique species is much different from all other cottids in the freshwaters of North America. Several marine and freshwater forms are recognized in a highly complex series.[593]

The deepwater sculpin is found only at depths of more than 50 fathoms, and its presence is frequently discovered only by studying the food habits of the lake trout and the burbot.[197,217]

Behavior Spawning apparently occurs in summer, judging by the condition of gonads examined.[200,591] Growth of this fish has not been studied, but a few fish grow to

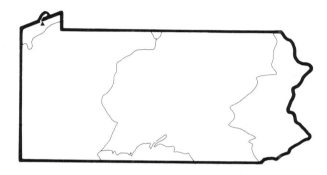

about 8 inches in freshwater, which is considerably smaller than marine forms.

Food The diet of this sculpin is mainly large copepods and midges, which are the most abundant invertebrates found at depths at which the sculpin is found.

Value This sculpin has some value as forage for lake trout and burbot, but little other value is apparent.

Literature Cited

1 Abbott, C. C. 1860. Descriptions of new species of American fresh-water fishes. Proc. Acad. Natur. Sci. Philadelphia 12: 325–328.

2 ———. 1862. Notes on the habits of *Aphredoderus sayanus*. Proc. Acad. Natur. Sci. Philadelphia 13(1861): 95–96.

3 ———. 1870. Notes on fresh-water fishes of New Jersey. Amer. Naturalist 4: 99–117.

4 ———. 1870. Mud-loving fishes. Amer. Naturalist 4: 385–391.

5 ———. 1874. Notes on the cyprinoids of central New Jersey. Amer. Natur. 8: 326–338.

6 ———. 1883. On the habits of certain sunfish. Amer. Natur. 17(2): 1254–1257.

7 Adams, C. C., and T. L. Hankinson. 1928. The ecology and economics of Oneida Lake fish. Bull. New York State College of Forestry 1(4a): 239–548.

8 Agassiz, J. L. R. 1850. Lake Superior. Its physical character, vegetation, and animals, compared with those of other and similar regions. Gould, Kendall, and Lincoln, Boston. 428 p.

9 ———. 1854. Notice of a collection of fishes from the southern bend of the Tennessee River, Alabama. Amer. J. Sci. 2nd ser. 17: 297–308; 353–369.

10 ———. 1855. Synopsis of the ichthyological fauna of the Pacific slope of North America, chiefly from the collections made by the expedition under the command of Capt. C. Wilkes, with recent additions and comparisons with eastern types. Amer. J. Sci. Arts. 2nd ser. 19(55): 71–99; 19(56): 215–232.

11 Aggus, L. R., and G. V. Elliott. 1975. Effects of cover and food on year-class strength of largemouth bass, p. 317–322. In: National symposium on the biology and management of the centrarchid basses. Henry Clepper, ed. Sport Fishing Institute, Washington, D. C. 534 p.

12 Allen, K. R. 1951. The Horokiwi Stream: a study of a trout population. New Zealand Marine Dept. Fish. Bull. 10. 238 p.

13 ———. 1961. Relations between salmonidae and the native freshwater fauna in New Zealand. N. Z. Ecological Soc. 8: 66–70.

14 Allen, W. R., and M. E. Clark. 1943. Bottom-preferences of fishes of northeastern Kentucky streams. Trans. Kentucky Acad. Sci. 11(2): 26–30.

15 Almy, G. 1978. Kokanee . . . the tiny tackle teasers of Upper Woods Pond. Pennsylvania Angler 47(4): 16–18.

16 Anas, R. E. 1959. Three-year-old pink salmon. J. Fish. Res. Bd. Canada 16(1): 91–94.

17 Anderson, L. R. 1948. Unusual items in the diet of the northern muskellunge, *Esox masquinongy immaculatus*. Copeia 1948(1): 63.

18 Anonymous. 1976. Glendale Lake produces world record Amur pike. Pennsylvania Angler 45(9): 32.

19 Applegate, R. L., J. W. Mullan, and D. I. Morais. 1967. Food and growth of six centrarchids from shoreline areas of Bull Shoals Reservoir. Proc. S-E Assn. Game Fish Comm. 20(1966): 469–482.

20 Applegate, V. C. 1943. Partial analysis of growth in a population of mudminnows, *Umbra limi* (Kirtland). Copeia 1943(2): 92–96.

21 ———. 1950. Natural history of the sea lamprey, *Petromyzon marinus*, in Michigan. U. S. Fish and Wildl. Serv. Spec. Sci. Rep. Fish. 55. 237 p.

22 ———. 1951. Sea lamprey investigations II. Egg development, maturity, egg production, and percentage of unspawned eggs of sea lampreys, *Petromyzon marinus*, captured in several Lake Huron tributaries. Pap. Michigan Acad. Sci. Arts Ltrs. 35 (1949): 71–90.

23 ———. 1961. Downstream movement of lampreys and fishes in Carp Lake River, Michigan. U. S. Fish and Wildl. Serv. Spec. Sci. Rep. Fish. 387. 71 p.

24 Atkinson, N. J. 1932. The destruction of grey trout eggs by suckers and bullheads. Trans. Amer. Fish. Soc. 61(1931): 183–188.

25 Atz, J. W. 1940. Reproductive behavior in the eastern Johnny darter, *Boleosoma nigrum olmstedi* (Storer). Copeia 1940(2): 100–107.

26 Backus, R. H. 1957. The fishes of Labrador. Bull. Amer. Mus. Nat. Hist. 113(4): 273–337.

27 Bailey, J. E. 1952. Life history and ecology of the sculpin *Cottus bairdi punctulatus* in southwestern Montana. Copeia 1952(4): 243–255.

28 ———. Alaska's fishery resources, the pink salmon. U. S. Fish Wildl. Serv., Fish. Leaflet 619. 8 p.

29 Bailey, R. M. 1938. The fishes of the Merrimack Watershed, p. 149–185. In: Biological survey of the Merrimack Watershed. Earl E. Hoover, ed. New Hampshire Fish and Game Comm. 238 p.

30 ———. 1941. Geographic variation in *Mesogonistius chaetodon* (Baird), with description of a new subspecies from Georgia and Florida. Univ. Michigan Mus. Zool. Occas. Pap. 454. 7 p.

31 ———. 1945. A review of "Some considerations of the distribution of fishes in Ontario," by Isobel Radforth. Copeia 1945(2): 125–126.

32 ———. 1951. A check list of the fishes of Iowa with keys for identification, p. 187–238. In: Iowa Fish and Fishing. Iowa State Cons. Comm.

33 ———. 1954. Distribution of the American cyprinid fish *Hybognathus hankinsoni* with comments on its original description. Copeia 1954 (4): 289–291.

34 ———. 1959. Distribution of the American cyprinid fish *Notropis anogenus*. Copeia 1959(2): 119–123.

35 Bailey, R. M., and M. O. Allum. 1962. Fishes of South Dakota. Univ. Michigan Mus. Zool. Misc. Publ. 119. 131 p.

36 Bailey, R. M., and F. B. Cross. 1954. River sturgeons of the American genus *Scaphirhynchus*: characters, distribution, and synonymy. Pap. Michigan Acad. Sci. Arts Ltrs. 39(1953): 169–208.

37 Bailey, R. M., and W. A. Gosline. 1955. Variation and systematic significance of vertebral counts in the American fishes of the family Percidae. Univ. Michigan Mus. Zool. Misc. Publ. 93. 44 p.

38 Baird, D. 1979. Rare fossil fish surfaces at The William Penn Memorial Museum. Pennsylvania Geology 10(2): 12–16.

39 Baird, S. F. 1855. Report on the fishes observed on the coast of New Jersey and Long Island during the summer of 1854. Ninth Ann. Rep. Smithsonian Inst. (1854): 317–337.

40 Baird, S. F., and C. Girard. 1854. Descriptions of new

species of fishes collected by Mr. John H. Clark on the U.S. and Mexican Boundary Survey, under Lt. Col. Jas. D. Graham. Proc. Acad. Natur. Sci. Philadelphia 6(1852–1853): 387–390.

41 ———. 1854. Descriptions of new species of fishes, collected by Captains R. B. Marcy and G. B. M'Clellan, in Arkansas. Proc. Acad. Natur. Sci. Philadelphia 6(1852–1853): 390–392.

42 Bajkov, A. 1927. Reports of the Jasper Park lakes investigations, 1925–26. I. The fishes. Contr. Canadian Biol. and Fish., n.s. 3(16): 379–404.

43 Baker, F. C. 1916. The relation of molluscs to fish in Oneida Lake. New York State College Forestry (Syracuse), Techn. Publ. 4. 16(21): 1–366.

44 Baldwin, N. S. 1950. The American smelt, Osmerus mordax (Mitchill) of South Bay, Manitoulin Island, Lake Huron. Trans. Amer. Fish. Soc. 78 (1948): 176–180.

45 Bardach, J. E., J. H. Todd, and R. Crickmer. 1966. Orientation by taste in fish of the genus Ictalurus. Science 155: 1276–1278.

46 Barker, E. E. 1918. The brook stickleback. Scientific Monthly 6: 526–529.

47 Barney, R. L. 1926. The distribution of the freshwater sheepshead, Aplodinotus grunniens Rafinesque, in respect to the glacial history of North America. Ecology 7(3): 351–364.

48 Barney, R. L., and B. J. Anson. 1923. Life history and ecology of the orange-spotted sunfish, Lepomis humilis. Rep. U.S. Commissioner of Fisheries for 1922, Appendix 15. 16 p. Bureau of Fisheries Document No. 938.

49 Barnickol, P. G. 1941. Food habits of Gambusia affinis from Reelfoot Lake, Tennessee, with special reference to malaria control. Report of Reelfoot Lake Biol. Sta. 5: 5–13.

50 Barnickol, P. G., and W. C. Starrett. 1951. Commercial and sport fishes of the Mississippi River between Caruthersville, Missouri, and Dubuque, Iowa. Bull. Illinois Nat. Hist. Surv. 25(5): 267–350.

51 Battle, H. I. 1940. The embryology and larval development of the goldfish (Carassius auratus L.) from Lake Erie. Ohio J. Sci. 40(2): 82–93.

52 Battle, H. I., and W. M. Sprules. 1960. A description of the semibuoyant eggs and early developmental stages of the goldeye, Hiodon alosoides (Rafinesque). J. Fish. Res. Bd. Canada 17(2): 245–266.

53 Bean, T. H. 1892. The fishes of Pennsylvania, p. 1–149. In: Rep. State Comm. Fish. (1889–90–91), Official Doc. 19, Harrisburg, Pa.

54 ———. 1894. Bibliography of the salmon of Alaska and adjacent regions. Bull. U. S. Fish. Comm. 12(1892): 39–49.

55 ———. 1903. Catalogue of the fishes of New York. Bull. New York State Mus. 60 (Zoology 9): 1–784.

56 Beckman, W. C. 1949. The rate of growth and sex ratio for seven Michigan fishes. Trans. Amer. Fish. Soc. 76: 63–81.

57 Beerbower, J. R., and M. H. Hait, Jr. 1959. Silurian fish in northeastern Pennsylvania and northern New Jersey. Proc. Pa. Acad. Sci. 33: 198–203.

58 Behmer, D. J. 1965. Spawning periodicity of the river carpsucker, Carpiodes carpio. Proc. Iowa Acad. Sci. 72: 253–262.

59 Bennett, G. W. 1954. Largemouth bass in Ridge Lake, Coles County, Illinois. Bull. Illinois Nat. Hist. Surv. 26(2): 217–275.

60 Bennett, G. W., and W. F. Childers. 1966. The lake chubsucker as a forage species. Progr. Fish-Cult. 28(2): 89–92.

61 Benson, N. G. 1953. The importance of ground water to trout populations in the Pigeon River, Michigan. Trans. North Amer. Wildl. Conf. 18: 269–281.

62 Berner, L. M. 1948. The intestinal convolutions: new generic characters for the separation of Carpiodes and Ictio-

bus. Copeia 1948(2): 140–141.

63 Berry, F. H. 1955. Food of the mudfish (Amia calva) in Lake Newman, Florida in relation to its management. Quart. J. Florida Acad. Sci. 18(1): 69–75.

64 ———. 1957. Age and growth of the gizzard shad (Dorosoma lacepedi) (LeSueur) in Lake Newman, Florida. Proc. S-E Assn. Game Fish. Comm. 11: 317–331.

65 ———. 1964. (Review and emendation of: Family Clupeidae, p. 257–454, in: Fishes of the western North Atlantic, by Samuel F. Hildebrand). Copeia 1964(4): 720–730.

66 Bersamin, S. V. 1958. A preliminary study of the nutritional ecology and food habits of the chubs (Leucichthys spp.) and their relation to the ecology of Lake Michigan. Pap. Michigan Acad. Sci. Arts Ltrs. 43: 107–118.

67 Bertin, L. 1956. Eels, a biological study. Cleaver-Hume Press Ltd., London. 192 p.

68 Bevelander, G. 1934. The gills of Amia calva specialized for respiration in an oxygen deficient environment. Copeia 1934(3): 123–127.

69 Bigelow, H. B., and W. C. Schroeder. 1953. Fishes of the Gulf of Maine. U. S. Fish and Wildl. Serv. Fish. Bull. 74, 1st revision. 577 p.

70 Birkhead, W. S. 1967. The comparative toxicity of stings of the ictalurid catfish genera Ictalurus and Schilbeodes. Comp. Biochem. Physiol. 22: 101–111.

71 Black, J. D. 1945. Natural history of the northern mimic shiner, Notropis volucellus volucellus Cope. Invest. Indiana Lakes and Streams 2: 450–469.

72 Blair, W. F., A. P. Blair, P. Brodkorb, F. R. Cagle, and G. A. Moore. 1957. Vertebrates of the United States. McGraw-Hill Book Co., New York. 819 p.

73 Bodola, A. 1966. Life history of the gizzard shad, Dorosoma cepedianum (LeSueur) in western Lake Erie. U. S. Fish and Wildl. Serv. Fish. Bull. 65(2): 391–425.

74 Boesel, M. W. 1938. The food of nine species of fish from the western end of Lake Erie. Trans. Amer. Fish. Soc. 67(1937): 215–223.

75 Bonham, K. 1941. Food of gars in Texas. Trans. Amer. Fish. Soc. 70(1940): 356–362.

76 Bonn, E. W. 1953. The food and growth rate of young white bass (Morone chrysops) in Lake Texoma. Trans. Amer. Fish. Soc. 82(1952): 213–221.

77 Borgeson, D. P., and G. W. McCammon. 1967. White catfish (Ictalurus catus) of the Sacramento-San Joaquin delta. California Fish Game 53(4): 254–263.

78 Bowen, E. S. 1931. The role of the sense organs in aggregations of Ameiurus melas. Ecological Monogr. 1: 1–35.

79 ———. 1932. Further studies of the aggregating behavior of Ameiurus melas. Biol. Bull. 63(2): 258–270.

80 Bowman, M. L. 1970. Life history of the black redhorse, Moxostoma duquesnei (Lesueur), in Missouri. Trans. Amer. Fish. Soc. 99(3): 546–559.

81 Branson, B. A. 1961. Observations on the distribution of nuptial tubercles in some catostomid fishes. Trans. Kansas Acad. Sci. 64(4): 360–372.

82 ———. 1962. Observations on the breeding tubercles of some Ozarkian minnows with notes on the barbels of Hybopsis. Copeia 1962(3): 532–539.

83 Branson, B. A., and G. A. Moore. 1962. The lateralis components of the acoustico-lateralis system in the sunfish family Centrarchidae. Copeia 1962(1): 1–108.

84 Breder, C. M., Jr. 1920. Some notes on Leuciscus vandoisulus (Cuv. & Val.). Copeia 1920(82): 85–88.

85 ———. 1920. Further notes on Leuciscus vandiosulus (Cuv. & Val.). Copeia 1920(87): 87–90.

86 ———. 1924. The little redfish (Oncorhynchus nerka) at Scranton, Pennsylvania. Copeia 1924(136): 97–99.

87 ———. 1928. On the appetite of Amiatus calva (Linnaeus). Copeia 1928(167): 54–56.

88 ———. 1935. The reproductive habits of the common catfish, Ameiurus nebulosus (Lesueur), with a discussion of their significance in ontogeny and phylogeny. Zoologica

19: 143–185.

89 ———. 1936. I. The reproductive habits of the North American sunfishes (family Centrarchidae). Zoologica 21: 1–48.

90 ———. 1939. Variations in the nesting habits of *Ameiurus nebulosus* (LeSueur). Zoologica 24(25): 367–377.

91 ———. 1940. The nesting behavior of *Eupomotis gibbosus* (Linnaeus) in a small pool. Zoologica 25(23): 353–360.

92 Breder, C. M., Jr., and D. R. Crawford. 1922. The food of certain minnows. A study of the seasonal dietary cycle of six cyprinoids with especial reference to fish culture. Zoologica 2(14): 287–327.

93 Breder, C. M., Jr., and R. F. Nigrelli. 1935. The influence of temperature and other factors on the winter aggregations of the sunfish, *Lepomis auritus,* with critical remarks on the social behavior of fishes. Ecology 16(1): 33–47.

94 Breder, C. M., and A. C. Redmond. 1929. The blue-spotted sunfish. A contribution to the life history and habits of *Enneacanthus* with notes on other Lepominae. Zoologica 9: 379–401.

95 Breder, C. M., Jr., and D. E. Rosen. 1966. Modes of reproduction in fishes. Natural History Press, Garden City, New York. 941 p.

96 Brezner, J. 1958. Food habits of the northern river carpsucker in Missouri. Progr. Fish-Cult. 20(4): 170–174.

97 Bridges, C. H., and J. W. Mullan. 1958. A compendium of the life history and ecology of the eastern brook trout *Salvelinus fontinalis* (Mitchill). Massachusetts Div. Fish Game. Fish. Bull. 23. 38 p.

98 Brigham, W. U. 1973. Nest construction of the lamprey, *Lampetra aepyptera.* Copeia 1973(1): 135–136.

99 Brown, B. E., and J. S. Dendy. 1961. Observations on the food habits of the flathead and blue catfish in Alabama. Proc. S-E Assn. Game Fish. Comm. 15(1961): 219–222.

100 Brown, C. J. D. 1971. Fishes of Montana. Big Sky Books, Montana State Univ., Bozeman. 207 p.

101 Brown, C. J. D., and A. C. Fox. 1966. Mosquitofish (*Gambusia affinis*) in a Montana pond. Copeia 1966(3): 614–616.

102 Brown, J. L. 1957. A key to the species and subspecies of the cyprinodont genus *Fundulus* in the United States and Canada east of the continental divide. J. Washington Acad. Sci. 47(3): 69–77.

103 Brown, W. H. 1951. Results of stocking largemouth black bass and channel catfish in experimental Texas farm ponds. Trans. Amer. Fish. Soc. 80(1950): 210–217.

104 Brummett, A. R. 1966. Observations on the eggs and breeding season of *Fundulus heteroclitus* at Beaufort, North Carolina. Copeia 1966(3): 616–620.

105 Bryant, W. L. 1934. New fishes from the Triassic of Pennsylvania. Proc. Amer. Philo. Soc. 73: 319–326.

106 Brynildson, O. M., V. A. Hacker, and T. A. Klick. 1963. Brown trout. Its life history, ecology and management. Wisconsin Cons. Dept. Publ. 234. 15 p.

107 Buchholz, M. 1957. Age and growth of the river carpsucker in Des Moines River, Iowa. Proc. Iowa Acad. Sci. 64: 589–600.

108 Burkhead, N. M., R. E. Jenkins, and E. G. Maurakis. 1980. New records, distribution and diagnostic characters of Virginia ictalurid catfishes with an adnexed adipose fin. Brimleyana (4): 75–93.

109 Burnet, A. M. R. 1968. A study of the relationships between brown trout and eels in a New Zealand stream. New Zealand Marine Dept. Fish. Tech. Rep. 26. 49 p.

110 Burr, B. M., and L. M. Page. 1979. The life history of the least darter, *Etheostoma microperca,* in the Iroquois River, Illinois. Illinois Natur. Hist. Surv. Biol. Notes 112: 1–15.

111 Burress, R. M. 1965. A quantitative creel census on two arms of Bull Shoals Reservoir, Missouri. Proc. S-E Assn. Game Fish Comm. 16: 387–398.

112 Buss, K. 1957. The controversial kokanee—a salmon for the lakes of northeastern United States. Pa. Fish Comm. Spec. Purpose Rep. 13 p.

113 Butler, R. L., and L. L. Smith, Jr. 1950. The age and rate of growth of the sheepshead, *Aplodinotus grunniens* Rafinesque, in the upper Mississippi River navigation pools. Trans. Amer. Fish. Soc. 79(1949): 43–54.

114 Cahn, A. R. 1929. The effect of carp on a small lake; the carp as a dominant. Ecology 10(3): 271–274.

115 Canfield, H. L. 1922. Care and feeding of buffalofish in ponds. U. S. Bur. Fish., Econ. Circ. 56. 3 p.

116 Carbine, W. F. 1939. Observations on the spawning habits of centrarchid fishes in Deep Lake, Oakland County, Michigan. Trans. North Amer. Wildl. Conf. 4: 275–287.

117 ———. 1942. Observations on the life history of the northern pike, *Esox lucius* L., in Houghton Lake, Michigan. Trans. Amer. Fish. Soc. 71: 149–164.

118 Carlander, K. D. 1950. Growth rate studies of saugers, *Stizostedion canadense canadense* (Smith) and yellow perch, *Perca flavescens* (Mitchill) from Lake of the Woods, Minnesota. Trans. Amer. Fish. Soc. 79(1949): 30–42.

119 Carlander, K. D., and R. E. Cleary. 1949. The daily activity patterns of some freshwater fishes. Amer. Midl. Naturalist 41(2): 447–452.

120 Carlson, D. R. 1966. Age and growth of the stonecat, *Noturus flavus* Rafinesque, in the Vermillion River. Proc. South Dakota Acad. Sci. 45: 131–137.

121 Carnes, W. C., Jr. 1958. Contributions to the biology of the eastern creek chubsucker, *Erimyzon oblongus oblongus* (Mitchill). MS thesis, North Carolina State Coll., Raleigh. 69 p.

122 Cartier, D., and E. Magnin. 1967. La croissance en longueur et en poids des *Amia calva* L. de la region de Montreal. Canadian J. Zool. 45(4): 797–804.

123 Carufel, L. H. 1963. Life history of saugers in Garrison Reservoir. J. Wildl. Manag. 27(3): 450–456.

124 Carver, D. C. 1967. Distribution and abundance of the centrarchids in the recent delta of the Mississippi River. Proc. S-E Assn. Game Fish. Comm. 20: 390–404.

125 Chamberlain, F. M. 1907. Some observations on salmon and trout in Alaska. U. S. Comm. Fish. (1906). 112 p.

126 Childers, W. F. 1967. Hybridization of four species of sunfishes (Centrarchidae). Bull. Illinois Nat. Hist. Surv. 29(3): 159–214.

127 Churchill, W. S. 1947. The brook lamprey in the Brule River. Trans. Wisconsin Acad. Sci. Arts Ltrs. 37(1945): 337–346.

128 Clary, J. R. 1972. Predation on the brown trout by the slimy sculpin. Progr. Fish-Cult. 34(2): 91–95.

129 Clay, W. M. 1975. The fishes of Kentucky. Kentucky Dept. Fish and Wildl. Resources, Frankfort. 416 p.

130 Claypole, E. W. 1885. Discovery of pteraspidian fish in the upper Silurian rocks of North America. Quart. J. Geol. Soc. London 41: 48–64.

131 Clemens, H. P., and K. E. Sneed. 1957. The spawning behavior of the channel catfish, *Ictalurus punctatus.* U. S. Fish and Wildl. Serv. Spec. Sci. Rep. Fish. 219. 11 p.

132 Clemens, W. A., J. R. Dymond, and N. K. Bigelow. 1923. Food studies of Lake Nipigon fishes. Univ. Toronto Studies. Publ. Ontario Fish Res. Lab. 25: 103–165.

133 Clemens, W. A., J. R. Dymond, N. K. Bigelow, F. B. Adamstone, and W. J. K. Harkness. 1923. The food of Lake Nipigon fishes. Publ. Ontario Fish. Res. Lab. 16: 171–188.

134 Clepper, H., ed. 1975. National symposium on the biology and management of the centrarchid basses. Tulsa, Oklahoma, 3–6 February 1975. Publ. by Sport Fishing Institute, Washington, D. C. 534 p.

135 Clinton, D. 1824. Description of a new species of fish from the Hudson River (*Clupea hudsoni*). Ann. Lyceum Natur. Hist. New York 1: 49–50.

136 Clugston, J. P. 1964. Growth of the Florida largemouth bass, *Micropterus salmoides floridanus* (LeSueur), and the northern largemouth bass, *M. s. salmoides* (Lacepede), in subtropical Florida. Trans. Amer. Fish. Soc. 93(2): 146–154.

137 ———. 1966. Centrarchid spawning in the Florida everglades. Quart. J. Florida Acad. Sci. 29(2): 137–144.

138 Clugston, J. P., and E. L. Cooper. 1960. Growth of the common eastern madtom, *Noturus insignis* in central Pennsylvania. Copeia 1960(1): 9–16.

139 Coker, R. E. 1930. Studies of common fishes of the Mississippi River at Keokuk. Bull. Bur. Fish. 45 (1929): 141–225.

140 Cole, C. F. 1965. Additional evidence for separation of *Etheostoma olmstedi* Storer from *Etheostoma nigrum* Rafinesque. Copeia 1965(1): 8–13.

141 ———. 1967. A study of the eastern Johnny darter, *Etheostoma olmstedi* Storer (Teleostei, Percidae). Chesapeake Sci. 8(1): 28–51.

142 Cole, L. J. 1905. The German carp in the United States, p. 523–641. In: U. S. Bur. Fish. Rep. Comm. Fish. for the year ending June 30, 1904. 641 p.

143 Collette, B. B. 1962. The swamp darters of the subgenus *Hololepis* (Pisces, Percidae). Tulane Studies in Zool. 9(4): 115–211.

144 ———. 1965. Systematic significance of breeding tubercles in fishes of the family Percidae. Proc. U. S. Nat. Mus. 117(3518): 567–614.

145 Collette, B. B., and P. Banarescu. 1977. Systematics and zoogeography of the fishes of the family Percidae. J. Fish. Res. Bd. Canada 34(10): 1450–1463.

146 Collins, G. B. 1952. Factors influencing the orientation of migrating anadromous fishes. U. S. Fish. Wildl. Serv., Fish Bull. 52: 375–396.

147 Constanz, G. D. 1979. Social dynamics and parental care in the tessellated darter (Pisces: Percidae). Proc. Acad. Natur. Sci. Philadelphia 131: 131–138.

148 Cooper, E. L. 1953. Returns from plantings of legal-sized brook, brown, and rainbow trout in the Pigeon River, Otsego County, Michigan. Trans. Amer. Fish. Soc. 82 (1952): 265–280.

149 Cooper, E. L., H. Hidu, and J. K. Andersen. 1963. Growth and production of largemouth bass in a small pond. Trans. Amer. Fish. Soc. 92(4): 391–400.

150 Cooper, E. L., C. C. Wagner, and G. E. Krantz. 1971. Bluegills dominate production in a mixed population of fishes. Ecology 52(2): 280–290.

151 Cooper, G. P. 1935. Some results of forage fish investigations in Michigan. Trans. Amer. Fish. Soc. 65: 132–142.

152 ———. 1936. Age and growth of the golden shiner (*Notemigonus crysoleucas auratus*) and its suitability for propagation. Pap. Michigan Acad. Sci. Arts Ltrs. 21(1935): 587–597.

153 ———. 1936. Importance of forage fishes. Proc. North Amer. Wildl. Conf. 1: 305–310.

154 ———. 1941. A biological survey of lakes and ponds of the Androscoggin and Kennebec River drainage systems in Maine. Maine Dept. Inland Fish. Game., Fish Surv. Rep. 4: 1–238.

155 Cooper, G. P., and G. N. Washburn. 1949. Relation of dissolved oxygen to winter mortality of fish in Michigan lakes. Trans. Amer. Fish. Soc. 76(1946): 23–33.

156 Cope, E. D. 1862. Observations on certain cyprinoid fish in Pennsylvania. Proc. Acad. Natur. Sci. Philadelphia 13(1861): 522–524.

157 ———. 1864. On a blind silurid, from Pennsylvania. Proc. Acad. Natur. Sci. Philadelphia 1864: 231–233.

158 ———. 1864. Partial catalogue of the cold-blooded Vertebrata of Michigan. Part 1. Proc. Acad. Natur. Sci. Philadelphia 16: 276–285.

159 ———. 1865. Partial catalogue of the cold-blooded Vertebrata of Michigan. Part 2. Proc. Acad. Natur. Sci. Philadel-

phia 17: 78–88.

160 ———. 1868. On the distribution of fresh-water fishes in the Allegheny region of southwestern Virginia. J. Acad. Natur. Sci. Philadelphia, ser. 2, 6: 207–247.

161 ———. 1869. Synopsis of the Cyprinidae of Pennsylvania. (Supplement: On some new species of American and African fishes). Trans. Amer. Philo. Soc. (Philadelphia) 13 (New Series): 351–410.

162 ———. 1870. Partial synopsis of the freshwater fishes of North Carolina. Proc. Amer. Philo. Soc. 11: 448–495.

163 ———. 1870. On some etheostomine perch from Tennessee and North Carolina. Proc. Amer. Philo. Soc. Philadelphia 11: 261–270.

164 ———. 1881. The fishes of Pennsylvania. Rep. Pa. Comm. Fish. 1879–80: 59–145.

165 Courtenay, W. R., Jr., and C. R. Robins. 1973. Exotic aquatic organisms in Florida with emphasis on fishes: a review and recommendations. Trans. Amer. Fish. Soc. 102(1): 1–12.

166 Coyle, E. E. 1930. The algal food of *Pimephales promelas* (Fathead minnow). Ohio J. Sci. 30(1): 23–35.

167 Cracraft, J. 1974. Continental drift and vertebrate distribution, p. 215–261. In: Annual Review of Ecology and Systematics, v. 5. 488 p.

168 Craig, P. C., and J. Wells. 1976. Life history notes for a population of slimy sculpin (*Cottus cognatus*) in an Alaskan stream. J. Fish. Res. Bd. Canada 33(7): 1639–1642.

169 Crass, R. S. 1964. Freshwater fishes of Natal. Shuter and Shooter, Pietermaritzburg, Natal. 167 p.

170 Crawshaw, L. I. 1975. Twenty-four hour records of body temperature and activity in bluegill sunfish (*Lepomis macrochirus*) and brown bullheads (*Ictalurus nebulosus*). Comp. Biochem. Physiol. 51A: 11–14.

171 Creaser, C. W. 1926. The establishment of the Atlantic smelt in the upper waters of the Great Lakes. Pap. Michigan Acad. Sci. Arts Ltrs. 5(1925): 405–424.

172 Cross, F. B. 1967. Handbook of fishes of Kansas. Univ. Kansas Mus. Natur. Hist. Misc. Publ. 45: 1–357.

173 Cross, F. B., and J. T. Collins. 1975. Fishes in Kansas. Univ. Kansas Mus. Natur. Hist. Pub. Ed. Ser. No. 3. 189 p.

174 Crossman, E. J. 1956. Growth, mortality and movements of a sanctuary population of maskinonge (*Esox masquinongy* Mitchill). J. Fish. Res. Bd. Canada 13(5): 599–612.

175 ———. 1962. The redfin pickerel, *Esox a. americanus* in North Carolina. Copeia 1962(1): 114–123.

176 ———. 1962. Predator-prey relationships in pikes (Esocidae). J. Fish. Res. Bd. Canada 19(5): 979–980.

177 ———. 1966. A taxonomic study of *Esox americanus* and its subspecies in eastern North America. Copeia 1966(1): 1–20.

178 ———. 1980. Chain pickerel, p. 137. In: D. S. Lee et al. 1980. Atlas of North American freshwater fishes. Publ. 1980-12, North Carolina Biol. Surv. 854 p.

179 Crossman, E. J., and K. Buss. 1965. Hybridization in the family Esocidae. J. Fish. Res. Bd. Canada 22(5): 1261–1292.

180 Crossman, E. J., and P. A. Larkin. 1959. Yearling liberations and change of food as affecting rainbow trout yield in Paul Lake, British Columbia. Trans. Amer. Fish. Soc. 88(1): 36–44.

181 Crowe, W. R. 1962. Homing behavior in walleyes. Trans. Amer. Fish. Soc. 91(4): 350–354.

182 Cuerrier, J. P., and G. Roussow. 1951. Age and growth of lake sturgeon from Lake St. Francis, St. Lawrence River. Canadian Fish Culturist 10: 17–29.

183 Cuvier, G. A., and M. A. Valenciennes. 1824–1849. Histoire naturelle des poissons. 22 vol. Levrault, Strasborg, Paris.

184 Cuvier, G. L. C. F. D. 1834. The animal kingdon arranged in conformity with its organization, with supplementary additions to each order, by Edward Griffith. Vol. 10. The Class Pisces arranged by the Baron Cuvier with supplemental additions, by Edward Griffith and Charles Hamil-

ton Smith. Whittaker and Co., London. 680 p.

185 Dadswell, M. J. 1975. Further new localities for certain coldwater fishes in eastern Ontario and western Quebec. Canadian Field-Naturalist 89(4): 447–450.

186 Daiber, F. C. 1952. The food and feeding relationships of the freshwater drum, *Aplodinotus grunniens* Rafinesque, in western Lake Erie. Ohio J. Science 52(1): 35–46.

187 ———. 1953. Notes on the spawning population of the freshwater drum (*Aplodinotus grunniens* Rafinesque) in western Lake Erie. Amer. Midl. Natur. 50(1): 159–171.

188 ———. 1956. A comparative analysis of the winter feeding habits of two benthic stream fishes. Copeia 1956(3): 141–151.

189 Darnell, R. M. 1958. Food habits of fishes and larger invertebrates of Lake Pontchartrain, Louisiana, an estuarine community. Univ. Texas Publ. Inst. Mar. Sci. 5: 353–416.

190 Darnell, R. M., and R. Meierotto. 1965. Diurnal periodicity in the black bullhead, *Ictalurus melas* (Rafinesque). Trans. Amer. Fish. Soc. 94(1): 1–8.

191 Davis, B. J., and R. J. Miller. 1967. Brain patterns in minnows of the genus *Hybopsis* in relation to feeding habits and habitat. Copeia 1967(1): 1–39.

192 Davis, C. C. 1959. A planktonic fish egg from fresh water. Limnol. Oceanogr. 4(3): 352–355.

193 Davis, J. R. 1972. The spawning behavior, fecundity rates and food habits of the redbreast sunfish in southeastern North Carolina. Proc. S-E Assn. Game Fish. Comm. 25(1971): 556–560.

194 Davis, R. M. 1972. Age, growth, and fecundity of the rosyside dace, *Clinostomus funduloides* Girard. Chesapeake Sci. 13(1): 63–66.

195 Deacon, J. E. 1961. Fish populations, following a drought, in the Neosho and Marais des Cygnes Rivers in Kansas. Univ. Kansas Mus. Natur. Hist. Publ. 13(9): 359–427.

196 Deacon, J. E., G. Kobetich, J. D. Williams, and S. Contreras. 1979. Fishes of North America endangered, threatened, or of special concern: 1979. Fisheries 4(2): 29–44.

197 Deason, H. J. 1939. The distribution of cottid fishes in Lake Michigan. Pap. Michigan Acad. Sci. Arts Ltrs. (1938) 24: 105–115.

198 Deelder, C. L., and D. W. Tucker. 1960. The Atlantic eel problem. Nature 185: 589–592.

199 DeKay, J. E. 1842. Natural history of New York. Part I. Zoology. Reptiles and Fishes. Part 4—Fishes. Appleton and Co., and Wilby and Putnam, Albany, N.Y. 415 p.

200 Delisle, C., and W. Van Vliet. 1968. First records of the sculpins *Myoxocephalus thompsonii* and *Cottus ricei* from the Ottawa Valley, southwestern Quebec. J. Fish. Res. Bd. Canada 25(12): 2733–2737.

201 Dence, W. A. 1948. Life history, ecology and habits of the dwarf sucker, *Catostomus commersonnii utawana* Mather, at the Huntington Wildlife Station. Roosevelt Wildl. Bull. 8(4): 83–150.

202 Dendy, J. S. 1946. Food of several species of fish, Norris Reservoir, Tennessee. J. Tennessee Acad. Sci. 21(1): 105–127.

203 Denoncourt, R. F. 1969. A systematic study of the gilt darter *Percina evides* (Jordan and Copeland) (Pisces: Percidae). Ph.D. thesis, Cornell Univ., Ithaca, N.Y. 216 p.

204 Denoncourt, R. F., and E. L. Cooper. 1975. A review of the literature and checklist of fishes of the Susquehanna River drainage above Conowingo Dam. Proc. Pa. Acad. Sci. 49: 121–125.

205 Denoncourt, R. F., C. H. Hocutt, and J. R. Stauffer, Jr. 1975. Extensions of the known ranges of *Ericymba buccata* Cope and *Etheostoma zonale* (Cope) in the Susquehanna River drainge. Proc. Pa. Acad. Sci. 49: 45–46.

206 ———. 1977. Notes on the habitat, description and distribution of the sharpnose darter, *Percina oxyrhyncha*. Copeia 1977(1): 168–171.

207 Denoncourt, R. F., T. B. Robbins, and R. Hesser. 1975. Recent introductions and reintroductions to the Pennsylvania fish fauna of the Susquehanna River drainage above Conowingo Dam. Proc. Pa. Acad. Sci. 49: 57–58.

208 DeWindt, J. T. 1973. The Landisburg Tongue of central Pennsylvania: a late Silurian delta. Proc. Pa. Acad. Sci. 47: 25–29.

209 Dineen, C. F. 1951. A comparative study of the food habits of *Cottus bairdii* and associated species of Salmonidae. American Midl. Nat. 46(3): 640–645.

210 Doan, K. H. 1938. Observations on dogfish (*Amia calva*) and their young. Copeia 1938(4): 204.

211 ———. 1941. Relation of sauger catch to turbidity in Lake Erie. Ohio J. Science 41(6): 449–452.

212 Dobie, J. 1956. Walleye pond management in Minnesota. Progr. Fish-Cult. 18(2): 51–57.

213 ———. 1959. Note on food of northern logperch. Trans. Amer. Fish. Soc. 88(3): 213.

214 ———. 1966. Food and feeding habits of the walleye, *Stizostedion v. vitreum,* and associated game and forage fishes in Lake Vermilion, Minnesota, with special reference to the tullibee, *Coregonus (Leucichthys) artedi.* Minnesota Fish. Invest. 4: 39–71.

215 Dobie, J., O. L. Meehean, S. F. Snieszko, and G. N. Washburn. 1956. Raising bait fishes. U. S. Fish and Wildl. Serv. Circ. 35. 123 p.

216 ———. 1948. Propagation of minnows and other bait species. U. S. Fish and Wildl. Serv. Circ. 12: 1–113.

217 Dryer, W. R. 1966. Bathymetric distribution of fish in the Apostle Islands region, Lake Superior. Trans. Amer. Fish. Soc. 95(3): 248–259.

218 Dryer, W. R., and J. Beil. 1964. Life history of lake herring in Lake Superior. U. S. Fish and Wildl. Serv., Fish. Bull. 63(3): 493–530.

219 Dybowski. 1869. Verh. zool. bot. Gesell. Wien 19: 956. Reference from: Berg, L. S. 1948. Freshwater fishes of the USSR and adjacent countries. Moscow Acad. Sci. USSR. Vol. 1, 504 p.

220 Dymond, J. R. 1922. A provisional list of the fishes of Lake Erie. Univ. Toronto Studies, Biol. Ser. 20. Publ. Ontario Fish. Res. Lab. 4: 57–73.

221 ———. 1926. The fishes of Lake Nipigon. Univ. Toronto Studies, Biol. Ser. 27. Publ. Ontario Fish. Res. Lab. 27: 1–108,

222 ———. 1932. Records of the alewife and steelhead (rainbow) trout from Lake Erie. Copeia 1932(1): 32.

223 Dymond, J. R., and J. L. Hart. 1927. The fishes of Lake Abitibi (Ontario) and adjacent waters. Univ. Toronto Studies, Biol. Ser. 29. Publ. Ontario Fish Res. Lab. 28: 1–19.

224 Dymond, J. R., J. L. Hart, and A. L. Pritchard. 1929. The fishes of the Canadian waters of Lake Ontario. Univ. Toronto Studies, Biol. Ser. 33. Publ. Ontario Fish. Res. Lab. 37: 1–35.

225 Eales, J. G. 1968. The eel fisheries of eastern Canada. Fish. Res. Bd. Canada Bull. 166. 79 p.

226 Eastman, C. R. 1917. Fossil fishes in the collections of the U. S. National Museum. Proc. U. S. Nat. Mus. 52(2177): 235–304.

227 Eddy, S., and J. C. Underhill. 1974. Northern fishes, with special reference to the Upper Mississippi Valley. Univ. Minnesota Press, Minneapolis. 3rd ed. 414 p.

228 Edsall, T. A. 1967. Biology of the freshwater drum in western Lake Erie. Ohio J. Science 67(6): 321–340.

229 Eigenmann, C. H., and R. S. Eigenmann. 1893. Preliminary descriptions of new fishes from the northwest. Amer. Natur. 27: 151–154.

230 Ellis, D. V., and M. A. Giles. 1965. The spawning behavior of the walleye, *Stizostedion vitreum* (Mitchill). Trans. Amer. Fish. Soc. 94(4): 358–362.

231 Emery, L. 1981. Range extension of pink salmon (*Oncorhynchus gorbuscha*) into the lower Great Lakes. Fisheries 6(2): 7–10.

232 Emig, J. W. 1966. Brown bullhead, p. 463–475. In: Inland fisheries management. Alex Calhoun, ed. California Dept. Fish and Game. 546 p.

233 Eschmeyer, P. H. 1950. The life history of the walleye, *Stizostedion vitreum vitreum* (Mitchill), in Michigan. Michigan Inst. Fish. Res. Bull. 3. 99 p.

234 ———. 1955. The reproduction of lake trout in southern Lake Superior. Trans. Amer. Fish. Soc. 84(1954): 47–74.

235 Eschmeyer, P. H., and R. M. Bailey. 1955. The pigmy white-fish, *Coregonus coulteri,* in Lake Superior. Trans. Amer. Fish. Soc. 84: 161–199.

236 Eschmeyer, P. H., and W. R. Crowe. 1955. The movement and recovery of tagged walleyes in Michigan, 1929–1953. Michigan Inst. Fish. Res. Misc. Publ. 8. 32 p.

237 Evans, H. E. 1952. The correlation of brain pattern and feeding habits in four species of cyprinid fishes. J. Compar. Neurol. 97(1): 133–142.

238 Everhart, W. H. 1950. Fishes in Maine. Maine Dept. Inland Fish Game. 53 p.

239 Evermann, B. W., and C. H. Bollman. 1886. Notes on a collection of fishes from the Monongahela River. Annals New York Acad. Sci. 3(11): 335–340.

240 Evermann, B. W., and H. W. Clark. 1920. Lake Maxinkuckee: a physical and biological survey. Indiana Dept. Cons. Publ. 7, vol. 1. 660 p.

241 Ewers, L. A. 1933. Summary report of crustacea used as food by the fishes of the western end of Lake Erie. Trans. Amer. Fish. Soc. 63: 379–390.

242 Ewers, L. A., and M. W. Boesel. 1935. The food of some Buckeye Lake fishes. Trans. Amer. Fish. Soc. 65: 57–70.

243 Faber, D. J. 1970. Ecological observations on newly hatched lake whitefish in South Bay, Lake Huron, p. 481–500. In: Biology of Coregonid Fishes. Univ. Manitoba Press, Winnipeg, 560 p.

244 Fabricius, E., and K. J. Gustafson. 1954. Further aquarium observations of the spawning behavior of the char, *Salmo alpinus* L. Rept. Inst. Freshwater Res. Drottningholm. 35: 58–104.

245 ———. 1958. Some new observations on the spawning behavior of the pike, *Esox lucius* L. Fish. Bd. Sweden, Inst. Freshwater Res. Rept. 39, p. 23–54.

246 Fahy, W. E. 1954. The life history of the northern green-side darter, *Etheostoma blennioides blennioides* Rafinesque. J. Elisha Mitchell Sci. Soc. 70(2): 139–205.

247 Fairchild, H. L. 1895. Glacial lakes of western New York. Bull Geol. Soc. Amer. 6: 353–374.

248 ———. 1934. Seneca Valley physiographic and glacial history. Bull. Geol. Soc. Amer. 45: 1073–1110.

249 Fajen, O. F. 1962. The influence of stream stability on homing behavior of two smallmouth bass populations. Trans. Amer. Fish. Soc. 91(4): 346–349.

250 Fava, J. A., Jr., and C. F. Tsai. 1974. The life history of the pearl dace, *Semotilus margarita,* in Maryland. Chesapeake Sci. 15(3): 159–162.

251 ———. 1976. Tuberculation of the pearl dace, *Semotilus margarita* (Pisces: Cyprinidae). Copeia 1976(2): 370–374.

252 Fenderson, O. C. 1964. Evidence of subpopulations of lake whitefish, *Coregonus clupeaformis,* involving a dwarfed form. Trans. Amer. Fish. Soc. 93(1): 77–94.

253 Ferguson, R. G. 1965. Bathymetric distribution of American smelt *Osmerus mordax* in Lake Erie. Univ. Michigan, Great Lakes Res. Div., Publ. 13: 47–60.

254 Fingerman, S. W., and R. D. Suttkus. 1961. Comparison of *Hybognathus hayi* Jordan and *Hybognathus nuchalis* Agassiz. Copeia 1961(4): 462–467.

255 Finnell, J. C., and R. M. Jenkins. 1954. Growth of channel catfish in Oklahoma waters: 1954 revision. Oklahoma Fish. Res. Lab. Rep. 41. 37 p.

256 Fitz, R. B. 1966. Unusual food of a paddlefish (*Polyodon spathula*) in Tennessee. Copeia 1966(2): 356.

257 Flemer, D. A., and W. S. Woolcott. 1966. Food habits and distribution of the fishes of Tuckahoe Creek, Virginia, with special emphasis on the bluegill, *Lepomis m. macrochirus* Rafinesque. Chesapeake Sci. 7(2): 75–89.

258 Foerster, R. E. 1968. The sockeye salmon, *Oncorhynchus nerka.* Fish. Res. Bd. Canada Bull. 162. 422 p.

259 Foltz, J. W. 1976. Fecundity of the slimy sculpin, *Cottus cognatus,* in Lake Michigan. Copeia 1976(4): 802–804.

260 Fontain, P. A. 1944. Notes on the spawning of the shovel-head catfish, *Pylodictis olivaris* (Rafinesque). Copeia 1944(1): 50–51.

261 Foote, L. E., and B. P. Blake. 1945. Life history of the eastern pickerel in Babcock Pond, Connecticut. J. Wildl. Manag. 9(2): 89–96.

262 Forbes, S. A. 1885. Description of new Illinois fishes. Bull. Illinois State Lab. Natur. Hist. 2(2): 135–139.

263 ———. 1890. Studies of the food of freshwater fishes. Bull. Illinois State Lab. Natur. Hist. 2: 433–473.

264 Forbes, S. A., and R. E. Richardson. 1920. The fishes of Illinois. Illinois Nat. Hist. Surv. Div. 357 p.

265 Forney, J. L. 1955. Life history of the black bullhead, *Ameiurus melas* (Rafinesque), of Clear Lake, Iowa. Iowa State Coll. J. Sci. 30(1): 145–162.

266 ———. 1957. Bait fish production in New York ponds. New York Fish and Game. J. 4(2): 150–194.

267 Forney, J. L., and C. B. Taylor. 1963. Age and growth of white bass in Oneida Lake, New York. New York Fish and Game J. 10(2): 194–200.

268 Forster, J. R. 1773. An account of some curious fishes, sent from Hudson Bay. Phil. Trans. Royal Soc. London 63(1): 149–160.

269 Fowler, H. W. 1907. Records of Pennsylvania fishes. Amer. Natur. 41: 5–21.

270 ———. 1909. A synopsis of the cyprinidae of Pennsylvania. Proc. Acad. Natur. Sci. Philadelphia 60(1908): 517–553.

271 ———. 1910. Note on some Pennsylvania fishes. Science 31 n.s. (792): 345–346.

272 ———. 1914. Notes on catostomid fishes. Proc. Acad. Natur. Sci. Philadelphia 65(1913): 45–60.

273 ———. 1917. Some notes on the breeding habits of local catfishes. Copeia 1917(42): 32–36.

274 ———. 1919. A list of the fishes of Pennsylvania. Proc. Biol. Soc. Washington 32: 49–74.

275 ———. 1921. The fishes of Bucks County, Pennsylvania. Copeia 1921(98): 62–68.

276 ———. 1938. Notes on Pennsylvania fishes. Rep. Pa. Bd. Fish. Comm. (1938): 101–108.

277 ———. 1940. A list of the fishes recorded from Pennsylvania. Pa. Bd. Fish. Comm., Biennial Report for period ending 31 May 1940, p. 59–78.

278 ———. 1945. A study of the fishes of the southern Piedmont and coastal plain. Acad. Natur. Sci. Philadelphia, Monogr. 7. 408 p.

279 ———. 1948. A list of the fishes recorded from Pennsylvania. Rev. ed. Bull. Pa. Bd. Fish. Comm. 7: 3–26.

280 Fowler, H. W., and J. G. Carlson. 1927. Fishes from McKean, Potter, and Cameron Counties, Pennsylvania. Proc. Biol. Soc. Washington 40: 65–74.

281 Franklin, D. R., and L. L. Smith, Jr. 1963. Early life history of the northern pike, *Esox lucius* L., with special reference to the factors influencing the numerical strength of year classes. Trans. Amer. Fish. Soc. 92(2): 91–110.

282 Franz, R., and D. S. Lee. 1976. A relict population of the mottled sculpin, *Cottus bairdi,* from the Maryland coastal plain. Chesapeake Sci. 17(4): 301–302.

283 Fremling, C. R. 1978. Biology and functional anatomy of the freshwater drum, *Aplodinotus grunniens* Rafinesque. Nasco, Fort Atkinson, Wisconsin. 46 p.

284 Fuchs, E. H. 1967. Life history of the emerald shiner, *Notropis atherinoides,* in Lewis and Clark Lake, South Dakota. Trans. Amer. Fish. Soc. 96(3): 247–256.

285 Funk, J. L. 1957. Movement of stream fishes in Missouri. Trans. Amer. Fish. Soc. 85(1955): 39–57.

286 Gage, S. H. 1928. The lampreys of New York State—life history and economics, p. 158–191. In: A biological survey of the Oswego River system. Suppl. to 17th Annual Rept. (1927), New York Cons. Dept.

287 Geen, G. H., T. G. Northcote, G. F. Hartman, and C. C. Lindsey. 1966. Life histories of two species of catostomid fishes in Sixteen-mile Lake, British Columbia, with particular reference to inlet stream spawning. J. Fish. Res. Bd. Canada 23(11): 1761–1788.

288 Gerald, J. W. 1966. Food habits of the longnose dace, Rhinichthys cataractae. Copeia 1966(3): 478–485.

289 Gerking, S. D. 1945. Distribution of the fishes of Indiana. Invest. Indiana Lakes and Streams 3. 165 p.

290 ———. 1947. The use of minor postglacial drainage connections by fishes in Indiana. Copeia 1947(2): 89–91.

291 ———. 1953. Evidence for the concepts of home range and territory in stream fishes. Ecology 34(2): 347–365.

292 Gibbs, R. H., Jr. 1957. Cyprinid fishes of the subgenus Cyprinella of Notropis. I. Systematic status of the subgenus Cyprinella, with a key to the species exclusive of the lutrensis-ornatus complex. Copeia 1957(3): 185–195.

293 ———. 1957. Cyprinid fishes of the subgenus Cyprinella of Notropis. II. Distribution and variation of Notropis spilopterus, with the description of a new subspecies. Lloydia 20(3): 186–211.

294 ———. 1963. Cyprinid fishes of the subgenus Cyprinella of Notropis. The Notropis whipplei-analostanus-chloristius complex. Copeia 1963(3): 511–528.

295 Gilbert, C. R. 1953. Age and growth of the yellow stone catfish, Noturus flavus (Rafinesque). MS thesis, Ohio State Univ. Columbus. 67 p.

296 ———. 1961. Hybridization versus intergradation: an inquiry into the relationship of two cyprinid fishes. Copeia 1961(2): 181–192.

297 ———. 1964. The American cyprinid fishes of the subgenus Luxilus (Genus Notropis). Bull. Florida State Mus. Biol. Sci. 8(2): 95–194.

298 ———. 1969. Systematics and distribution of the American cyprinid fishes Notropis ariommus and Notropis telescopus. Copeia 1969(3): 474–492.

299 ———. 1980. Cycleptus elongatus (LeSueur), blue sucker, p. 396. In: D. S. Lee et al., Atlas of North American Freshwater Fishes. North Carolina State Mus. Natur. Hist., Raleigh. 854 p.

300 ———. 1980. Notropis ariommus (Cope), Popeye shiner, p. 229 In: D. S. Lee et al., Atlas of North American freshwater fishes. North Carolina State Mus. Natur. Hist., Raleigh. 854 p.

301 Gilliams, J. 1824. Description of a new species of fish of the Linnaean genus Perca. J. Acad. Natur. Sci. Philadelphia 4(1): 80–81.

302 Girard, C. F. 1850. A monograph of the freshwater Cotti. Proc. Amer. Assn. Adv. Sci. 2nd meeting (1849): 409–411.

303 ———. 1852. Contributions to the natural history of the freshwater fishes of North America. I. A monograph of the cottoids. Smithsonian Contrib. Knowl. 3(3): 80 p.

304 ———. 1856. Description of some new species of fish from the State of Massachusetts. Proc. Boston Soc. Natur. Hist. 5(1854–1856): 39–41.

305 ———. 1857. Researches upon the cyprinoid fishes inhabiting the freshwaters of the United States of America, west of the Mississippi Valley, from specimens in the Museum of the Smithsonian Institution. Proc. Acad. Natur. Sci. Philadelphia 8(1856): 165–213.

306 ———. 1858. Notice upon new genera and new species of marine and fresh-water fishes from western North America. Proc. Acad. Natur. Sci. Philadelphia 9(1857): 200–202.

307 ———. 1860. Ichthyological notices. Proc. Acad. Natur. Sci. Philadelphia (1859) 11: 56–68; 100–104; 113–122; 157–161.

308 Gmelin, J. F. 1788. Caroli A Linne, systema naturae per regna tria naturae, secundum classes, ordines, genera, species, cum characteribus, differentiis, synonymis, locis. vol. 1 (Regnum animale). 13th ed. aucta, reformata. Lipsiae. Georg Emmanuel. Beer.

309 Godfrey, H. 1957. Feeding of eels in four New Brunswick salmon streams. Fish. Res. Bd. Canada. Progr. Rep. Atlantic 67: 19–22.

310 Goldsborough, E. L., and H. W. Clark. 1908. Fishes of West Virginia. Bull. Bur. of Fish. 27(1907): 29–39.

311 Goode, G. B. 1886. American fishes. Smithsonian Inst., Washington, D.C. 496 p.

312 Goodyear, C. P. 1967. Feeding habits of three species of gars, Lepisosteus, along the Mississippi Gulf coast. Trans. Amer. Fish. Soc. 96(3): 297–300.

313 Gorham, S. W., and D. E. McAllister. 1974. The shortnose sturgeon, Acipenser brevirostrum, in the Saint John River, New Brunswick, Canada, a rare and possible endangered species. Syllogeus, National Museums of Canada, Ottawa, No. 5. 18 p.

314 Gosline, W. A. 1949. The sensory canals of the head in some cyprinodont fishes, with particular reference to the genus Fundulus. Univ. Michigan Mus. Zool. Occas. Pap. 519. 17 p.

315 ———. 1966. The limits of the fish family Serranidae, with notes on other lower percoids. Proc. California Acad. Sci. 4th Ser. 33(6): 91–112.

316 Graham, J. J. 1956. Observations on the alewife, Pomolobus pseudoharengus (Wilson), in fresh water. Publ. Ontario Fish. Res. Lab. 74 (Univ. Toronto Studies Biol. Ser. 62). 43 p.

317 Graham, K., and P. Bonislawsky. 1978. An indexed bibliography of the paddlefish (Polyodon spathula). Missouri Dept. Conservation, Columbia. 14 p.

318 Grainger, E. H. 1953. On the age, growth, migration, reproductive potential and feeding habits of the Arctic char (Salvelinus alpinus) of Frobisher Bay, Baffin Island. J. Fish. Res. Bd. Canada 10(6): 326–370.

319 Gray, J. W. 1942. Studies of Notropis atherinoides atherinoides Rafinesque in the Bass Islands region of Lake Erie. MS thesis, Ohio State University, Columbus. 29 p.

320 Gray, W. B. 1923. Umbra pygmaea. Aquatic Life 7(6): 67.

321 Greeley, J. R. 1927. Fishes of the Genesee Region with annotated list, p. 47–66. In: A biological survey of the Genesee River System. Suppl. to 16th Annual Rep. (1926). New York Cons. Dept. 100 p.

322 ———. 1929. VI. Fishes of the Erie-Niagara watershed, p. 150–179. In: A biological survey of the Erie-Niagara system. Suppl. to 18th Annual Rep. New York Cons. Dept. 244 p.

323 ———. 1933. The spawning habits of brook, brown and rainbow trout, and the problem of egg predators. Trans. Amer. Fish. Soc. 62 (1932): 239–248

324 ———. 1935. Fishes of the watershed, with annotated list, p. 63–101. In: A biological survey of the Mohawk-Hudson watershed. Suppl. to 24th Annual Rep. (1934). New York Cons. Dept. Biol. Surv. 9.

325 ———. 1936. Fishes of the area with annotated list, p. 45–88. In: A biological survey of the Delaware and Susquehanna watersheds. Suppl. to 25th Annual Rep. (1935). New York Cons. Dept. Biol. Surv. 10. 356 p.

326 ———. 1937. Fishes of the area with annotated list, p. 45–103. In: A biological survey of the lower Hudson watershed. Suppl. to 26th Annual Rep. (1936). New York Cons. Dept. Biol. Surv. 11. 373 p.

327 ———. 1938. Fishes of the area with annotated list, p. 48–73. In: A biological survey of the Allegheny and Chemung watersheds. Suppl. to 27th Annual Rep. (1937). New York Cons. Dept. 287 p.

328 ———. 1940. II. Fishes of the watershed with annotated list, p. 42–81. In: A biological survey of the Lake Ontario watershed. New York Cons. Dept. Biol. Surv. 16(1939),

261 p.

329 Greenbank, J., and P. R. Nelson. 1959. Life history of the threespine stickleback, *Gasterosteus aculeatus* Linnaeus, in Karluk Lake and Bare Lake, Kodiak Island, Alaska. U.S. Fish. Wildl. Serv., Fish. Bull. 153: 537–559.

330 Greene, C. W. 1930. The smelts of Lake Champlain, p. 105–129. In: A biological survey of the Champlain watershed. Suppl. to 19th Annual Rep. (1929). New York Cons. Dept. 321 p.

331 ———. 1935. The distribution of Wisconsin fishes. Wisconsin Cons. Comm., Madison. 235 p.

332 Greenwood, P. H., D. E. Rosen, S. H. Weitzman, and G. S. Myers. 1966. Phyletic studies of teleostean fishes, with a provisional classification of living forms. Bull. Amer. Mus. Nat. Hist. 131(4): 1–455.

333 Griswold, B. L. 1963. Food and growth of spottail shiners and other forage fishes of Clear Lake, Iowa. Iowa Acad. Sci. 70: 215–223.

334 Griswold, B. L., and R. A. Tubb. 1977. Food of yellow perch, white bass, freshwater drum, and channel catfish in Sandusky Bay, Lake Erie. Ohio J. Sci. 77(1): 43–47.

335 Grosslein, M. D., and L. L. Smith, Jr. 1959. The goldeye, *Amphiodon alosoides* (Rafinesque), in the commercial fishery of the Red Lakes, Minnesota. U.S. Fish Wildl. Serv. Fish. Bull. 60: 33–41.

336 Gruchy, C. G., R. H. Bowen, and I. M. Gruchy. 1973. First records of the silver shiner, *Notropis photogenis,* from Canada. J. Fish. Res. Bd. Canada 30(9): 1379–1382.

337 Gunn, J. M., S. U. Qadri, and D. C. Mortimer. 1977. Filamentous algae as a food source for the brown bullhead (*Ictalurus nebulosus*). J. Fish. Res. Bd. Canada 34(3): 396–401.

338 Gunter, G. 1945. Studies on marine fishes of Texas. Publ. Inst. Marine Sci. 1(1). 190 p.

339 Günther, A. 1859. Catalogue of fishes of the British Museum. London. Vol. 1, 264 p.

340 Hackney, P. A., W. M. Tatum, and S. L. Spencer. 1967. Life history study of the river redhorse, *Moxostoma carinatum* (Cope), in the Cahaba River, Alabama, with notes on the management of the species as a sport fish. Proc. S-E Assn. Game Fish. Comm. 21: 324–332.

341 Hagen, D. W. 1967. Isolating mechanisms in threespine sticklebacks (*Gasterosteus*). J. Fish. Res. Bd. Canada 24(8): 1637–1692.

342 Hall, A. J. 1978. The Hudson: "That river's alive." National Geographic 153(1): 62–88.

343 Hall, G. E., and R. M. Jenkins. 1954. Notes on the age and growth of the pirateperch, *Aphredoderus sayanus,* in Oklahoma. Copeia 1954(1): 69.

344 Hallam, J. C. 1959. Habitat and associated fauna of four species of fish in Ontario streams. J. Fish Res. Bd. Canada 16(2): 147–173.

345 Hankinson, T. L. 1908. A biological survey of Walnut Lake, Michigan. Rep. State Biol. (Geol.) Survey, Michigan, 1907, p. 153–288.

346 ———. 1919. Notes on life-histories of Illinois fish. Trans. Illinois State Acad. Sci. 12: 132–150.

347 ———. 1920. Report on investigations of the fish of the Galien River, Berrien County, Michigan. Univ. Michigan Mus. Zool. Occas. Pap. 89: 1–14.

348 ———. 1932. Observations on the breeding behavior and habitats of fishes in southern Michigan. Pap. Michigan Acad. Sci. Arts Ltrs. 15: 411–425.

349 Hann, H. W. 1927. The history of the germ cells of *Cottus bairdii* Girard. J. Morphology and Physiology 43(2): 427–497.

350 Hansen, D. F. 1943. On nesting of the white crappie, *Pomoxis annularis.* Copeia 1943(4): 259–260.

351 ———. 1951. Biology of the white crappie in Illinois. Bull. Illinois Nat. Hist. Surv. 25(4): 211–265.

352 ———. 1965. Further observations on nesting of the white crappie, *Pomoxis annularis.* Trans. Amer. Fish. Soc. 94(2): 182–184.

353 Hardisty, M. W., and I. C. Potter. 1971–1972. Biology of lampreys. Academic Press, New York. Vol. 1, 400 p.; vol. 2, 432 p.

354 Harrington, R. W., Jr. 1947. The breeding behavior of the bridled shiner, *Notropis bifrenatus.* Copeia 1947(3): 186–192.

355 ———. 1948. The life cycle and fertility of the bridled shiner, *Notropis bifrenatus* (Cope). Amer. Midl. Nat. 39(1): 83–92.

356 ———. 1948. The food of the bridled shiner, *Notropis bifrenatus* (Cope). Amer. Midl. Nat. 40(2): 353–361.

357 ———. 1956. An experiment on the effects of contrasting daily photo-periods on gametogenesis and reproduction in the centrarchid fish, *Enneacanthus obesus* (Girard). J. Exp. Zool. 131(3): 203–224.

358 Harrington, R. W., Jr., and E. S. Harrington. 1961. Food selection among fishes invading a high subtropical salt marsh: from onset of flooding through the progress of a mosquito brood. Ecology 42(4): 646–666.

359 Harris, R. H. D. 1962. Growth and reproduction of the longnose sucker, *Catostomus catostomus* (Forster), in Great Slave Lake. J. Fish. Res. Bd. Canada 19(1): 113–126.

360 Hart, J. L. 1928. Data on the rate of growth of pikeperch (*Stizostedion vitreum*) and sauger (*S. canadense*) in Ontario. Univ. Toronto Studies, Biol. Ser. 34: 45–55.

361 Hart, J. L. 1973. Pacific fishes of Canada. Fish. Res. Bd. Canada. Bull. 180. 740 p.

362 Hartman, G. F. 1965. The role of behavior in the ecology and interaction of underyearling coho salmon (*Oncorhynchus kisutch*) and steelhead trout (*Salmo gairdneri*). J. Fish. Res. Bd. Canada 22(4): 1035–1081.

363 Hasler, A. D., R. M. Horrall, W. J. Wisby, and W. Braemer. 1958. Sun-orientation and homing in fishes. Limnol. Oceanogr. 3(4): 353–361.

364 Hasler, A. D., and J. R. Villemonte. 1953. Observations on the daily movements of fishes. Science 118(3064): 321–322.

365 Hasler, A. D., and W. J. Wisby. 1958. The return of displaced largemouth bass and green sunfish to a "home" area. Ecology 39(2): 289–293.

366 Held, J. W. 1969. Some early summer foods of the shovelnose sturgeon in the Missouri River. Trans. Amer. Fish. Soc. 98(3): 514–517.

367 Henshall, J. A. 1881. Book of the black bass. Robert Clarke and Co., Cincinnati. 463 p.

368 Hergenrader, Gary L. 1969. Spawning behavior of *Perca flavescens* in aquaria. Copeia 1969(4): 839–841.

369 Hermann, J. 1804. Observationes zoologicae, quibus novae complures, aliaeque animalium species describuntur et illustrantur. IV. Pisces. Amandus Koenig, Strasbourg and Paris. 332 p.

370 Hervey, G. F., and J. Hems. 1968. The goldfish. Faber and Faber, London. 271 p.

371 Hester, F. E. 1970. Phylogenetic relationships of sunfishes as demonstrated by hybridization. Trans. Amer. Fish. Soc. 99(1): 100–104.

372 Hildebrand, S. F. 1963. Family Clupeidae, p. 257–454. In: Fishes of the western North Atlantic. Mem. Sears Found. Mar. Res. 1(3). 630 p.

373 Hildebrand, S. F., and W. C. Schroeder. 1928. Fishes of Chesapeake Bay. Bull. U. S. Bur. Fish 43(1): 1–366.

374 Hile, R. 1937. Morphometry of the cisco, *Leucichthys artedi* (LeSueur), in the lakes of the northeastern highlands, Wisconsin. Int. Rev. de. ges. Hydr. U. Hydr. Leipzig 36(1/2): 57–130.

375 ———. 1941. Age and growth of the rock bass, *Ambloplites rupestris* (Rafinesque), in Nebish Lake, Wisconsin. Trans. Wisconsin Acad. Sci. Arts Ltrs. 33: 189–337.

376 Hoar, W. S. 1951. The chum and pink salmon fisheries of British Columbia, 1917–1947. Fish. Res. Bd. Canada Bull. 90. 46 p.

377 Hocutt, C. H., and P. S. Hambrick. 1973. Hybridization between the darters *Percina crassa roanoka* and *Percina oxyrhyncha* (Percidae, Etheostomatini), with comments on the distribution of *Percina crassa roanoka* in the New River. Amer. Midl. Natur. 90: 397–405.

378 Hoese, H. D. 1963. Salt tolerance of the eastern mudminnow, *Umbra pygmaea.* Copeia 1963(1): 165–166.

379 Holbrook, J. E. 1855. An account of several species of fish observed in Florida, Georgia, etc. J. Acad. Natur. Sci. Philadelphia 3 (2d. ser.) (5): 47–58.

380 Hollis, E. H. 1952. Variations in the feeding habits of the striped bass, *Roccus saxatilis* (Walbaum) in Chesapeake Bay. Bull. Bingham Oceanogr. Collect. (Yale Univ.) 14(1): 111–131.

381 Holloway, A. D. 1954. Notes on the life history and management of the shortnose and longnose gars in Florida waters. J. Wildl. Manag. 18(4): 438–449.

382 Hooper, F. F. 1949. Age analysis of a population of the Ameiurid fish *Schilbeodes mollis* (Hermann). Copeia 1949(1): 34–38.

383 Hoopes, D. T. 1960. Utilization of mayflies and caddisflies by some Mississippi River fish. Trans. Amer. Fish. Soc. 89: 32–34.

384 Hoover, E. E. 1936. Contributions to the life history of the chinook and landlocked salmon in New Hampshire. Copeia 1936(4): 193–198.

385 Horak, D. L., and H. L. Tanner. 1964. The use of vertical gill nets in studying fish depth distribution, Horsetooth Reservoir, Colorado. Trans. Amer. Fish. Soc. 93(2): 137–145.

386 Hourston, A. S. 1952. The food and growth of the maskinonge (*Esox masquinongy* Mitchill) in Canadian waters. J. Fish. Res. Bd. Canada 8(5): 347–368.

387 Houser, A., and C. Collins. 1962. Growth of black bullhead catfish in Oklahoma. Oklahoma Fish. Res. Lab. Rep. 79: 1–18.

388 Howland, J. W. 1932. Studies on the Kentucky black bass (*Micropterus pseudaplites* Hubbs). Trans. Amer. Fish. Soc. 61(1931): 89–94.

389 ———. 1932. The spotted or Kentucky black bass of Ohio. Ohio Dept. Agr. Div. Cons. Bull. 1(4): 1–9.

390 ———. 1933. Experiments in the propagation of spotted black bass. Trans. Amer. Fish. Soc. 62(1932): 185–188.

391 Hoyt, R. D. 1970. Food habits of the silverjaw minnow, *Ericymba buccata* Cope, in an intermittent stream in Kentucky. Amer. Midl. Nat. 84(1): 226–236.

392 ———. 1971. Age and growth of the silverjaw minnow, *Ericymba buccata* Cope, in Kentucky. Amer. Midl. Nat. 86(2): 257–275.

393 ———. 1971. The reproductive biology of the silverjaw minnow, *Ericymba buccata* Cope, in Kentucky. Trans. Amer. Fish. Soc. 100(3): 510–519.

394 Hubbs, C. L. 1921. An ecological study of the life-history of the fresh-water atherine fish *Labidesthes sicculus.* Ecology 2(4): 262–276.

395 ———. 1921. Geographical variation of *Notemigonus crysoleucas*—an American minnow. Trans. Illinois State Acad. Sci. 11(1918): 147–151.

396 ———. 1929. The Atlantic American species of the fish genus *Gasterosteus.* Univ. Michigan Mus. Zool. Occas. Pap. 200. 9 p.

397 ———. 1930. Materials for a revision of the catostomid fishes of eastern North America. Univ. Michigan Mus. Zool. Misc. Publ. 20:1–47.

398 ———. 1931. *Parexoglossum laurae,* a new cyprinid fish from the Upper Kanawha River system. Univ. Michigan Mus. Zool. Occas. Pap. 234. 12 p.

399 ———. 1951. The American cyprinid fish *Notropis germanus* Hay interpreted as an intergeneric hybrid. Amer. Midl. Natur. 45(2): 446–454.

400 Hubbs, C. L., and R. M. Bailey. 1938. The small-mouthed bass. Cranbrook Inst. Sci. Bull. 10. 92 p.

401 ———. 1940. A revision of the black basses (*Micropterus* and *Huro*) with descriptions of four new forms. Univ. Michigan Mus. Zool. Misc. Publ. 48. 51 p.

402 ———. 1952. Identification of *Oxygeneum pulverulentum* Forbes, from Illinois, as a hybrid cyprinid fish. Pap. Michigan Acad. Sci. Arts Ltrs. 37(1951): 143–152.

403 Hubbs. C. L., and J. D. Black. 1940. Percid fishes related to *Poecilichthys variatus,* with descriptions of three new forms. Univ. Michigan Mus. Zool. Occas. Pap. 416. 30 p.

404 ———. 1947. Revision of *Ceratichthys,* a genus of American cyprinid fishes. Univ. Michigan Mus. Zool. Misc. Publ. 66. 56 p.

405 Hubbs, C. L., and D. E. S. Brown. 1929. Materials for a distributional study of Ontario fishes. Trans. Royal Canadian Inst. 17(1): 1–56.

406 Hubbs, C. L., and M. D. Cannon. 1935. The darters of the genera *Hololepis* and *Villora.* Univ. Michigan Mus. Zool. Misc. Publ. 30. 93 p.

407 Hubbs, C. L., and G. P. Cooper. 1935. Age and growth of the long-eared and the green sunfishes in Michigan. Pap. Michigan Acad. Sci. Arts Ltrs. 20(1934): 669–696.

408 ———. 1936. Minnows of Michigan. Cranbrook Inst. Sci. Bull. 8. 95 p.

409 Hubbs, C. L., and W. R. Crowe. 1956. Preliminary analysis of the American cyprinid fishes, seven new, referred to the genus *Hybopsis,* subgenus *Erimystax.* Univ. Michigan Mus. Zool. Occas. Pap. 578. 8 p.

410 Hubbs, C. L., and C. W. Greene. 1928. Further notes on the fishes of the Great Lakes and tributary waters. Pap. Michigan Acad. Sci. Arts Ltrs. 8: 371–392.

411 Hubbs, C. L., and L. C. Hubbs. 1932. Experimental verification of natural hybridization between distinct genera of sunfishes. Pap. Michigan Acad. Sci. Arts Ltrs. 15: 427–437.

412 Hubbs, C. L., L. C. Hubbs, and R. E. Johnson. 1943. Hybridization in nature between species of catostomid fishes. Contr. Lab. Vert. Biol. Univ. Michigan 22. 76 p.

413 Hubbs, C. L., and K. F. Lagler. 1958. Fishes of the Great Lakes region. Cranbrook Inst. Sci. Bull. 26 (rev.). 213 p.

414 Hubbs, C. L., and T. E. B. Pope. 1937. The spread of the sea lamprey through the Great Lakes. Trans. Amer. Fish. Soc. 66(1936): 172–176.

415 Hubbs, C. L., and I. C. Potter. 1971. Distribution, phylogeny, and taxonomy, p. 1–65. In: The Biology of lampreys. Vol. 1., M. W. Hardisty and I. C. Potter, eds., Academic Press. New York.

416 Hubbs, C. L., and E. C. Raney. 1939. *Hadropterus oxyrhynchus,* a new percid fish from Virginia and West Virginia. Univ. Michigan Mus. Zool. Occas. Pap. 396. 9 p.

417 ———. 1944. Systematic notes on North American siluroid fishes of the genus *Schilbeodes.* Univ. Michigan Mus. Zool. Occas. Pap. 487. 36 p.

418 ———. 1947. *Notropis alborus,* a new cyprinid fish from North Carolina and Virginia. Univ. Michigan Mus. Zool. Occas. Pap. 498. 17 p.

419 Hubbs, C. L., and M. B. Trautman. 1937. A revision of the lamprey genus *Ichthyomyzon.* Univ. Michigan Mus. Zool. Misc. Publ. 35. 109 p.

420 Hubbs. C. L., B. W. Walker, and R. E. Johnson. 1943. Hybridization in nature between species of American cyprinodont fishes. Contr. Lab. Vert. Biol. Univ. Michigan 23: 1–21.

421 Hubbs, C., and S. M. Dean. 1979. Growth and reproductive responses of *Menidia beryllina* (Atherinidae) inhabiting Lake Texoma. Southwestern Naturalist 24(3): 546–549.

422 Hubert, W. A. 1976. Age and growth of three black bass species in Pickwick reservoir. Proc. S-E Assn. Game Fish. Comm. 29(1975): 126–134.

423 Huggler, T. E. 1979. Pink salmon: the new midwest sport fish. Fishing World 26(4): 29–31.

424 Huish, M. T. 1957. Food habits of three Centrarchidae in Lake George, Florida. Proc. S-E Assn. Game Fish. Comm. 11: 293–302.

425 Huish, M. T., and D. F. Hoffmeister. 1947. The short-tailed shrew (*Blarina*) as a source of food for the green sunfish. Copeia 1947(3): 198.

426 Hunter, J. G. 1966. The Arctic char. Fish. Canada 19(3): 17–19.

427 Hunter, J. R. 1963. The reproductive behavior of the green sunfish, *Lepomis cyanellus*. Zoologica 48(1): 13–24.

428 Hunter, J. R., and A. D. Hasler. 1965. Spawning association of the redfin shiner, *Notropis umbratilis*, and the green sunfish, *Lepomis cyanellus*. Copeia 1965(3): 265–281.

429 Hunter, J. R., and W. J. Wisby. 1961. Utilization of the nests of green sunfish (*Lepomis cyanellus*) by the redfin shiner (*Notropis umbratilis cyanocephalus*). Copeia 1961(1): 113–115.

430 Huntsman, G. R. 1967. Nuptial tubercles in carpsuckers (Carpiodes). Copeia 1967(2): 457–458.

431 Hynes, H. B. N. 1950. The food of freshwater sticklebacks (*Gasterosteus aculeatus* and *Pygosteus pungitius*), with a review of methods used in studies of the food of fishes. J. Animal Ecology 19(1): 36–58.

432 Innes, W. T. 1947. Goldfish varieties and water gardens. Innes Publ. Co., Philadelphia. 381 p.

433 ———. 1951. Black-banded sunfish, p. 146–148. In: Aquarium Highlights, Innes Publ. Co., Philadelphia. 519 p.

434 Jackson, S. W., Jr. 1957. Comparison of the age and growth of four fishes from Lower and Upper Spavinaw Lakes, Oklahoma. Proc. S-E Assn. Game Fish. Comm. 11: 232–249.

435 Jaffa, B. B. 1917. Notes on the breeding and incubation periods of the Iowa darter, *Etheostoma iowae* Jordan and Meek. Copeia (47): 71–72.

436 Jenkins, R. E. 1970. Systematic studies of the catostomid fish tribe Moxostomatini. Ph.D. thesis, Cornell Univ., Ithaca, N.Y. 800 p.

437 Jenkins, R. E., and E. A. Lachner. 1971. Criteria for analysis and interpretation of the American fish genera *Nocomis* Girard and *Hybopsis* Agassiz. Smithsonian Contr. Zool. 90. 15 p.

438 Jenkins, R. E., E. A. Lachner, and F. J. Schwartz. 1971. Fishes of the central Appalachian drainages: their distribution and dispersal, p. 43–117. In: The distributional history of the biota of the southern Appalachians, Part III, Vertebrates. Virginia Poly. Inst. and State Univ., Res. Div. Monogr. 4.

439 Jenkins, R. E., L. A. Revelle, and T. Zorach. 1975. Records of the blackbanded sunfish, *Enneacanthus chaetodon*, and comments on the southeastern Virginia freshwater ichthyofauna. Virginia J. Sci. 26: 128–134.

440 Jenkins, R. E., and T. Zorach. 1970. Zoogeography and characters of the American cyprinid fish *Notropis bifrenatus*. Chesapeake Sci. 11(3): 174–182.

441 Jenkins, R. M. 1953. Growth histories of the principal fishes in Grand Lake (O' the Cherokees), Oklahoma, through thirteen years of impoundment. Oklahoma Fish. Res. Lab. Rep. 34. 87 p.

442 ———. 1956. Growth of blue catfish (*Ictalurus furcatus*) in Lake Texoma. Southwestern Naturalist 1(4): 166–173.

443 Jobes, F. W. 1949. The age, growth and distribution of the longjaw cisco, *Leucichthys alpenae* Koelz, in Lake Michigan. Trans. Amer. Fish. Soc. 76(1946): 215–247.

444 John, K. R., and A. D. Hasler. 1956. Observations on some factors affecting the hatching of eggs and the survival of young shallow-water cisco, *Leucichthys artedi* LeSueur, in Lake Mendota, Wisconsin. Limnol. Oceanogr. 1(3): 176–194.

445 Johnson, F. H. 1977. Responses of walleye (*Stizostedion vitreum vitreum*) and yellow perch (*Perca flavescens*) populations to removal of white sucker (*Catostomus commersoni*) from a Minnesota lake, 1966. J. Fish. Res. Bd. Canada 34: 1633–1642.

446 Johnson, L. D. 1958. Pond culture of muskellunge in Wisconsin. Wisconsin Cons. Dept. Tech. Bull. 17. 53 p.

447 Johnson, M. G. 1965. Estimates of fish populations in warmwater streams by the removal method. Trans. Amer. Fish. Soc. 94(4): 350–357.

448 Johnson, M. S. 1975. Biochemical systematics of the atherinid genus *Menidia*. Copeia 1975(4): 662–691.

449 Johnson, R. P. 1963. Studies on the life history and ecology of the bigmouth buffalo, *Ictiobus cyprinellus* (Valenciennes). J. Fish. Res. Bd. Canada. 20(6): 1397–1429.

450 Jones, J. W. 1959. The salmon. Harper and Brothers, New York. 192 p.

451 Jones, J. W., and H. B. N. Hynes. 1950. The age and growth of *Gasterosteus aculeatus*, *Pygosteus pungitius* and *Spinachia vulgaris*, as shown by their otoliths. J. Animal Ecology 19(1): 59–73.

452 Jordan, D. S. 1877. A partial synopsis of the fishes of upper Georgia with supplementary papers on fishes of Tennessee, Kentucky and Indiana. Ann. New York Lyceum Natur. Hist. 11: 307–377.

453 ———. 1877. On the fishes of northern Indiana. Proc. Acad. Natur. Sci. Philadelphia 29: 42–82.

454 ———. 1877. Notes on Cottidae, Etheostomatidae, Percidae, Centrarchidae, Aphredoderidae, Dorysomatidae and Cyprinidae, with revisions of the genera and descriptions of new or little known species. In: Contributions to North American ichthyology based primarily on the collection of the U. S. National Museum. Bull. U. S. Nat. Mus. 1877–78, 10: 1–116.

455 ———. 1878. A synopsis of the family Catostomidae. Bull. U. S. Nat. Mus. 12: 97–230.

456 ———. 1885. A catalogue of the fishes known to inhabit the waters of North America, north of the tropic of Cancer, with notes on the species discovered in 1883 and 1884. Rep. U. S. Comm. Fish and Fisheries 1884: 787–973.

457 ———. 1886. Note on the scientific name of the yellow perch, the striped bass, and other North American fishes. Proc. U. S. Nat. Mus. (1885) 8: 72–73.

458 ———. 1888. A manual of the vertebrate animals of the northern United States, including the district north and east of the Ozark mountains, south of the Laurential hills, north of the southern boundary of Virginia, and east of the Missouri river; inclusive of marine species. 5th ed. A. C. McClurg, Chicago. 375 p.

459 Jordan, D. S., and B. W. Evermann. 1890. Description of a new species of fish from the Tippecanoe River, Indiana. Proc. U. S. Nat. Mus. 13: 3–4.

460 ———. 1904. American food and game fishes. Doubleday, Page and Co., New York. 572 p.

461 Karr, J. R. 1963. Age, growth and food habits of Johnny, slenderhead and blacksided darters of Boone County, Iowa. Proc. Iowa Acad. Sci. 70: 228–236.

462 ———. 1964. Age, growth, fecundity and food habits of fantail darters in Boone County, Iowa. Proc. Iowa Acad. Sci. 71: 274–280.

463 Keast, A. 1965. Resource subdivision amongst cohabitating fish species in a bay, Lake Opinicon, Ontario. Univ. Michigan, Great Lakes Res. Div. 13: 106–132.

464 Keast, A., and D. Webb. 1966. Mouth and body form relative to feeding ecology in the fish fauna of a small lake, Lake Opinicon, Ontario. J. Fish. Res. Bd. Canada 23(12): 1845–1874.

465 Keast, A., and L. Welsh. 1968. Daily feeding periodicities, food uptake rates, and dietary changes with hour of day in some lake fishes. J. Fish. Res. Bd. Canada 25(6): 1133–1144.

466 Kelly, H. A. 1924. *Amia calva* guarding its young. Copeia (133): 73–74.

467 Kendall, W. C. 1902. Notes on the silversides of the genus *Menidia* of the east coast of the United States, with descriptions of two new subspecies. Rep. U.S. Fish Comm. (1901): 241–267.

468 ———. 1914. The fishes of New England. The Salmon Family. Part I.—The trout or charrs. Mem. Boston Soc. Nat. Hist. 8(1): 1–103.

469 ———. 1917. The pikes: their geographical distribution habits, culture, and commercial importance. U. S. Comm. Fish. Rep. for 1917, Bur. Fish. Doc. 853. 45 p.

470 ———. 1918. The Rangeley Lakes, Maine, with special reference to the habits of the fishes, fish culture and angling. Bull. U. S. Bur. Fish. 35(1915–1916): 487–594.

471 ———. 1927. The smelts. Bull. U. S. Bur. Fish. 42(1926): 217–375.

472 Kendall, W. C., and W. A. Dence. 1929. The fishes of the Cranberry Lake region. Roosevelt Wildl. Bull. 5(2): 219–276.

473 Kendall, W. C., and E. L. Goldsborough. 1908. The fishes of the Connecticut lakes and neighboring waters, with notes on the plankton environment. U. S. Bur. Fish. Doc. 633. 77 p.

474 Kennedy, W. A. 1943. The whitefish, *Coregonus clupeaformis* (Mitchill), of Lake Opeongo, Algonquin Park, Ontario. Univ. Toronto Studies, Biol. Ser. Publ. Ontario Fish. Res. Lab. 51: 23–66.

475 ———. 1949. Relationship of length, weight and sexual maturity to age in three species of Lake Manitoba fish. Fish. Res. Bd. Canada Bull. 81. 5 p.

476 ———. 1954. Growth, maturity and mortality in the relatively unexploited lake trout, *Cristivomer namaycush,* of Great Slave Lake. J. Fish. Res. Bd. Canada 11(6): 827–852.

477 Kennedy, W. A., and W. M. Sprules. 1967. Goldeye in Canada. Fish. Res. Bd. Canada Bull. 161. 45 p.

478 Keup, L., and J. Bayless. 1964. Fish distribution at varying salinities in Neuse River Basin, North Carolina. Chesapeake Sci. 5(3): 119–123.

479 Kinney, E. C., Jr. 1954. A life history study of the silver chub, *Hybopsis storeriana* (Kirtland), in western Lake Erie with notes on associated species. Ph.D. thesis, Ohio State Univ., Columbus. 99 p.

480 Kirtland, J. P. 1838. Report on the zoology of Ohio, p. 157–200. In: 2nd Ann. Rep. Geol. Surv. State of Ohio (by W. W. Mather, principal geologist, and the several assistants).

481 ———. 1841. Description of four new species of fishes. Boston J. Natur. Hist. 3(3): 273–279.

482 ———. 1841. Descriptions of the fishes of the Ohio River and its tributaries. Boston J. Natur. Hist. 3: 338–352, 469–482; 4: 16–26, 303–308; 5: 21–32.

483 ———. 1844. Descriptions of *Acipenser rubicundus, A. platyrhynchus* and *Rutilus storeianus.* Proc. Boston Soc. Natur. Hist. (1841–1844)1: 71.

484 Kitchell, J. F., and J. T. Windell. 1970. Nutritional value of algae to bluegill sunfish, *Lepomis macrochirus.* Copeia 1970(1): 186–190.

485 Klarberg, D. P., and A. Benson. 1975. Food habits of *Ictalurus nebulosus* in acid polluted water of northern West Virginia. Trans. Amer. Fish. Soc. 104(3): 541–547.

486 Klawe, W. L. 1957. Common mummichog and newt in a lake on Digby Neck, Nova Scotia. Canadian Field-Naturalist 71(3): 154–155.

487 Kleinert, S. J., and D. Mraz. 1966. Life history of the grass pickerel (*Esox americanus vermiculatus*) in southeastern Wisconsin. Wisconsin Cons. Dept. Techn. Bull. 37. 39 p.

488 Kneib, R. T. 1972. The effects of man's activity on the distribution of five stream fishes in Little Pine Creek, Pennsylvania. Proc. Pa. Acad. Sci. 46: 49–51.

489 Koelz, W. 1924. Two new species of cisco from the Great Lakes. Univ. Michigan Mus. Zool. Occas. Pap. 146. 8 p.

490 ———. 1929. Coregonid fishes of the Great Lakes. Bull. Bur. Fish. 43(1927): 297–643.

491 ———. 1931. The coregonid fishes of northeastern America. Pap. Michigan Acad. Sci. Arts Ltrs. 13(1930): 303–432.

492 Koshinsky, G. D. 1965. Limnology and fisheries of five Precambrian headwater lakes near Lac la Ronge, Saskatchewan. Sask. Dept. Natur. Res. Fish Rep. 7. 52 p.

493 Koski, R. T., E. C. Kenney, and B. E. Turnbaugh. 1971. A record-sized shortnose sturgeon from the Hudson River. New York Fish and Game J. 18(1): 75.

494 Koster, W. J. 1936. The life history and ecology of the sculpins (Cottidae) of central New York. Ph.D. thesis, Cornell Univ., Ithaca, N.Y.

495 ———. 1937. The food of sculpins (Cottidae) in central New York. Trans. Amer. Fish. Soc. 66(1936): 374–382.

496 ———. 1939. Some phases of the life history and relationships of the cyprinid, *Clinostomus elongatus* (Kirtland). Copeia 1939(4): 201–208.

497 Kott, E. 1974. a morphometric and meristic study of a population of the American brook lamprey, *Lethenteron lamottei* (LeSueur), from Ontario. Canadian J. Zool. 52(8): 1047–1055.

498 Kraatz, W. C. 1923. A study of the food of the minnow *Campostoma anomalum.* Ohio J. Sci. 23(6): 265–283.

499 ———. 1924. The intestine of the minnow *Campostoma anomalum* (Rafinesque), with special reference to the development of its coiling. Ohio J. Sci. 24(6): 265–298.

500 ———. 1928. Study of the food of the blunt-nosed minnow, *Pimephales notatus.* Ohio J. Sci. 28(2) 86–98.

501 Kramer, R. H., and L. L. Smith, Jr. 1960. Utilization of nest of largemouth bass, *Micropterus salmoides,* by golden shiners, *Notemigonus crysoleucas.* Copeia 1960(1): 73–74.

502 Krueger, W. H. 1961. Meristic variation in the fourspine stickleback, *Apeltes quadracus.* Copeia 1961(4): 442–450.

503 Krumholz, L. A. 1948. Reproduction in the western mosquitofish, *Gambusia affinis affinis* (Baird & Girard), and its use in mosquito control. Ecological Monogr. 18: 1–43.

504 ———. 1981. Observations on changes in the fish population of the Ohio River from Rafinesque to 1980. Trans. Kentucky Acad. Sci. 42(1–2): 1–15.

505 Kruse, K. C., and M. G. Francis. 1977. A predation deterrent in larvae of the bullfrog, *Rana catesbeiana.* Trans. Amer. Fish. Soc. 106(3): 248–252.

506 Kwain, W., and A. H. Lawrie. 1981. Pink salmon in the Great Lakes. Fisheries 6(2): 2–6.

507 Lacépède, B. G. 1802. Histoire naturelle des poissons. Vol. 4. Plassan, Paris. 728 p.

508 ———. 1803. Histoire naturelle des poissons. Vol 5. Plassan, Paris. 803 p.

509 Lachner, E. A. 1950. The comparative food habits of the cyprinid fishes *Nocomis biguttatus* and *Nocomis micropogon* in western New York. J. Washington Acad. Sci. 40(7): 229–236.

510 ———. 1952. Studies of the biology of the cyprinid fishes of the chub genus *Nocomis* of northeastern United States. Amer. Midl. Nat. 48(2): 433–466.

511 ———. 1956. The changing fish fauna of the Upper Ohio Basin, p. 64–78. In: Man and the Waters of the Upper Ohio Basin, C. A. Tryon, Jr., and M. A. Shapiro, eds. Special Publ. 1, Pymatuning Lab. of Field Biology, Univ. Pittsburgh. 100 p.

512 Lachner, E. A., and R. E. Jenkins. 1967. Systematics, distribution, and evolution of the chub genus *Nocomis* (Cyprinidae) in the southwestern Ohio River basin, with the description of a new species. Copeia 1967(3): 557–580.

513 ———. 1971. Systematics, distribution, and evolution of the chub genus *Nocomis* Girard (Pisces, Cyprinidae) of eastern United States, with descriptions of new species. Smithsonian Contr. Zool. 85. 97 p.

514 ———. 1971. Systematics, distribution and evolution of the *Nocomis biguttatus* species group (Family Cyprinidae: Pisces) with a description of a new species from the Ozark Upland. Smithsonian Contr. Zool. 91. 28 p.

515 Lachner, E. A., E. F. Westlake, and P. S. Handwerk. 1950.

Studies on the biology of some percid fishes from western Pennsylvania. Amer. Midl. Nat. 43(1): 92–111.

516 Lagler, K. F. 1956. The pike, *Esox lucius* Linnaeus, in relation to waterfowl on the Seney National Wildlife Refuge, Michigan. J. Wildl. Manag. 20(2): 114–124.

517 Lagler, K. F., and V. C. Applegate. 1942. Further studies of the food of the bowfin (*Amia calva*) in southern Michigan, with notes on the inadvisability of using trapped fish in food analyses. Copeia 1942(3): 190–191.

518 ———. 1943. Age and growth of the gizzard shad, *Dorosoma cepedianum* (Lesueur), with a discussion of its value as a buffer and as forage of game fishes. Invest. Indiana Lakes and Streams 2(1942): 99–110.

519 Lagler, K. F., and C. Hubbs. 1943. Fall spawning of the mud pickerel, *Esox vermiculatus* LeSueur. Copeia 1943(2): 131.

520 Lagler, K. F., and F. V. Hubbs. 1940. Food of the longnosed gar (*Lepisosteus osseus oxyurus*) and the bowfin (*Amia calva*) in southern Michigan. Copeia 1940(4): 239–241.

521 Lagler, K. F., C. B. Obrecht, and G. V. Harry. 1943. The food and habits of gars (*Lepisosteus spp.*) considered in relation to fish management. Invest. Indiana Lakes and Streams (1942) 2: 117–135.

522 Lagler, K. F., and W. E. Ricker. 1943. Biological fisheries investigations of Foots Pond, Gibson County, Indiana. Invest. Indiana Lakes and Streams 2(1942): 47–72.

523 Lake, C. T. 1936. The life history of the fan-tailed darter. Amer. Midl. Naturalist 17: 816–830.

524 Lambou, V. W. 1961. Utilization of macrocrustaceans for food by freshwater fishes in Louisiana and its effects on the determination of predator-prey relations. Progr. Fish-Cult. 23(1): 18–25.

525 Lamsa, A. 1963. Downstream movements of brook sticklebacks, *Eucalia inconstans* (Kirtland), in a small southern Ontario stream. J. Fish. Res. Bd. Canada 20(2): 587–589.

526 Langlois, T. H. 1929. Breeding habits of the northern dace. Ecology 10(1): 161–163.

527 ———. 1954. The western end of Lake Erie and its ecology. Edwards Bros. Ann Arbor, Michigan. 479 p.

528 Larimore, R. W. 1952. Home pools and homing behavior of smallmouth black bass in Jordan Creek. Illinois Nat. Hist. Surv. Div. Biol. Notes 28. 12 p.

529 ———. 1957. Ecological life history of the warmouth (Centrarchidae). Bull. Illinois Nat. Hist. Surv. 27(1): 1–83.

530 Larimore, R. W., and P. W. Smith. 1963. The fishes of Champaign County, Illinois, as affected by 60 years of stream changes. Bull. Illinois Natur. Hist. Surv. 28(2): 299–382.

531 Larsen, A. 1954. First record of the white perch (*Morone americana*) in Lake Erie. Copeia 1954(2): 154.

532 Latta, W. C. 1963. The life history of the smallmouth bass, *Micropterus d. dolomieui*, at Waugoshance Point, Lake Michigan. Bull. Inst. Fish. Res. Michigan, 5. 56 p.

533 Lawler, G. H. 1954. Observations on the trout-perch *Percopsis omiscomaycus* (Walbaum), at Heming Lake, Manitoba. J. Fish. Res. Bd. Canada 11(1): 1–4.

534 ———. 1960. A mutant pike, *Esox lucius*. J. Fish. Res. Bd. Canada 17(5): 647–654.

535 ———. 1965. Fluctuations in the success of year-classes of whitefish populations with special reference to Lake Erie. J. Fish. Res. Bd. Canada 22(5): 1197–1227.

536 Legendre, P. 1969. Two natural hybrids of the cyprinid fish *Chrosomus eos*. MS thesis, McGill Univ., Montreal, Quebec. 119 p.

537 Leidy, J. 1899. Notice and description of fossils in caves and crevices of the limestone rocks of Pennsylvania. Pa. Geol. Surv. Annual Rep. for 1887. p. 1–20.

538 Leim, A. H., and W. B. Scott. 1966. Fishes of the Atlantic Coast of Canada. Fish. Res. Bd. Canada Bull. 155. 485 p.

539 Lennon, R. E. 1954. Feeding mechanism of the sea lamprey and its effect on host fishes. U. S. Fish Wildl. Serv.,

Fish. Bull. 56: 247–293.

540 Lennon, R. E., and P. S. Parker. 1960. The stoneroller, *Campostoma anomalum* (Rafinesque), in Great Smoky Mountains National Park. Trans. Amer. Fish. Soc. 89(3): 263–270.

541 Leonard, A. K. 1927. The rate of growth and the food of the horned dace (*Semotilus atromaculatus*) in Quebec, with some data on the food of the common shiner (*Notropis cornutus*) and of the brook trout (*Salvelinus fontinalis*) from the same region. Publ. Ontario Fish. Res. Lab. 30: 35–44.

542 LeSueur, C. A. 1817. A short description of five (supposed) new species of the genus *Muraena*, discovered by Mr. LeSueur in the year 1816. J. Acad. Natur. Sci. Philadelphia 1(1): 81–83.

543 ———. 1817. Description of a new species of the genus *Cyprinus*. J. Acad. Natur. Sci. Philadelphia 1(1): 85–86.

544 ———. 1817. A new genus of fishes of the order Abdominales, proposed under the name of *Catostomus*, and the characters of this genus, with those of its species, indicated. J. Acad. Natur. Sci. Philadelphia 1(1): 88–96; 102–111.

545 ———. 1817. Descriptions of four new species, and two varieties, of the genus *Hydrargira*. J. Acad. Natur. Sci. Philadelphia 1(1): 126–134.

546 ———. 1818. Description of several new species of North American fishes. J. Acad. Nat. Sci. Philadelphia 1(2): 222–235, 359–368.

547 ———. 1818. Description of several new species of the genus *Esox*, of North America. J. Acad. Natur. Sci. Philadelphia 1(2): 413–417.

548 ———. 1818. Description of several species of chondropterygious fishes of North America, with their varieties. Trans. Amer. Phil. Soc. n.s. 1:383–394.

549 ———. 1819. Notice sur quelques poissons découverts dans les lacs du haut Canada, durant l'été de 1816. Mem. Mus. Hist. Natur. Paris 5: 148–161.

550 ———. 1828. In: G. A. Cuvier and M. A. Valenciennes. 1828–1849. Histoire naturelle des poissons. Vol. 22. Levrault, Strasborg, Paris.

551 Leverett, F. 1934. Glacial deposits outside the Wisconsin terminal moraine in Pennsylvania. Pa. Geol. Surv. 4th Ser. Bull. G7. 123 p.

552 Lewis, W. M., and D. Elder. 1953. The fish population of the headwaters of a spotted bass stream in southern Illinois. Trans. Amer. Fish. Soc. 82(1952): 193–202.

553 Lewis, W. M., and T. S. English. 1949. The warmouth, *Chaenobryttus coronarius* (Bartram), in Red Haw Hill Reservoir, Iowa. Iowa State Coll. J. Sci. 23(4): 317–322.

554 Lindsey, C. C. 1956. Distribution and taxonomy of fishes in the Mackenzie drainage of British Columbia. J. Fish. Res. Bd. Canada 13(6): 759–789.

555 Lindsey, C. C., J. W. Clayton, and W. G. Franzin. 1970. Zoogeographic problems and protein variation in the *Coregonus clupeaformis* whitefish species complex, p. 127–146. In: Biology of coregonid fishes. C. C. Lindsey and C. S. Woods, eds. Univ. Manitoba Press, Winnipeg. 560 p.

556 Lindsey, C. C., T. G. Northcote, and G. F. Hartman. 1959. Homing of rainbow trout to inlet and outlet spawning streams at Loon Lake, British Columbia. J. Fish. Res. Bd. Canada 16(5): 695–719.

557 Lindsey, C. C., and C. S. Woods, eds. 1970. Biology of coregonid fishes. Univ. Manitoba Press, Winnipeg. 560 p.

558 Linnaeus, C. 1758. Systema naturae per regna tria naturae, secundum classes, ordines, genera, species, cum characteribus, differentiis, synonymis, locis. 10th ed. Vol. 1. Laurentii Salvii, Holmiae. 824 p.

559 ———. 1766. Systema naturae per regna tria naturae, secundum classes, ordines, genera, species, cum characteribus, differentiis, synonymis, locis. 12 ed. Vol. 1. Laurentii Salvii, Holmiae. 532 p.

560 Lippson, A. J., and R. L. Moran. 1974. Manual for identification of early developmental stages of fishes of the Potomac River estuary. Martin Marietta Corp., Baltimore. 282 p.

561 Loftus, K. H. 1958. Studies on river-spawning populations of lake trout in eastern Lake Superior. Trans. Amer. Fish. Soc. 87(1957): 259–277.

562 Loos, J. J., and W. S. Woolcott. 1969. Hybridization and behavior in two species of *Percina* (Percidae). Copeia 1969(2): 374–385.

563 Luce, W. M. 1933. A survey of the fishery of the Kaskaskia River. Bull. Illinois Natur. Hist. Surv. 20(2): 71–123.

564 MacCrimmon, H. R., T. L. Marshall, and B. L. Gots. 1970. World distribution of brown trout, *Salmo trutta:* further observations. J. Fish. Res. Bd. Canada 27: 811–818.

565 MacCrimmon, H. R., and E. Skobe. 1970. The fisheries of Lake Simcoe. Ontario Dept. Lands Forests, Fish. Wildl. Branch, Toronto. 140 p.

566 Maciolek, J. A., and P. R. Needham. 1952. Ecological effects of winter conditions on trout and trout foods in Convict Creek, California, 1951. Trans. Amer. Fish. Soc. 81(1951): 202–217.

567 Magnin, E. 1963. Notes sur la répartition, la biologie et particulièrement la croissance de l'*Acipenser brevirostris* LeSueur 1817. Naturaliste Canadien 90(3): 87–96.

568 ———. 1964. Validité d'une distinction specifique entre le deux acipenserides: *Acipenser sturio* L. d'Europe et *Acipenser oxyrhynchus* d'Amerique du nord. Naturaliste Canadien 91(1): 5–20.

569 Magnuson, J. L., and L. L. Smith. 1963. Some phases of the life history of the trout-perch. Ecology 44(1): 83–95.

570 Malick, R. W., Jr., P. C. Ritson, and J. L. Polk. 1978. First records of the silvery minnow, *Hybognathus nuchalis* Agassiz, in the Susquehanna River drainage of Pennsylvania. Proc. Acad. Natur. Sci. Philadelphia 129(5): 83–85.

571 Manion, P. J. 1967. Diatoms as food of larval sea lampreys in a small tributary of northern Lake Michigan. Trans. Amer. Fish. Soc. 96: 224–226.

572 Mansueti, A. J. 1963. Some changes in morphology during ontogeny in the pirateperch, *Aphredoderus s. sayanus.* Copeia 1963(3): 546–557.

573 Mansueti, A. J., and J. D. Hardy, Jr. 1967. Development of fishes of the Chesapeake Bay Region. Part 1. Natur. Res. Inst., Univ. Maryland, Baltimore. 202 p.

574 Mansueti, R. J. 1951. Occurrence and habitat of the darter *Hololepis fusiformis erochrous* in Maryland. Copeia 1951(4): 301–302.

575 ———. 1958. The hickory shad unmasked. Nature Magazine 51(7): 351–354.

576 ———. 1961. Movements, reproduction, and mortality of the white perch, *Roccus americanus,* in the Patuxent Estuary, Maryland. Chesapeake Sci. 2(3–4): 142–205.

577 ———. 1962. Eggs, larvae, and young of the hickory shad, *Alosa mediocris,* with comments on its ecology in the estuary. Chesapeake Sci. 3(3): 173–205.

578 Mansueti, R. J., and H. J. Elser. 1953. Ecology, age and growth of the mud sunfish, *Acantharchus pomotis,* in Maryland. Copeia 1953 (2): 117–119.

579 Mansueti, R. J., and H. Kolb. 1953. A historical review of the shad fisheries of North America. Chesapeake Biol. Lab. Publ. 97. 293 p.

580 Markle, D. F. 1976. The seasonality of availability and movements of fishes in the channel of the York River, Virginia. Chesapeake Sci. 17(1): 50–55.

581 Markus, H. C. 1934. Life history of the blackhead minnow (*Pimephales promelas*). Copeia 1934(3): 116–122.

582 Marshall, N. 1947. Studies on the life history and ecology of *Notropis chalybaeus* (Cope). Quarterly J. Florida Acad. Sci. 9(3–4): 163–188.

583 Martin, N. V. 1966. The significance of food habits in the biology, exploitation, and management of Algonquin Park, Ontario, Lake trout. Trans. Amer. Fish. Soc. 95(4): 415–422.

584 Martin, N. V., and N. S. Baldwin. 1960. Observations on the life history of the hybrid between eastern brook trout and lake trout in Algonquin Park, Ontario. J. Fish. Res. Bd. Canada 17(4): 541–551.

585 Martin, R. G., and R. S. Campbell. 1953. The small fishes of Black River and Clearwater Lake, Missouri. Univ. Missouri Studies 26(2): 45–66.

586 Massmann, W. H. 1961. A Potomac River shad fishery, 1814–1824. Chesapeake Sci. 2(1-2): 76–81.

587 ———. 1967. A bibliography of the striped bass. Sport Fishing Institute, Washington, D.C. 15 p.

588 Massmann, W. H., and R. S. Bailey. 1956. The shad in Virginia waters. Virginia Wildlife, April 1956. 4 p.

589 Mauch, W. L., and D. W. Coble. 1971. Vulnerability of some fishes to northern pike (*Esox lucius*) predation. J. Fish. Res. Bd. Canada 28(7): 957–969.

590 McAllister, D. E. 1960. The twospine stickleback *Gasterosteus wheatlandi,* new to the Canadian freshwater fauna. Canadian Field-Naturalist 74(4): 177–178.

591 ———. 1961. The origin and status of the deepwater sculpin *Myoxocephalus thompsonii,* a nearctic glacial relict. Bull. Nat. Mus. Canada 172: 44–65.

592 ———. 1964. Distinguishing characters for the sculpins, *Cottus bairdi* and *C. cognatus,* in eastern Canada. J. Fish. Res. Bd. Canada 21(5): 1339–1342.

593 McAllister, D. E., and J. Aniskowicz. 1976. Vertebral number in North American sculpins of the *Myoxocephalus quadricornis* complex. J. Fish. Res. Bd. Canada 33(12): 2792–2799.

594 McAllister, D. E., and C. C. Lindsey. 1961. Systematics of the freshwater sculpins (*Cottus*) of British Columbia. Bull. Nat. Mus. Canada 172: 66–89.

595 McCammon, G. W., and C. M. Seeley. 1961. Survival, mortality, and movements of white catfish and brown bullheads in Clear Lake, California. Calif. Fish Game 47(3): 237–255.

596 McCann, J. A. 1959. Life history studies of the spottail shiner of Clear Lake, Iowa, with particular reference to some sampling problems. Trans. Amer. Fish. Soc. 88(4): 336–343.

597 McCarraher, D. B. 1960. Pike hybrids (*Esox lucius × E. vermiculatus*) in a sandhill lake, Nebraska. Trans. Amer. Fish. Soc. 89(1): 82–83.

598 McComish, T. S. 1967. Food habits of bigmouth and smallmouth buffalo in Lewis and Clark Lake and the Missouri River. Trans. Amer. Fish. Soc. 96(1): 70–74.

599 McConnell, W. R. 1906. Preliminary report of the investigation of certain waters of Pennsylvania. Rep. Pennsylvania Dept. Fish. 1905: 172–179.

600 McCrimmon, H. R. 1958. Observations on the spawning of lake trout, *Salvelinus namaycush,* and the post-spawning movement of adult trout in Lake Simcoe. Canadian Fish Cult. 23: 3–11.

601 ———. 1968. Carp in Canada. Fish. Res. Bd. Canada Bull. 165. 93 p.

602 McCrimmon, H. R., and O. E. Devitt. 1954. Winter studies on the burbot, *Lota lota lacustris,* of Lake Simcoe, Ontario. Canadian Fish-Cult. 16: 34–41.

603 McInerney, J. E. 1969. Reproductive behaviour of the blackspotted stickleback, *Gasterosteus wheatlandi.* J. Fish. Res. Bd. Canada 26(8): 2061–2075.

604 McKenzie, J. A., and M. H. A. Keenleyside. 1970. Reproductive behavior of ninespine sticklebacks (*Pungitius pungitius*(L.)) in South Bay, Manitoulin Island, Ontario. Canadian J. Zool. 48(1): 55–61.

605 McPhail, J. D. 1961. A systematic study of the *Salvelinus alpinus* complex in North America. J. Fish. Res. Bd. Canada 18(5): 793–816.

606 McPhail, J. D., and C. C. Lindsey. 1970. Freshwater fishes of northwestern Canada and Alaska. Fish. Res. Bd. Canada Bull. 173. 381 p.

607 Meade, J. W. 1976. Meet the Amur pike. Pennsylvania Angler 45(5): 8–11.

608 Meek, S. E. 1896. A list of fishes and mollusks collected in Arkansas and Indian territory in 1894. Bull. U. S. Fish. Comm. 15(1895): 341–349.

609 Menzel, R. W. 1945. The catfish fishery of Virginia. Trans. Amer. Fish Soc. 73(1943): 364–372.

610 Merriman, D. 1937. Notes on the life history of the striped bass (Roccus lineatus). Copeia 1937(1): 15–36.

611 Merriner, J. V. 1971. Development of intergeneric centrarchid hybrid embryos. Trans. Amer. Fish. Soc. 100(4): 611–618.

612 Metcalf. A. L. 1959. Fishes of Chautauqua, Cowley and Elk Counties, Kansas. Univ. Kansas Mus. Natur. Hist. Publ. 11(6): 345–400.

613 Meyer, W. H. 1962. Life history of three species of redhorse (Moxostoma) in the Des Moines River, Iowa. Trans. Amer. Fish. Soc. 91(4): 412–419.

614 Miller, E. E. 1966. White catfish, p. 430–440. In: Inland Fisheries Management. Alex Calhoun, ed. California Dept. Fish and Game. 546 p.

615 ———. 1966. Channel catfish, p. 440–463. In: Inland Fisheries Management. Alex Calhoun, ed. California Dept. Fish and Game. 546 p.

616 Miller J. G. 1962. Occurrence of ripe chain pickerel in the fall. Trans. Amer. Fish. Soc. 91(3) 323.

617 Miller, R. B. 1952. A review of the Triaenophorus problem in Canadian lakes. Fish. Res. Bd. Canada Bull. 95. 42 p.

618 Miller, R. B., and R. C. Thomas. 1957. Alberta's pothole trout fisheries. Trans. Amer. Fish. Soc. 86(1956): 261–268.

619 Miller, R. J. 1962. Reproductive behavior of the stoneroller minnow, Campostoma anomalum pullum. Copeia 1962(2): 407–417.

620 ———. 1968. Speciation in the common shiner: an alternate view. Copeia 1968(3): 640–647.

621 Miller, R. R. 1950. Notes on the cutthroat and rainbow trouts with the description of a new species from the Gila River, New Mexico. Univ. Michigan Mus. Zool. Occas. Pap. 529. 42 p.

622 ———. 1950. A review of the American clupeid fishes of the genus Dorosoma. Proc. U. S. Nat. Mus. 100(3267): 387–410.

623 ———. 1955. An annotated list of the American cyprinodontid fishes of the genus Fundulus, with the description of Fundulus persimilis from Yucatan. Univ. Michigan Mus. Zool. Occas Pap. 568. 25 p.

624 ———. 1957. Origin and dispersal of the alewife, Alosa pseudoharengus, and the gizzard shad, Dorosoma cepedianum, in the Great Lakes. Trans. Amer. Fish. Soc. 86: 97–111.

625 ———. 1960. Systematics and biology of the gizzard shad (Dorosoma cepedianum) and related fishes. U. S. Fish and Wildl. Serv. Fish. Bull. 60: 371–392.

626 ———. 1965. Quaternary freshwater fishes in North America, p. 569–581. In: The Quaternary of the United States. H. E. Wright, Jr. and David G. Frey, eds. VII Congress of the Intern. Assn. Quaternary Res., Princeton Univ. Press. 922 p.

627 ———. 1972. Threatened freshwater fishes of the United States. Trans. Amer. Fish. Soc. 101(2): 239–252.

628 Miller, R. V. 1968. A systematic study of the greenside darter, Etheostoma blennioides Rafinesque (Pisces: Percidae). Copeia 1968(1): 1–40.

629 Minckley, W. L. 1959. Fishes of the Big Blue River basin, Kansas. Univ. Kansas Mus. Natur. Hist. Publ. 11(7): 401–442.

630 ———. 1963. The ecology of a spring stream, Doe Run, Meade County, Kentucky. Wildl. Monogr. 11:1–124.

631 Minckley, W. L., and J. E. Deacon. 1959. Biology of the flathead catfish in Kansas. Trans. Amer. Fish. Soc. 88(4): 344–355.

632 Minckley, W. L., J. E. Johnson, J. N. Rinne, and S. E. Willoughby. 1970. Foods of buffalofishes, Genus Ictiobus, in central Arizona reservoirs. Trans. Amer. Fish. Soc. 99(2): 333–342.

633 Ming, A. D. 1968. Life history of the grass pickerel, Esox americanus vermiculatus in Oklahoma. Okla. Fish. Res. Lab. Bull. 8. 66 p.

634 Mitchill, S. L. 1814. Report in part of Samuel L. Mitchill, M.D., on the fishes of New York. D. Carlisle, N.Y. 28 p.

635 ———. 1815. Fishes of New York, Trans. Lit. Phil. Soc. New York 1: 355–492.

636 ———. 1815. On the fishes of New York. Notice in Trans. Linn. Soc. London 11(2): 424.

637 ———. 1817. Report on the ichthyology of the Walkill, from specimens of fishes presented to the Society (Lyceum of Natural History) by Dr. B. Akerly. Amer. Month. Mag. Crit. Rev. 1(4): 289–290.

638 ———. 1818. Memoir on ichthyology. The fishes of New York described and arranged. Amer. Month. Mag. Crit. Rev. 1817–1818, 2: 241–248; 321–328.

639 Moen, T. 1954. Food of the bigmouth buffalo, Ictiobus cyprinellus (Valenciennes), in northwest Iowa lakes. Proc. Iowa Acad. Sci. 61: 561–569.

640 Moody, H. L. 1957. A fisheries study of Lake Panasoffkee, Florida. Quart. J. Florida Acad. Sci. 20(1): 21–88.

641 Moore, G. A., and F. B. Cross. 1950. Additional Oklahoma fishes with validation of Poecilichthys parvipinnis (Gilbert and Swain). Copeia 1950(2): 139–148.

642 Moore, G. A., and R. C. McDougal. 1949. Similarity in the retinae of Amphiodon alosoides and Hiodon tergisus. Copeia 1949(4): 298.

643 Moore, G. A., and J. M. Paden. 1950. The fishes of the Illinois River in Oklahoma and Arkansas. Amer. Midl. Natur. 44(1): 76–95.

644 Moore, J. W., and F. W. H. Beamish. 1973. Food of larval sea lamprey (Petromyzon marinus) and American brook lamprey (Lampetra lamottei). J. Fish Res. Bd. Canada 30(1): 7–15.

645 Morrow, J. E. 1964. Populations of pike, Esox lucius, in Alaska and northeastern North America. Copeia 1946(1): 235–236.

646 Mount, D. I. 1959. Spawning behavior of the bluebreast darter, Etheostoma camurum (Cope). Copeia 1959(3): 240–243.

647 Moyle, J. B., and W. D. Clothier. 1959. Effects of management and winter oxygen levels on the fish population of a prairie lake. Trans. Amer. Fish. Soc. 88(3): 178–185.

648 Moyle, P. B. and R. D. Nichols. 1973. Ecology of some native and introduced fishes of the Sierra Nevada foothills in central California. Copeia 1973(3): 478–490.

649 Mraz, D., S. Kmiotek, and L. Frankenberger. 1961. The largemouth bass, its life history, ecology and management. Wisconsin Cons. Dept. Publ. 232. 13 p.

650 Mullan, J. S., R. L. Applegate, and W. C. Rainwater. 1968. Food of the logperch, Percina caprodes, and brook silverside, Labidesthes sicculus, in a new and old Ozark reservoir. Trans. Amer. Fish. Soc. 97(3): 300–305.

651 Muth, K., and L. L. Smith, Jr. 1974. The burbot fishery in Lake of the Woods. Univ. Minnesota Agri. Exp. Sta. Techn. Bull. 269. 68 p.

652 Myers, G. S. 1931. The primary groups of oviparous cyprinodont fishes. Stanford Univ. Publ. University Series, Biological Sci. 6(3): 241–254.

653 Needham, P. R. 1930. Studies on the seasonal food of brook trout. Trans. Amer. Fish. Soc. 60: 73–88.

654 Needham, P. R., and R. Gard. 1959. Rainbow trout in Mexico and California with notes on the cutthroat series. Univ. California Publ. Zool. 67(1): 1–124.

655 Neill, W. T. 1950. An estivating bowfin. Copeia 1950(3): 240.

656 Nelson, E. W. 1876. A partial catalogue of the fishes of Illinois. Illinois State Lab. Natur. Hist. Bull. 1(1): 33–52.

657 Nelson, J. S. 1968. Life history of the brook silverside, *Labidesthes sicculus,* in Crooked Lake, Indiana. Trans. Amer. Fish. Soc. 97(3): 293–296.

658 ——. 1968. Salinity tolerance of brook sticklebacks, *Culaea inconstans,* freshwater ninespine sticklebacks, *Pungitius pungitius,* and freshwater fourspine sticklebacks, *Apeltes quadracus.* Canadian J. Zool. 46(4): 663–667.

659 ——. 1969. Geographic variation in the brook stickleback, *Culaea inconstans,* and notes on nomenclature and distribution. J. Fish. Res. Bd. Canada 26(9): 2431–2447.

660 ——. 1971. Comparison of the pectoral and pelvic skeletons and of some other bones and their phylogenetic implications in the Aulorhynchidae and Gasterosteidae (Pisces). J. Fish. Res. Bd. Canada 28(3): 427–442.

661 ——. 1971. Absence of the pelvic complex in ninespine sticklebacks, *Pungitius pungitius,* collected in Ireland and Wood Buffalo National Park region, Canada, with notes on meristic variation. Copeia 1971(4): 707–717.

662 Nelson, W. R. 1968. Reproduction and early life history of sauger, *Stizostedion canadense,* in Lewis and Clark Lake. Trans. Amer. Fish. Soc. 97(2): 159–166.

663 Netboy, A. 1968. The Atlantic salmon. A vanishing species? Faber and Faber, London. 457 p.

664 Netsch, N. F. 1967. Food and feeding habits of longnose gar in central Missouri. Proc. S-E Assn. Game Fish. Comm. 18: 506–511.

665 Netsch, N. F., and A. Witt, Jr. 1962. Contributions to the life history of the longnose gar, *Lepisosteus osseus,* in Missouri. Trans. Amer. Fish. Soc. 91(3): 251–262.

666 New, J. G. 1962. Hybridization between two cyprinids, *Chrosomus eos* and *Chrosomus neogaeus.* Copeia 1962(1): 147–152.

667 ——. 1966. Reproductive behavior of the shield darter, *Percina peltata,* in New York. Copeia 1966(1): 20–28.

668 Newberry, J. S. 1889. The Paleozoic fishes of North America. U. S. Geol. Surv. Monogr. 16. 340 p.

669 Newman, H. H. 1907. Spawning behavior and sexual dimorphism in *Fundulus heteroclitus* and allied fish. Biol. Bull. 12(5): 314–348.

670 ——. 1908. The process of heredity as exhibited by the development of *Fundulus* hybrids. J. Exper. Zool. 5(4): 503–561.

671 Niemuth, W., W. Churchill, and T. Wirth. 1959. The walleye. Its life history, ecology and management. Wisconsin Cons. Dept. Publ. 227. 14 p.

672 Nikolskii, G. V. 1956. Fishes of the Amur Basin. Moscow, Acad. Sci. U.S.S.R. 551 p.

673 Noble, R. L. 1965. Life history and ecology of western blacknose dace, Boone County, Iowa, 1963–1964. Proc. Iowa Acad. Sci. 72: 282–293.

674 Norden, C. R. 1970. Evolution and distribution of the genus *Prosopium,* p. 67–80. In: Biology of coregonid fishes. C. C. Lindsey and C. S. Woods, eds. Univ. Manitoba Press, Winnipeg. 560 p.

675 Normandeau, D. A. 1969. Life history and ecology of the round whitefish, *Prosopium cylindraceum* (Pallas), of Newfoundland Lake, Bristol, New Hampshire. Trans. Amer. Fish. Soc. 98(1): 7–13.

676 Norris, T. 1862. Remarks on a species of *Osmerus* taken in the Schuylkill, below Fairmount Dam. Proc. Acad. Nat. Sci. Phila. 13(1861): 58–59.

677 Northcote, T. G., and H. W. Lorz. 1966. Seasonal and diel changes in food of adult kokanee (*Oncorhynchus nerka*) in Nicola Lake, British Columbia. J. Fish. Res. Bd. Canada 23(8): 1259–1263.

678 Nurnberger, P. K. 1928. A list of the plant and animal food of some fishes of Jay Cooke Park. Trans. Amer. Fish. Soc. 58: 175–177.

679 Odell, T. T. 1934. The life history and ecological relationships of the alewife (*Pomolobus pseudoharengus* (Wilson) in Seneca Lake, New York. Trans. Amer. Fish. Soc. 64: 118–126.

680 Oehmcke, A. A., L. Johnson, J. Klingbiel, and C. Wistrom 1958. The Wisconsin muskellunge, its life history, ecology and management. Wisconsin Cons. Dept. Publ. 225. 12 p.

681 Okkelberg, P. 1922. Notes on the life history of the brook lamprey, *Ichthyomyzon unicolor.* Univ. Michigan Mus. Zool. Occas. Pap. 125. 14 p.

682 Page, L. M. 1974. The subgenera of *Percina* (Percidae: Etheostomatini). Copeia 1974(1): 66–86.

683 ——. 1977. The lateralis system of darters (Etheostomatini). Copeia 1977(3): 472–475.

684 ——. 1978. Redescription, distribution, variation and life history notes on *Percina macrocephala* (Percidae). Copeia 1978(4): 655–664.

685 Page, L. M., and P. W. Smith. 1971. The life history of the slenderhead darter, *Percina phoxocephala,* in the Embarras River, Illinois. Illinois Nat. Hist. Surv. Biol. Notes 74: 1–14.

686 Pallas. In: T. Pennant. 1784 Artic zoology. Vol. 1. Henry Hughes, London. 185 p.

687 Paloumpis, A. A. 1958. Responses of some minnows to flood and drought conditions in an intermittent stream. Iowa State Coll. J. Sci. 32(4): 547–561.

688 Parker, H. L. 1964. Natural history of *Pimephales vigilax* (Cyprinidae). Southwestern Naturalist 8(4): 228–235.

689 Parker, M. V. 1939. A note on the food of the short-nosed gar at Reelfoot Lake. Rep. Reelfoot Lake Biol. Sta. 3: 186–187.

690 Parsons, J. W. 1959. Muskellunge in Tennessee streams. Trans. Amer. Fish. Soc. 88(2): 136–140.

691 Patriarche, M. H. 1953. The fishery in Lake Wappapello, a flood-control reservoir on the St. Francis River, Missouri. Trans. Amer. Fish Soc. 82(1952): 242–254.

692 Pearse, A. S. 1915. On the food of the small shore fishes in the waters near Madison, Wisconsin. Bull. Wisconsin Natur. Hist. Soc. 13(1): 7–22.

693 ——. 1919. Habits of the black crappie in inland lakes of Wisconsin. Rep. U. S. Commissioner of Fisheries for 1918. Bur. Fish. Doc. 867. 16 p.

694 Peckham, R. S., and C. F. Dineen. 1957. Ecology of the central mudminnow, *Umbra limi* (Kirtland). Amer. Midl. Nat. 58(1): 222–231.

695 Perlmutter, A. 1963. Observations on fishes of the genus *Gasterosteus* in the waters of Long Island, New York. Copeia 1963(1): 168–173.

696 Perry, W. G. 1973. Notes on the spawning of blue and channel catfish in brackish water ponds. Prog. Fish-Cult. 35(3): 164–166.

697 Petravicz, J. J. 1936. The breeding habits of the least darter, *Microperca punctulata* Putnam. Copeia 1936(2): 77–82.

698 Petravicz, W. P. 1938. The breeding habits of the blacksided darter, *Hadropterus maculatus.* Copeia 1938(1): 40–44.

699 Petrosky, C. E., and T. F. Waters. 1975. Annual production by the slimy sculpin population in a small Minnesota trout stream. Trans. Amer. Fish. Soc. 104(2): 237–244.

700 Pfeiffer, R. A. 1955. Studies on the life history of the rosyface shiner, *Notropis rubellus.* Copeia 1955(2): 95–104.

701 Pflieger, W. L. 1965. Reproductive behavior of the minnows *Notropis spilopterus* and *Notropis whipplii.* Copeia 1965(1): 1–8.

702 ——. 1966. Reproduction of the smallmouth bass (*Micropterus dolomieui*) in a small Ozark stream. Amer. Midl. Nat. 76(2): 410–418.

703 ——. 1971. A distributional study of Missouri fishes. Univ. Kansas Mus. Nat. Hist. Publ. 20(3): 225–270.

704 ——. 1975. The fishes of Missouri. Missouri Dept. Cons. 342 p.

705 Potter, G. E. 1924. Food of the short-nosed gar-pike (*Lepidosteus platystomus*) in Lake Okoboji, Iowa. Proc. Iowa Acad. Sci. 30(1923): 167–170.

706 ———. 1927. Ecological studies of the short-nosed gar-pike (*Lepidosteus platystomus*). Univ. Iowa Stud. Nat. Hist. 11(9): 17–27.

707 Power, G. 1969. The salmon of Ungava Bay. Arctic Inst. North America, Tech. Pap. 22: 1–72.

708 Prakash, A. 1962. Seasonal changes in feeding of coho and chinook (spring) salmon in southern British Columbia waters. J. Fish. Res. Bd. Canada 19(5): 851–866.

709 Prather, E. E., and H. S. Swingle. 1960. Preliminary results on the production and spawning of white catfish in ponds. Proc. S-E Assn Game Fish. Comm. 14: 143–145.

710 Price, J. W. 1963. A study of the food habits of some Lake Erie fish. Bull. Ohio Biol. Surv. 2(1): 1–89.

711 Priegel, G. R. 1962. Plentiful but unknown. Wisconsin Cons. Bull. 27(3): 13.

712 ———. 1963. Food of walleye and sauger in Lake Winnebago, Wisconsin. Trans. Amer. Fish. Soc. 92(3): 312–313.

713 ———. 1969. The Lake Winnebago sauger. Age, growth, reproduction, food habits and early life history. Wisconsin Dept. Nat. Res. Tech. Bull. 43. 63 p.

714 ———. 1970. Reproduction and early life history of the walleye in the Lake Winnebago region. Wisconsin Dept. Nat. Res. Tech. Bull. 45. 105 p.

715 Pritchard, A. L., and A. L. Tester. 1944. Food of spring and coho salmon in British Columbia. Fish. Res. Bd. Canada Bull. 65: 1–23.

716 Probst, R. T., and E. L. Cooper. 1955. Age, growth, and production of the lake sturgeon (*Acipenser fulvescens*) in the Lake Winnebago region, Wisconsin. Trans. Amer. Fish. Soc. 84: 207–227.

717 Purkett, C. A., Jr. 1958. Growth rates of Missouri stream fishes. Missouri Cons. Comm., Fish and Game Div. D-J Series 1. 46 p.

718 ———. 1961. Reproduction and early development of the paddlefish. Trans. Amer. Fish. Soc. 90(2): 125–129.

719 ———. 1963. Paddlefish fishery of the Osage River and the Lake of the Ozarks, Missouri. Trans. Amer. Fish. Soc. 92(3): 239–244.

720 Putnam, F. W. 1863. List of the fishes sent by the Museum to different institutions, in exchange for other specimens, with annotations. Bull. Harvard Mus. Comp. Zool. 1(1): 2–16.

721 ———. 1866. Remarks on a supposed nondescript species of *Gasterosteus* from Massachusetts. Proc. Essex Inst. 5: 4.

722 Radforth, I. 1944. Some considerations on the distribution of fishes in Ontario. Contr. Royal Ontario Mus. Zool. 25. 116 p.

723 Rafinesque, C. S. 1817. Additions to the observations on the sturgeons of North America. Amer. Month. Mag. Crit. Rev. 1(4): 288.

724 ———. 1817. First decade of new North American fishes. Amer. Month. Mag. Crit. Rev. 2(2): 120–121.

725 ———. 1818. Descriptions of two new genera of North American fishes, *Opsanus* and *Notropis*. Amer. Month. Mag. Crit. Rev. 2(3): 203–204.

726 ———. 1818. Discoveries in natural history made during a journey through the western region of the United States. Amer. Month. Mag. Crit. Rev. 3(5): 354–356.

727 ———. 1818. Further account of discoveries in natural history in the western states, by Constantine Samuel Rafinesque, Esq., communicated in a letter from that gentleman to the editor. Amer. Month. Mag. Crit. Rev. 4: 39–42.

728 ———. 1819. Prodrome de 70 nouveaux genres d'animaux découverts dans l'intérieur des Etats-Unis d'Amerique durant l'année 1818. J. Physique, Paris 88: 417–429.

729 ———. 1820. Description of the silures or catfishes of the river Ohio. Quart. J. Sci. Lit. Arts, Royal Inst. London 9: 48–52.

730 ———. 1820. Fishes of the Ohio. Western Rev. and Misc. Mag. 1: 361–377.

731 ———. 1820. Fishes of the River Ohio. Western Rev. and Misc. Mag. 2: 48–57, 169–177, 235–242, 299–307.

732 ———. 1820. Ichthyologia Ohiensis, or natural history of the fishes inhabiting the River Ohio and its tributary streams. Printed for the author by W. O. Hunt, Lexington, Kentucky. Reprint edition 1899, Burrows Brothers Co., Cleveland, Ohio. 175 p.

733 Raney, E. C. 1938. The distribution of fishes of the Ohio drainage basin of western Pennsylvania. Ph.D. thesis, Cornell Univ., Ithaca, N.Y. 102 p.

734 ———. 1939. The breeding habits of the silvery minnow, *Hybognathus regius* Girard. Amer. Midl. Nat. 21(3): 674–680.

735 ———. 1939. The breeding habits of *Ichthyomyzon greeleyi* Hubbs and Trautman. Copeia 1939(2): 111–112.

736 ———. 1939. Observations on the nesting habits of *Parexoglossum laurae* Hubbs and Trautman. Copeia 1939 (2): 112–113.

737 ———. 1940. The breeding behavior of the common shiner, *Notropis cornutus* (Mitchill). Zoologica 25(1): 1–14.

738 ———. 1940. Reproductive activities of a hybrid minnow. *Notropis cornutus* × *Notropis rubellus*. Zoologica 25(24): 361–367.

739 ———. 1940. Comparison of the breeding habits of two subspecies of black-nosed dace, *Rhinichthys atratulus* (Hermann). Amer. Midl. Nat. 23(2): 399–403.

740 ———. 1940. *Rhinichthys bowersi* from West Virginia a hybrid, *Rhinichthys cataractae* × *Nocomis micropogon*. Copeia 1940(4): 270–271.

741 ———. 1941. Range extensions and remarks on the distribution of *Parexoglossum laurae* Hubbs. Copeia 1941(4): 272.

742 ———. 1942. Propagation of the silvery minnow (*Hybognathus nuchalis regius* Girard) in ponds. Trans. Amer. Fish. Soc. 71: 215–218.

743 ———. 1942. The summer food and habits of the chain pickerel (*Esox niger*) of a small New York pond. J. Wildl. Manag. 6(1): 58–66.

744 ———. 1943. Unusual spawning habitat for the common white sucker, *Catostomus c. commersonnii*. Copeia 1943(4): 256.

745 ———. 1947. Subspecies and breeding behavior of the cyprinid fish *Notropis procne* (Cope). Copeia 1947(2): 103–109.

746 ———. 1949. Nests under the water. Canadian Nature 11(3): 71–78.

747 ———. 1950. Freshwater fishes of the James River basin, Virginia, p. 151–194. In: The James River basin, past, present and future. Virginia Acad. Sci. Richmond.

748 ———. 1952. The life history of the striped bass, *Roccus saxatilis* (Walbaum). Bull. Bingham Oceanogr. Collect. (Yale Univ.) 14(1): 5–97.

749 ———. A new lamprey, *Ichthyomyzon hubbsi,* from the upper Tennessee River system. Copeia 1952(2): 93–99.

750 ———. 1955. Natural hybrids between two species of pickerel (*Esox*) in Stearns Pond, Massachusetts, p. 405–419. In: Richard H. Stroud. Fisheries report for some central, eastern, and western Massachusetts lakes, ponds, and reservoirs, 1951–1952. Massachusetts Div. Fish. Game. 447 p.

751 ———. 1965. Some pan fishes of New York—rock bass, crappies and other sunfishes. The Conservationist, New York Cons. Dept. 19(6): 19–35.

752 Raney, E. C., and C. L. Hubbs. 1948. *Hadropterus notogrammus,* a new percid fish from Maryland, Virginia, and West Virginia. Univ. Michigan Mus. Zool. Occas. Pap. 512. 26 p.

753 Raney, E. C., and E. A. Lachner. 1939. Observations on the life history of the spotted darter, *Poecilichthys maculatus* (Kirtland). Copeia 1939(3): 157–165.

754 ———. 1946. Age, growth, and habits of the hog sucker,

Hypentelium nigricans (LeSueur), in New York. Amer. Midl. Nat. 36(1): 76–86.

755 Raney, E. C., and W. H. Massmann. 1953. The fishes of the tidewater section of the Pamunky River, Virginia. J. Washington Acad. Sci. 43(12): 424–432.

756 Raney, E. C., and D. A. Webster. 1940. The food and growth of the young of the common bullhead, *Ameiurus nebulosus nebulosus* (LeSueur), in Cayuga Lake, New York. Trans. Amer. Fish. Soc. 69(1939): 205–209.

757 ———. 1942. The spring migration of the common white sucker, *Catostomus c. commersonnii* (Lacepede), in Skaneateles Lake inlet, New York. Copeia 1942(4): 139–148.

758 Rathjen, W. F., and L. C. Miller. 1957. Aspects of the early life history of the striped bass (*Roccus saxatilis*) in the Hudson River. New York Fish and Game J. 4(1): 43–60.

759 Rawson, D. S. 1951. Studies of the fish of Great Slave Lake. J. Fish. Res. Bd. Canada 8(4): 207–240.

760 ———. 1957. The life history and ecology of the yellow walleye. *Stizostedion vitreum,* in Lac la Ronge, Saskatchewan. Trans. Amer. Fish. Soc. 86(1956): 15–37.

761 ———. 1959. Limnology and fisheries of Cree and Wollaston lakes in northern Saskatchewan. Saskatchewan Dept. Nat. Res. Fish. Rep. 4: 1–73.

762 Rawson, D. S., and C. A. Elsey. 1950. Reduction in the longnose sucker population of Pyramid Lake, Alberta, in an attempt to improve angling. Trans. Amer. Fish. Soc. 78(1948): 13–31.

763 Reckahn, J. A. 1970. Ecology of young lake whitefish (*Coregonus clupeaformis*) in South Bay, Manitoulin Island, Lake Huron, p. 437–460. In: Biology of Coregonid Fishes. Univ. Manitoba Press, Winnipeg. 560 p.

764 Redmond, L. C. 1964. Ecology of the spotted gar (*Lepisosteus oculatus* Winchell) in southeastern Missouri. MS thesis, Univ. Missouri. 144 p.

765 Reed, E. B. 1962. Limnology and fisheries of the Saskatchewan River in Saskatchewan. Saskatchewan Dept. Nat. Res. Fish. Rep. 6. 48 p.

766 Reed, H. D. 1907. The poison glands of *Noturus* and *Schilbeodes*. Amer. Naturalist 41: 553–566.

767 Reed, R. J. 1957. The prolonged spawning of the rosyface shiner, *Notropis rubellus* (Agassiz), in northwestern Pennsylvania. Copeia 1957(3): 250.

768 ———. 1957. Phases of the life history of the rosyface shiner, *Notropis rubellus,* in northwestern Pennsylvania. Copeia 1957(4): 286–290.

769 ———. 1959. Age, growth, and food of the longnose dace, *Rhinichthys cataractae,* in northwestern Pennsylvania. Copeia 1959(2): 160–162.

770 ———. 1971. Biology of the fallfish, *Semotilus corporalis* (Pisces, Cyprinidae). Trans. Amer. Fish. Soc. 100(4): 717–725.

771 Reeves, C. D. 1907. The breeding habits of the rainbow darter (*Etheostoma caeruleum* Storer), a study in sexual selection. Biological Bull. 14(1): 35–59.

772 Regier, H. A., V. C. Applegate, and R. A. Ryder. 1969. The ecology and management of the walleye in western Lake Erie. Great Lakes Fish. Comm. Tech. Rep. 15, 101 p.

773 Reid, G. K., Jr. 1950. Notes on the centrarchid fish *Mesogonistius chaetodon elizabethae* in peninsular Florida. Copeia 1950(3): 239–240.

774 Reighard, J. E. 1900. The breeding habits of the dogfish, *Amia calva.* Rep. Michigan Acad. Sci. 1(1894–1899): 133–137.

775 ———. 1906. The breeding habits, development and propagation of the black bass (*Micropterus dolomieui* Lacepede and *Micropterus salmoides* Lacepede). Bull. Michigan Fish. Comm. 7: 1–73.

776 ———. 1910. Methods of studying the habits of fishes, with an account of the breeding habits of the horned dace. Bull. (U.S.) Bur. Fish. 28(1908): 1111–1136.

777 ———. 1920. The breeding behavior of the suckers and minnows. Biol. Bull. 38(1): 1–32.

778 ———. 1943. The breeding habits of the river chub, *Nocomis micropogon* (Cope). Papers Mich. Acad. Sci. Arts Ltrs. 28(1942): 397–423.

779 Reighard, J. E., and H. Cummins. 1916. Description of a new species of lamprey of the genus *Ichthyomyzon*. Univ. Michigan Mus. Zool. Occas. Pap. 31: 1–12.

780 Reisman, H. M. 1963. Reproductive behavior of *Apeltes quadracus*. including some comparisons with other gasterosteid fishes. Copeia 1963(1): 191–192.

781 ———. 1968. Reproductive isolating mechanisms of the blackspotted stickleback, *Gasterosteus wheatlandi.* J. Fish. Res. Bd. Canada 25(12): 2703–2706.

782 Reno, H. W. 1966. The infraorbital canal, its lateral-line ossicles and neuromasts, in the minnows *Notropis volucellus* and *N. buchanani* Copeia 1966(3): 403–413.

783 ———. 1969. Cephalic lateral-line systems of the cyprinid genus *Hybopsis*. Copeia 1969(4): 736–773.

784 Repsys, A. J., R. L. Applegate, and D. C. Hales. 1976. Food and food selectivity of the black bullhead, *Ictalurus melas,* in Lake Poinsett, South Dakota. J. Fish. Res. Bd. Canada 33: 768–775.

785 Resh, V. H., R. D. Hoyt, and S. E. Neff. 1971. The status of the common shiner, *Notropis cornutus chrysocephalus* (Rafinesque), in Kentucky. Proc. S-E Assn. Game Fish. Comm. 25: 550–556.

786 Richardson, J. 1836. Fauna Boreali-Americana; or the zoology of the northern parts of British America: part third, the fish. Richard Bentley, London. 327 p.

787 Richardson, L. R. 1939. The spawning behavior of *Fundulus diaphanus* (LeSueur). Copeia 1939(3): 165–167.

788 Richardson, R. E. 1913. Observations on the breeding habits of fishes at Havana, Illinois, 1910 and 1911. Bull. Illinois Natur. Hist. Surv. 9: 405–416.

789 Richmond, N. D. 1940. Nesting of the sunfish, *Lepomis auritus* (Linnaeus), in tidal waters. Zoologica 25(21): 329–330.

790 Ricker, W. E. 1930. Feeding habits of speckled trout in Ontario waters. Trans. Amer. Fish. Soc. 60: 64–72.

791 ———. 1934. An ecological classification of certain Ontario streams. Univ. Toronto Studies, Biol. Ser. 37. 114 p.

792 ———. 1937. The food and the food supply of sockeye salmon (*Oncorhynchus nerka* Walbaum) in Cultus Lake, British Columbia. J. Biol. Bd. Canada 3(5): 450–468.

793 Rickett, J. D. 1976. Growth and reproduction of largemouth bass and black bullheads cultured together. Progr. Fish-Cult. 38(2): 82–85.

794 Riggs, C. D. 1955. Reproduction of the white bass, *Morone chrysops*. Invest. Indiana Lakes and Streams 4: 87–110.

795 Roach. L. S., and I. M. Evans. 1948. Growth of game and pan fish in Ohio. 2. Crappies. Ohio Div. Cons., Sec. Fish Mgmt. 29 p.

796 Robins, C. R. 1954. A taxonomic revision of the *Cottus bairdi* and *Cottus carolinae* species groups in eastern North America (Pisces, Cottidae). Ph.D. thesis, Cornell Univ. 230 p.

797 ———. 1961. Two new cottid fishes from the fresh waters of eastern United States. Copeia 1961(3): 305–315.

798 Robins, C. R., R. M. Bailey, C. E. Bond, J. R. Brooker, E. A. Lachner, R. N. Lea, and W. B. Scott. 1980. A list of common and scientific names of fishes from the United States and Canada. 4th ed. Amer. Fish. Soc. Spec. Publ. No. 12. 174 p.

799 Robins, C. R., and E. E. Deubler, Jr. 1955. The life history and systematic status of the burbot, *Lota lota lacustris* (Walbaum), in the Susquehanna River system. New York State Mus. and Sci. Serv. Circ. 39. 49 p.

800 Robins, C. R., and E. C. Raney. 1956. Studies of the catostomid fishes of the genus *Moxostoma,* with descriptions of two new species. Cornell Univ. Agri. Exp. Sta. Memoir 343. 56 p.

801 Robinson, D. T. 1959. The ichthyofauna of the lower Rio

Grande, Texas and Mexico. Copeia 1959(3): 253–256.

802 Rohde, F. C., R. G. Arndt, and J. C. S. Wang. 1974. Additional records of the least brook lamprey, Okkelbergia aepyptera (Abbott), from the Delmarva Peninsula. Chesapeake Sci. 15(3): 154–155.

803 ———. 1975. Records of the freshwater lampreys, Lampetra lamottenii and Okkelbergia aepyptera, from the Delmarva Peninsula (East Coast, United States). Chesapeake Sci. 16(1): 70–72.

804 ———. 1976. Life history of the freshwater lampreys, Okkelbergia aepyptera and Lampetra lamottenii (Pisces: Petromyzonidae), on the Delmarva Peninsula (East Coast, United States). Southern California Acad. Sci. Bull. 75: 99–111.

805 Romer, A. S. 1942. Notes on certain American Paleozoic fishes. Amer. J. Sci. 240: 216–228.

806 Roos, J. F. 1960. Predation of young coho salmon on sockeye salmon fry at Chignik, Alaska. Trans. Amer. Fish. Soc. 89(4): 377–379.

807 Ross, R. D. 1958. Races of the cyprinid fish Campostoma anomalum pullum (Agassiz) in eastern United States. Virginia Agri. Exp. Sta. Techn. Bull. 136. 20 p.

808 ———. 1958. Some taxonomic problems of Shenandoah River fishes. Virginia Agri. Exp. Sta. Techn. Bull. 137. 10 p.

809 Rostlund, E. 1952. Freshwater fish and fishing in native North America. Univ. California Publ. Geography 9:1–313.

810 Rounsefell, G. A., and L. D. Stringer. 1945. Restoration and management of the New England alewife fisheries with special reference to Maine. Trans. Amer. Fish. Soc. 73: 394–424.

811 Roussow, G. 1957. Some considerations concerning sturgeon spawning periodicity. J. Fish. Res. Bd. Canada 14(4): 553–572.

812 Rupp, R. S. 1965. Shore-spawning and survival of eggs of the American smelt. Trans. Amer. Fish. Soc. 94(2): 160–168.

813 Ryder, J. A. 1886. The development of the mud-minnow. Amer. Naturalist 20: 823–824.

814 ———. 1890. The sturgeon and sturgeon industries of the eastern coast of the United States, with an account of experiments bearing upon sturgeon culture. Bull. U. S. Fish. Comm. (1888), 8: 231–328.

815 Savage, T. 1962. Cottus girardi Robins, a synonym of Cottus bairdi Girard. Copeia 1962(4): 848–850.

816 ———. 1963. Reproductive behavior of the mottled sculpin, Cottus bairdi Girard. Copeia 1963(2): 317–325.

817 Sawyer, P. J. 1957. Laboratory care and feeding of larval lampreys. Copeia 1957(3): 244.

818 Schloemer, C. L. 1947. Reproductive cycles of five species of Texas centrarchids. Science 106: 85–86.

819 Schneider, H., and A. D. Hasler. 1960. Laute und lauterzeugung beim susswassertrommler Aplodinotus grunniens Rafinesque (Sciaenidae, Pisces). Zeitschrift fur vergleichende Physiologie 43: 499–517.

820 Schoffman, R. J. 1939. Age and growth of the red-eared sunfish in Reelfoot Lake. J. Tennessee Acad. Sci. 14(1): 61–71.

821 ———. 1940. Age and growth of the black and white crappie, the warmouth bass, and the yellow bass in Reelfoot Lake. Report of Reelfoot Lake Biol. Sta. 4: 22–42.

822 ———. 1941. Age and growth of the drum in Reelfoot Lake. J. Tennessee Acad. Sci. 16(1): 100–110.

823 ———. 1944. Age and growth of the smallmouth buffalo in Reelfoot Lake. J. Tennessee Acad. Sci. 19(1): 3–9.

824 ———. 1955. Age and rate of growth of the yellow bullhead in Reelfoot Lake, Tennessee. J. Tennessee Acad. Sci. 30(1): 4–7.

825 Schultz, L. P. 1927. Temperature-controlled variation in the golden shiner, Notemigonus crysoleucas. Pap. Michigan Acad. Sci. Arts Ltrs. 7(1926): 417–432.

826 Schwartz, F. J. 1959. Records of the Allegheny brook lam-

prey, Ichthyomyzon greeleyi Hubbs and Trautman, from West Virginia, with comments on its occurrence with Lampetra aepyptera (Abbott). Ohio J. Sci. 59(4): 217–220.

827 ———. 1961. Food, age, growth, and morphology of the blackbanded sunfish, Enneacanthus c. chaetodon, in Smithville Pond, Maryland. Chesapeake Sci. 2(1–2): 82–88.

828 ———. 1963. The fresh-water minnows of Maryland. Maryland Conservationist 40(2): 19–29.

829 ———. 1965. The distribution and probable postglacial dispersal of the percid fish, Etheostoma b. blennioides, in the Potomac River. Copeia 1965(3): 285–290.

830 ———. 1965. Age, growth, and egg complement of the stickleback Apeltes quadracus at Solomons, Maryland. Chesapeake Sci. 6(2): 116–118.

831 Schwartz, F. J., and R. Jachowski. 1965. The age, growth, and length-weight relationship of the Patuxent River, Maryland, ictalurid white catfish, Ictalurus catus. Chesapeake Sci. 6(4): 226–229.

832 Schwartz, F. J., and J. Norvell. 1958. Food, growth, and sexual dimorphism of the redside dace, Clinostomus elongatus (Kirtland), in Linesville Creek, Crawford County, Pennsylvania. Ohio J. Sci. 58(5): 311–316.

833 Scofield, E. C. 1931. The striped bass of California (Roccus lineatus). California Div. Fish and Game, Fish Bull. 29. 84 p.

834 Scott, D. C. 1949. A study of a stream population of rock bass, Ambloplites rupestris. Invest. Indiana Lakes and Streams 3(3): 169–234.

835 Scott, D. M. 1955. Additional records of two fishes, Erimyzon sucetta kennerlyi and Hadropterus copelandi, from southern Ontario, Canada. Copeia 1955(2): 151.

836 Scott, W. B. 1952. Records of the western lake chub-sucker, Erimyzon sucetta kennerleyi, from Ontario, Canada. Copeia 1952(3): 203.

837 ———. 1967. Freshwater fishes of eastern Canada. 2d. ed. Univ. Toronto Press, Toronto. 137 p.

838 Scott, W. B., and W. J. Christie. 1963. The invasion of the lower Great Lakes by the white perch, Roccus americanus (Gmelin). J. Fish. Res. Bd. Canada 20(5): 1189–1195.

839 Scott, W. B., and E. J. Crossman. 1973. Freshwater fishes of Canada. Fish. Res. Bd. Canada Bull. 184. 966 p.

840 Scott, W. B., and S. H. Smith. 1962. The occurrence of the longjaw cisco, Leucichthys alpenae, in Lake Erie. J. Fish. Res. Bd. Canada 19(6): 1013–1023.

841 Seaburg, K. G., and J. B. Moyle. 1964. Feeding habits, digestive rates, and growth of some Minnesota warmwater fishes. Trans. Amer. Fish. Soc. 93(3): 269–285.

842 Seguin, R. L. 1956. Limites geographiques et facteurs climatiques de la distribution naturelle de la truite mouchetée. Revue canadienne de Geographie 10(2–3): 113–117.

843 Self, J. T. 1940. Notes on the sex cycle of Gambusia affinis affinis, and on its habits and relation to mosquito control. Amer. Midl. Nat. 23(2): 393–398.

844 Seversmith, H. F. 1953. Distribution, morphology and life history of Lampetra aepyptera, a brook lamprey in Maryland. Copeia 1953(4): 225–232.

845 Shannon, E. H. 1967. Geographical distribution and habitat requirements of the redbreast sunfish, Lepomis auritus, in North Carolina. Proc. S-E Assn. Game Fish. Comm. 20(1966): 319–323.

846 Shapovalov, L. 1951. A remarkable sea journey by a rainbow trout (Salmo gairdnerii) of interior stock. California Fish Game 37(4): 489–490.

847 Shapovalov, L., and A. C. Taft. 1954. The life histories of the steelhead rainbow trout (Salmo gairdneri gairdneri) and silver salmon (Oncorhynchus kisutch) with special reference to Waddell Creek, California, and recommendations regarding their management. California Dept. Fish and Game, Fish Bull. 98. 375 p.

848 Sheri, A. N., and G. Power. 1968. Reproduction of white

perch, *Roccus americanus,* in the Bay of Quinte, Lake Ontario. J. Fish. Res. Bd. Canada 25(10): 2225–2231.

849 Shetter, D. S., and G. R. Alexander. 1965. Results of angling under special and normal trout fishing regulations in a Michigan trout stream. Trans. Amer. Fish. Soc. 94(3): 219–226.

850 Shields, J. T. 1955. Report of fisheries investigations during the second year of impoundment of Fort Randall Reservoir, South Dakota, 1954. South Dakota Dept. Game Fish Parks, Dingell-Johnson Proj. F-1-R-4. 102 p.

851 Shoemaker, H. H. 1947. Pickerel and pumpkinseed coaction over the sunfish nest. Copeia 1947(3): 195–196.

852 Sibley, C. K. 1929. The food of certain fishes of the Lake Erie drainage basin, p. 180–188. In: A biological survey of the Erie-Niagara system. New York Cons. Dept., Suppl. to 18th Annual Rep. (1928). 244 p.

853 Siefert, R. E. 1968. Reproductive behavior, incubation and mortality of eggs, and postlarval food selection in the white crappie. Trans. Amer. Fish. Soc. 97(3): 252–259.

854 Sigler, W. F. 1949. Life history of the white bass, *Lepibema chrysops* (Rafinesque) of Spirit Lake, Iowa. Iowa State Agri. Exp. Sta. Res. Bull. 366: 201–244.

855 Silliman, R. P. 1941. Fluctuations in the diet of the chinook and silver salmons (*Oncorhynchus tshawytscha* and *O. kisutch*) off Washington, as related to the troll catch of salmon. Copeia 1941(2): 80–87.

856 Sisk, M. E. 1966. Unusual spawning behavior of the northern creek chub, *Semotilus atromaculatus* (Mitchill). Trans. Kentucky Acad. Sci. 27(1–2): 3–4.

857 Slipp, J. W. 1943. The rock bass, *Ambloplites rupestris,* in Washington State. Copeia 1943(2): 132.

858 Smallwood, W. M., and P. H. Struthers. 1928. Carp control studies in Oneida Lake, p. 67–83. In: A biological survey of the Oswego River system. Suppl. 17 Ann. Rep. (1927), New York Cons. Dept. 248 p.

859 Smith, B. G. 1908. The spawning habits of *Chrosomus erythrogaster* Rafinesque. Biol. Bull. 15(1): 9–18.

860 ———. 1923. Notes on the nesting habits of *Cottus.* Pap. Michigan Acad. Sci. Arts Ltrs. 2: 221–225.

861 Smith, L. L., Jr., and R. H. Kramer. 1964. The spottail shiner in Lower Red Lake, Minnesota. Trans. Amer. Fish. Soc. 93(1): 35–45.

862 Smith, M. W. 1952. Limnology and trout angling in Charlotte County lakes, New Brunswick. J. Fish. Res. Bd. Canada 8(6): 381–452.

863 Smith, P. W., and L. M. Page. 1969. The food of spotted bass in streams of the Wabash River drainage. Trans. Amer. Fish. Soc. 98(4): 647–651.

864 Smith, S. H. 1956. Life history of the lake herring of Green Bay, Lake Michigan. U. S. Fish Wildl. Serv. Fish. Bull. 57: 87–138.

865 ———. 1968. The alewife. Limnos 1(2): 1–9.

866 Snelson, F. F., Jr. 1968. Systematics of the cyprinid fish *Notropis amoenus,* with comments on the subgenus *Notropis.* Copeia 1968(4): 776–802.

867 ———. 1972. Systematics of the subgenus *Lythrurus,* genus *Notropis* (Pisces: Cyprinidae). Bull. Florida State Mus. Biol Sci. 17(1): 1–92.

868 Snelson, F. F., Jr., and W. L. Pflieger. 1975. Redescription of the redfin shiner, *Notropis umbratilis,* and its subspecies in the central Mississippi River basin. Copeia 1975(2): 231–249.

869 Snow, H., A. Ensign, and J. Klingbiel. 1960. The bluegill, its life history, ecology and management. Wisconsin Cons. Dept. Publ. 230. 14 p.

870 Spoor, W. A. 1935. On the sexual dimorphism of *Catostomus commersonnii* (Lacepede). Copeia 1935(4): 167–171.

871 Starrett, W. C. 1950. Distribution of the fishes of Boone County, Iowa, with special reference to the minnows and darters. Amer. Midl. Natur. 43(1): 112–127.

872 ———. 1950. Food relationships of the minnows of the Des Moines River, Iowa. Ecology 31(2): 216–233.

873 ———. 1951. Some factors affecting the abundance of minnows in the Des Moines River, Iowa. Ecology 32(1): 13–27.

874 Stauffer, J. 1864. (Description of *Percina peltata*). In: E. D. Cope. On a blind silurid from Pennsylvania. Proc. Acad. Natur. Sci. Philadelphia 16: 231–233.

875 Stevens, R. E. 1959. The white and channel catfishes of the Santee-Cooper Reservoir and tailrace sanctuary. Proc. S-E Assn. Game Fish. Comm. 13: 203–219.

876 Stewart, N. H. 1926. Development, growth, and food habits of the white sucker, *Catostomus commersonnii* LeSueur. Bull. (U.S.) Bur. Fish. 42: 147–184.

877 Stockard, C. R. 1907. Observations on the natural history of *Polyodon spathula.* Amer. Naturalist 41: 753–766.

878 Stone, F. L. 1948. MS. A study of the taxonomy of the blue and the yellow pikeperches (*Stizostedion*) of Lake Erie and Lake Ontario. Ph.D. thesis, Univ. Rochester, Rochester, N.Y. 164 p.

879 Storer, D. H. 1844. Descriptions of two new species of fishes. Boston J. Natur. Hist. 4 (1843–1844): 58–62.

880 ———. 1845. Description of hitherto undescribed fishes. Proc. Boston Soc. Natur. Hist. 2: 47–49.

881 Stout, J. F. 1963. The significance of sound production during the reproductive behavior of *Notropis analostanus* (Family Cyprinidae). Animal Behavior 11: 83–92.

882 Strauss, R. E. 1977. Morphometric and electrophoretic analysis of the systematic status of *Cottus girardi* Robins (Pisces: Cottidae). MS thesis, Pennsylvania State Univ. 125 p.

883 Stroud, R. H., and H. Bitzer. 1955. Harvests and management of warm-water fish populations in Massachusetts' lakes, ponds and reservoirs. Progr. Fish-Cult. 17(2): 51–63.

884 Summerfelt, R. C., and C. O. Minckley. 1969. Aspects of the life history of the sand shiner, *Notropis stramineus* (Cope), in the Smoky Hill River, Kansas. Trans. Amer. Fish. Soc. 98(3): 444–453.

885 Suttkus, R. D. 1958. Status of the nominal cyprinid species *Moniana deliciosa* Girard and *Cyprinella texana* Girard. Copeia 1958(4): 307–318.

886 ———. 1963. Order Lepisostei, p. 61–88. In: Fishes of the western North Atlantic. Mem. Sears Found. Marine Res. 1(3): 1–630.

887 Svardson, G. 1970. Significance of introgression in coregonid evolution, p. 33–59. In: Biology of coregonid fishes. C. C. Lindsey and C. S. Woods, eds. Univ. Manitoba Press, Winnipeg. 560 p.

888 Swingle, H. S., and E. V. Smith. 1950. Factors affecting the reproduction of blue-gill bream and largemouth black bass in ponds. Alabama Poly. Inst. Agri. Exp. Sta. Circ. 87. 8 p.

889 Sykes, J. E., and B. A. Lehman. 1957. Past and present Delaware River shad fishery and considerations for its future. U. S. Fish Wildl. Serv. Res. Rep. 46. 25 p.

890 Talbot, G. B., and J. E. Sykes. 1958. Atlantic Coast migrations of of American shad. U. S. Fish Wildl. Serv. Fish. Bull. 58: 473–490.

891 Tanyolac, J. 1973. Morphometric variation and life history of the cyprinid fish *Notropis stramineus* (Cope). Occas. Pap. Mus. Nat. Hist. (Kansas): 12: 1–28.

892 Taylor, W. R. 1969. A revision of the catfish genus *Noturus* Rafinesque, with an analysis of higher groups in the Ictaluridae. U. S. Nat. Mus. Bull. 282. 315 p.

893 Thoits, C. F., III. 1958. A compendium of the life history and ecology of the white perch. Massachusetts Div. Fish Game Fish. Bull. 24. 16 p.

894 Thomas, B. O. 1962. Behavioral studies of the brook stickleback, *Eucalia inconstans* (Kirtland). Amer. Zool. 2(3): 452.

895 Thomas, D. L. 1970. An ecological study of four darters of the genus *Percina* (Percidae) in the Kaskaskia River, Illi-

nois. Illinois Nat. Hist. Surv. Biol. Notes 70: 1–18.

896 Thorpe, J. E. 1977. Morphology, physiology, behavior and ecology of *Perca fluviatilis* L. and *P. flavescens* Mitchill. J. Fish. Res. Bd. Canada 34(10): 1504–1514.

897 Tiffany, L. H. 1921. The gizzard shad in relation to plants and game fishes. Trans. Amer. Fish. Soc. 50(1920): 381–386.

898 Tilton, J. E., and R. L. White. 1964. *Menidia beryllina* from several central Texas impoundments. Texas J. Sci. 16: 120.

899 Todd, J. H., J. Atema, and J. E. Bardach. 1967. Chemical communication in social behavior of a fish, the yellow bullhead (*Ictalurus natalis*). Science 158: 672–673.

900 Trautman, M. B. 1931. *Parexoglossum hubbsi*, a new cyprinid fish from western Ohio. Univ. Michigan Mus. Zool. Occas. Pap. 235. 11 p.

901 ————. 1948. A natural hybrid catfish, *Schilbeodes miurus* × *Schilbeodes mollis*. Copeia 1948(3): 166–174.

902 ————. 1957. The fishes of Ohio, with illustrated keys. Ohio State Univ. Press, Columbus. 683 p.

903 Traver, J. R. 1929. The habits of the blacknosed dace, *Rhinichthys atronasus* (Mitchill). J. Elisha Mitchell Sci. Soc. 45(1): 101–129.

904 Trembley, F. J. 1930. The gar-pike of Lake Champlain, p. 139–145. In: A biological survey of the Champlain watershed. Suppl. 19th Ann. Rep. (1929). New York Cons. Dept. 321 p.

905 Trent, L., and W. W. Hassler. 1966. Feeding behavior of adult striped bass, *Roccus saxatilis*, in relation to stages of sexual maturity. Chesapeake Sci. 7(4): 189–192.

906 Tsai, C. 1972. Life history of the eastern Johnny darter, *Etheostoma olmstedi* Storer, in cold tailwater and sewage-polluted water. Trans. Amer. Fish. Soc. 101(1): 80–88.

907 Tsai, C., and E. C. Raney. 1974. Systematics of the banded darter, *Etheostoma zonale* (Pisces: Percidae). Copeia 1974(1): 1–24.

908 Turner, C. L. 1921. Food of the common Ohio darters. Ohio J. Sci. 22(2): 41–62.

909 Tyler, A. V. 1963. A cleaning symbiosis between the rainwater fish, *Lucania parva*, and the stickleback, *Apeltes quadracus*. Chesapeake Sci. 4(1): 105–106.

910 Underhill, A. H. 1941. Estimation of a breeding population of chub suckers. Trans. 5th North Amer. Wildl. Conf. p. 251–256.

911 ————. 1949. Studies on the development, growth and maturity of the chain pickerel, *Esox niger* LeSueur. J. Wildl. Manag. 13(4): 377–391.

912 Van Cleave, H. J., and H. C. Markus. 1929. Studies on the life history of the blunt-nosed minnow. Amer. Naturalist 63: 530–539.

913 Vandermeer, J. H. 1966. Statistical analysis of geographic variation of the fathead minnow, *Pimephales promelas*. Copeia 1966(3): 457–466.

914 Van Duzer, E. M. 1939. Observations on the breeding habits of the cut-lips minnow, *Exoglossum maxillingua*. Copeia 1939(2): 65–75.

915 Vanicek, D. 1961. Life history of the quillback and highfin carpsuckers in the Des Moines River. Proc. Iowa Acad. Sci. 68: 238–246.

916 Van Meter, H. D., and M. B. Trautman. 1970. An annotated list of the fishes of Lake Erie and its tributary waters exclusive of the Detroit River. Ohio J. Sci. 70(2): 65–78.

917 Van Oosten, J. 1929. Life history of the lake herring (*Leucichthys artedi* LeSueur) of Lake Huron as revealed by its scales, with a critique of the scale method. Bull. Bur. Fish. 44 (1928): 265–428.

918 ————. 1937. First records of the smelt, *Osmerus mordax*, in Lake Erie. Copeia 1937(1): 64–65.

919 ————. 1942. The age and growth of the Lake Erie white bass, *Lepibema chrysops* (Rafinesque). Pap. Michigan Acad. Sci. Arts Ltrs. 27: 307–334.

920 ————. 1947. Mortality of smelt, *Osmerus mordax* (Mitchill), in Lakes Huron and Michigan during the fall and winter of 1942–1943. Trans. Amer. Fish. Soc. 74(1944): 310–337.

921 ————. 1961. Records, ages, and growth of the mooneye, *Hiodon tergisus*, of the Great Lakes. Trans. Amer. Fish. Soc. 90(2): 170–174.

922 Van Oosten, J., and H. J. Deason. 1938. The food of the lake trout (*Cristivomer namaycush*) and of the lawyer (*Lota maculosa*) of Lake Michigan. Trans. Amer. Fish. Soc. 67(1937): 155–177.

923 Vasey, F. W. 1967. Age and growth of walleye and sauger in Pool 11 of the Mississippi River. Iowa State J. Sci. 41(4): 447–466.

924 Vladykov, V. D. 1949. Quebec lampreys (Petromyzonidae). I. List of species and their economical importance. Quebec Dept. Fish. Contr. No. 26. 67 p.

925 ————. 1950. Larvae of eastern American lampreys (Petromyzonidae). I. Species with two dorsal fins. Naturaliste Canadien 77(3–4): 73–95.

926 ————. 1955. Fishes of Quebec. Sturgeons. Quebec Dept. Fisheries, Album 5. 11 p.

927 ————. 1955. Fishes of Quebec. Eels. Quebec Dept. Fisheries, Album 6. 12 p.

928 ————. 1964. Quest for the true breeding area of the American eel (*Anguilla rostrata* LeSueur). J. Fish. Res. Bd. Canada 21(6): 1523–1530.

929 Vladykov, V. D., and G. Beaulieu. 1946. Etudes sur l'esturgeon (*Acipenser*) de la province de Quebec. Naturaliste Canadien 73: 143–204.

930 Vladykov, V. D., and J. R. Greeley. 1963. Order Acipenseroidei, p. 24–60. In: Fishes of the western North Atlantic. Vol. 1. Mem. Sears Found. Marine Res.

931 Vladykov, V. D., and E. Kott. 1976. Is *Okkelbergia* Creaser and Hubbs 1922 (Petromyzontidae) a distinct taxon? Canadian J. Zool. 54(3): 421–425.

932 Vladykov, V. D., and J. M. Roy. 1948. Biologie de la lamproie d'eau douce (*Ichthyomyzon unicuspis*) après la metamorphose. Revue Canadienne de Biologie 7(3): 483–485.

933 Vladykov, V. D., and D. H. Wallace. 1938. Is the striped bass (*Roccus lineatus*) of Chesapeake Bay a migratory fish? Trans. Amer. Fish. Soc. 67(1937): 67–86.

934 von Geldern, C., Jr., and D. F. Mitchell. 1975. Largemouth bass and threadfin shad in California, p. 436–449. In: National symposium on the biology and management of the centrarchid basses. Henry Clepper, ed. Sport Fishing Institute, Washington, D.C. 534 p.

935 Vrat, V. 1949. Reproductive behavior and development of eggs of the three-spined stickleback (*Gasterosteus aculeatus*) of California. Copeia 1949(4): 252–260.

936 Wagner, C. C., and E. L. Cooper. 1963. Population density, growth, and fecundity of the creek chubsucker, *Erimyzon oblongus*. Copeia 1963(2): 350–357.

937 Wagner, W. C., and T. M. Stauffer. 1980. Three-year-old pink salmon in Lake Superior tributaries. Trans. Amer. Fish. Soc. 109(4): 458–460.

938 Walbaum, M. J. J. 1792. Petri Artedi renovati, i.e., bibliotheca et philosophia ichthyologica. Ichthyologiae pars III. Grypeswaldiae. Ant. Ferdin. Roese. 723 p.

939 Walburg, C. H. 1964. Fish population studies, Lewis and Clark Lake, Missouri River, 1956 to 1962. U. S. Fish Wildl. Serv. Spec. Sci. Rep. Fish. 482. 27 p.

940 Walburg, C. H., and J. E. Sykes. 1957. Shad fishery of Chesapeake Bay with special emphasis on the fishery of Virginia. U. S. Fish Wildl. Serv. Res. Rep. 48. 26 p.

941 Wallace, C. R. 1967. Observations on the reproductive behavior of the black bullhead (*Ictalurus melas*). Copeia 1967(4): 852–853.

942 Wallace, D. C. 1972. The ecology of the silverjaw minnow, *Ericymba buccata* Cope. Amer. Midl. Nat. 87(1): 172–190.

943 ————. 1973. The distribution and dispersal of the silver-

jaw minnow, *Ericymba buccata* Cope. Amer. Midl. Nat. 89(1): 145–155.

944 Walters, V. 1955. Fishes of western Arctic America and eastern Arctic Siberia. Taxonomy and zoogeography. Bull. Amer. Mus. Nat. Hist. 106(5): 255–368.

945 Ward, H. C. 1951. A study of fish populations, with special reference to the white bass, *Lepibema chrysops* (Rafinesque), in Lake Duncan, Oklahoma. Proc. Oklahoma Acad. Sci. 30(1949): 69–84.

946 Wascko, H., and C. F. Clark. 1948. Pond propagation of bluntnose and blackhead minnows. Ohio Div. Cons. and Natur. Res. Wildl. Cons. Bull. 4. 16 p.

947 Watson, J. E. 1955. The Maine smallmouth. Maine Dept. Inland Fish. Game, Augusta. 31 p.

948 Webb, J. F., and D. D. Moss. 1967. Spawning behavior and age and growth of white bass in Center Hill Reservoir, Tennessee. Proc. S-E Assn. Game Fish. Comm. 21: 343–357.

949 Webster, D. A. 1954. Smallmouth bass, *Micropterus dolomieui*, in Cayuga Lake. Part 1, Life history and environment. Cornell Univ. Agr. Exp. Sta. Memoir 327. 39 p.

950 ———. 1962. Artificial spawning facilities for brook trout, *Salvelinus fontinalis*. Trans. Amer. Fish. Soc. 91: 168–174.

951 Wells, L., and R. House. 1974. Life history of the spottail shiner (*Notropis hudsonius*) in southeastern Lake Michigan, the Kalamazoo River, and western Lake Erie. U. S. Bur. Sport Fish Wildl. Res. Rep. 78. 10 p.

952 Werner, R. G. 1972. Bluespotted sunfish, *Enneacanthus gloriosus*, in the Lake Ontario drainage, New York. Copeia 1972(4): 878–879.

953 Westman, J. R. 1938. Studies on the reproduction and growth of the blunt-nosed minnow, *Hyborhynchus notatus* (Rafinesque). Copeia 1938(2): 57–61.

954 Wich, K., and J. W. Mullan. 1958. A compendium of the life history and ecology of the chain pickerel *Esox niger* (LeSueur). Massachusetts Div. Fish Game Fish. Bull. 22. 27 p.

955 Wigley, R. L. 1959. Life history of the sea lamprey of Cayuga Lake, New York. Bull. U. S. Fish Wildl. Serv. 59: 561–617.

956 Wiley, E. O. 1976. The phylogeny and biogeography of fossil and recent gars (Actinopterygii: Lepisosteidae). Univ. Kansas Mus. Nat. Hist. Misc. Publ. 64. 111 p.

957 Willard, B. 1965. Pennsylvania geology summarized. Pa. Topogr. and Geol. Surv. Ed. Ser. No. 4. 17 p.

958 Williams, E. H. 1895. Notes on the southern ice limit in eastern Pennsylvania. Amer. J. Sci. 49: 174–185.

959 Williams, E. H., Jr. 1902. Kansas glaciation and its effects on the river systems of northern Pennsylvania. Proc. and Coll. of Wyoming Hist. and Geol. Soc. (Wilkes-Barre, Pa.) 7: 21–28.

960 ———. 1920. The deep Kansan pondings in Pennsylvania and the deposits therein. Proc. Amer. Philo. Soc. 59: 49–84.

961 Williams, J. D. 1975. Systematics of the percid fishes of the subgenus *Ammocrypta*, genus *Ammocrypta*, with descriptions of two new species. Bull. Alabama Mus. Nat. Hist. 1: 1–56.

962 Wilson, A. In: Rees' New Cyclopedia, 9. (No pagination) ca. 1811 (Type locality probably Philadelphia).

963 Wilson, A. W. G. 1907. Chub's nests. Amer. Naturalist 41: 323–327.

964 Winchell, A. 1864. Description of a garpike, supposed to be new—Lepidosteus (*Cylindrosteus*) *oculatus*. Proc. Acad. Natur. Sci. Philadelphia 16: 183–185.

965 Winn, H. E. 1953. Breeding habits of the percid fish *Hadropterus copelandi* in Michigan. Copeia 1953(1): 26–30.

966 ———. 1958. Observations on the reproductive habits of darters (Pisces-Percidae). Amer. Midl. Nat. 59: 190–211.

967 ———. 1958. Comparative reproductive behavior and ecology of fourteen species of darters (Pisces-Percidae). Ecological Monogr. 28(2): 155–191.

968 ———. 1960. Biology of the brook stickleback *Eucalia inconstans* (Kirtland). Amer. Midl. Nat. 63(2): 424–438.

969 Winn, H. E., and J. F. Stout. 1960. Sound production by the satinfin shiner, *Notropis analostanus*, and related fishes. Science 132 (3421): 222–223.

970 Wirth, T. L. 1958. Lake Winnebago freshwater drum. Wisconsin Cons. Bull. 23(5): 1–3.

971 Witt, A., Jr. 1960. Length and weight of ancient freshwater drum, *Aplodinotus grunniens*, calculated from otoliths found in Indian middens. Copeia 1960(3): 181–185.

972 Witt, A., Jr., and R. C. Marzolf. 1954. Spawning and behavior of the longear sunfish, *Lepomis megalotis megalotis*. Copeia 1954(3): 188–190.

973 Wynne-Edwards, V. C. 1933. The breeding habits of the black-headed minnow (*Pimephales promelas* Raf.) Trans. Amer. Fish. Soc. 62(1932): 382–383.

974 Yant, D. R., R. O. Smitherman, and O. L. Green. 1976. Production of hybrid (blue × channel) catfish and channel catfish in ponds. Proc. S-E Assn. Game Fish. Comm. 29(1975): 82–86.

975 Young, R. T., and L. J. Cole. 1900. On the nesting habits of the brook lamprey. Amer. Natur. 34(404): 617–620.

976 Zimmerman, C. J. 1970. Growth and food of the brook silverside, *Labidesthes sicculus*, in Indiana. Trans. Amer. Fish. Soc. 99(2): 435–438.

977 Zorach, T. 1972. Systematics of the percid fishes, *Etheostoma camurum* and *E. chlorobranchium* new species, with a discussion of the subgenus *Nothonotus*. Copeia 1972(3): 427–447.

978 Zorach, T., and E. C. Raney. 1967. Systematics of the percid fish *Etheostoma maculatum* Kirtland, and related species of the subgenus *Nothonotus*. Amer. Midl. Natur. 77(2): 296–322.

Index to Common and Scientific Names